ISBN 978-1-332-82576-9
PIBN 10088879

English
Français
Deutsche
Italiano
Español
Português

www.forgottenbooks.com

Mythology Photography **Fiction**
Fishing Christianity **Art** Cooking
Essays Buddhism Freemasonry
Medicine **Biology** Music **Ancient
Egypt** Evolution Carpentry Physics
Dance Geology **Mathematics** Fitness
Shakespeare **Folklore** Yoga Marketing
Confidence Immortality Biographies
Poetry **Psychology** Witchcraft
Electronics Chemistry History **Law**
Accounting **Philosophy** Anthropology
Alchemy Drama Quantum Mechanics
Atheism Sexual Health **Ancient History**
Entrepreneurship Languages Sport
Paleontology Needlework Islam
Metaphysics Investment Archaeology
Parenting Statistics Criminology
Motivational

RAMBLES ABOUT BATH

AND ITS NEIGHBOURHOOD.

BASED ON THE ORIGINAL WORK BY DR. TUNSTALL,

CONTAINING

Two Maps, Sixteen Wood-cuts, and Eight Autotypes.

REVISED AND RE-EDITED,

WITH BIOGRAPHICAL NOTICES AND HISTORICAL NOTES.

Sixth Edition.

LONDON: SIMPKIN, MARSHALL, AND CO.
BATH: R. E. PEACH, 8, BRIDGE STREET.

MDCCCLXXVI.

[ENTERED AT STATIONERS' HALL.]

DEDICATION.

To ROBERT STICKNEY BLAINE, Esquire,

SUMMER HILL.

Dear Sir,

Accept the dedication of this New Edition of Rambles about Bath and its Neighbourhood as the expression of my sincere personal respect—a sentiment shared, I believe, by the great body of your fellow citizens—but more especially as a recognition of your steady efforts to promote the interests of the city and the general good of all classes of the community.

Believe me,

Dear Sir,

Your faithful Servant,

R. E. PEACH.

LIST OF ILLUSTRATIONS.

AUTOTYPES.

WOOD-CUTS.

Map of the City and Borough of Bath after Introductory Chapter.
Map of the Neighbourhood at the end of the Book.

INTRODUCTORY CHAPTER.

" Meadows trim with daisies pied,
Shallow brooks and rivers wide ;
Towers and battlements it sees
Bosom'd high in tufted trees,
Where perhaps some beauty lies,
The cynosure of neighbouring eyes."

" Great men have liv'd among us, heads that plann'd
And tongues that utter'd wisdom—better none."

IN presenting a new edition of RAMBLES ABOUT BATH to
the Public, we are fully conscious of the defects, both of
omission and commission, which will be found in it. The
difficulties of adapting a book of this character—for the most
part essentially a relation of fact, the text of which was written
nearly thirty years ago—to the present time, are too obvious to
need demonstration. Every page in the old edition contains
inaccuracies—the inevitable result of time—statements modified
by local changes, and circumstances needing to be corrected, or to
be re-stated. Fresh information and new facts were to be engrafted
on, or fitted to, the old text; new subjects were to be introduced :
and all these various elements required to be woven into a homo-
geneous, and, so far as practicable, harmonious whole. If in this
attempt an approximate success has been achieved, we shall feel
that something has been done towards keeping alive, and enhanc-
ing, the interest which must always be felt in a city whose natural
beauties, architectural elegance, unique traditions, and historical
records, still entitle her to the proud distinction of " Queen of the
West."

The arrangement of the present edition of Rambles about
Bath is based, for the most part, on the lines of the former edition
—an arrangement always regarded by the public with general

approbation. Any departure from the original plan has been made with the view rather of rendering the work more consistent and complete than of effecting any radical change. For instance the chapters in the old edition have been arranged in the present as *Walks*, and although these Walks are *radial* in character, some of them embrace a much larger area than is intended to be covered in a single excursion.

A few of the Wood-cuts of the former edition have been omitted, while those that have been retained, together with others not before used, are worked in the letter-press. The chief embellishments, however, and those probably most deserving of notice, from their novelty in local pictorial illustration, are the autotypes, effectively and faithfully representing subjects of interest in the city and its neighbourhood.

A new feature has been introduced to supply a desideratum often felt by the disciples of Isaac Walton, namely, a short sketch of the angling to be found within the compass of a day's excursion from Bath.

While giving the fullest description (compatible with the space at our command) of each object demanding notice, we have passed over others which the tourist can see for himself as well without as with our aid. We have not thought it desirable to encumber our columns with churchyard literature, most of which is a disgrace to "God's Acre." We have endeavoured to present in an attractive form the historical and archæological interest of each place included in our book—and this, as a rule, is the only information worth preserving for the intelligent tourist, who, from time to time, may wish to refresh his memories of the past, or who is for the first time visiting the scenes described.

The Index has been rendered as complete as possible—in some respects its very copiousness may detract from its value, but in such a case it is rather difficult to draw the line, and it is perhaps better to err on the side of redundancy than meagreness.

It has been very much of late the fashion for anonymous writers to abuse and decry Bath. We think without reason. .

We must, in justice to our subject, quote the reference to Bath from Lord Macaulay's famous dissertation on the state of England, at the close of the seventeenth century, in which the historian draws a comparison between Bath and all other Watering Places of that period, and between Bath in 1685 and what it was thirty years ago when he wrote—

"But at the head of English watering places, without a rival, was Bath.

"The springs of that city had been renowned from the days of the Romans. It had been, during many centuries, the seat of a Bishop. The sick repaired thither from every part of the realm. The King sometimes held his court there. Nevertheless, Bath was then a maze of only four or five hundred houses, crowded within an old wall in the vicinity of the Avon.

"Pictures of what were considered as the finest of those houses are still extant, and greatly resemble the lowest rag shops and pot houses of Ratcliffe Highway. Travellers, indeed, complained loudly of the narrowness and meanness of the streets. That beautiful city which charms even eyes familiar with the master-pieces of Bramante and Palladio, and which the genius of Anstey and Smollett, of Frances Burney and of Jane Austin, has made classic ground, had not begun to exist. Milsom Street itself was an open field lying far beyond the walls; and hedgerows intersected the space which is now covered by the Crescent and the Circus. The poor patients to whom the waters had been recommended lay on straw in a place which, to use the language of a contemporary physician, was a covert rather than a lodging.

"As to the comforts and luxuries which were to be found in the interior of the houses of Bath by the fashionable visitors who resorted thither in search of health or amusement, we possess information more complete and minute than can generally be obtained on such subjects. A writer who published an account of that city about sixty years after the Revolution has accurately described the changes which had taken place within his own recollection. He assures us that, in his younger days, the gentlemen who visited the springs slept in rooms hardly as good as the garrets which he lived to see occupied by footmen. The floors of the dining-rooms were uncarpeted, and were coloured brown with a wash made of soot and small beer, in order to hide the dirt. Not a wainscot was painted. Not a hearth or a chimney-piece was of marble. A slab of common freestone, and fire-irons which had cost from three to four shillings, were thought sufficient for any fireplace.   The best apartments were hung with coarse woollen stuff, and were furnished with rush-bottomed chairs.

"Readers who take an interest in the progress of civilisation, and of the useful arts, will be grateful to the humble topographer who has recorded these facts, and will perhaps wish that historians of far higher pretentions had sometimes spared a few pages from military evolutions and political intrigues, for the purpose of letting us know how the parlours and bed-chambers of our ancestors looked."*   .

The inference from the foregoing is obvious.   Let any candid reader, who will take the trouble to go through these pages attentively, and compare the Bath of to-day with the Bath of thirty years ago, say whether the result of his observation does not bear out the fact that in all respects the pre-eminence accorded to Bath by Lord Macaulay is fully maintained.   Having regard to the elements which alone can be taken as the criteria of the progress and material prosperity of a large city, namely, its general condition and its institutions—educational, philanthropic, religious, and secular—it may be safely asserted that Bath runs neck and neck in these particulars with other places of a similar character.

The perpetually recurring phrase used, in nine cases out of ten, by persons who scarcely think of its meaning—"the palmy days of Bath," would be as well forgotten, since it refers to a time when Bath, if it were prosperous, was so with a prosperity which, to use Thackeray's words in describing a drinking bout, left "vanitas vanitatum written on the bottom of the pot." Such times are happily not only departed from Bath, but from all other English cities.

Bath is more prosperous, and dispenses infinitely more general happiness in its present position, as a place of residence, than when it was chiefly the fitful abode of men and women of fashion and pleasure, the haunt of the well-born gambler, and the hunting-ground of the well-bred roué.

The fact that Bath has not greatly advanced in population during the past thirty years has been used as an argument to prove that it has fallen in public estimation.

* Macaulay's History of England, Chap. III.

There cannot be a greater fallacy than the inference drawn from this statement. In the first place the assertion is incorrect. Beyond the legal boundaries of the city, in almost every direction, suburbs have sprung up inhabited by persons, who, if not in Bath, are of it, and who do not count in the population returns.

What, a few years ago, were fields or cabbage gardens in the direction of Weston, Lansdown (Charlcombe), Newbridge and other localities, are now covered by villas and mansions, "vying with each other in the comfort and luxury of their appointments," and the cry is not for tenants to occupy them, but for more eligible sites and more villas for tenants who are always ready to take them. All this, be it observed, is new since Lord Macaulay conversed with us thirty years ago on the "exquisite beauties of Bath," which even then " charmed eyes familiar with the masterpieces of Bramante and Palladio." It must be remembered, too, that Bath is the centre of a large and rich agricultural district abounding with populous villages, small towns, country seats, and manufactories of some importance, and that these help to stimulate and sustain a spirit of enterprise amongst the tradesmen of the city, whose warehouses, shops, and goods are equal to, if they do not outvie, those of any other place out of London.

Nor is it in the suburbs alone that progress has been made. A brief summary of what has been done, in the city, may be permitted.

Within the period under consideration the Royal United and General Hospitals have been enlarged, and they may now challenge comparison with analogous institutions in any other city.

The older institutions have been remodelled and brought into harmony with modern ideas of economy and general usefulness. Various eleemosynary societies, supported by voluntary aid, and answering ends more or less useful, are carried on with careful regard to the public good.

Many improvements have been made in the streets and street arrangements. A sum of £70,000 has been expended upon works for increasing and improving the sources of the Water supply, the cost of which to the ratepayers is relatively lower than in almost any other place that can be named.

If, as a recent writer has said, the "character, habits, and mode of life of the Bath people have undergone of late years a very decided change . . . . and its old glories, its Public Balls, its Card Assemblies, belong only to history," it means that Bath no longer depends as it formerly did upon these amusements as its chief sources of prosperity, though they are still important adjuncts.

Nor, in the educational institutions of Bath, is there any occasion to shrink from comparison with other large cities. Since Macaulay wrote, many schools of the first importance have been established in the city: for example, the Wesleyan College, for training young men for the ministry as well as for secular professions; the Royal School, for the education of daughters of Officers of the British Army—both handsome buildings, nearly opposite each other, on Lansdown; the Bath Proprietary College, near Pulteney Street, and the Somersetshire College, in the Circus, each of which, in its own special line, has reason to be proud of its achievements. If we pause to express a regret it is to the effect, that the promoters of these two Colleges have not been able to effect an amalgamation by which Bath might possess a College equal in importance and magnitude to those of Clifton, and Cheltenham. The Grammar School, during the past thirty years, has not sustained the credit and glories of its old traditions. In times past, under Dr. Morgan and Mr. Pears, and others before them, it was the only Public School of eminence in the city. Men who distinguished themselves in the senate, in arms, in Indian politics, and other branches of professional life, received their education wholly, or in part, at this School. It promises, however, to have a useful career in the future, under the modified scheme settled by the Endowed School Commissioners, adapting it to "middle class" education, directed by the able Head Master now appointed. Besides these, there are Private Schools— some for advanced scholars preparing for Universities—others preparatory, most of which are well supported, showing that they are adequately grappling with the educational wants of the day, as developed by competition for the public service, as well as for professional life.

Commensurate, too, with the provision for boys are the educational facilities afforded for girls. In every part of the city Ladies'

Schools of the highest character have multiplied, the success of which, we are justified in saying, has been proportionate to their increase. Not only has each its resident teachers, but the higher work is supplemented and completed by visiting masters and mistresses—professors than whom no place can boast a more accomplished staff than Bath.

If there has been a want—a pressing want—long felt in Bath —it has been that of a School in which the daughters of every class of citizens could receive a thoroughly good education, the only conditions of admission into which should be character and due preliminary training. In a little work published in the early part of last year entitled "Go to Bath," which we have already quoted, this suggestion was embodied in the following words :—

" The establishment of a Ladies' College on a large scale would be an invaluable addition to the *attractions* as well as to the material advantages of the place, and would meet a want generally felt by its inhabitants.

" We only throw out this proposition as a hint, a suggestion— to be passed on, to be thought over, talked over, argued upon, made subject of newspaper correspondence, and moulded into shape if it be deemed worthy of consideration. The idea is not our own, not a new one—we know that the subject has already excited a good deal of attention among those who are fully competent to be judges of the probable success of an institution of the kind and its especial applicability to Bath. Let the thing be fairly set before the public, and there will not be wanting some one to come to the front with a programme of the design contemplated.

" In a few words, the outline of the scheme is as follows :—To promote an extended system of teaching in classes, after the manner of the Scotch Universities, by a staff of able Professors attached to the foundation. The Collegiate buildings would not be adapted for the reception of Boarders, but would consist rather of a number of well appointed Lecture Rooms, with Laboratory, Elementary Museum of Natural History, Geology, and whatever may be illustrative of the different sciences comprehended in the courses of Lectures."

We confess when this suggestion was promulgated, we had

hoped that it would have been carried out by the private
enterprise of Bath citizens, by which the direction would have
been vested in a local body. If this idea has not been literally
realized, the main object has been practically attained by the
establishment of the High School. At all events we are ready to
admit that our judgment in this respect may have been biased
by local considerations, and that, after all, greater independence,
and a more perfect system of management and discipline may
be attained by the local management being subordinate to a
central supreme authority in London. One thing is clear, the
principle of a "Mixed School" will be fairly tried, and no respectable parents, in future, will have reason to complain that,
without sending their daughters to Schools remote from Bath,
they cannot obtain for them the greatest of all advantages at the
outset of life—a good education.

When Lord Macaulay penned his eulogium on Bath, the Great
Western was the only Railway connected with the city ; since
that time two other lines and an important junction have been
constructed, viz., the Wilts, Somerset and Dorset Railway, connecting Bath with Salisbury, Weymouth, Southampton, and the
South West, &c. ; the Somerset and Dorset line, which is, practically, an extension of the Midland, viâ Evercreech, Southward ; and
the Mangotsfield Junction, which brings Bath into direct communication with the North, North-West and Midland districts,
without the awkward "elbow" of Bristol.

Much has been done in Church Building and Church Restoration
during the period in which we are especially interested. The
records in this book will bear witness that never in any previous
thirty years of its History has Bath accomplished so much as it
has between the years 1845 and 1875. The Abbey stands first,
and proclaims with silent eloquence what it was, and what it is.*

* We do not forget the removal, by the old Corporation, of
the buildings and alleys by which the Abbey was formerly surrounded. This act was but a tardy undoing of what it had either
directly done or sanctioned others in doing. Such an aggregation
of dens, filthy alleys, and abominations of every description,
especially in such a locality, could never have been possible,
unless permitted by the Corporate body, and the marvel is that
these evils could have been tolerated so long.

The amount, in the aggregate, expended in work of this nature, including Nonconformists' Chapels, exceeds £150,000—a sum raised entirely by voluntary subscriptions. We do not desire to make more of this fact than it legitimately warrants. Building Churches and Chapels does not necessarily imply religious zeal or worldly prosperity, but we may at least claim that, in the present instance, this work has been done with a quiet, steady energy, and an absence of ostentation which imply the highest motives, and that it has kept pace only with the recognized advancement of the city in all other important matters.

We have laid ourselves under the strongest obligation to many friends; and should be guilty of ingratitude if we did not emphatically thank them for their valuable assistance so cheerfully and generously given on all occasions. If there be any whose names are not included in the following list, we would offer our apologies in anticipation :—

Rev. Canon BERNARD	Rev. C. C. LAYARD
,, H. B. BURNEY	,, H. T. PERFECT
,, E. Ll. DAVIES	,, T. POYNTON
,, F. S. FORSS	,, Prebendary SCARTH
,, Canon JACKSON	,, G. TUGWELL.
,, W. L. NICHOLS	

Sir BERNARD BURKE, *Ulster King-at-Arms.*

Messrs. GILL & BROWNE	Mr. PLAYER ISAAC
Mr. W. L. COURTNEY	,, CHARLES MOORE
,, C. E. DAVIS	,, J. W. MORRIS
,, Mr. C. EKIN	,, MURCH
Dr. FALCONER	,, TURNER PAYNE
Mr. GEE	,, C. P. RUSSELL
,, A. GOODRIDGE	,, P. C. SHEPPARD
,, JOSIAH GOODWIN	,, F. SHUM
,, E. L. HILL	,, SKRINE
Dr. HUNTER	

Mr. W. WILLCOX.

In conclusion, while thanking our numerous subscribers for their encouragement in our enterprise, we hope we shall not have disappointed their expectations, and that the book, now produced, may be regarded as not unworthy of their approbation.

ERRATA

Page 2 line 12 for Badonca read *Badonica*.

Page 5 line 24 for date of Romans leaving Britain 444 read 409-10.

Page 24 line 2 for vestage read *vestige*.

Page 89 line 20 for and showed them &c. read *whom he had shown*.

Page 108 line 5 for prevent read *prevents*.

Page 127 line 6 from bottom for Middleton read *Midleton*.

Page 137 in second note line 3 for have read *has*.

Page 206 line 11 for parellel read *parallel*.

Page 263 bottom line for widows read *windows*.

Page 288 line 4 for accomodation read *accommodation*.

Page 321 line 4 for floreated read *foliated*.

Page 348 line 12 for goverment read *government*.

Page 423 lines 3 and 4 for improbability in attributing to this site the account given &c. read *improbability in regarding this as the site mentioned by* &c.

Page 432 line 5 from bottom for Externally to the west end of the church read *Externally, to the west end of the church*, &c.

During the progress of the book through the press the Rev. C. Lloyd has resigned the living of Englishcombe and is succeeded by the Rev. James Smart. The Rev. F. Pocock has resigned Monckton Combe and is succeeded by the Rev. A. G. Grigstock. The Rev. W. J. Pollock has resigned the living of St. Saviours.

A RAMBLE ABOUT OLD BATH.

G ENTLE READER, I have been a wanderer—
one of poor Goldsmith's philosophic vaga-
bonds ; and though I have not earned pence on the
high roads of Europe by flute-playing, yet I have
visited many lands, trudging weary miles in search of
those beauties of Nature and Art which none but he
who walks amongst them can fully enjoy. Yet,
to me, few possess such charms as the picturesque
ruins and romantic scenery of my native land, over
which history has thrown the sober mantle of calm
narration, and fiction has sported with in its wild
day dream !

Aquæ Solis, Caer Akeman, or Akemannesceaster,
as modern Bath has been successively designated by
Roman, Romanised Briton, and Saxon, was also
called Caer Pallidar, but not till after its Roman
occupancy, for the Goddess Pallas was unknown to
the Ancient Britons who named the vale in which
the City lies Caer Badon.

From immemorial time the valley of the Avon
has been a favourite with its masters. Very charming

B

are the surrounding hills; the breezy downs; the rich meadows. The busy crowd can never spoil such beauties, and though Mount Beacon, Beechen Cliff, and Bathwick hill are now studded with houses, the scene has and ever will have, that varied loveliness which makes it well deserving the praise bestowed on it.

Let us pause for a moment to contrast its present aspect with the appearance it must have presented to the Roman Soldier marching to join the Camp, which with its walled enclosure formed the infant city. From Mons Badonca, now Beacon Hill, he would have looked down on the spot where the Abbey —aptly named from its lightness the lanthorn of England—now stands. He would have seen the temple of Minerva, of which many interesting memorials are still preserved. Stretching southwards to the river he would have noted the parallel streets of the camp with its walls and gateways, and beyond, the everlasting hills the same yesterday, to-day, and for ever, now in sunshine, now in shadow, framing the picture in purple and gold.

What mist is that which rises near the temple of Minerva? It comes from those healing springs which gave to Bath its Roman name of AQUÆ SOLIS,

The City of the Waters of the Sun.

Let us walk round the site of the Roman city, of which many interesting remains have been, from time to time, discovered. When the foundations of the Royal Mineral Water Hospital were excavated in 1738, what by some was conjectured to have been the Prætorium, with mosaic pavements and an altar, were exposed to view. In close proximity were found grains of wheat, the *debris* of the market, usually held near the Prætorium, and immediately opposite, in 1796, vestiges of Roman walls, composed of square blocks of stone laid in cement, were unearthed, the cavities being filled with smaller stones strongly cemented together by liquid mortar.

The Roman baths were discovered in 1757, when the Duke of Kingston pulled down the priory. In clearing the foundations, stone coffins, and the bones of animals used in sacrifices, were found at a considerable depth below the building. When the workmen reached the Roman sewers, the mineral waters flowed in and interrupted the work of excavation. These baths are known under the name of the Kingston, or old Roman baths. Kingston Buildings occupy a portion of the site of the priory.

The reputed Principia of the Romans, afterwards called St. Mary's Rampier—now the Upper Borough-walls—passed due east and west, and the principal street, now Union and Stall Streets, stood at right angles, directly south. "The name of Stall," says Wood, "arose from the stables of the Roman cavalry being situated there." This is a manifest error. The name is derived from a church, long since destroyed, which, being dedicated to St.

Mary of Bethlehem, was called St. Mary de Stall, *i.e.*, St. Maria de Stabula, or the Virgin at the manger. The continuation of this street from South gate to St. Lawrence's, now the Old Bridge, was until lately called Horse Street, in consequence of its leading to the bath for horses. At the bottom of Stall Street we turn round the Lower Borough Walls, through Westgate Buildings to Gascoyne Place, where formerly stood a tower of that name, over-looking the King's mead, long since covered with houses, and thence pass along the Upper Borough Walls to the back of the Market. In a lane below, leading to the slaughter houses, the east gate is still seen, together with a large portion of the ancient wall. Proceeding through the Grove to St. James's Church, we complete the circuit of the ancient city.

Of the CITY GATES, formerly four in number, three are destroyed, and the one remaining promises to be, ere long, consigned to oblivion. These gates will first occupy our attention.

Leland the antiquary, visited the city in 1530. Entering it through a "*great stone arch*," which stood "on the centre of a bridge of five fair stone arches, between which and south gate" he marked "the meadows on either hand."

South gate, which stood at the bottom of Stall Street, was the handsomest of the four structures. It was rebuilt in 1362, the dimensions being eleven feet wide and fifteen feet high. Its south side was ornamented with an enthroned statue of King

Edward III, having on the one side the figure of Bishop Ralf de Salopia, and on the other, that of Prior John de Walcot. It was destroyed in 1755.

The north gate, termed by Leland the "toune gate," in consequence of Queen Elizabeth having there received the formal presentation of the keys, is described by him, and all succeeding writers, as surmounted by a tower, which, as appears from Dr. Jones's Map (A.D. 1572), was part of St. Mary's Church. The principal entrance, ten feet wide by fifteen high, was surmounted by a grotesque painted figure of King Bladud. This gate was pulled down in 1776.

West gate was re-built in the year 1572, and was made sufficiently commodious to lodge the Royal Family on their visits to Bath. It was occupied by King James II. in 1687, by the Princess Amelia in 1728, and by the Prince of Wales in 1734. It was pulled down in 1776.

At the south side of the Market is a deep and narrow lane, which led to the Monk's Mill. In this ancient roadway stood the east gate.

The Romans held the city till their departure from Britain, A.D. 444. They left it adorned with baths and temples, one of the latter, dedicated to Minerva, partially coinciding with the present sites of the Abbey and the Pump Room.

The native possessors of the soil occupied the place until the year 577, when the Saxons ravaged it with fire and sword. In 676, Osric king of

Northumbria founded the monastery, which, after numerous vicissitudes, was restored by Offa king of Mercia in 775.

In 907, the city was first governed by a sheriff, and afterwards by a provost or bailiff. Its ancient charters were confirmed by Edward III, Richard II, Henry V. and VI.

King Edgar was crowned in the ancient church of St. Peter in 973 ; and from this time Bath began to take an important position. Leland says that " King Eadgar was crounid with much joy and honor at St. Peter's, in Bath, whereupon he bare a great zeale to the towne, and gave very great fraunchises and principles onto it ; in knowlege whereof, they pray in al there ceremonies for the soule of King Eadgar. And at Whitsunday-tide, at which tyme menne say Eadgar was crounid, ther is a king elected in Bath, every yere, of the townes menne, in the joyfulle remembrance of king Eadgar, and the privileges gyven to the towne by hym. This king is fested and his adherentes by the richest menne of the towne."

In the reign of Alfred the Great, the city, within the walls, consisted of three parishes—St. Peter's, St. James's and St. Michaels. The last no longer exists. The church stood near the Cross Bath, and the name is perpetuated in the passage leading from Westgate Street to St. John's Hospital, the chapel of which is dedicated to St. Michael. The present parish of St. Michael was then situated without the old north gate, and was called St. Michael Outwich.

In Edward the Confessor's time, the city was divided into three portions. That bounded by Cheap and Stall Streets belonged to the monks; the opposite part, between Westgate and Stall Streets, was under the jurisdiction of the barons; while the portion, northward to the Upper Borough Walls, was held by the king's burgesses.

At the Norman Conquest, out of 178 burgesses, sixty-four held under the king, ninety under the barons, while twenty-four were tenants to the monastery. The population was then 570 souls.

" The king," says Domesday Book, " holds Bade. In the time of king Edward, it was held by queen Edith, and gelded for twenty hides, when the county of Somerset was assessed. The king has there LXIV burgesses, rendering four pounds; and there are four score and ten burgesses of other men paying yearly to the borough LX shillings. The king has there six unoccupied houses.

" This borough, with Estone (now Batheaston), renders sixty pounds by tale, and one mark of gold. Besides this, a mint yields one hundred shillings. Edward accounts eleven pounds for the third penny of this borough.

" From the same borough, one house is taken away. Hugh, the interpreter, holds it, and it is worth 2s.

" The church of Saint Peter in Bade, has in that borough 24 burgesses who pay twenty shillings."

In the time of William Rufus, the city, during Odo's rebellion, was totally destroyed by fire.   In his reign, a native of France named John of Tours, or John de Villula,* who then practised physic in Bath, purchased the bishopric of Wells, and determined to unite that see to the Abbey of Bath.   The King, being mindful of his soul's health, and in consideration of the sum of five hundred marks to him in hand paid, granted the diocese to the Abbey of St. Peter's, together with the whole city of Bath, with its mint, baths, tolls, markets, and other privileges, for ever in perpetuity, for a yearly rent of twenty pounds, payable to the king.

In the reign of Edward I, A.D. 1297, the city sent its two first members to Parliament.

The walls, which had been strongly rebuilt in 1090 on their old foundations, were repaired in 1369, in obedience to a precept from King Edward III.

---

* When these papers first appeared, we were much criticised for calling him John de Pillula, his name having, we believe, in all previous works, been spelled John de Villula.   His proper name was (from his birth-place) John of Tours ; and, as a nickname, he received the other appellation in consequence of his skill in physic ; it being always to be remembered that the Saxon P. V. and W. are represented by very similar characters, as the coins of William the Conqueror and manuscripts of the period plainly show.—J. T.—[The foregoing note is retained in deference to the writer ; but the point contended for is by no means conceded by the present Editor.]

In 1412, the name of John Savage occurs as the first mayor on record.

In 1447, King Henry VI. granted a charter enabling the mayor to determine the assize of bread and beer.

In 1590, Queen Elizabeth, who had previously visited the city, gave it a new charter, which enlarged its boundaries with jurisdiction over the priory lands, baths, and suburbs. Under this charter the municipality extended from Walcot Church on the one side, to the end of the present Park on the Weston Road, and thence to the river, which formed its eastern and southern boundaries.

In 1640, King Charles I. fortified the city at an expense of £7,000; it nevertheless opened its gates to the Parliamentarians on the 29th of July, 1645, when Sir William Waller fixed his head-quarters in the city, then considered the most important stronghold in the county. During the civil wars it was in turn held by both parties, its position in the valley rendering its tenure of little use to either.

In 1673, as stated by Captain Henry Chapman, who was then mayor of Bath, the city and suburbs, occupying about fifty acres, paid only £30 to the poor's rates.

Those desirous of reading the monkish fable, which early historians have woven round the origin of this ancient city, are recommended to peruse the certificate which Mr. Wood hoped would have been signed by the citizens in 1741, recording the authenticity of his history of Bladud and the swine, or his life and marvellous adventures in Wood's own veritable history — a work as interesting to the antiquary as fairy tale to youthful maiden.

A MIDST the many records of the ancient monastery, it is difficult to select such an account of its fate and fortunes as shall interest the general reader, without encumbering the narration with extraneous details.

The Abbey of Bath was originally consecrated as a nunnery by king Osric, who, in 676, gave to Bertona, an abbess, one hundred of his tenants to erect a dwelling for herself and sisterhood, "for the salvation of his soul, and satisfaction of his sins." This pious lady doubtless employed her able-bodied men in the erection of the building, selling the others, with their wives, families, and possessions, to enable her to purchase building materials with the proceeds. In those days the "*Manentes*" belonged absolutely to the king and nobility; mere tillers of the earth, they and theirs were to all intents and purposes slaves.

The Danish incursions soon afterwards laid waste the city, and the nuns were driven from their peaceful abode. King Offa, in 775, finding their house in ruins and the church destroyed, rebuilt it, and converted it into a college for secular priests.   To this foundation the Danish kings were great benefactors. Athelstan in 931, and Edwy in 956, endowed it with various lands in the adjacent county.

In 970, King Edgar, urged by St. Dunstan, archbishop of Canterbury, expelled the secular clergy, who being allowed to marry, brought their wives and families into the convents, and employed themselves in works unconnected with religion.   From this period may be dated the strife between the regular and secular priests, which continued until the Reformation, and was aggravated during the reigns of the Norman, Plantagenet, and Tudor kings, by the promotion of foreign monks to English benefices, to the exclusion of the native clergy.   This rule proved so irksome to the lower orders that they frequently rebelled against it.   The contest led to two great evils—the introduction of a foreign language (the Latin) into public devotion, and the establishment of vows of celibacy from the clergy.   Of this latter, the reformed religion still possesses one relic in its colleges, the fellows of which are compelled to resign on their marriage.

To return from our digression.   Edgar, having expelled the priests, founded a college or monastery for an abbot and twenty monks of the Benedictine order.

The Parker Collection of Manuscripts, relating to Bath, preserved in Corpus Christi College,

Cambridge, contains the following memoranda of redemption from slavery, which from their curiosity we translate :—

" In this page of the book of Christ, Leofnoth, a peasant, attached to the glebe of Corston, the son of Egelnoth, has, with five oxen and twelve sheep, purchased himself and family from Elfsig, the abbot, and all the monks of Bath.   Witness, KEASKILL, *the bailiff, and all the citizens."*

" In this book of Christ it is written that Edric, of Ford, has purchased his daughter, Sæfrig, from Elfsig, the abbot, and convent of Bath, in perpetual liberty, and all her progeny."

" It is written, &c., that Elfric and Egilric Scot are free, for the perpetual liberty of the soul of Elfsig, the abbot; by the testimony of the whole convent."

These manumissions occur during the reign of William the Conqueror.   In his time, as appears from Domesday Book, the lands of the Abbey were valued at eighty pounds yearly.   They extended not only over a third part of the city, but included no less than seventeen adjacent villages, with their manorial rights and privileges.   In 1106, John of Tours, its most bountiful benefactor, having laboured, and at length effected, " with all decent authority," as he himself declares, " so that the head and mother church of Somerset shall be in the city of Bath," restored to the monks all that he had appropriated to himself, together with the lands he had purchased of Hugo cum Barbâ, which consisted of five manors, devoting all his revenues derived from the city, to the perfecting of the building of the church and monastery. He also erected a stately palace for himself and successors. From this time to the Reformation, the Abbey increased in riches, by the gifts, not only of the kings, but also of the nobility and pious individuals.

It possessed great privileges as the following curious letter of King Henry I. will shew; the original is in Latin :—

"HENRY, *King of England, to Walter, of Gloucester, and Waren, Viscount of Somerset, and their Officers, greeting. I command that the whole lands, and men of the monks of Bath, shall be in peace and quiet from all decrees and complaints in your shires and hundreds, and in other things, murder and theft excepted, when they shall be in my hand. Witness,* NIGEL DE ALBIN, *at Gloucester.*"

King John was a great patron of the monks. He annexed a priory at Cork and another at Waterford to the monastery, and gave them his royal farm of Barton with a separate jurisdiction and the privileges of execution and ordeal, exempting both themselves and their tenants from suit and service, assizes and juries, as well as from toll at Bristol.

In 1223, the prior rented the city during the pleasure of King Henry III., at a yearly rental of £30. In 1304, King Edward gave him the toll of the two fairs then established. In 1330, the monks established a woollen manufactory in Bath, and the cloth became celebrated throughout England. About this time the prior had to pay a fine to the king for infringing the statute of Mortmain, passed in 1279, to restrain the cupidity of the church, which threatened even then to absorb all the lands in the kingdom. The succeeding century found them a small body, rich, luxurious, and extravagant; too indolent even to keep their own houses in repair; so that when Oliver King became bishop in 1495, he was compelled to pension the monks, and devote their income to the rebuilding of the church and monastery.

The priory had a southern aspect, protected from the public gaze by a wall. Its gardens extended as far as the present vestry-room, and a gate led to the Abbey Green, which formed its first court. Below this was the orchard, and St. James's Street occupies the site of the ancient Lear lands, so called from their being the place where poor strangers were entertained without the gate of the priory. The grounds extended along the east side of Stall Street, from which it was approached by an elegant arch called the Abbey gate, and the walls ran along the present Galloway Buildings to the city wall, with a narrow entrance to the Grove, through St. Peter's gate. Immediately adjoining were two baths—one for the monks, and one for the poor; and next to these was a tennis-court. The Orange Grove was divided into two portions, one running eastward from the north side of the church belonged to the monks, and was called the *Abbey-litten*, while the other portion was called *Mitre-green.* These, in Beau Nash's time, were planted with three rows of trees, and called the Orange Grove, in consequence of the erection of a column in 1734, recording the cure of the Prince of Orange. It then formed the most delightful promenade within the walls. In addition to this, the monks possessed all the land, including the Mill, to the east and south of the city, the Ham barton, and the Ambrey mead. This property, with Prior Park, the mansion at Combe, and other tenements at Bridgwater, Dunster, and Walcot, King Henry VIII. sold to Colles for £962 17s. 4d.

The parish of St. Peter and St. Paul, commonly called the Abbey, was endowed at the dissolution of the monastery. The church has been frequently rebuilt. On its present site once stood a Roman temple dedicated to Minerva, a portion of which, it is said, may still be seen under the eastern buttresses; but these remains have rather the character of early Norman. Be this as it may, the heathen temple was, we are told, consecrated to Christianity by St. David in 596. Osric founded the monastery in 676. This building was totally destroyed by the Danes in 678; restored by Offa in 775; and its constitution reformed by Edgar in 970. The church was rebuilt in 1010; burned in 1137; and again restored. To this edifice, the present noble structure succeeded, which, although commenced in 1499, was not practically completed until 1608. Elphage, a learned monk of Glastonbury, a native of Weston, near Bath, and subsequently Archbishop of Canterbury, was the first abbot appointed by King Edgar. He was scarcely dead, when John of Tours annexed the Abbey to the bishop's see, and from this period to the Reformation, it was governed by priors. Among them we find John de Tellisford, a monk of Dunster (then a cell belonging to the Bath Abbey), elected in 1411, who had a fierce quarrel with the mayor relative to the ringing of the city bells, which was quelled only by a decree from the bishop, forbidding any bells to ring before the prior's in the morning, or after his at night. John de Cantlow, elected in 1489, deserves our notice and respect. He not only repaired the Abbey, but restored St. Catherine's Church, and the Chapel of St. Mary Magdalen's Hospital, in Holloway. To him, in 1499, succeeded prior Wm. Birde, Oliver King being then bishop. The church notwithstanding its recent reparation, was in a ruinous condition. These good men devoted themselves to the task of rebuilding it—a work neither lived to complete. The prior died poor, in consequence of having devoted the greater part of his income to the erection of the beautiful chapel which bears his name.

William Holway, otherwise Gibbs, succeeded Prior Birde in 1525. He continued the building, which was scarcely completed, when the monastery was suppressed, its church, lands, and revenues, being granted by letters patent to Humphrey Colles, who sold them to the family of Colthurst. Having en-

c

tirely despoiled the church of everything that could
be turned into use, or converted into money, the
roofless shell of the building was given to the citizens
for a parish church.   Sir John Harington, of Kelston,
in a poetical epistle to Bishop Montague, first drew
public attention to the propriety of re-edifying it.
One day, during a shower of rain, he was conversing
with the bishop near the church, and asked his lordship to step in for shelter, special care being taken
to convey the prelate into the north aisle, then nearly
roofless, and despoiled of its lead.   This situation
not sheltering his lordship, he remonstrated with
Sir John.   "Doth it rain, my lord?   Then let me see
your bounty towards covering our poor church, for
if it keep us not safe from the waters above the earth,
how shall it ever save others from the fire beneath?"
The bishop generously gave £1,000, and applied
himself sedulously to the task.   Private charity alone
prevented this noble building from sharing the fate
of other monastic edifices, reduced to ruin by the
cupidity of those to whom the king had granted or
sold them.   In 1606, Thomas Bellot (founder of
the hospital which bears his name), nobly aided in
the good cause, together with many other generous
benefactors.

The rector, John Pelling, entered warmly into the
work, so much so, that his life bore testimony to
the truth of his motto, *Non mihi, sed ecclesiæ*—"not
for me, but for my church."

The west front is ornamented with the representation of the dream of Bishop King, wherein he saw

angels ascending and descending a ladder, and calling on him to rebuild the church. Near these are mutilated statues of the twelve apostles, and some almost obliterated inscriptions. His name being Oliver King, his mark was an olive tree crowned with the motto, *De sursum est*—"it is from above." Here, also, are the arms of King Henry VII., with the united red and white rose, surmounted by a crown and a crowned portcullis. The west door is beautifully carved with the arms of the bishopric impaling Montague. On either side are stone statues of the bishop and prior, as their ecclesiastical robes plainly indicate, and not of St. Peter and St. Paul, as former writers have asserted. Over the north door of the west front is a small statue of King Edgar, with a roll representing the charter, and above, the inscription, " Domus mea." A statue of King Osric ornaments the south door, and represents him bearing a purse of money, in allusion to the wealth with which he endowed the original foundation. Above this figure is a scroll, bearing the inscription, "*Domus orationis*," finishing the sublime inscription, " My house is the house of prayer." On the eastern buttress of the south transept is the almost obliterated date of 1557, marking the repairs then completed by Mr. Peter Chapman. Francis Allen, in 1616, gave a sum of money to make the buttresses of the north side of the east end uniform with the southern, as appears by a date stone, recently recut.

Having briefly sketched the history of the Abbey, we will glance at the building as it was, and as it is.

THE ABBEY AS IT WAS.

FEW ancient structures perhaps have suffered more from panegyric than the Abbey. Beautiful as it unquestionably is, it seems equally unquestionable that local writers have done their best to disappoint the expectations of visitors by raising them to an extravagant pitch ; and could the stones of the building cry out, we can fancy they would with one voice exclaim, "save us from our friends."

As the Abbey Church of Bath is the latest specimen of ecclesiastical Gothic Architecture erected in the kingdom, it might not unreasonably be expected that it should display a happy combination of the graces of the great school to which it belongs. Nor is this expectation likely to be disappointed, as few visitors, probably, will fail to recognise the chaste uniformity, the proportion, and harmony of the several parts. As regards its surroundings, our Abbey has led rather a chequered life. In its early days it was not so closely associated with upstart neighbours as at a later date, while its present state is a decided improvement on what may be called its middle period. Slender and graceful, rather than broad and massive, the Abbey, nevertheless, would have made a pretty picture at all times, with its towers, flying buttresses, and many windows. Very different, however, must it have appeared when, fresh from the builders' hands, its unsullied walls showed their creamy hues amidst blossoming orchards and pleasant gardens.

But Bath was soon destined to become the fashion, and royalty, courtiers, fine ladies, and tinselled gentlemen, required food and lodging. Lines of houses grew up in the neighbourhood of the springs, and petty shops pressed closer and closer to the sacred walls, hustling them, as it were, into dismal courts and foul alleys. Time and ignorance gradually did their work. The west front of the building, beautiful with the vision seen in dreamland, by the good bishop, Oliver King, and by him written and graven on stones, had become well-nigh illegible. At no very distant date, we venture to predict that the public, "that self-constituted patron of ancient ecclesiastical buildings," will restore the angelic messengers in their pristine grace and beauty, ascending and descending upon the slumbering prelate. While the exterior of the building suffered from greed and vandalism, the interior felt the influence of the churchwarden period. The architectural ability of this august body was largely displayed in whitewash, and so liberally was this material employed, that niches were lost, delicate tracery effaced, and the structure from east to west, from north to south,

at length wore the cleanly but depressing aspect of a
whited sepulchre.   At this time, every pier in the
church was crowded with monumental tablets.
But the building had yet to reach the lowest depth
of architectural degradation.   This, however, was
gained when the Corporation, in a moment of ill-
directed generosity, made a grant for the purpose
of re-pewing the choir, as well as for erecting
galleries and "improving" the organ loft.   The
result of this final effort of bad taste was that the
choir was supremely disfigured, and that the *coup
d'œil* was destroyed.   Such was the aspect presented
by the Abbey, to the archæological students who
visited it, almost up to the end of the first quarter
of the present century.

There is a popular aphorism to the effect that
when things come to the worst they are likely to
mend.   Vandalism was dying out, and the churchwarden dynasty was rapidly drawing to a close.
Corporations, too, began to bestir themselves in the
direction of city improvements, and so far as the
Abbey is concerned, that body commenced operations in the year 1823, by the gradual removal of
Wades' Passage, together with other close and un-
wholesome dens, that almost literally leaned against
the north aisle for support.   In our early boyhood
we were familiar with these "passages," visiting
them, especially in the winter evenings, in quest of
forbidden game, which at that time was only to be
found lurking in secret places.   Even then the

applicability of the emphatic words of Scripture to these unlicensed dealers passed through our mind— " My house is the house of prayer, but ye have made it a den of thieves."

The church, " a favourable example of the pointed style," is thus described by Mr. John Wood, architect, in his work, entitled " An Essay towards a Description of Bath," vol. 1, p. 309 :—" This structure was formed upon a triple square of 75 feet, so that the length of the edifice from east to west became 225 feet. But the nave within, made a figure of six squares upon its area, that part of the church being 31 feet in breadth, and 186 feet in length. Now the outside of the Abbey Church, in Bath, is within a trifle of 225 feet in length, from east to west; and the nave within, to the centres of the pillars on each side of it, makes a figure of six squares upon its area, or very near it; that part of the building being 34 feet 10 inches in breadth, and 211 feet in length."

THE ABBEY AS IT IS.

FAIR indeed is the Abbey as we see it to-day. No vestage of whitewash mars the delicate beauty of pillar, wall, or roof. The monumental tablets are arranged in seemly order along the aisles; no screen destroys the symmetry of the building; the galleries have disappeared; the windows, which a few years' since presented a cold uniformity of dull green glass, now glow in all the beauty of colour and richness of design. Of these we shall presently speak more at length when we have sketched some of the stages through which, during the last few years, the building has rapidly past from approaching decay to the strength and beauty of its original perfection in 1616.

The propriety of several considerable alterations in the interior of the building was seriously discussed in the year 1834, such for example as removing the galleries, and re-pewing the church. The time, however, was scarcely ripe for such changes, and the idea

was abandoned.   Five-and-twenty years later, when
Bishop Carr was rector, various suggestions were
made as to the necessity of arresting further decay,
the estimate for the probable outlay being about
£900.   This scheme, like the preceding, fell to the
ground. ⸱ After the death of Bishop Carr, the Rev.
Charles Kemble succeeded to the living, and to this
gentleman we are mainly indebted for the restorations
which have made the Abbey what it is.   Mr. Kemble
was eminently fitted to bring this important work to
a successful completion.   Possessed of considerable
wealth, of great administrative powers, of indomit-
able resolution, and unwearied energy, the esteem
in which he was held added largely to the effect of
so many natural advantages.   Sympathy and interest
were gradually enlisted in the good cause, and at
length Sir George Gilbert Scott was privately requested by the Rector to survey the building.   This
was done, and the cost of restoration was estimated
at £20,000.

Sir George Gilbert Scott's plan being approved,
and liberal contributions having been promised,
operations were commenced in 1864.   For the sake
of convenience, the work may be classed in three ⸱
divisions.   The first consisted of external repairs,
and embraced the foundations, roof, windows, and
battlements.   The second part, which consisted of a
stone-groined ceiling, was commenced in 1868.   The
third and last portion, namely, the adaptation of the
entire building for public worship, repairing and

cleaning the walls and pillars of the nave, as well as heating, lighting, and pewing with new carved oak seats, was finished in 1873.

In a work like the present, it would be out of place to enter into tedious details as to the sums expended. Suffice it to say, that about £30,000 have been spent in bringing the Abbey to its present state. Of this sum the late Rector and his family contributed between £11,000 and £12,000. It may be added that no debt of any kind, in connection with restoration, exists. We have spoken of the many attributes which rendered the Rev. Charles Kemble so well fitted for the prominent part he played in the restoration of the Abbey. It remains to mention one more, namely, generosity, and this was taxed to the full. He is gone to his rest, and needs no human praise. But his name, as connected with the church in question, belongs to us and to posterity, nor, were he at hand to hear, could he object to our concluding phrase, " Honour to whom honour is due."

The stranger, who enters by the west door, may well pause for a moment in order to glance at the general harmony of the noble picture before him, at the admirable lightness of the groined roof, at the shields of arms—a history in themselves,—on the ceiling of the nave and aisles, at the tall pillars, at the narrow transept, and at the many coloured lights that chequer the almost spotless creamy whiteness of the stone.

Passing from the general to the particular, the first object that arrests attention is Prior Birde's Chapel, or Oratory. We extract the following description of it from the work of its restorer, the late Mr. Edward Davis, formerly architect of this city, entitled "Gothic Ornaments, illustrative of Prior Birde's Oratory in the Abbey Church of Bath :"—

"This chapel is almost coeval with the Abbey in which it stands. The first stone was laid about 1515, by Prior Wm. Birde, under whom the design was, for some time, diligently prosecuted. When, however, nearly completed, its progress was interrupted (probably from the ecclesiastical reforms of that period), and the structure still affords unquestionable evidence of the abruptness with which the work was abandoned. Part of the front next the choir is left unfinished, and portions, intended to be decorated, remain still as they were prepared for the carver. Hence we learn the method of executing carved work at that period. The stone was first shaped as required, a black coat of water-colour was laid on, and the drawing being pricked through, the outline was obtained on the stone by the application of white pounce. For this information, as well as for the very perfect state of much of the carved work, we are indebted to the coatings of lime-wash, beneath which it was, until lately, concealed.

"Its subsequent history is soon told. Remarkable alike for its purity and richness of decoration, it was fated to experience the same neglect to which all

architecture of a Gothic character was so long exposed. For three centuries it was left to the mercy
of parish officers, the fronts defaced by monuments,
the lower compartments of the windows blocked up,
while those parts permitted to remain exposed were
washed and rewashed with coats of different hues,
until all the sharpness of the carved work was lost,
and much of the delicate tracery obliterated."

Thus it remained until the year 1833, when a subscription was commenced for its renovation, which
Mr. Davis was enabled to complete in strict conformity with its pristine condition. The cornice is
sculptured with running vine branches in bold relief;
the south side consists longitudinally of two divisions,
rising from a basement ornamented with quatrefoils
in panels, separated by octangular buttresses, which
Mr. Davis considered were carried higher than the
present straight line, and that they supported grotesque figures bearing bannerets, their object being to
break the monotony. These buttresses are divided
into four compartments of small panelled arches.
The divisions between the buttresses are composed
of two four-centered arches, with three mullions
and tracery, having a plinth of several mouldings,
and a dado of enriched quatrefoils in panels, with
an open rosette in the centre of each; the spandrils
are enriched with finely-wrought foliage, among
which the *bird* is frequently repeated. At the north-
west angle are two niches, one above the other,
having duplex canopies crowned with pinnacles; at

the exterior angle of the north-west corner is a double panel, crowned with an ogee arch moulding, with crockets, from which springs one of the angular groins. This elaborately beautiful oratory is now completely restored, according to the original design, at the expense of the family of the late rector.

The church is remarkable for its many punning devices—a conceit then common with the learned. Thus Prior Birde's mark is a bird in a W. Bellot, giving the glass in the great east window, must needs perpetuate his name by causing it to be glazed in very small pieces, inserted, as the heralds call it, "bellot-wise." Malet, of Enmore, also glazed a window, decorating it with his coat-of-arms and motto, "Malet Meliora"—"he would wish to do better." Biss, of Spargrove, ornamented a window with his arms and motto, "Bis fecit, sis felix bis"— "Biss did this, do thou twice as much."

The organ was built by Smith, of Bristol, in 1837. The restoration of the church necessitated a change in the position of the instrument. At the time of its removal, it was enlarged by Messrs. Hill and Son, of London. The entire cost of the improvements being defrayed by the late Rev. Charles Kemble. The position in which it is placed, however, is singularly unfortunate, inasmuch as it blocks up the north transept, and thus destroys the harmony of the building. It would have been practicable to have con-structed a graceful gallery, on which to have placed it.

Painted Windows.

The first window is the gift of Thomas Gill, Esq.,

"in memory of his daughter, Louisa Gignac Waring, widow of Captain Waring, of Chewton Priory, Somerset." The work is by Clayton and Bell.

The second window is heraldic, and contains the shields of arms belonging to the St. Barbes. An ancestor of the family gave the original plain window in the year 1614. The following description is happy in its simplicity—"In memory of her late husband and his ancestors and her own, this window was restored by Harriet St. Barbe."

The third window is to the memory of John Smith Soden, F.R.C.S., and like the preceding, is by Messrs. Clayton and Bell.

The fourth window was presented by Mrs. Colonel Madox, of Bath, as a memorial to her husband, Colonel Henry Madox. The subject is Our Lord appearing to his Disciples after his Resurrection. The work is by Ward and Hughes. In these pictures the drawing is good, and the draperies admirably easy. The canopies and scrolls, above and below the central lights, are tasteful and harmonious.

The last window, next to the north transept, is the gift of the late rector, the Rev. Prebendary Kemble. It contains various illustrations of youthful piety, such as Samuel before Eli, and Timothy instructed by his mother. The subjects are executed by Messrs. Clayton and Bell.

Passing the organ, the first window, eastward of the obliterated transept, is erected by his widow to the memory of her husband, Edward Barrow Evans,

Esq., of Cheltenham, by whom the adjoining window was given in memory of his brother, the late Rev. Harry Barrow Evans, Hygrove, near Gloucester. Both are by Bell, of Bristol.

The third window is in memory of Maria Ann Doveton, widow of Lieut-Colonel Charles Jackson Doveton. It tells the story of Our Lord's First Miracle—the Conversion of Water into Wine—at Cana of Galilee.

The small window above the east door of this aisle, is by O'Connor, of London, and is dedicated by his brother officers to their sometime comrade, Humphrey Newman, Esq., 2nd Battalion, 6th Royal Regiment.

The paintings in the east window, which is the largest square-headed window in the kingdom, deserve special notice. Like so many of those already alluded to, they are the work of Messrs. Clayton and Bell, and were erected through the instrumentality of the Bath Literary Club, backed by the indefatigable energy of Jerom Murch, Esq., of Cranwells, by whom a large proportion of the funds was collected. The window contains four graduated tiers of seven lights each, the main subject being the prominent events in the life of Our Lord—from the Annunciation to the Ascension. The cost of the entire work was £1,270. The harmony of colour is very beautiful.

A reredos, admirable in taste and design, has been promised. Only one of the screens is as yet put up. Four more are required, the entire cost of which will be £1,432. The simplicity and beauty of the future work may be seen from the solitary specimen that has been placed *in situ.*

The window, at the east end of the south aisle, was presented by Mrs. Card and the Misses Jamieson. The four principal compartments are filled with figures representing the Evangelists.

The first window, in the south aisle of the choir, will shortly be filled with Munich glass, in memory of the late S. Brooke, Esq. (maternal uncle of the late rector), of Cowbridge. It was the last of the munificent gifts of the late Rev. Charles Kemble to the Abbey.

The second window was executed by Messrs. Burlison and Grylls, London. It contains the following inscription :—" To the glory of the Holy Trinity, and in the memory of William Gomm, of St. Petersburgh, and of his descendants buried in this church—this window is placed by his grandson, Sir William Maynard Gomm, K.C.B."

The third window will shortly be filled with a subject at the cost of a relative of the late rector. This window, which stands above the vestry door, was given in 1614 by " the Company of Tailors of Bath." At present it contains the arms of the company in the centre light.

The end window in the south transept is the munificent gift of Mrs. Rowland Elliott, of this city, as a memorial to her father Robert Scott, Esq., and of the restoration to health of the Prince of Wales. The lower compartments illustrate the sickness and recovery of King Hezekiah. The whole of the upper compartments represent what is termed a "Jesse window," showing the genealogy of Our Lord from the stem of Jesse. It is the work of Messrs. Clayton and Bell ; the entire cost was little short of £1,000.

The first window, west of the transept, bears the following inscription :—" In memory of James Heywood Markland, D.C.L., F.R.S., F.S.A." It is the work of Messrs. Clayton and Bell. The main subject, which occupies the entire width of the picture, illustrates the " Offering of the Magi."

The second window, erected to the memory of Admiral Duff, is by Messrs. Ward and Hughes, London. Among other scrolls and devices is the appropriate one, " They that go down to the sea in ships, and occupy their business in great waters, these men see the works of the Lord, and his wonders in the deep."

The third window is to the memory of the late George Norman, Esq., surgeon, F.R.C.S. The subject, which contains twenty-two figures, is very appropriate, namely, " Our Lord Healing the Sick."

The next window is the gift of Mrs. Slack, in memory of her husband, E. F. Slack, Esq., who died during his Mayoralty, in 1867.

The last window, in the south aisle, is the gift of the late Mrs. Robert Brooke, Royal Crescent, and is in memory of her son, Robert Arthur Brooke. It is the work of Ward and Hughes, London.

D

The small window above the south-west door, was presented by the contractors engaged in the restoration. It is by Bell, of Bristol, and consists of four compartments severally containing Moses, the builder of the Tabernacle, and David, Solomon, and Zerubbabel, the builders and restorers of the Temple.

The west window is unfinished, the three centre lights and a portion of the tracery being all that is at present *in situ*. A complete design has been prepared by Messrs. Clayton and Bell, illustrating the Old Testament History. Two of these lights have been put in by subscription, one of them being a memorial to Mr. John Hulbert. The tracery commemorative of Mr. Edward Jones, late churchwarden.

The small window above the north-west door, was given by some friends in memory of the late Mr. Charles Empson. It was painted by Chance, Birmingham.

The Freemasons of Bath and the Province of Somerset set on foot a movement to restore the west front of the structure, in imitation of the liberal and spirited enterprise of the Bristol brethren in connection with S. Mary Redcliff, the north-east corner of which was built at their expense. The attempt was, we regret to say, only partially successful. Still good service was rendered, and it may be hoped that what was so well begun may ultimately be completely accomplished at no distant day.

It would be scarcely just not to notice the merit of the carving of the stalls, and the delicacy of the work that enriches the pulpit, a memorial in honour of the former rector, the gentle and much beloved Bishop Carr.

The Communion Table is the gift of T. F. W. Walker, Esq.; the reading desk of several ladies of Bath; and the lectern of Mrs. Bligh. The font, which stands at the south-west end of the church, was designed by Sir Gilbert Scott, and the cost defrayed by subscription, in honour of the late rector during his lifetime. It may be stated that the sum spent upon the restoration and decoration of the Abbey, including the painted windows and other gifts, amounts to about £37,000.

Great credit is due to the Honorary Secretaries— William Long,* Frederick Shum,† and Richard

---

* William Long, M.A., F.S.A,, D.L., and Justice of the Peace, West Hay, Wrington, near Bristol, was for many years a resident in Bath, and took an active part in all that concerned its higher interests. As a churchman, he was regarded by the laity as a wise and judicious leader. Firm in his own convictions, he felt and expressed a tender regard for the opinions of those whose views differed from his own. When defending the Church, he maintained her cause modestly, but with unswerving resolution. Nothing that he said or did was calculated to embitter the controversy, or to wound the feelings of his opponents. Mr. Long's literary tastes are well known. Well read in general literature, in archæology and topography he is *facile princeps*. His exhaustive essay on Abury, published in the *Wiltshire Magazine*, and subsequently in an enlarged and separate form in 1862, is full of learning and interest. The Duties and Responsibilities of Magistrates, published in 1855, is an admirable treatise. Mr. Long's latest work consists of two papers on the Catacombs of Rome, read before the Literary Club in 1867-68, but not published till 1875. Embracing as it does the results of historical learning and conscientious local

Stothert, Esqrs., for the perseverance, energy, and zeal with which they co-operated with the Rector during the progress of the work.

We mention a few of the monuments most worthy of notice. Among them are Lady Waller's monument, those of Beau Nash, Admiral Sir William Hargood, Quin the actor, Caleb Hillier Parry, M.D., and the elaborate altar tomb of " the good Bishop Montague." It needs little guidance for the visitor to discern others worthy of notice besides these. Prior to 1834, every pillar in the church was surrounded with monumental tablets, placed in the most incongruous manner. These have all been transferred to the walls.

The Rev. Richard England Brooke, M.A., Canon of York, and late Vicar of Holy Trinity Church, Hull, succeeded the late Rev. Charles Kemble in the Rectory of Bath, of which the Simeon Trustees are the patrons, in 1875.

---

research, the work will prove interesting to students possessed of kindred tastes. Mr. Long has collected an extensive general library, as well as a valuable series of works on the topography and archæology of Bath.

† Mr. F. Shum, F.S.A., is a gentleman of considerable literary acquirements. In his paper on Barker, the Painter, he has done much to give that artist his true place amongst painters, whilst in his essay on Gainsborough, he has displayed considerable powers of analysis and a true appreciation of the rise and development of English art, and English artists, of which Gainsborough was one of the brightest types. Like his coadjutor, Mr. Long, he is a collector of " Bath Books," a taste to which may be attributed the fact that the fine library of local literature, collected by the late Mr. Charles Godwin, is now possessed by Mr. Shum in its entirety.

OLD CHURCHES AND OTHER BUILDINGS.

A CHAPTER ON RUINS.

THE church of **Saint Mary de Stall**, once the parish church of that part of the city which now forms the parish of St. Peter and St. Paul, occupied a portion of the ground extending from the end of the Pump Room portico, round Cheap Street to the passage leading to the Abbey Yard, and back again to Stall Street. Its exact position is unknown. Antiquaries have erroneously described it as standing on the site of the temple of Minerva, but the head of Apollo, found near the spot in 1727, and now on the mantel-piece in the Lecture Room of the Royal Institution, seems to prove it to have been the temple of Apollo, destroyed by St. David in 596, when the first Christian church was built. The vicarage of Stall, with Widcombe attached, was given to the convent of Bath by Bishop Button in 1236. In 1322, an ordinance was made requiring the vicar to reside constantly in the parish, a house and glebe-lands being given him in Parsonage Lane. He was also obliged to provide a curate for the church of Widcombe. For this service he received the tithes of Lyncombe, Widcombe, and Berewyke, paying the yearly sum of fifty shillings and fourpence to the prior. It is only within the last quarter of a century that Lyncombe and Widcombe have been constituted separate ecclesiastical parishes.

A portion of this building, we believe, may still be seen. In October, 1845, while Messrs. Arnold were at work in their cellars, they found that the pavement gave a hollow sound. A mason cut through a three-inch pennant stone and discovered beneath it a crypt of well-built masonry. This cellar is of ancient workmanship, having numerous apertures built up. There is little doubt that the vault formed a portion of the old church.

The will of Alderman John Chapman was proved in this church in 1544, as appears in the registry of Wells. "In 1584, the Mayor and Corporation," says Warner, "gave Sir Richard Meredith* the consolidated rectory. He, in return, presented them with all the church property, with the exception of the parsonage-house, on a lease for fifty years, at a rental of £62. This opportunity for erecting buildings was not lost; the sites of the ancient churches were destroyed, while the Abbey was polluted, disgraced, and spoiled by the mean residences and shops which

* Sir Richard Meredith appears to have been used by the Corporation merely as a convenient tool.

were attached to its august walls." In 1819, the Corporation resolved not to renew the leases; in 1823, two houses were taken down, and all were removed in 1834, when the building, as we have said, underwent considerable repairs.

At the dissolution, Stall's Church paid the monastery £8 15s. per annum.

The church of Saint Michael *intra muros*, said to have been erected on the site of a temple dedicated to Diana, was situated in Westgate Street at the corner of Cross Bath Lane, near an alley occupied by armourers' shops, called, from that circumstance, Spurrier's Lane, a name afterwards changed to Bridewell, in consequence of an ancient prison occupying the site of the present charity schools. This church was a large building, with tower, nave, and aisles, erected at the same time as Stall's Church. In 1180, it was thoroughly repaired by Bishop Fitzjocelyne, who attached the hospital of St. John the Baptist to the living. The church was destroyed in the sixteenth century.

The church of Saint Mary *intra muros*, (called by Sir Thomas Speke in his certificate to King Edward in 1553, the "paryshe of our ladye within the gate of Bathe,") was thoroughly repaired by Fitzjocelyne in 1180. Godwin, " *De presulibus Angliæ*," declares it to have been of great antiquity. We find that so late as 1541 rectors were appointed to it. The building joined the north gate, and the tower formed the city prison from 1590 to 1770. In Emmanuel Bowen's Map it is called the Free School.

Of the church of Saint Mary *extra muros*, no further record can be obtained than that it stood on the banks of the river eastward. It is supposed to have been at the bottom of Al'vord, afterwards Boat-stall, and now Slippery Lane, where a ferry, leading to Bathwick, formerly existed.

The chapel of Saint James was situated on the south east rampart, and another, dedicated to Saint Helena, the mother of Constantine the Great, stood between the north gate and Walcot, in Ladymead.

There was a chapel, dedicated to Saint Lawrence, on the Old Bridge, which gave its name to that structure. It was built in 1362. Before this time, the only passage was by a ford or ferry. Previous to the erection of the dams at Twerton, the river was easily fordable.

The Sanctuary Chapel, dedicated to St. Wære-burgh, who died in 699, as well as to St. John the Evangelist, and to St. Catherine, the patroness of the city of Bath, was founded by Nicholas, bishop of Llandaff in 1170, at the request of the prior and monks. In the Commissioners' Accounts, filed in the Augmentation Office, London, in 1553, it is called "Wayborough Chapel,"—an erroneous orthography, arising from an error in transcribing the ancient manuscript. The dipthong æ was anciently a e, in separate letters, while the r represented the modern y, or written *g*. "Lada" and "wære" are synonymous, both meaning "sanctuary." This chapel, which occupied the site of the present Fountain Buildings, was completely dilapidated at the Reformation, when

King Edward gave it to the Grammar School. Its yearly rental was, *for the church*, sixpence; for the garden, one shilling; and six shillings for Lady or St. Wæreburgh's mead. If the plot of ground, extending to Hay Hill, paid one shilling and sixpence, the mead, paying six shillings, must have been of considerable extent. In 1670, this property, without the mead, was leased by the Corporation for ninety-nine years, at a yearly rental of eightpence. In 1749, Wood describes Broad Street as extending as far northward as Wæreburgh Church, then an alehouse over the cistern which supplied the conduits in the upper part of the old city.

In 1766, another building lease was granted to various parties, at a rental (as appears from the report of the Charity Commissioners) amounting in all to £36. It was then denominated Fountain Buildings, from their occupying the site of the cistern.

Saint Winifred's was a small chapel, near a spring on the High Common, below Somerset Place.

Among the religious buildings which have been destroyed, two deserve our notice. In Frog Lane (now New Bond Street) stood the PRESBYTERIAN MEETING-HOUSE, which, after having being used for a variety of purposes, was converted into an equestrian circus, where Ducrow, when a boy, performed in 1805. This building was pulled down in 1810. The FRIENDS' MEETING-HOUSE stood at the west end of Marchant's Court (now Northumberland Place), and was removed in 1806, when Union Street was laid out.

PUBLIC CONDUITS.

WHILE ecclesiastics provided for the spiritual welfare of the city, they were not unmindful of the health and cleanliness of the inhabitants. To effect these desirable objects they erected conduits—no mean specimens of architectural skill.

Wood describes them as all situated in open and exposed situations. The first he mentions is Carn Well, of which remains now exist opposite the Bladud's Head Inn, Walcot Street. From the back of an alcove surmounted by a tower, the water issued into a basin for public use. It was destroyed about 1740.

Broad Street had a stone conduit in its centre.

St. Michael's stood in an open space in front of the ancient church. It was a handsome structure. The base formed a cube, having a dome-shaped tower of considerable height, bearing a square pedestal with coats of arms, the whole being surmounted by an hour-glass. Each front was ornamented with a niche from which the water issued.

Immediately within the north gate was an elegant building called St. Mary's conduit. It was quadrangular, surmounted by a domed roof, with a globe above, on which was placed a pinnacle; smaller globes ornamented each of the corners, from which the water constantly issued.

The Market Place was adorned with a High Cross conduit, which stood between the ancient Guildhall and the Abbey; Stall's conduit, between Cheap Street and Westgate Street, with another at the bottom of Stall Street, opposite St. James's Church, and from which it derived its name, complete the list.

These conduits appear to have been copiously supplied with water from a well on the slope of Beacon Hill, which Wood describes as a remarkable spring. "Persons," says he, "from great distances, come to fill their bottles and pitchers at Carn Well. Its water is of singular efficacy in weak eyes."

In Sir Thomas Speke's report to King Edward (to which we have already referred) it is called Walcot's water, returning, in 1553, a rental of sixteen pence. It was given by that amiable monarch to the Grammar School, having, previously to the Reformation, been rented by the priory of Bath for the supply of their conduits, at a variable rental payable in bread to the poor of Walcot parish.

Leland, in 1530, describes Holloway as a "rocky hill, full of fair springs of water;" and Henry Chapman, in 1673, begins his description of Bath by informing us of the bountiful supply of pure water,

"especially in the village adjoining it southwards,
where," says he, "there are fifty, if not more, habita-
tions, where scarce one house makes use of the water
that served another, each one enjoying a particular
spring to itself. From two of its hills the city, by
pipes of lead, is not only plentifully served into
common conduits, but also not a few of the private
houses are supplied within doors at such easy rates
that few places enjoy the like; and this, being carried
through streets, lanes, and byeways, is not only for
indoor occasions, but, in case of fire, very ready
to be made use of."

Wood informs us, in 1739, that most of the conduits had become useless, some of them being
replaced by single taps fixed against houses. They
were all removed when the various streets were
widened and improved. At this time no care was
taken to insure a free public supply.

In the year 1835, the Report of the Corporation
Reform Commissioners was published, and from it
we learn that the Corporation possessed the springs
of Beacon Hill and Beechen Cliff, and that the Sham
Castle springs were vested in them by Act of Parliament in 1769, but that every great landed proprietor
continued to supply his own tenants. In 1791, a
public company was formed for the benefit of St.
James's Square and the neighbourhood ; seven years
later the Corporation purchased the plant. In 1816,
this body modified the water rents, and in 1832,
expended £3,000 in increasing the supply and laying down new pipes.

In 1845, a Report on the Sanitary Condition of Bath, drawn up by Sir Henry de la Beche, was published by authority of Parliament. The document tells us that there were seven water companies, all independent of the Corporation; that unprotected by parliamentary sanction, no competition could take place, and that much of the water was wasted, Mr. Little stating in evidence that the surplus water of the Circus Company was sufficient to supply the population of Avon Street and Milk Street (the poorest portions of the city) for seven months in the year, and that no further outlay than the laying down of pipes was required. He also states that " he knows but of three stand pipes for the use of the poor, and that these only supplied for certain hours in the morning; the others get their supply how they can." It is obvious, therefore, that a better system was required.

With a few trifling exceptions, the water supply of the city is now vested in the Corporation by Act of Parliament. The supply is derived from various sources. There are three reservoirs in the immediate neighbourhood of the town, namely, in Cleveland Walk, Beechen Cliff, and at the rear of Camden Crescent. In Chilcombe Bottom, a beautiful and sequestered glen lying between Charmey Down and Little Solsbury, there is a chain of three reservoirs, which contain collectively about ten million gallons of water. Two of the tanks were constructed in 1846, the third in 1852. Other sources of supply are Monks' Wood, Oakford, and Cold Ashton, near the picturesque Valley of St. Catherine, a few miles from Bath.

These are now the largest and most important sources of supply. An Act of Parliament was obtained in 1870 to construct the works. Under this Act, a capital of £70,000 was raised, *i.e.*, £56,000 for the cost of the works, in addition to an annual rent-charge payment of £700 upon the Duke of Cleveland's springs in Bathwick, which, when capitalized at 5 per cent. per annum, represents a capital sum of £14,000.

The Corporation is about to apply to Parliament for powers to raise a further sum of £12,000, for the completion of the works authorised by the Act of 1870.

It may be added that while the supply is ample, and the quality good, the water rate of the borough is the lowest in the kingdom, Cheltenham, we believe, excepted.

THE BATHES OF BATHE AYDE.[*]

W E will not pause to inquire whether the hot springs led the Romans to form a settlement here, or whether, attracted by the beauty of the vale and the strong positions afforded by the surrounding hills, they selected it as an important military station, for both reasons appear to have had their influence. Inhabitants of a more genial clime, they loved spots sheltered from bleak winds, and were accustomed to look on baths as daily necessaries.

The *Roman* Baths were lost for ages, as the monks, unaware of their existence, built the monastery on their site, erecting baths adjoining Stall's Churchyard, where the Grand Pump Room stands. The remains were discovered in 1755. The foundations lay twenty feet below the surface, the walls being of wrought stone, eight feet high. The semi-circular bath was fifteen feet in diameter, floored with smooth flag-stones, having a stone seat running round it eighteen inches high. The descent was by seven steps. A

---

[*] By this name Dr. Jones, the first author who wrote on the use of the Bath Waters, described the mineral springs in 1572.

channel ran along the bottom, at a right angle towards the present King's Bath. Near it was a large oblong bath, having a colonnade on three sides, with pilasters intended to support the roof. On one side were two square sudatories. The walls were furnished with tubulated bricks, about eighteen inches long, with an orifice opening inwards to communicate heat to the apartment. The fireplace, a small conical arch, was placed near the outer wall, on each side of which were two sudatories, with smaller baths, and rooms used preparatory to entering the bath or the sudatory. These rooms communicated with each other, and were paved with small die-stones, of various colours, forming tesseræ. The waste water was conveyed to the Avon by a regular set of channels. Above these baths several stone coffins, with various relics of a later period, were discovered.

It may appear strange to us, of modern times, that Bishop Beckyngton should threaten with fine and excommunication all who bathed without proper clothing; but for the sake of decency, such a rule was adopted in 1449. Nash abolished the custom of both sexes bathing together. Even now bathers, in the King and Queen's Baths, are exposed to observation from the neighbouring houses.

Dr. Jones gives us an idea of the baths when Queen Elizabeth visited them. The proprietors beset visitors, each recommending his own bath. This nuisance became so intolerable that the Corporation petitioned King James (his consort, Queen Anne, having used the bath which Bellot enclosed in 1610, and from which circumstance it was called the Queen's Bath) to enclose them. This intention was frustrated by the King's death, and the subsequent civil wars.

In 1624, Sir Francis Stoner gave a sum of money for improving the King's Bath.

In 1628, Dr. Venner says "the baths were so fairly built that they exceeded all others."

In 1631, Dr. Jordan says, "he is sorry he cannot recommend their internal use, as they could not be procured clear enough for drinking." "The streets," he tells us, "are dunghills, slaughter-houses, and pig-styes. The butchers dress the meat at their own doors, while pigs wallow in the mire. The baths are bear-gardens, where both sexes bathe promis-cuously; while the passers-by pelt them with dead dogs, cats, and pigs."

In 1644, Queen Henrietta, the wife of Charles I., came for the benefit of the waters. In 1663, King Charles II. brought Queen Catherine to Bath for the same purpose.

The next year, under Captain Henry Chapman, the baths, pumps, &c., were improved.

In 1673, Sir Alexander Frazer, the King's physician, caused "drinking pumps" to be attached to the springs.

In 1688, Dr. Guidott calls the springs "the metro-politan waters of all England," and in the same year the Earl of Melfort erected a cross in the bath used by

E

Mary, the consort of King James II., from which circumstance it is supposed to derive its name; but Leland, in 1538, described it as then having a cross in the centre. "There be 2 springes of whote wather in the west-south-west part of the towne, whereof the bigger is caullid the *Crosse Bath*, because it hath a a cross erectid in the middle of it. This bath is much frequentid, and is temperate and pleasant, having 11 or 12 arches of stone for menne to stonde under yn tyme of reyne."

Queen Anne, with Prince George, her consort, visited Bath in 1702, when the old Pump Room was erected under the auspices of Beau Nash. This building was enlarged in 1751, and after several repairs and improvements, was taken down by the Corporation in 1796, and replaced by the present commodious structure. On its pediment is inscribed, in gilt letters, a pithy sentence from Pindar, of which Sir William Boyd gives us the following paraphrase :—

> Chief of Nature's works divine,
> Water claims the highest praise.

Dr. Sutherland thus describes the baths in 1760 :— "The slips resemble cells for the dead, rather than rooms for the living; their avenues are dark and narrow, far less conspicuous than the entrances of the meanest inns. The baths are unseemly ponds, exposed to wind and rain, as well as to the public gaze."

In May, 1788, Leonard Coward, then mayor, laid the foundation of the present private baths in Stall Street.

Near the Cross Bath is the Hot Bath and Pump Room, where the water rises from the earth at a temperature of 117 degrees Fahrenheit. Here, also, are seven very comfortable baths, fitted with white marble and glazed white tiles. Each bath contains more than fourteen hogsheads of water, and can be filled in about five minutes. To every bath there is a separate dressing-room. A douche, with reclining, vapour, and shower baths, of a very commodious description, are among the arrangements, as well as a tepid swimming bath, sixty-two feet long and twenty-three feet wide, which contains six hundred and seventy hogsheads of water, at a temperature of 88°.

The King's Bath is very ancient, for, in 1236, we find the prior disbursing a sum of money for its enclosure. It is sixty feet long, by forty-one feet wide. It is filled daily to the height of four feet seven inches, and contains something more than than three hundred and fourteen tons of water.*

* The natural temperature of the waters at the King's Bath, varies between 117 and 114 degrees Fahrenheit. The springs yield about 186,000 gallons every twenty-four hours. At the other three springs the temperature is lower. Upon chemical analysis of the Bath waters, they are found to contain in each pint, according to Mr. Walcker :—

	Grains.
Chloride of Sodium	1.89031
—— Magnesium	1.66744

The Queen's Bath adjoins the King's, and is supplied from the same spring. It is twenty-five feet square.

The private baths are also supplied from this spring, each bath being ten feet long, by six feet wide. They contain respectively thirteen hogsheads of water.

The baths in connection with the Grand Pump Room Hotel, are as it were erections of to-day. Fitted with all modern appliances, they are beyond question, as commodious and luxurious as any in the world. The Hotel offers special advantages to those who are crippled by gout, rheumatism, or palsy, as they can be lowered to the level of the baths by means of an hydraulic lift.

The diseases which are benefited by the Bath waters are—palsy, gout, rheumatism, nervous de-rangements, in which the brain is not materially affected, leprosy, chronic diseases of the skin, palsy from lead, poisonous effects produced by mercury

Sulphate of Potassa	0.36588
———— Soda	2.42145
———— Lime	10.20303
Carbonate of Lime	1.33339
Protocarbonate of Iron	0.03032
Allumina	0.01885
Silica	0.40419
Extractive matter	,, ,,
Grains	18.33486

Carbonic acid gas...... { at a temp. } ......0.05 cub. in.
Atmospheric air......... { of 114° } ......1.74 cub. in.

or other minerals; pain, weakness or contraction of limbs, dyspeptic complaints, biliary and visceral obstructions, etc.

Dr. Granville, after noticing the efficacy of the waters in the above complaints, adds :—" There is another class of diseases not mentioned in the foregoing enumeration of those benefited by the Bath waters, which ought not to be passed over lightly : I allude to those referable to the female constitution. During nineteen years' practice as an accoucheur in the Metropolis, I can safely aver that I have had reason to be highly satisfied on very many occasions with the Bath waters. Baden-Baden does not afford better results in such cases, although so much vaunted on that score ; and Tonbridge Wells water is decidedly inferior to it."

These baths do not relax the system, diminish the strength, or exhaust the spirits, even in persons previously weakened by disease, for, after remaining in the water twenty or thirty minutes, they come out refreshed, and find their spirits lighter and more cheerful. Dr. Lucas says, " The Bath waters, from the nature of their contents, are found particularly beneficial in a relaxed state of the fibres, by bracing and strengthening the solids."

Sir George Gibbes, Dr. Spry, Dr. Barlow, and other distinguished physicians, bear testimony to the benefit dyspeptic patients derive from their use ; and Dr. Falconer observes, that " every medical practitioner at this place has seen instances of people labouring under want of appetite, pain, and spasm of the stomach and bowels, with all the symptoms of depraved digestion, joined to a very great degree of weakness, both of body and spirits, relieved by the use of the Bath waters. The recovery in such cases is particularly remarkable, taking place quickly after the commencement of the remedy. A few days will frequently work such a change as would be scarcely credible were it of less common occurrence."*

When, however, any of these complaints are accompanied with pain in the chest, spitting of blood, palpitation of the heart, undue determination of blood to the head, or by a tendency to epileptic attacks, the waters are injurious.†

The whole of the Baths and Pump Rooms are under the management of the Corporation.

* The Reader is referred to a Work by Dr. Falconer, entitled " *The Baths of Bath,*" for a more exhaustive account of the waters.

† As many of these symptoms may be referable to causes requiring very opposite modes of treatment, those who suffer from any of the above affections are advised to consult some medical man before deciding that the waters are *un*suited to their case.

THE HOSPITALS.

BATH, says Dr. Guidott, writing in 1673, "is one great hospital;" and most truly may it be said, that no city, ancient or modern, possesses so many noble charities. Here, indeed, misery has always sought and obtained that relief which no other place can afford.

In the following sketch we purpose to give such an account of these institutions, as may explain the object of their foundation.

We have undoubted evidence that from the earliest periods, provision was made for poor strangers resorting to the mineral springs. The *Lear lands*, within the south gate, but without the walls of the convent, were appropriated to the sick, and John of Tours erected a bath for them in the Abbey Churchyard.

The oldest charity is the 𝕷epers' 𝕳ospital, founded by Bishop Robert de Lewes, who embroiled himself in state affairs during King Stephen's commotions with the Empress Maude. Having taken Geoffrey de Talebot, one of her spies, and placed him in " durance vile," the people of Bristol (warm adherents of the Empress) came unexpectedly to Bath, and took, as the old chronicler has it, " the Bishop away with them to Bristol." The Knight and the Bishop were both soon after released.

A hospital was built in 1138 near the Hot Bath, for the accommodation of seven lepers. In Wood's time it had fallen into decay. The building stood at the corner of " No where-lane," so called in consequence of Mr. Robert Chapman, mayor in 1669, having a servant girl fond of slipping out at the back door, who when discovered, said she had been "no where." Being traced to this spot, which had previously no name, it was called " No where-lane." The passage led from the Hot Bath to Westgate Buildings.

In 1712, Miss Strode, of Downside, gave £5 yearly to this hospital, directing it to be paid between eleven and twelve o'clock on Lady-day in the chancel of the Abbey church, that is to say, during morning service. This payment was continued until 1786, when the hospital was destroyed. In 1825, a decree was obtained from the Court of Chancery that this sum, with the arrears, should be paid to the president and governors of the Bath Hospital, who now annually receive the sum above mentioned out of the Tadwick estate.

The next in point of antiquity is the hospital of St. John the Baptist, founded by Bishop Fitzjocelyne in 1174, who endowed it with £22 19s. 6d. yearly.

Sir Thomas Speke examined its revenues in 1553. "There is," says he, in his report to the King, "an hospital called St. John's, having lands, tenements, and hereditaments thereunto belonging, of the clear yearly value of £25 13s. 8d. This hospital was erected, it is said, for the relief of six poor men, and one priest, or master, to serve them, having their continual living upon the same. The hospital is annexed to the parish church of St. Michael, *intra muros*, and the parson is master of the hospital; the residue of the profits is employed and received by the said master. No foundation shown, nor would the master appear."

This charity survived the Reformation, and with similar institutions becoming vested in the Crown by act of Parliament, King Edward VI. dispatched commissioners throughout the kingdom to discover what were then called "concealed lands." Being suffered to dilapidate, Queen Elizabeth granted it a share of the money raised by brief for the restoration of the Abbey in the year 1573. The Corporation, in whom the patronage had been vested by Queen Elizabeth, resolved that the mayor, for the time being, should be master of the hospital, and should dispose of its revenues as he pleased. This continued until 1662, when the Corporation omitting to present, King Charles II. gave the hospital to his chaplain, John Rustat, who in 1665, granted his brother Tobias a lease of the property at a rental of £130. This lease terminating in 1711, the master, Mr.

Clement, leased it to his son on the same terms. In 1716, the Rev. John Chapman, who succeeded him, filed a bill and gained a decree which set this lease aside, directing the rent to be £163 15s. 2d., and the fine not less than £3,922. In 1727, Wood was employed to rebuild the hospital. It was his first work in the city. The leases granted after the decree expired in 1813, when the fines, amounting to £5,000, were fairly divided between the master and almspeople, he receiving two-thirds, and they one. The master is bound to keep the building in repair, to provide for the regular performance of divine worship, and to pay a nurse. There are six men and six women, who have each a separate apartment, receiving £2 a year for clothes and coal, and five shillings weekly. Applicants must be fifty years of age, unmarried, ten years resident in Bath, and members of the Church of England, of good report. The appointment rests with the master. The Charity Commissioners reported, in 1820, that the affairs of this hospital were well managed. The rooms over the hospital are now let in tenements, to artizans, labourers, and the like, although they were originally erected by the Duke of Chandos for the accommodation of the nobility and gentry. They are unconnected with the hospital, excepting in so far as they increase its revenues.

"Improvement," says the Rev. John Earle in his "Guide to the Knowledge of Bath Ancient and Modern," "is still the order of the day in Bath.

One of the aims now before the local Charity Trustees is the obtaining a new scheme for making St. John's Hospital more useful. Eleven years ago, in 1855, the Court of Chancery determined that the foundation was a municipal, and not an ecclesiastical one, and made an order that the Trustees of the Municipal Charities should be appointed Trustees of the patronage, which at that time the Corporation were about to sell. In the meantime the matter had been before the Charity Commissioners, and there it seemed likely to stay, when Mr. E. T. Payne (secretary to the Bath Charity Trustees) came into office. By a vigorous correspondence with the Commissioners, he has got the business so far matured that they have 'certified' the Attorney-General that he may institute legal proceedings in the matter."

After protracted litigation the "St. John's Hospital Scheme," for the future management of this important Charity has at length been settled. As the document which now lies before us is infinitely too long for insertion, we must content ourselves with one or two extracts. "The Charity, and property thereof, shall be under the management and control of trustees."

"As the income of the charity increases the trustees may, by making the requisite arrangements in the present hospital building or by appropriating for the purpose other adjacent houses or buildings belonging to the Charity, the leases whereof shall have expired, provide accommodation for an increased number of almspeople, and may increase the number of almspeople accordingly. The trustees may also, if they shall think fit and the income of the Charity allow, appoint persons, who would be qualified under the provisions of this scheme to be almspeople, as out-pensioners. Such additional almspeople and out-pensioners respectively shall receive the like stipend of ten shillings a week, and be subject to the same conditions and regulations (so far as applicable) as the original almspeople. They shall also (except with the previous consent of the trustees) reside within the limits of the city and borough of Bath, or within three miles of such limits, under penalty of forfeiture of their pensions."

"When, by the falling in of the existing leases of the Charity property or otherwise, the income of the Charity shall be increased to a sum which, in the opinion of her Majesty's Attorney-General, shall make it desirable that a new or further scheme should be settled for the administration of this charity, application shall be made by him, or by the trustees with his sanction, to the Court of Chancery for the purpose."

Regarding the scheme in question, Sir Roundell Palmer* writes :—" We have heard that opposition is expected from the lessees who hold under the hospital, but surely they have no right to complain if their legal rights are not encroached on and their

---

* Now Lord Selborne.

reasonable claims treated in a fair and liberal spirit. At all events such claims must not be allowed to stand in the way of any scheme which, whilst dealing honourably with all existing rights, shall remove the reproach which now exists that a property intended for the use of the poor, and which ought to yield £8,000 per annum, only produces £1,260." Such figures render comments unnecessary. Some years probably must elapse before all the funds derivable from the Charity can be disposed of according to the intention of the founder. It can, however, only now be a question of time.

St. Catherine's Hospital is stated to have been built by seven sisters, of the name of Binbury, on some arable land within the town wall, called by Sir Thomas Speke in his report, "Bynburye landes," anciently belonging to a family of that name. Wood is in error when he says it derived its name from Catherine of Arragon, Queen Mary's mother. We have already said that St. Catherine was patroness of the city of Bath, it being part of the ancient oath that every freeman should keep her day holy, as may be seen in the *Codex Ruber Bathoniæ*, now preserved in the library at Longleat. The manuscript is interesting, and contains the legend of St. Catherine, written by one of the monks in the 15th century. We take the liberty of modernising the following :—

> " Sovereigns and friends that be now here,
> And that would like your souls to save,
> List to a lesson of heart'ly cheer,
> With heart'ly cheer ye shall it have.

So shall a lesson of health be taught,
How that ye shall heaven win ;
Have it, and learn it, forget it not,
Of the maid and martyr, St. Katerynne."

The Hospital derives its other name, "The Black
Alms," from the colour of the gowns worn by the
almspeople. It was included in the grant of lands
given to the Corporation for charitable uses by King
Edward in 1552. These consisted of eighty-two tenements, including the White Hart Inn,* Fountain
Buildings, Bladud Buildings, (these two forming the
old Wæreburgh Mead), the Monks' Mill, and many
others. "The same spirit," says Warner, "which
had been manifested with respect to St. John's,
appeared in this case also, so that in 1735, a decree
was obtained from the Court of Chancery for the
restoration of lands ;" and a long Chancery suit was
terminated by the Corporation agreeing to surrender
certain property to the Charity Trustees, for the use
of the hospital and the Free School founded by
King Edward VI.

Wood describes the hospital as a "mean edifice,
two stories high, with a frontage of eighty-five feet
in Bynburye Lane." He says, "it receives thirteen
poor people, inhabitants of Bath, ten of whom are
clothed in sable garments, and receive an allowance
of fourteen pence weekly." In 1825, this building
was pulled down to make room for the United
Hospital, the Corporation erecting another near its

* The Grand Pump Room Hotel now stands on the site of
this once celebrated Inn.

site. It is a collegiate building of the Elizabethan style. The Charity Commissioners report in 1820, that ten poor women receive 3s. 6d. weekly, with a black gown once in two years, and that the vacancies are filled up by the Mayor for the time being. This continued until the Corporation Reform Bill of 1835, since which period the charity property has been vested in the hands of trustees, who require that candidates for vacancies shall have been house-keepers, except in very urgent cases, and that they shall be recommended by at least twenty ratepayers. The full number of fourteen pensioners is now clothed and maintained.*

In the extensive grants of land given by by King Edward, the 𝔊rammar 𝔖chool largely participated. In the year 1553, he gave them the west gate for their school-room. Some years later, it was removed to the body of the desecrated church of St. Mary, by the north gate, where it continued until the present school-house was built by the Corporation in 1752. The following is a copy of the petition of the citizens for these lands :—

" *Memorandum,— That I, the Mayor of Bath, with the citizens of the same town, do desire the lands and tenements hereunto annexed, of the king's majesty's gift, to us and our successors for ever, to teach a free Grammar School there, and also for the relief of the poor people: in witness, &c., by me,* EDWARD LUDWELL."

* The weekly payments to each pensioner at present amounts to 5s., and biennially a black cloth cloak or gown, value 30s.

King Edward, reciting this petition in his grant, declares it to be a free Grammar School for ever, for the education and instruction of boys and young men.

Prior to the Reformation, the tithes were in the hands of the clergy. One-third of the sum was expended on the church itself; another third went to the poor; and the remaining third was the priest's. The youth were educated by the ecclesiastics, and the monasteries formed schools. Young ladies were received into nunneries, for their education; while religious persons, of both sexes, taught the children of the poor. This system was changed by Henry VIII.; the Church lands being sequestrated by gift or sale, so that the tithes passed into the possession of the Laity. In King Edward's reign, therefore, a petition for the poor was to be expected, and many of the Church lands remaining in the hands of the Crown, were devoted to their service, and to the foundation of free schools. In the reign of Queen Elizabeth, compulsory assessments for the relief of the poor became necessary, and were enforced by acts of parliament, which continued until the passing of the poor law in 1834. The Churches, also dilapidated by time, became ruinous, and King Charles I., a century afterwards, at the request of Archbishop Laud, issued a 'king's letter, calling on parishes to repair the buildings "dedicated by their pious ancestors to the service of the Most High."

No sooner, however, had the Corporations throughout the kingdom obtained possession of these lands, than fraud and sequestration became apparent, so that an act of parliament was passed, in 1601, "to redress the misemployment of lands, &c., heretofore given for charitable uses." Under this act, king George II. issued a commission in 1734 to inquire into the state of the Bath Grammar School, and a decree was made by Queen Caroline (regent during the King's absence in Hanover) "that, for thirty-five years, the master should instruct *gratis*, ten sons of freemen, or inhabitants of Bath, during which time he should receive £10 per annum; and that, after the expiration of that term, he should receive £50 yearly." In 1811, the Master received £80 per annum, together with the benefice of Charlcombe, which was annexed to the School by a decree of the Court of Chancery, in 1738, at the instance of the Rev. Walter Robins, then Master, who also successfully resisted some of the abuses of his day.

The school is now under the management of a Board of Governors who are partly ex-officio, partly elective, and partly co-operative, and is conducted in accordance with the scheme prepared in 1872 by the Endowed Schools Commissioners, and ratified by the Queen in Council. This scheme sanctioned the sale of the advowson of Charlcombe, prior to the death of the late Head-Master in 1874, and the appropriation of the purchase money to

F

the augmentation of the Endowment Fund of the
School. The stipend of the Head-Master is now
fixed at £150 per annum, but besides this sum
he receives one-third of the capitation fees, and a
house,* rent free. It may be added, that the capitation fees are £9 per annum in the senior, and £6
in the junior department. Boys who gain exhibitions are exempted from this charge. The system
of education, which was formerly the rigid Grammar
School curriculum, has, under the above scheme,
been greatly modified and brought more into harmony with the requirements, or supposed requirements, of the present day. The School is open to
all classes. The Head-Master is the Rev. H. E.
Sanderson, M.A.

Bellot's Hospital. In the year 1609, Thomas
Bellot, steward of the household to Queen Elizabeth,
purchased an estate in Wiltshire for £300, and with
it, endowed a hospital in Bell Tree Lane, at the
corner of the "Bynburye" lands, for the reception of
twelve of the poorest strangers who should come to
Bath for the benefit of the waters. Queen Elizabeth,
in 1590, vested the springs in the Corporation, and
in 1597 an act was passed, giving the poor of the
kingdom a right to their free use. This act, enforced
by subsequent acts passed in 1603, 1628, and 1642,
empowered justices to license such persons to travel
to Bath. Limiting their expenses, it authorised them

---

* Built in 1752.

to demand assistance from the parishes through which they passed. In 1714, these acts became extinct, so that Bath was infested with vagrants at the very time when the rich were beginning to patronize it. For the following particulars we are indebted to Wood. vol. 2, p. 206 :—

BELLOT'S HOSPITAL AS IT WAS.

"For the benefit of the poor, to whom the legislature had given the free use of the baths, Mr. Bellot purchased a piece of the priory land, joining the south side of the King's Bath, and made a cistern for them to bathe in temperate water. This cistern received the overflowing of the King's bath; and, taking the name of the New Bath, retained it until the year 1615, when it was joined to the King's Bath by means of an aperture, and then it was dignified by the name of the Queen's Bath on this remarkable occasion :—As Anne, the queen of James I., was bathing, one day, in the King's Bath, there arose from the bottom of the cistern, by Her Majesty's side, a flame like a candle, which had no sooner ascended to the top of the water, than it spread itself upon the surface into a large circle of light, and then became extinct. This so frightened the queen that she betook herself to the New Bath, and from thence the cistern was called the Queen's Bath."

"In order that the poor," continues Wood, "might not be destitute of instructions how to use the water, Elizabeth, Viscountess Scudamore, in 1652, gave £8 annually to a physician, that he might gratuitously advise the poor." This salary has been slightly augmented, and the annual stipend of £10 is now paid to the medical officer by the Charity Trustees, who nominate the inmates of the Hospital.

An erroneous impression prevails that Bellot acted only as trustee to Robert Cecil, Earl of Salisbury, to whom the honour of this foundation has been assigned. The following quotation, however, from Sir

John Harington's poetical address to Bishop Montague, seems to place the point beyond dispute :—

" So far has Bellot's star outshin'd,
 Whoever has to church been kind,
 As doth full moon, in starry night,
 Exceed the lesser torch's light.
 The church's ornaments, the floor,
 The benches, windows, seats, and door
 Call Bellot father ; and the bell
 Rings Bellot, though it ring a knell.
 Hospitals, baths, streets, and highways
 Sound out the noble Bellot's praise,
 'Cause he was pious, and hath given
 Much, whose reward shall be in heaven.
 Let bounteous Bellot take the palm,
 And after age his name embalm ;
 I envy not, but more rejoice,
 And give him, too, my thankful voice."

We well remember this hospital with its venerable quadrangle and antiquated chambers, eloquent of the olden time ; nor do we forget the entrance gate, rich with shields, ornaments, and inscriptions.

Worn out with long service, it was pulled down in 1859, and re-opened in the following year. The dilapidated but picturesque quadrangle is no more, and a modern erection, less ornamental than useful, now represents the Bellot's Hospital of 1609. A portion of the old gateway, however, has been preserved.

It seems strange that no memento of the founder should have existed on the original building. Above the old doorway were placed the arms of Rustat, surmounting a marble tablet, which relates that the ground, being a portion of the land belonging to St.

John's Hospital, was freely granted, without fine, to the mayor, aldermen, and citizens, by Tobias Rustat, brother and lessee to John Rustat, clerk, master of St. John's Hospital, to the end that it may be restored and continued to the same use to which it had been applied by Thomas Bellot, gentleman, since his first obtaining the same of the master, co-brethren, and sisters of the said hospital. This tablet bears date March 25, 1672, and, being all the record of the charity visible to the public, caused it to be misnamed "Rustat's Charity."

The rents in 1820, amounted to £76 per annum. At the present time the annual income is about £220. The hospital is open for the reception of patients, from Lady-day to Michaelmas, or longer if the funds permit. Each inmate (of whom there are 11, when the Hospital is full) has a furnished apartment, and receives a weekly payment of two shillings and four-pence. A new bath has lately been erected inside the Hospital for the patients. The ancient bath for Lepers is also appropriated to their use, as well as to that of all poor persons, who procure orders from the Mayor, or any medical man. The different sexes bathe on alternate days.

The Mineral Water Hospital. In 1715, a scheme was put forth for the establishment of a general hospital, but from a variety of circumstances, it was not carried into effect until 1737. Among the foremost of its supporters were Dr. Oliver, Beau Nash, and Ralph Allen, who gave all the stone from his quarries, while John Wood contributed the plans, and superintended the erection of the building. By an Act of Parliament, passed in 1739, for its incorporation and government, the institution may possess freehold property to the extent of £1,000 a year. The hospital was opened for the reception of patients on the 21st May, 1742; since which period, 49,411 patients have been admitted, of whom 39,711 were either cured or greatly relieved.

To increase its usefulness, the waters were introduced into the interior of the building in 1830. Powerful steam machinery was erected, not only for pumping, but also for ventilation, washing, and cooking. These improvements have rendered the treatment of disease more successful. In 1835, the inhabitants of Bath, previously excluded, were allowed, under certain conditions to become in-patients.

The beneficiaries of this charity require no recommendation but that of poverty, and the case being suitable for the use of the waters. It is open to the United Kingdom, the eligibility of each case being ascertained by a circumstantial report, which must contain—

1. The name, age, and parish of the applicant.

2. A brief history of the disease, comprising its origin, progress, and present symptoms.

3. A correct statement of the general health, particularly mentioning the absence of all disorders, which render the Bath waters inapplicable.

When practicable, these facts should be stated by

a medical man, and addressed to the Registrar of the
hospital, who submits them to the Medical Board.
Accuracy of report is necessary, for when, from
defective or erroneous statements, cases are found
to be unsuitable, the patients are sent home. Soldiers
may be admitted by certificates from their commanding officers, who shall also agree to receive them when
discharged, in whatever state of health they may be.
The same regulation applies to pensioners of Chelsea
and Greenwich.

On receipt of a notice of vacancy, the patient
brings a certificate, duly executed, and the caution-
money (three pounds), for those who come from any
part of England or Wales, and five pounds for those
from Scotland or Ireland. The object of this regulation is to ensure the means of returning patients to
their homes, when discharged; or to defray the
cost of interment in the event of death. When not
required for these purposes, or for clothing, the whole
is returned. All persons coming to Bath on pre-
tence of seeking admission, without having their
cases previously approved, and receiving notice of
vacancy, are treated as vagrants.

In 1874, out of 851 patients discharged, no fewer
than 747 were cured, or greatly relieved; while 89
were either incurable by the waters, or unsuited for
their use.

Within the past few years this institution has
been greatly enlarged and improved. The founda-

tion stone of the new building was laid June 4th, 1859, and the work was completed June 11th, 1861. The new part has been very happily united with the original structure. The entire cost of the addition amounted to £18,000. At present the hospital contains 145 beds of which **88 are** appropriated to males and 57 to females. For light, air, space, and convenience, the Bath Mineral Water Hospital may compare favourably with any similar building in the kingdom.

It is to be regretted that an erroneous opinion prevails that this hospital is independent of public support; its average expenses, for the last ten years, were £4,472 yearly, while its permanent income has averaged only £2,581 per annum.

The Royal United Hospital, situated in Beau Street, was erected in 1826, at an expense of £7,000. It receives its name from the union of the Casualty Hospital, founded in 1788, by James Norman, Esq., with the Bath City Infirmary and Dispensary, on the Lower Borough Walls. The building has recently been enlarged by the addition of the "Albert Wing," the cost of which amounted to about £8,000. The entrance-hall contains a fine bust of the late Prince Consort. Beneath the pediment is the following: "The Prince's Wards, erected in memory of Albert the Good, A.D. 1864."

The number of in-patients admitted during the year 1874 was 1,018; of which 465 were medical, and 553 surgical cases. Of these 543 were discharged cured; 307 relieved; 94 died; and 74 remained in the hospital on the 31st December, 1874.

The number of medical out-patients was 5,062; of surgical and dental, 3,323; 515 out-patients were visited at their own homes; making a total of 8,900 out-patients. This, added to the number of in-patients, gives a total of 9,918 patients during the year 1874.

The total income of the hospital from funded property does not exceed £425 per annum. The total expenditure during the past year amounted to £4,760 12s. 9d., which was defrayed by receipts from annual subscriptions, donations, collections in churches and chapels, and legacies. The amount required from voluntary sources to meet the annual average expenses is little less than £4,500.

IN AND OUT OF BATH.

WALK THE FIRST.

THE ORANGE GROVE; THE PARADES; ACROSS THE
BRIDGE; UNDER THE RAILWAY ARCH; THROUGH
CLEVELAND WALK; UP THE NORTH ROAD TO
SHAM CASTLE; HAMPTON DOWN; HOME BY
THE CANAL OR THE WARMINSTER ROAD.

BATH, pre-eminently distinguished for the
variety and beauty of its suburban walks,
presents an almost endless succession of delightful
prospects.   Every hill gives us new features, every
ramble new views.   The valleys, with neat cottages
clustering around village churches, have each a charm
of their own.   Nor is this all, for the taste of the
citizens has, in many cases, by the formation of
public walks, rendered these beauties easily available.

Leaving the Orange Grove by the site of St. Peter's
Gate, we reach the Walks, on the left of which
stands the Royal Literary Institution.   This portion

of the city (erected partly within, and partly beyond, the ancient walls) is full of interest for the student. In an alley, beyond what used to be the Freemasons' Hall, stands Ralph Allen's town house—a fine specimen of Wood's architectural talent. The portico is imposing, and the front richly carved.

Wood began the improvement of the city by the erection of the North Parade, the first stone of which was laid on the 10th March, 1740. According to the original design the Parades were to have been adorned with three hundred columns and pilasters of the Corinthian order; at each corner there was to have been a tower, and in each front, a centre house and pediment. In the inner square, it was proposed to build a superb ball room, ninety feet long, by fifty-two broad, with an assembly room of the same dimensions. The plan was never completed. Here formerly might be seen the pomps and vanities of Bath; the ladies, with their hoops and towering head-dresses, followed by pert abigails and pampered lap-dogs, each fair dame attended by her powdered beau, reciting vapid rhymes, or the last naughty scandal.

Pierrepont Street, from the centre house of which Lord Chesterfield wrote some of his questionable letters to his son, is classic ground. Previous to the opening of the railroad, it was the dullest street in Christendom. Now it forms a busy highway. Opposite Pierrepont House, an opening (which Wood calls St. James's portico) led to the theatre, since converted into a Roman Catholic Chapel, and more recently into a Masonic Hall.

From the South Parade may be seen the Roman Catholic Church, a beautiful structure, St. Matthew's Church, Widcombe, the Great Western Railway Station, Beechen Cliff, the Cemetery, Prior Park, and Bathwick Hill. The foreground comprises the old Ham Gardens, where formerly stood the Abbey Grange, around whose walls the chapmen congregated to hold the chartered fair of Bath. Here grapes, for the cultivation of which the city was famous, were trained on standards in the foreign manner.

Passing through Duke Street, we cross the North Parade Bridge. The Abbey and St. Michael's Church are seen to advantage from this spot. Bathwick Church, and many neat villas occupy our attention, till we reach the railway bridge, under which a footway leads to the Canal. Crossing it by a small iron bridge, a steep path leads to Cleveland Walk. This walk which derives its name from the Cleveland family, extends from Bathwick Hill to the North Road, and forms one of the most agreeable promenades in the neighbourhood of the city. It commands an extensive view.

From Sham Castle, which stands conspicuously on the slope of the hill, there is a more extensive, though scarcely a more beautiful prospect. The building was originally erected by Ralph Allen, in order to break the monotony of the view from his house on the Parade. Following the North Road for about a quarter of a mile, we pass through a small gate, and soon reach the crest of the hill. On every side, the heights which encircle the city, slope somewhat abruptly into the valley. Squares and cres-

SHAM CASTLE.

cents, streets and terraces, lie mapped out with marvellous distinctness. The sluggish Avon flashes for a moment over the weir, and then pursues its tranquil way. The train speeds westward, decked with a plume of snowy vapour, and far away the Mendips and the Cotswolds, mingle their blue distance with the sky.

The view comprises the whole country between Alfred's Monument at Stourton, and Beckford's Tower on Lansdown. Englishcombe Barrow, and Kelston Round Hill, are striking objects in the picture.

HAMPTON DOWN.

THE walk over the turf is delightful. From this point the valley, east of the city, is seen to great advantage. Yonder, is the old British fortress of Solsbury; Batheaston nestles in the meadows; and further to the east is Banagh Down or Holy Hill. A few hundred yards to the south-east may still be traced a portion of the WANSDYKE—an intrenchment erected as a boundary between two tribes, whose names are now well nigh forgotten. The view from Hampton Rocks was considered unrivalled by the celebrated painter, Sir Benjamin West.

The old British city of Caer Badon stood a little to the north-west of these rocks.

The Celtic Britons held possession of the country until it was invaded and conquered by the Belgæ, 350 years before the Christian era. These being subdued by the Romans, the country became an integral portion of the empire. From the remotest period the ancient Britons carried on an extensive trade with the Phœnicians in tin and other mineral productions; indeed, many of their mining implements, are still met with both in Cornwall and

Somerset. Diodorus Siculus informs us their tribes were well governed, skilful in various arts, more particularly in navigation; and that the whole of the southern coast of Britannia was a busy scene of industry, wealth, and comparative civilization. Religious principles, embracing a system of morality, honour, and virtue, were assumed to have been inculcated by the Druids.

The mines were sedulously guarded; every available height was fortified by the Belgic Britons. Many of these fortifications may still be traced in the vicinity of Bath. "These," as Sir Richard Colt Hoare tells us, "must not be confounded with Roman camps, which were built in more convenient localities, and of more regular form, the Britons depending on the strength of their position, the Romans on the courage of their soldiers." •

From this digression we return to Caer Badon, which occupied a projecting point of the down. The entrenchments surrounded a space of thirty acres, and sloped abruptly northward. On the side of the hill are the remains of a vallum or earthwork, which probably afforded additional security to the inhabitants. The approaches were guarded by outworks of various sizes. Many trackways may still be traced, which communicated with distant settlements; some of these form our present pathways, while others have become modern highways. On the north of the down are two long barrows, or places of sepulture; and on its southern side two circular mounds. The numerous elevations of earth which intersect each other in every direction, preserve a regular form, and seem to point out the site of various buildings.*

Sir Richard Colt Hoare opened and examined many barrows, and deserves the thanks of all British antiquaries for his indefatigable researches. "From their contents," he says, "the early progress of civilization may be traced. The most ancient, which may reasonably be referred to the Celtic period, contain the stone hammer and flint spear-head of the tenant of the grave, together with clay urns, formed by the hand alone, rudely ornamented with crossed lines, evidently produced by a stick before exposure to heat."

The Belgic Britons, we are told, reduced the bodies of their warriors to ashes. These were carefully collected. A covered receptacle was formed of un-cemented stones, over which was raised a pile of earth, varying in size according to the rank of the deceased. In these barrows we find brass weapons, ivory pins, beads, rings, and pottery. This custom of burying the weapons and other valuable articles with the deceased continued for some centuries after this period; many of the coffins of our early kings and ecclesiastics containing both the vestments and in-signia of authority.

* The Editor does not hold himself responsible for the fore-going statements. The Rev. Prebendary Scarth, in his able work, "Aquæ Solis," dismisses the subject in little more than a single line. "Hampton Down, where there are vestiges of an ancient British settlement," p. 16.

G

As neither the tiller of the land, nor the quarry-man, have obliterated its features, Caer Badon may, as far as its outlines and general aspect are concerned, be still traced, and will repay a visit.

"In 1835," says Mr. Mendenhall, of the Bath Athenæum, in his communication to the Society of Antiquaries, "this spot was partially broken into, to procure material for the new Warminster Road, which runs along the valley below; but as none offered, it was spared further molestation. A short time afterwards I collected a quantity of ancient pottery, which was thickly strewed about, of various qualities, from the coarse black, or brown, to the more delicate Roman, but of this latter few and small fragments; with them, portions of Roman bricks and burned bones, a boar's tusk, and animals' teeth in abundance; with a curvilinear notched ornament of dress; a small blue bead, of transparent glass, decidedly British. I also found black vegetable mould, totally differing from the neighbouring soil; the portions of stone about in no case resembling the kind found in the vicinity, clearly indicating that they were brought from a considerable distance. I found, also, some rusty nails, of various forms and sizes."

"These various works," says the Rev. Mr. Phelps,* of Bicknoller, the latest historian of the county, "prove, in connection with the numerous fortifications in this county and the neighbouring one of

* This work, it is to be regretted, he did not live to complete.

Wilts, the great skill of the Belgic-British engineers."
They are the works, indeed, if not of a great, at
least of a semi-civilized people.

If we follow the straight line of the tramway
through the wood—the spot is very charming—
we shall be enabled to return either by the Canal
or the Warminster Road. The entire distance is
between four and five miles.

IN AND OUT OF BATH.

WALK THE SECOND.

Through Pulteney Street; up Bathwick Hill; Claverton as it was, and as it is. Duelling; Homewards by the Banks of the Canal; Bathampton; the Parish of Bathwick; length of Walk.

IT is much to be regretted that the high walls on the south side of Bathwick Hill hide from the pedestrian the beautiful prospects he would otherwise enjoy. To those who can, without inconvenience, manage a sharp incline, Bathwick Hill forms an agreeable walk, the pavement being continued to the summit. Its position shelters it from the north-east wind; while the sun, even in the winter, renders it both warm and pleasant. These advantages, with the exception of the pavement, are shared by the North Road, which however far exceeds it in beauty, embracing as it does a view of Beechen Cliff, Saint Matthew's Church, and the quiet valley of Smallcombe, so called to distinguish it from its neighbour, Widecombe, or Widcombe. On reaching the summit of the hill, a road, diverging to the left, conducts us to the village of

CLAVERTON.

The first portion of the way, fenced in by plantations and pleasant hedgerows, runs over the Down. Presently, we reach the Italian lodge of Claverton Manor, and find ourselves *vis a vis* with a lovely bit of genuine English scenery. On the opposite side of the valley, peeping from the foliage of the hillside, is the picturesque village of Conkwell, with its breezy down, on which weather-beaten blocks of stone harmonize with the verdure of the turf, the rich hue of the corn fields, and the many tinted forest trees.

Here, in early spring, may be seen a variety of flowers but rarely met with in less favoured spots, luxuriating in the sheltered copse woods:—anemones, orchids, hyacinths, with the more humble, but not less fragrant, violet and primrose, while one or two species of veronica cling to the low wall that skirts the road.

Mr. Charles Terry, M.R.C.S., in a sketch of the Zoology of Bath, embracing a radius of little more than six miles from the city, says, "in the open down, old quarry grounds, hill-sides, dotted with plantations and underwood, and luxuriant well timbered valley, watered by innumerable streams, and intersected for nearly its whole length by the river Avon, is the favorite habitat of birds and insects. The spot is well worth a visit from the naturalist, who may here. enrich his collection by some rare specimens; want of space has compelled the writer to confine his account of insects to that of one tribe, the Lepidoptera, which more generally engages the attention of collectors from the beauty and variety of its members, and for whose use there is appended to each specimen the name of the month in which the perfect insect makes its appearance."*

The name of Claverton (spelled Clafterton in Domesday Book) has given rise to many rather fanciful ideas with respect to its derivation. Wood says, that it is "compounded of the Roman *clavis*—a key, and the Saxon *tun*—a town; Collinson, that it is "derived, no doubt, from some Saxon owner." The Saxon word, clæfter, or claver, signifying cleft-grass, or clover, together with a further reference to William the Conqueror's survey, gives us at least a plausible reason for its name: it then contained a large extent of pasture, and was called "The Village of the Clover Down."

The moralist and man of letters will pause to contemplate the character and actions of those whose names are connected with the records and traditions of Claverton, as Bishop Warburton, Ralph Allen, Pope, Shenstone, and Graves.

At the conquest, this manor was worth £7, and William bestowed it on his interpreter, Hugoline.

---

* See Appendix to "Wright's Historic Guide." Bath: R. E. Peach.

Reverting to the crown, it was given to Hugo cum Barbâ, who sold it to John of Tours, and he gave it to the Abbey of Bath ; shortly after it was annexed to to the bishopric. In 1257, Bishop Button obtained a charter of free warren from King Henry III., and a grant that, together with Hampton, it should form a liberty exempt from the jurisdiction of the hundred of Bathforum. In 1548, it was alienated from the see by Bishop Barlowe, who exchanged it with King Edward VI. for other lands. The King granted it to Matthew Colthurst, whose son sold it, in 1588, to Edward Hungerford, from whose family it passed into the possession of that of Estcourt. In 1609, Sir Thomas Estcourt sold it to the Bassets. In 1701, Robert Holder became the purchaser, whose son disposed of it, in 1714, to William Skrine. In 1758, it was purchased by Ralph Allen, who bequeathed it at his death, in 1764, to his niece, the wife of Bishop Warburton, who afterwards married the Rev. Martin Stafford Smith. At her death, the estate, together with property. in Widcombe, came into the possession of Allen Tucker, Esq., son of Captain Tucker, Ralph Allen's Nephew, who died in 1816. The Claverton property was then purchased by the late John Vivian, Esq., who was for many years Solicitor to the Excise, and by whom the mansion was built. He bequeathed it to his second son, the late George Vivian, Esq.,* a gentle-

* The whole of the estate was purchased by I. Carr, Esq., of this gentleman, in 1869. Since then, a considerable portion of the property has passed into the possession of Henry Duncan Skrine, Esq., of Warleigh Manor.

man of great literary taste, as well as an accomplished artist.* The Widcombe property is now in the possession of Major Ralph S. Allen, M.P.

In the centre of the Village, a narrow pathway leads to the church—an unpretending Gothic structure, of the fifteenth century, consisting of a nave, chancel, and north aisle. It boasts a charming porch, a tower; stained glass; various emblems; coats of arms; and some good open carved work around the manor pew. The church has been recently restored.

On the north wall of the chancel is an alabaster monument of the early part of the seventeenth century, representing a knight, a lady and a child. Near it is the monument of Graves, who died in 1804, at the advanced age of ninety years.

On the south wall is the monument of John Clutterbuck, of Widcombe, who died in 1766. It represents a female figure reclining gracefully in a mourning attitude on an urn. The family of Skrine, and others, have monuments here.

Humphrey Chambers, one of the divines appointed by Parliament to sit at Westminster, was rector during the civil wars, and died here in 1646. The parish register contains the following memorandum,

---

* Mr. Vivian published a volume illustrative of the Hungerford Mansion, (referred to on page 91,) together with Kingston House, Bradford-on-Avon, besides a folio vol. on Portugal and two series of folio illustrations of Spain ; these bear evidence of his fine taste and artistic skill.

written by him :—

" Mem.—That I, Humphrey Chambers, parson of Claverton, did grant a licence to eat flesh this day to William Basset, Esq., of Claverton, by reason of his notorious sickness; which sickness of his yet continuing, I do now continue his said licence, according to the statute; and have, according to the law, here registered the same, the day and year above written. In witness whereof I have hereunto set my hand, HUMPHREY CHAMBERS*."*

The churchyard is a great attraction. It has been the theme of poets and historians. Here, perhaps, Pope sought solitude for contemplation. Fielding, too, may have strolled hither, when sick of the feeble twaddle of fine ladies, and trim gentlemen in the city. Here Shenstone* may sometimes have caught a poetic gleam of pastoral inspiration; while Graves, pursuing the even tenor of his way, lived to bury successive generations of his parishioners, and showed them the way to heaven.

> For he, God's messenger, who taught the vale,
> No schoolman's subtilties e'er used, nor sought
> By learning's phantasies to dazzle those
> Who hear the preacher and forget the Word.

* Shenstone, frequently left his pretty retreat "The Leasowes," near Hales Owen, to visit his friend Graves at Claverton. Cunningham happily expressed the character of the Poet in the following couplet—

> '' He marked in his elegant strains,
> The graces that glowed in his mind."

Richard Graves was born in 1715, of an ancient family at Mickleton, Gloucestershire. He originally intended to practise medicine, but subsequently turned his attention to the church. At the University of Oxford he was the intimate friend of Sir William Blackstone and Shenstone, and in 1748, was presented to the living of Claverton. He possessed a mind cultivated with great care; a natural politeness, and a simplicity of manners which concealed a spirit ardent in search of truth. His prevailing eccentricity was an exaggerated love of order; his friendships were ennobled by cheerfulness and piety, his classical learning was extensive, his poetry chaste, and his writings breathe the true spirit of Christianity. He held the living for fifty-six years, without one month's absence from his ministerial duties. As an author, his fame rests on the "Spiritual Quixote," a satire on the religious revivalism of the day, a work replete with elegance and wit, and which still commands admiration.

Here, too, are the remains of Ralph Allen. His monument is covered by creeping plants, and shaded by trees. It is raised on three steps, and terminates in a pyramidal roof, supported on either side by three arches; it is surrounded with an iron rail. There are one or two sepulchral slabs of the 12th century in the churchyard.

The present Manor House has had two predecessors. The first stood in a field south of the church; no vestiges of it, we believe, remain. It was erected by Bishop Ralf de Salopia, about the year 1340. This prelate was one of the most munificent of the early bishops. He built the Vicars' Close and some of the choristers' houses at Wells, as well as the church of Winscombe. To this " court house " succeeded a noble mansion, erected by Sir Edward Hungerford, of Heytesbury, in 1588. No portion of it now remains except the flights of steps upon the terrace walk. " Here, Sir William Basset," says Aubrey, in his Natural History of Wiltshire, "hath made the best vineyard I have heard of in England." The Manor House now stands on the crest of the hill, and contains some elaborate and beautiful stone and other work, belonging to the house built by Sir Edward Hungerford.

In 1643, while Sir William Basset was entertaining Sir Edward Hungerford, of Farley Castle, and other knights and gentlemen of the king's party, a cannon ball, directed from the opposite down, passed through the wall as they sat at dinner. There was a call to " boot and saddle;" a skirmish took place in a field near the ferry, in which neither party was victorious ; three roundhead soldiers and one royalist were left dead upon the field, and were buried under the west wall of the churchyard.

In 1771, the poor rates amounted to £43 5s. 3d. ; in 1780, to £11 19s. 6d. ; in 1839, to £40; and at present, average £175 yearly. The population, at the census of 1871, was 165. The parish contains an area of 1,243 statute acres, and its rental for union calculations is £2817.

Claverton Down was occasionally the scene of duels during the last century, most of which were occasioned by disputes at the gaming tables and other places of public resort. One must be here recorded. In the year 1778, many foreign nobles made Bath their residence, and, among others, were the Viscount du Barré, with his wife* and her sister, two ladies of great beauty and accomplishments, and Count Rice, an Irish gentleman, who had borne arms in the service of France. A house was taken in the Royal Crescent, where for a time they lived together on the most amicable terms. They kept open house, where play was allowed to a ruinous extent. Quarrelling at cards, words ran high between Du Barré and Rice, and an immediate challenge was given and accepted. At one o'clock in the morning, a coach was procured from the Three Tuns, in Stall Street, and Claverton Down was reached in moody silence, at the first dawn of day.

A contemporary account describes the combat as follows:—" Each armed with two pistols and a sword. The ground being marked out by the seconds, the Viscount du Barré fired first, and lodged a ball in Count Rice's thigh, which penetrated as far as the bone ; Count Rice fired his pistol, and wounded the Viscount in the breast. He went back two or three steps, then came forward again, and both, at the same time, presented their pistols to each other ;

* The Viscount's wife was the notorious Madame du Barré, née Jeanne Vaubernier, mistress of Louis XV. She returned to France in 1793, and was guillotined the same year.

the pistols flashed together in the pan, though only one was discharged. Then they threw away their pistols, and took to their swords; when Count Rice had advanced within a few yards of the Viscount, he saw him fall, and heard him cry out, 'Je vous demande ma vie,' to which Count Rice answered, 'Je vous la donne;' but in a few seconds the Viscount fell back, and expired. Count Rice was brought with difficulty to Bath, being dangerously wounded, though now he is in a fair way of recovery. The Coroner's inquest sat on the Viscount's body last Saturday, and after a mature examination of the witnesses and the Viscount's servants, brought in their verdict 'Manslaughter.'"

The Viscount's body was left exposed the whole day on the Down, and was subsequently buried in Bathampton churchyard. Count Rice recovered; was tried at Taunton for murder, and acquitted. He died in Spain in 1809. At that part of the Down where the yeomanry were formerly reviewed, a bank slopes towards the wall. It was on the *other side* of this wall, and a few yards from the gate, that the duel took place, where a stone slab marks the spot. The ivory hilt of the sword once belonging to Count Rice, is now attached to the city seal in the Town Clerk's office.

We can diversify our return from Claverton by many pleasant paths, and may ramble again and again to the Village without the necessity of returning by the same route; for example by the Warminster Road, or the towing path of the Canal, or returning over Hampton Down *viâ* the old tramway and so reaching the banks of the Canal, or over the Down, descending by the road which crosses the Warminster Road, we can reach

BATHAMPTON.

The village retains much of its ancient appearance. We at once enter the churchyard, where many interesting memorials, and some curious epitaphs may be seen. Time will soon efface the following record:—

> " Here rest the remains of
> John Baptiste, Viscount du Barré,
> Obt. 18th November, 1778." *

The Lych Gate was erected from a design by Mr. C. E. Davis, at the time of the restoration of the church and enlargement of the churchyard, by the late Rev. Edward Duncan Rhodes.

The Church, with a well proportioned battle-mented tower, of the perpendicular order, was entirely rebuilt in 1754-5, with the exception of the chancel, by Ralph Allen, at a total cost of £619 11s. 5d., reduced by the sale of old lead to £518. It consisted, until lately, of merely a nave, chancel, and manor chantry chapel on the south. It was of little architectural character, although an attempt was made at Gothic. A few years since a north aisle was added,† and still more

* For particulars respecting the duel, see pages 92 and 93.

† The cost of the work was raised by subscription, the architect being Mr. Alfred Goodridge.

15

Bathampton Church, near Bath.

recently, under the care of Mr. C. E. Davis, architect, instructed by the late Incumbent, the chantry chapel has been embellished with traceried windows, the chancel* restored as nearly as possible upon its ancient model, and a chancel arch built. On the west side of the porch a recess has been added for the reception of two very well executed but unfortunately mutilated figures of a knight and his wife, temp. Edward II. or early Edward III. Until the erection of this recess these figures hung on either side the doorway, being turned out from the church when it was rebuilt. Beneath the east window, on the exterior, is a valuable specimen of an early effigy. It is carved in one piece of stone, the block being incised to admit of the figure in low relief of a bishop or abbot of the eleventh century. The head and pastoral staff are much mutilated, but the vestments are perfect, consisting of the chasuble, stole, dalmatic, and albe. The chancel was the property of the Fishers, who were lay rectors since the reign of Elizabeth until recently, when it was sold, with the rectory house, to the present lord of the manor, Major Ralph S. Allen, M.P., who resides at the Manor House.

In the tower are five bells, some of which are very ancient, and bear curious Latin inscriptions.

* The east window was erected (there was none before), and a portion of the chancel restored, in memory of the late George Edward Allen, Esq., as may be seen by an inscription on a brass at the north side. Amongst the contributors to this work were the late Ladies Cawdor, Carteret and Caroline Thynne, Miss Allen, and P. C. Sheppard, Esq.

The pretty school house at the east corner of the churchyard was built at the cost of Miss Sheppard.

The living was united with that of the adjoining parish of Bathford for about 70 years. In 1855, on the death of the Rev. James Carter, Vicar, the patrons (the Dean and Chapter of Bristol) agreed to the separation of the parishes, and appointed the Rev. E. D. Rhodes incumbent of Bathampton. It would be impossible in a work of this description to do justice to the character and memory of this estimable and accomplished man, but the church and village of Bathampton must long bear the impress of his energy and devotedness; the large-heartedness of his liberality, and the excellence of his taste and judgment.

The organization of a long neglected parish, the complete restoration and enlargement of the church, and tasteful improvement of the churchyard, though the most prominent, were by no means the only evidences of Mr. Rhodes' care for his pastoral charge.

Up to the date of the separation of the parishes, there had been no parsonage house, and the Patrons assented to the division on the condition that such provision should be made by the parishioners. To carry this arrangement, therefore, into effect, the late Mr. Vivian, of Claverton, gave two acres of land, which were exchanged with Major Allen for the present site, around which Mr. Rhodes built the boundary wall; a sum of £400 and upwards was raised by subscription, which, together with other sums, and £100 given by the Patrons, were invested in the names of Trustees, and accumulated during the eleven years of Mr. Rhodes' incumbency. Subsequently Miss Rhodes gave £100; the balance required to meet the cost of building the house being defrayed by the present Vicar, the Rev. Henry Girdlestone. For the purpose of augmenting the endowment, the lay rectorial tithes were purchased by Mr. Rhodes, and a neighbouring land-owner contributed £300 to meet the £200 given by the Commissioners of Queen Anne's Bounty.

Mr. Rhodes died suddenly in 1866 to the grief of his parishioners, among whom he had for eleven years most affectionately ministered, and to the especial sorrow of that larger circle of friends who far and near had experienced the privilege of his personal friendship. The simple dignity and sweet courtesy of his manner were such as to win the confidence and love of all whose good fortune it was to know him. He was a ripe scholar and an excellent divine. Few men were so thoroughly imbued with a love of poetry as he, or possessed a more complete knowledge of poets and poetic literature, especially of an early date. And though one of the least ostentatious of men, he was ever ready to allow others to profit by the almost boundless resources of his literary knowledge. " He was a man, take him for all in all [we] shall not look upon his like again."

. . . " His church and parish of Bathampton were the home of his thoughts and affections, as of the labour of his later years. That church, a model

H

of an English country church, restored to its present perfection, mainly by his liberality, stands the centre of what he had made a model English country parish—the fittest monument to his memory. No truer heart than his was ever laid to rest 'in sure and certain hope' within its shadow; no dearer or more honoured memory of teacher, pastor, friend, will ever be cherished by those who yet may worship beneath its roof."

He who wrote these beautiful words—the Bishop of Peterborough—also wrote the no less appropriate inscription which was placed in the church, and was as follows :—

"To the dear and honoured memory of EDWARD DUNCAN RHODES, B.D., Prebendary of Wells, and for the last 11 years of his life Vicar of this Parish of Bathampton. Born 17th October, 1797, Died 18th September, 1866. A zealous pastor, a wise and thoughtful teacher, a preacher of rare eloquence, an affectionate and generous relative and friend, a large-hearted, noble-minded man ; he consecrated, first, to the Saviour whom he loved, and then, for His sake, to the flock for whom he laboured, and to the church of which he was a devotedly attached member, the ripened fruits of a cultivated intellect and a pious and reverent spirit. This church, restored in large measure by his liberality and taste, is his fittest and most lasting monument. These lines record the love and grief of those to whom within these walls, and from house to house, he ministered so faithfully and well."

Close to the church is the conventual barn, built at the same period as the church tower. The roof will repay inspection, on account of the strength and simplicity with which the rafters are connected together. Some years ago the barn was reduced in size, and the pitch of the roof and doorway greatly altered.

Among the old-fashioned houses in the village, the rectory bears evident marks of antiquity. There is an archway surmounted by a floriated cross of stone, which was formerly the "hip-knob" on the conventual barn.*   In the garden may still be seen the bowl of the early church font.   The house has undergone many restorations, but has never, we believe, been used as a residence by any clergyman of the Church of England since the Reformation.

The house, now the Post Office, is a most picturesque remnant of a much larger house, probably the ancient manor house or grange of the Priors of of Bath.

Many hewn stone steps remain in the main street, their worn condition proving them to be very ancient. They were erected for the use of the yeomens' wives, when wheel carriages were rare, to enable them to mount the pillion behind their husbands.

The manor of Bathampton belonged to the Abbey of Bath from time immemorial.   In the year 1548, Bishop Barlow included it with Claverton in a bargain of exchange for other lands, formerly the property of the Prior of Bath.   In 1553, King Edward granted it to William Crowch, from whom it came into the possession of the family of Popham. Subsequently it passed to the Hungerfords, and afterwards to the Bassets.   In 1701, it was purchased by Richard Holder, through whom it came into the

* A copy of this singular cross is placed on the porch of Claverton Church.

632906 A

hands of Ralph Allen, who devised it to his brother, Philip Allen, postmaster of Bath, who was succeeded by his son Ralph, father of the late George Edward and Henry Allen, the latter of whom was the father of the present possessor.

In the time of William the Conqueror, this manor, then called Hantone, was worth one hundred and ten shillings.　In 1292, it was valued at ten marks and a half; its name was then "Bathentuna."　In 1790, the population was 150; in 1871, it had increased to 387.　In 1770, the poor rates were £36; in 1780, £74.　The average annual expenditure, previous to the formation of the Union, was £158; while at present it is £377 per annum on an area of 932 statute acres.　The rateable value for apportioning Union expenditure is £5,943.

Pursuing our route to the city by the high road, on the brow of the hill, beyond the turnpike a fine specimen of the sycamore is seen.　From this spot we obtain a charming view of the tributary valley which winds between Lansdown and Solsbury into Gloucestershire.　To the right are the river, railroad, and canal; the towing-path of the latter affords an agreeable walk.

BATHWICK.

BATHWICK, called *Wiche* in Domesday Book, a word signifying "a retreat," to which *Bath* was added, to distinguish it from other places of the same name, was given by King William the Conqueror to

Geoffrey, Bishop of Coutance, in Normandy, together with a number of other lordships, amounting in all to 280, situated in various parts of the country, as a reward for his military services.

According to Dugdale, this bishop—more skilful in arms than in divinity—was of noble Norman extraction, and held a distinguished command at the Battle of Hastings. Dying in 1093, many of his estates reverted to the Crown; among others Bathwick, which was shortly afterwards bestowed on the nunnery of Wherwell, in Hampshire, from which circumstance we find that, in 1293, it was called Wick-Abbas. At the dissolution of religious houses it again became the property of the Crown, and Queen Mary granted it to Sir Edmond Neville, from whom it came to Capel, Earl of Essex, whose descendant sold it in 1726 to Sir William Pulteney, created Earl of Bath 1742,* in whose family it

* The Earldom of Bath, with the minor dignities of Viscount Pulteney, of Wrington, County of Somerset, and Baron of Hedon, County of York, were conferred 14th July, 1742, on the famous statesman William Pulteney, with remainder to the heirs male of his body. His lordship married Anna Maria, daughter of John Gumley, Esq., of Isleworth, Middlesex, and had issue one son, William, Viscount Pulteney, who died unmarried in the lifetime of his father, 1763, and one daughter, who died 1741, aged 14. The Earl died in 1764, when all his honours became extinct, but his great estates devolved on his brother, General Henry Pulteney, who died in 1765. At the General's death, the Pulteney property devolved on Frances, daughter of Daniel Pulteney, Esq., son of John Pulteney, Esq., uncle of the Earl of Bath. This lady was wife of Sir William Johnstone, Bart., of Westerhall, Dumfriesshire, who took the name of Pulteney. Their only child,

remained until 1808, when, on the death of the
Countess of Bath, the estate devolved to the Earl of
Darlington, created afterwards first Duke of Cleveland, upon whose father it was entailed in remainder
by the Earl of Bath.   The Duke, at his death
in 1841, devised it to his second son, Lord William
Vane, who for family reasons assumed the name of
Powlett, the maiden name of his mother, who was the
younger daughter and co-heiress of the last Duke of
Bolton.   In 1864, Lord William succeeded to the
Dukedom on the death of Henry, second Duke, and,
dying the same year, the estate reverted to Harry,
now fourth Duke of Cleveland, youngest son of the
first Duke.   His Grace is patron of the living, which
has been annexed to that of Woolley since the
Conquest.

According to Collinson, the population of Bathwick, in 1781, amounted only to 150 souls.   It is
difficult to point out a place in the kingdom which
has improved so rapidly as this once quiet and retired village.   About ninety years ago, it consisted
of an irregular street of forty-five houses, near the
ancient village church.   A stream of water, arising in
Claverton Down, ran through the village in an open

Henrietta Laura Pulteney, succeeded to the great Pulteney property, and was created Baroness of Bath 26th July, 1792, and
Countess of Bath 26th October, 1803.   Her ladyship married
General Sir James Murray, Bart., who assumed the surname and
arms of Pulteney ; and pre-deceased her ladyship.   She died 14th
August, 1808, without issue, when her peerage honours became
extinct, and Bathwick estate, together with Wrington and Burring-
ton, as above stated, devolved to the Cleveland family.

stone channel. Children sported in the meadows which lay between the village and the city, while crowds of visitors crossed the ferry, at the bottom of Boatstall Lane, to enjoy a ramble in the meadows. At this period, in addition to the mill, a broad cloth factory stood near the river.

It requires some stretch of imagination to believe that the foregoing passage contains a tolerably accurate description of Bathwick in 1780. We look in vain for the old-fashioned irregular village, of which but one house (the Crown Inn) in Bathwick Street remains. The ancient church, having fallen to decay, was pulled down, on the building of the new church, and the materials used in the construction of the Mortuary Chapel, in which are preserved an early English font and a pulpit of more recent date.

Collinson, in his history, gives many of the inscriptions which, in his time, ornamented the walls of the old church. Here was interred Mackinnon, of Skye, who accompanied the Pretender to Culloden, and carried him off the field. The exposure and privations to which this gallant Highland Chieftain was subjected during his perilous escape, caused him to lose the use of his limbs; and, some years afterwards, coming to Bath for the sake of the waters, he died here.

Here, too, rests Edward Barlow, M.D., who died A.D. 1844. Possessed of rare gifts and great professional ability he used each alike for the benefit of the poor, the sick, and the friendless. The Hospitals of the city were especially a pride and a pleasure to him, and no consideration ever induced him to forget their claim on his time and attention. No public memorial of his services has, we believe, been ever erected.

Near this chapel stands the church, dedicated to S. John Baptist, the first portion of which was built from the design of Mr. C. E. Giles, architect, in the year 1862. The cost of the building was borne by the late Rev. L. R. Hamilton, with the exception of £270 contributed by the Church Building Societies, and £330 from private donors. For some time, in accordance with the original intention, it was used as a chapel-of-ease to the parish church. In addition to the munificent liberality above referred to, Mr. Hamilton, who was appointed the first perpetual curate, provided, with the assistance of friends, a small endowment of £1,500. Sometime after Mr. Hamilton's death, successful efforts were made to enlarge the church, and, under the direction of Mr. Blomfield, architect, a south aisle and chancel were added, at a cost, including the organ, vestry, and interior fittings and decorations, of between £7,000 and £8,000. That portion of Bathwick, which had been assigned as a district, is now an independent ecclesiastical parish, of which the Rev. A. Douglas is the first vicar. The patronage is vested in the Rector of Bathwick. All sittings are free, and the church and its parochial organisation are maintained by the offertories. Within the last two years (1873-5) the endowment has been increased by £2,000.

The site was given by the late Lord William Powlett (afterwards third Duke of Cleveland).

On the south side of the church, the building, formerly the old Rectory House, was purchased, in 1873, by a lady, repaired and enlarged, and given to the parish as a Vicarage House. The congregation have built a Schoolroom for the choir in connection with the church, on a site formerly part of the old Rectory buildings and waste, which is also used as a Sunday School. The parish is indebted to the liberality of the same lady for the gift of this site.

The church grounds are kept in beautiful order by the " church servants."

Bathwick Parish Church,
Dedicated to S. Mary the Virgin.

This church is well placed in an open and commanding situation at the base of Bathwick Hill.

At the commencement of the present century, the need of more efficient church accommodation in the parish was urgently felt, and a special Act of Parliament was at length obtained to enable the parishioners to borrow money, on the security of church rates, to build the present edifice. The old parish church was therefore demolished, and the present mortuary chapel in S. John's parish was erected from its materials, but not on its site. The ancient structure stood upon the ground now occupied by the chancel.

The Earl of Darlington (first Duke of Cleveland) gave the ground of the new building. The foundation stone was laid in 1814, and the church was consecrated in February, 1820, the Rev. Peter Gunning being rector.

The late Mr. John Pinch was the architect, and while it is to be regretted that he selected late Third Pointed as the style of the building, and still more that the work was executed at a period when the Gothic revival was in its infancy, it must be admitted that he succeeded under adverse circumstances in producing a structure of very considerable merit, both as to its proportions and its acoustic properties. The east end was temporarily finished with an apse—space being left within the walls of the surrounding enclosure for a chancel in the future : and in accordance with the fashion of the day, a huge structure of woodwork, at the west end, provided three elevated rostra for reader, parish clerk, and preacher, all the pews facing towards this unwieldly arrangement.

The cost of the building, including the Act of Parliament above mentioned, and another, which it became necessary to procure, amounted to £14,262 6s. 1d.

In 1866, the pews were removed and low seats substituted, and a new pulpit and reading desk were placed at the east end on either side of the apse, at a cost to the parishioners of £598 2s. 9d.

The pulpit, reading desk, and a new stone font, were the gift of a lady, who devoted some jewels which had been bequeathed to her, as a thankoffering for the use of the church.

A small sum, which remained in hand after this alteration, was made the nucleus of a fund for the further addition of a chancel : and when the Rev. Prebendary Scarth resigned the living, on his promotion to the rectory of Wrington, it had increased to £400, which sum, together with plans furnished by the late Mr. Gill, of Bath, to cost £800, was handed over to the present rector, the Rev. George Tugwell, on his appointment to Bathwick at Easter, 1871.

He, however, feeling the necessity of dealing with so important a building in a larger and more complete manner, at once placed the matter in the hands of Mr. G. E. Street, R.A., by whom the plans of the existing chancel were prepared and estimated to cost £3,000.

The foundation stone was laid on October 11, 1873, by the Rev. Prebendary Scarth,* and the chancel was consecrated on February 2, 1875.

* The Rev. Harry Mengden Scarth, M.A., Prebendary of Wells, was Rector of Bathwick for 30 years, and resigned in 1871, on his appointment to the rectory of Wrington, Somerset. An

It would be presumptuous to criticise Mr. Street's work, but we may be allowed to admire the masterly way in which a new building, perfect in every detail, has been adapted to the former structure, which in detail at all events was full of faults. An inferior artist would have made a mere addition, a patch of good on bad work. Mr. Street has completed the building with a chancel, which is a harmony and not a contrast, which leads the eye from that which is wrong to that which is right, and which has converted a mere place of meeting into an obvious and symmetrical church.

The chancel is half the length of the nave, and of great height. It is raised by two steps above the level of the main building, and three steps lead to the sacrarium, on which the footpace stands. So that the altar is elevated by seven steps above the ground line.

The east window of seven lights is filled with stained glass of great excellence and jewel-like quality, and is the work of Messrs. Clayton and Bell. It cost between £400 and £500, and was the gift of Mrs. Roscoe, of Elms Lea. In the head are seven emblems of the Blessed Virgin Mary—the Rose, Lily, Star, Moon, Burning Bush, and Mirror, surrounding an Agnus Dei—the emblem of Christ. Beneath are figures of the four Evangelists. The seven lights, in their upper portion, are filled with the following subjects, commencing on the north side :—The Annunciation, Salutation, Adoration of the Magi, Nativity, Presentation in the Temple, Christ found in the Temple, Christ blessing Children ; and under these occur :— The Prophecy of Simeon, the Flight into Egypt, Christ bearing the Cross, the Crucifixion, the Betrayal, Christ lost by His Mother, the Maries at the Sepulchre.

The altar cross and other furniture of the re-table are from Messrs. Barkenten and Krall, of London. The brass eagle lectern is from Mr. Street's drawings, and was furnished by Messrs. Potter and Son, of London.

---

able and diligent archæologist, he made important discoveries during his sojourn in this city, and embodied the chief results of his own and others' researches in his *Magnum Opus*—"Aquæ Solis : Notices of Roman Bath," quarto. Besides this work he extended his researches to other localities, and contributed valuable papers to the Archæological Journal, the Journal of the Archæological Association, the Somersetshire Archæological Journal, as well as to other periodicals.

An organ chamber is in process of completion, and the plan contemplates additional vestries for the clergy and choir.

It should be stated that the element of colour is sparingly introduced. It has not, however, been forgotten. Lack of funds alone prevent the addition of a reredos in stone with diapered backgrounds, the colouring of the roof and of the principal mouldings, a screen of illuminated metal-work, and many other points of detail, which, when carried out, will render this church one of the principal ornaments of the city.

The **Bathwick Parochial National Schools**, situated at the bottom of Henrietta Street, are under the management of a committee of the clergy of Bathwick, S. John, and lay churchmen, and are supported entirely by voluntary contributions. The average number of boys attending the school is upwards of 100, and of girls upwards of 60. These receive an excellent secular education, besides being instructed in the distinctive principles and teaching of the Church of England. The schools are visited by the clergy of Bathwick, and of S. John the Baptist, and a special service for the schools is held at S. Mary's, on the second Sunday in each month, when an address is given to the children by the clergy of each parish alternately. Mr. H. A. Simmons is the Hon. Secretary and Treasurer. Mr. Hale is master, and Miss Kingman mistress.

The **Victoria Infant School** (near the above) is for children of both sexes, between the ages of 4 and 7, and is under the management of a committee of gentlemen, assisted by a number of lady visitors. It is supported by voluntary contributions. It is an admirable institution, and the management deserve every praise.

There are three streets in this parish in which there neither are, nor in all probability ever will be, any houses. One of them, William Street, opens upon a beautiful prospect towards Widcombe, embracing Prior Park, and a wide stretch of upland scenery; while the other two, Sutton and Sunderland Streets, were intended to lead to Frances Square. This plan, however, not having been carried out, the vacant ground has been enclosed, and is traversed by a broad gravel walk. The enclosure, now called Bathwick Park, affords a beautiful view of the higher parts of the city, the grey tint of the buildings blending happily with the trees scattered on the heights. This improvement was completed in 1833. In 1817, Queen Charlotte resided at No. 93, Sydney Place; his Majesty King William IV., then Duke of Clarence, occupying the house at the opposite end. During her visit to the city, her Majesty held daily levees in the Pump Room, endearing herself to all by her affability and condescension, as well as by her munificent contributions to the local charities. One of her Majesty's visits was to the studio of the celebrated flower painter, Hewlett, whose success in this department of his art was attributed to his professional wanderings about the sheltered nooks and valleys round the city.

It was originally intended that Sydney Place should completely surround the Gardens. Two sides of the square, • however, were only erected. Had the original plan been carried out, Bathwick would

have been one of the most attractive suburban
parishes in the kingdom.

A large number of the labouring population of
the parish inhabit a primitive spot called the
Villa Fields, which lies between the railroad and
the river. The cottages are detached, each being
built on its own plot of ground, just as the whim of
the settler suggested. It is said that this curious
suburb somewhat resembles a young settlement in the
Western States of the Union. In its centre is situated
Bathwick Villa, which was inhabited, during a portion
of the last century, by the Rev. Dr. John Trusler, a man
noted for his eccentricity. He dedicated one of
his works to the rising generation, by whom it seems
not to have been appreciated, for it not unfrequently
happened that, on his return from the city, he found
his full-bottomed wig bristling with butcher's skewers
—"like quills upon the fretful porcupine,"—placed
therein, without his knowledge, during his progress
through the market. The Villa is now let to the
poor in tenements.

Bathwick Villa was a favourite place of public resort, as the following advertisement, copied from the
Bath Journal, of 1788, proves :—

"VILLA GARDENS.

"The nobility and gentry are respectfully informed that the
ingenious Signor John Invetto intends to display the most superb
and brilliant fireworks, this present Monday, May 19th, 1788.
The gardens will be brilliantly illuminated ; the music will begin
at six; and the fireworks at half-past eight.

"N.B.—A good coach road ; and, for the convenience cf the
upper town, a ferry is kept opposite Walcot Parade."

In 1808, the late Duke of Gloucester reviewed the Bath Regiment of Volunteers in the Villa Fields.

Bathwick and Walcot are connected by a handsome cast-iron bridge, erected in 1827, after a design by Mr. Goodridge. In digging the foundations, twenty-one Roman coins of the lower empire were discovered, and still more recently some important Roman remains have been found on the Walcot side. It is conjectured that two forts stood at this point for the protection of the ferry.

In this parish, and near the river, stood "Spring Gardens," formerly one of the most celebrated places of public resort in the neighbourhood of the city. In course of time it became necessary to build on a portion of the ground, when its gaieties were gradually transferred to Sydney Gardens. The grounds were laid out by Mr. Harcourt in 1795, and still constitute one of the chief attractions of the city. The railroad and canal, which pass through the Gardens, increase rather than detract from the beauty of the promenades. Here, during the summer season, are held the horticultural shows, for which the city is famous. These exhibitions, which attract the rank and fashion of the neighbourhood, are held under the spirited management of the Hanoverian Band Committee, under whose auspices also an excellent Band performs, on certain days in the week, during the summer, both in the Gardens and the Victoria Park.

Many years since, a gentleman—influenced, perhaps, by the Greek motto placed on the north front of the Pump Room, and which declares water to be the best element—established a set of baths on the hydropathic system in the Pulteney Hotel. The design failed, and the hotel returned to its pristine habits. The late Emperor of France, Louis Napoleon, resided here for a considerable time after his escape from Ham.   On coming to Bath again in 1871, he revisited his former residence, pointing out to his son, from his carriage, the rooms he occupied.   .

The Hotel has long ceased to exist, and is now known as the 𝕭𝖆𝖙𝖍 𝕻𝖗𝖔𝖕𝖗𝖎𝖊𝖙𝖆𝖗𝖞 . 𝕮𝖔𝖑𝖑𝖊𝖌𝖊. The property is held in 120 shares, which entitle their posessors to nominate one pupil for each share. The course of instruction, while it is adapted to the standard of Classical and Mathematical attainments required at the Universities, is such as, at the same time, to secure the complete preparation of candidates for entrance into Woolwich and Sandhurst, and for marine and naval cadetships.   This college also is recognised by the Secretary of State for India in Council as possessing an efficient class for civil engineering.

A public examination is held before the summer vacation, and an exhibition of £50 is awarded at this examination to that pupil proceeding to the University of Oxford, Cambridge, or Dublin, who shall have shown sufficient proficiency in his studies.

One scholarship of £20 a year, tenable for three years, and two of £15 a year, tenable for two years, if the scholar remains a pupil of the college, with a free nomination, competed for in July. These scholarships are pen to all, whether pupils of the college, or others eligible to become pupils, whose age on the 1st July shall not exceed fifteen years.

The profits of the college are devoted to the advancement and interests of the pupils.

Several exhibitions have been gained by the pupils at Oxford and Cambridge, where many also have obtained high honours at the final examinations. The larger number of boys, however, enter the army, in the examinations for which they have been very successful ; or engage in the other professions.

In no part of the environs of the city did the improvements of the last century make such rapid progress as in Bathwick. Pulteney Bridge, which connected the suburb with the city, was built in 1770. The houses on either side of the roadway have since been converted into shops of various kinds. Their removal would be a great improvement to the locality, inasmuch as it would open up a suburban view of rare beauty.

𝕬rgyle 𝕮hapel, of which the Rev. William Jay was minister for fifty-six years, was built for the Independents in 1789, the first stone being laid in 1788, by the Rev. Thomas Tuppen, a popular preacher, distinguished for his biblical learning. Mr. Jay preached the opening sermon on the 4th of October, 1789; and on the 30th of January, 1791, was ordained as the minister. Two pillars stand in the chapel, one to commemorate the erection of the building, the other the fifty years' faithful service of its distinguished pastor. It has been thrice enlarged; once in 1814, and again in 1821. In 1862, the sum of £2,000 was expended on improvements, both internal and external. The schools attached to the chapel were built about thirty years ago. On Sundays, there are 300 children under instruction; and on other days, a mixed school is held. At present the number of pupils amounts to 110. The school is supported by the members of the congregation, without any Government aid. The Rev. Henry Tarrant was appointed minister of the chapel in 1875.

The plan of Laura Place having been drawn by Baldwin, the city architect, was begun in 1788. After the passing of the Reform Bill in 1832, it was proposed to erect a column in the centre. Happily the suggestion was not carried out, and the beautiful vista of Great Pulteney Street remains unobstructed by any extraneous ornament.

Laura Chapel (Episcopal) in Henrietta Street, was opened in 1796. Many eminent men have officiated here, amongst whom the late Rev. E. Tottenham, B.D.,* Prebendary of Wells, may especially be named.

* The Rev. E. Tottenham, B.D., eminent as a preacher and a controversialist, was quite a young man when he took part in the famous "Downside Discussion" in 1834. Mr. Tottenham was for some years after this minister of Kensington Chapel, when his

The 𝕭𝖆𝖙𝖍𝖜𝖎𝖈𝖐 𝕮𝖊𝖒𝖊𝖙𝖊𝖗𝖞, which lies at the west end of Smallcombe wood, makes a fitting termination to the present walk. No burial place in the kingdom boasts a more picturesque site. It was formed in the year 1856, by the the then Rector, the Rev. Prebendary Scarth. The western portion of the ground, which contains an elegant chapel, is set apart for the use of Nonconformists.

The rateable value of this parish is £33,273 on an area of 570 acres. In 1780, the poor rates were £52; they now average £1,550. The population in 1871 was 5,271. It forms under the Reform and Boundary Acts of 1832, a part of the Parliamentary Borough.

Our calculation of distance must not always be regarded as absolute. A tourist is a sort of knight-errant in search of the beautiful, and is apt to stray out of bounds in order to catch a view here, or to gather a flower there. "Rambles" scarcely imply straight walking. The stretch just taken does not probably exceed six miles.

---

many admirers, in 1841, purchased Laura Chapel for the sum of £2,500, and presented it to him, and shortly after he was created Prebendary of Wells. He continued to officiate in Laura Chapel until his death, in June, 1853. Such was the estimation in which he was held that a public subscription, amounting to about £3000, was afterwards raised, a part of which sum (£250) was appropriated to the purchase of his library, and the balance presented to his widow. The library contains about 2,000 vols. of theology and miscellaneous literature (with many curious Romish catechisms), and at present is deposited at the Athenæum, in the Orange Grove, where it is open to the free use of the public on certain conditions.

IN AND OUT OF BATH.

WALK THE THIRD.

S. JAMES.

WITHIN the last century, Stall Street contained many interesting houses, some of which are engraved round the borders of the large map of the city now in the Reading Room of the Royal Literary Institution.

The church of S. James was formerly an ecclesiastical dependency attached to the Abbey. The first steps towards a separation were taken in June,

1860, and in 1862 it became an independent ecclesiastical parish. The endowment, which amounts
in all to about £350 per annum, is derived from
the following sources :—The Ecclesiastical Commissioners granted £1,000; £1,500 was raised from
other sources, and the interest of these sums, with
fees and pew rents, together with £50 received
annually from the Abbey on the separation taking
place, brings the income derived for the living to
the amount above mentioned.

The old perpendicular church tower, which was
in the same style as that at Bathampton, of similar
date, has been removed, and another one built,
rather more in harmony with the body of the church.
This tower is 150 feet high, and classic in character,
in style similar to the Italian Campaniles, with a
small octagonal cupola, supported by pilasters
of the Corinthian order.

The church contains 1,173 sittings, of which 600
are free.

When the Rev. Charles Kemble severed S. James's
from S. Peter and S. Paul's (Abbey), the latter
became the smallest parish in the city, and the rector
thereof bears clerical jurisdiction over the smallest
ecclesiastical area in the borough, though still titular
Rector of Bath, much the same as for many years
our kings were titular kings of France after they
had ceased to possess territorial power.

The Bath Free Library (near the south-west corner
of the Abbey) is in many respects an exceptional

institution, and owes its existence to exceptional efforts. The burgesses of the city having on two occasions, when convened for the purpose of adopting the Free Libraries' Act, refused to avail themselves of its provisions, the friends of popular education in the city addressed themselves to the accomplishment of their object by other means. A Free History Class, which in 1875 numbered upwards of 500 members, was conducted for seven years by Mr. J. W. Morris, and in connection with this a small library was formed. Steadily fostering the idea that a Free Library would be yet secured if a taste for reading were cultivated and the desire for information increased, an amount of public interest was at length excited, to which the present institution is largely indebted.

The munificence and public spirit of an occasional visitor to Bath, Mr. Charles Mackillop, who placed the sum of £1,500 at the disposal of the President of the Class for this purpose, enabled the committee to purchase the premises, now admirably adapted to the wants of readers of every class, and to furnish them with a considerable and appropriate library. To this Library, Mr. I. Pitman, the inventor of the well known system of phonetics, added a collection of 2,000 volumes, and the Library and Reading Room were opened at a public meeting, presided over by the Mayor (Admiral Paynter), February 16th, 1875.

It is not, however, in the power of the Trustees of the Library to continue it for more than three years upon its present basis of voluntary support. If at the expiration of the time mentioned the burgesses, conversant with its advantages, should vote the rate necessary for its permanent support, the building and its contents will then be presented absolutely to the city, but if the application of the act to Bath should unhappily be again refused, the institution will be closed and its collections dispersed.

At present the Library is steadily progressing in popular favour.

𝕱𝖗𝖎𝖊𝖓𝖉𝖘' 𝕸𝖊𝖊𝖙𝖎𝖓𝖌 𝕳𝖔𝖚𝖘𝖊 (York Street), Mr. W. Wilkins, of London, architect. This building, the sacrarium of which is in the Doric style, was originally erected and used by the various lodges of Freemasons in Bath. The late Duke of Sussex, M.W.G.M., attended by upwards of 700 members of the fraternity, opened and dedicated the Hall August 4th, 1817. In 1842, the late Rev. J. B. Wallinger having seceded from the Established Church, his friends of the Baptist persuasion leased the property, when it was called " Bethesda Chapel," and he carried on his ministrations here ; after his resignation, the Society of Friends, who had for some years held their religious worship in a building on the Lower Borough Walls, purchased the building in which their services have been ever since conducted.

The 𝕽𝖔𝖞𝖆𝖑 𝕷𝖎𝖙𝖊𝖗𝖆𝖗𝖞 𝖆𝖓𝖉 𝕾𝖈𝖎𝖊𝖓𝖙𝖎𝖋𝖎𝖈 𝕴𝖓𝖘𝖙𝖎𝖙𝖚𝖙𝖎𝖔𝖓 was established in the year 1824, on the site of the Lower Assembly Rooms, which were burned down in 1820. The building is a classical structure in the

Doric style of architecture, and includes a spacious
and elegant Reading Room and Library—a large
room originally intended and used for Lectures,
but now appropriated as a Geological Museum—
and other rooms, galleries, and lobbies devoted
to purposes connected with the Museum. The
institution, which is under the management of a

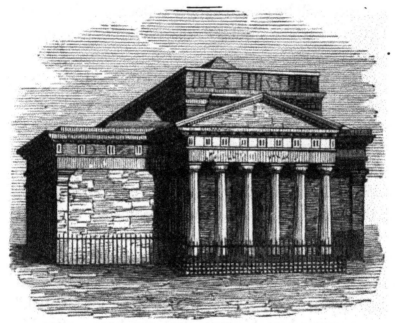

ROYAL LITERARY AND SCIENTIFIC INSTITUTION.

committee and trustees, chosen from the body of
subscribers, forms a centre for the promotion of
objects connected with science and literature.*

* An interesting account of the formation of this Institution
will be found in "The Connection of Bath with the Literature
and Science of England: a Paper read before the Literary and
Philosophical Association of the Bath Institution, on November
6th, 1826, by the Rev. Joseph Hunter, F.S.A., with an account of
the formation of the Institution, and Notes on the Paper; written
in 1853 by the Author."—Published by R. E. Peach, Bath.

The library consists of above 9,000 volumes of standard literature and books of reference. An important addition has recently been made to it through the presentation, by the Rev. Leonard Blomefield, of his well-selected library of natural history and science, including his Herbarium of British Plants. This part of the collection is now known as the "Jenyns Library."

The large room of the Museum has been appropriated to the valuable and extensive geological collection of Mr. Charles Moore, F.G.S., who has deposited it at the institution for general inspection and for the edification of the public, who have free admittance to it during four days in the week. The fine specimens of saurians and fishes from the lias, as well as the organic remains from the Rhætic and other beds — many of which are unique and new to science—are of great value, and give evidence of the untiring energy and perseverance, as well as the scientific knowledge, of Mr. Moore. An addition has lately been made to this part of the museum, through the liberality of Mr. Handel Cossham, who has erected a gallery for the reception of cases in order to increase the collection. The ceiling of this room is enriched by four paintings byCasala, which were formerly at Fonthill.

In the vestibule and lobbies of the institution are arranged the unique collections of Roman antiquities found in the neighbourhood, and deposited by the Corporation in the year 1827. A full description of these remains will be found in a work written by the Rev. Prebendary Scarth in 1864, entitled "Aquæ Solis, or Notices of Roman Bath."*

The "Godfrey Ornithological Collection" is placed in the galleries of the building, and consists of a numerous collection of British and foreign birds and animals, made by the late Lieutenant - Colonel John Race Godfrey. Many years of unremitting labour and perseverance were employed by this gentleman in collecting specimens from all parts of the world. After his death in 1856, his widow —unwilling that the museum, which had so long been the cherished object of her husband's care and regard, should be scattered or dispersed—presented the entire collection to his native city. Since its presentation it has been re-arranged, with many additions, and forms an attractive feature in the museum.

In connection with these galleries is a room appropriated to the "Duncan Museum of Local Natural History," founded through the liberality of Mrs. J. and Miss Duncan, containing a collection of the local fauna, carefully and scientifically arranged by the Rev. Leonard Blomefield.

The Museum has also lately been enriched by a bequest from the late Miss E. Lockey, of Swainswick, consisting of cabinets of British insects, medals and minerals; numerous models, and an ethnological collection of foreign weapons and implements, which are in course of arrangement.

* Bath : R. E. Peach.

The Literary and Philosophical Association, and the Bath Naturalist and Antiquarian Field Club, hold their meetings in the Reading Room of the Institution, when papers are read on subjects connected with science and literature.

S. John's Church and Priory (Roman Catholic) —built from the design of Mr. Hansom, of Clifton— stands in a conspicuous position at the end of the South Parade, and is the first object of architectural interest that arrests the attention of visitors entering Bath by the Great Western Railway. The site was purchased from Earl Manvers. The first stone was laid in October, 1861. The internal dimensions of the building are one hundred and forty feet by sixty, increased at the transept to seventy-three feet. The spire is two hundred feet high. The arcade, separating the nave from the aisles, has circular pillars of polished red Devonshire marble, surmounted by elaborately-carved capitals of Ancaster stone. The walls are faced on both sides with freestone. The chancel is the same height and width as the nave, and is terminated by a semi-octagonal apse. On each side of the chancel are chapels, which are connected by moulded arches. Around the lower portion of the chancel walls is an arcade of moulded arches, resting on marble shafts. Marble shafts are also employed in the window jambs above. The sacristies are placed at the south-east, and connected with the chancel by a corridor running round the apse, and entering behind the reredos of the high altar. The ground at

the east end being considerably lower than that at
the west end, a second range of rooms is obtained
under the sacristies, having a corridor communicating
with the adjoining priory, the residence of the priests.

The New Church (Swedenborgian), situated in
Henry Street, was opened on the 21st July, 1844,
where the centenary of their foundation was celebrated in 1856. Six hundred sittings are provided
for the congregation, and beneath the chapel is a
lofty, spacious Schoolroom for 100 children, besides
a valuable lending library of works in polemic
divinity. Mr. Underwood, of Bath, furnished the
design, and the cost of its erection was about
£2,000.

A Baptist Chapel has recently been completed on
the eastern side of Manvers Street, from the design
of Messrs. Wilson and Willcox of Bath.

The ancient street, called Horse Street, now
Southgate Street (its old name having been changed
about fifty years ago, at the suggestion of Mr. Barnes),
was a narrow road, having, on either side, houses of
a mean appearance, and covered with thatch so late
as 1726. It crossed the Barton of Bath, from St.
Lawrence's Bridge to the South Gate. Leland, in
1542, describes the meadows as touching the street
on both sides. The west side still preserves the
name of *Ambrey*, denoting a cupboard or storehouse
for provisions, to which purpose the buildings
were devoted by the monks. In 1726, a great
fire occurred, which destroyed a large part of the

ancient houses. The present street is a decided improvement on its predecessor.

In 1727, Wood proposed that the General Hospital should be built in the Ambrey Mead, then used as a kitchen garden; and as this spot was contiguous to the hot spring, it was resolved to make a new bath in the centre of the building; but no sooner was the plan proposed, than the land passed into other hands, and ten years elapsed before a site could be obtained.

Southgate Street is terminated by the Old Bridge, which was enlarged in 1754, and again in 1847.* It is built on or near the site of St. Lawrence's Bridge, which was constructed in 1304, to enable the inhabitants to attend the chartered fair, annually held in Holloway, on the 3rd of May. Upon it Prior John de Walcot placed a small oratory, or chapel, wherein the priest said a short prayer for the sick, the lame, and others who passed into the city in search of health or profit. For this service he received the alms of the faithful. Such chapels may still be seen in Roman Catholic countries, although long since unknown in our own. The bridge had a tower, with portcullis, on its south side. According to a custom common at the time, a line of houses stood on either side the roadway of the bridge. The centre piers were surmounted by two stone figures, the one representing a lion, the

* It is now in contemplation by the Corporation to widen the water way, remove the present bridge, and to replace it by a more commodious structure.

other a bear, which were mischievously destroyed in 1799, and thrown into the river. This approach to the city was further guarded by a drawbridge, which crossed the moat in front of the south gate.

WIDCOMBE.

LITTLE less than a century ago, the first house on the "beach," as Claverton Street was formerly called, was the Old Pack Horse—an ancient inn, where, it is said, Allen, Pope, Graves, Warburton, Fielding, and other worthies were wont to smoke their pipes, and enjoy agreeable converse. This house was removed in 1824.

The curiously-constructed wooden bridge, by which the Great Western railroad passes over the river, here attracts our attention. Crossing in an oblique direction, it required, at the time it was built, much engineering ability to overcome the difficulty; for, although the river at this point is but eighty feet wide, the bridge has two arches, each of eighty feet span.

For the convenience of persons passing to and from Widcombe there is a foot-bridge over the Avon. The entrance from the Widcombe side is near the bottom of Lyncombe Hill. The bridge offers a short cut to the Great Western Railway Station, and to certain parts of the city on the north bank of the river.

The rectory of Bath originally comprehended the Abbey, S. Mary de Stall, long since desecrated, the rectory of S. Michael, the rectory of S.

James, and the vicarge of Lyncombe and Widcombe.
S. Michael's was first separated 1842. To serve
all these parishes there was the Abbey, then confined to the choir within the aisles, S. James's, with
its old western tower, Widcombe Church (of
Thomas à Becket), and the Chapel of Prior Cantlow
in Holloway. The accommodation was manifestly insufficient, and the first step towards meeting the want
was an attempt made to provide fifty extra sittings
in Holloway Chapel; then followed the building of
S. Mark's Church in 1830, and, strange to say, the
closing of the Prior's chapel, during the incumbency
of the Rev. Charles Crook.

S. Mark's Church was built by the late city architect, Mr. Manners, and although at the time it was
built the principles of "Christian Architecture" were
pretty well understood by a few of our architects
they were not yet common property. S. Mark's,
fortunately, is not a pretentious building, consisting
of a nave, aisles, and western tower, a small recess
at the east end being the apology for a chancel. The
style is "four centered." The Rev. J. W. Sproule
is the vicar.

The Hon. and Rev. W. J. Brodrick (the late Viscount Middleton) was instituted Rector of Bath in
1839, and he sometime after took steps to separate
the Vicarage of Lyncombe and Widcombe from the
Abbey and to constitute two distinct and independent vicarages, namely, those of S. Mark and S.
Matthew.

𝔖. 𝔐𝔞𝔱𝔱𝔥𝔢𝔴'𝔰 𝔠𝔥𝔲𝔯𝔠𝔥,* at the bottom of Widcombe Hill, from the designs of Messrs. Manners and Gill, was built in 1847. The site is sloping, and unfortunately has not afforded a sufficient area for so large a church, the consequence being that the ecclesiastical arrangements of the plan are very much cramped. Externally the church, with its gabled roof and broach spire, in the decorated style, lends much to the landscape. The building within is a plane parallelogram, divided by two rows of pillars and arches, with a nave and side aisles ; a sort of transept on one side giving accommodation for the parish children in a gallery. A division of the nave is separated off as a chancel by a handsome stone screen right and left, with a stone pulpit in its usual place. Funds were wanting when the church was built, which will account for its plain character ; but the late vicar, the Rev. G. E. Tate, has enriched the eastern window, filled it with coloured glass, and erected a reredos from the drawings of Mr. C. E. Davis, of tolerably good design (though scarcely important enough); and in the cornice of which is the following inscription :—" Christ is all in all ; The same yesterday, to-day, and for ever; Head over all things to the Church." In 1873, the Rev. G. E.

* The bells in the tower, six in number, are fine, some bearing inscriptions. They were formerly in the tower of " Old Widcombe Church," whence, on the building of S. Matthew's, they were removed. We are familiar with the proverb " robbing Peter to pay Paul ;" *mutatis mutandis*—a ringing of the changes—and the proverb receives a new illustration, S. Matthew being enriched at the expense of S. Thomas à Becket.

Tate resigned the benefice, and was succeeded by the present vicar, the Rev. W. A. Cornwall.

At the bottom of Lyncombe hill, nearly opposite the mill, stands what was once a villa, formerly occupied, it is said, by the poet Pope. It is seen to the best advantage from the bank of the river. A little beyond was Ralph Allen's stone wharf, to which was conveyed the freestone from the quarries on Combe Down. A tramway ran down the Carriage Road to the river side. In an old view, still extant, ladies and gentlemen may be seen walking to Prior Park by the side of the tramroad.

At the end of Widcombe Parade we turn the corner leading to Prior Park Buildings. From this point a short walk conducts us to the Cemetery connected with the parish of St. Peter and St. Paul, commonly called the Abbey parish. It was laid out by a former Rector of Bath, the Hon. and Rev. W. J. Brodrick, afterwards Dean of Exeter, and who, on the death of his brother, Viscount Midleton, in 1863, succeeded to the title. He died in 1870. It now forms an integral portion of the Abbey parish, under an Act of Parliament, enabling city parishes to incorporate certain suburban districts for cemeteries. This city of the dead boasts scenic surroundings of unusual beauty.

The chapel is a fair specimen of the Anglo-Norman style. Mr. Manners' original design comprehended cloisters for the erection of monuments. These cloisters would have formed three sides of an ex-

K

tensive quadrangle, the non-completion of which
has thrown the building out of proportion.

A little below is a stone, representing a Roman
altar, which tells us of three skeletons found during
the formation of·the Cemetery. In the course of
the work some coins of Constantine the Great and
Carausius were discovered.

From the Cemetery, as already implied, varied
and extensive views are obtained. The back of
Beechen Cliff towers 360 feet above the city, which,
stretches up the slopes of Lansdown. To the westward is "Bagatelle" formerly a public tea garden.
Below lies Perrymead, with a road leading through
an archway to Pope's favourite walk.

Eastward are the **Manor House** and plantations,
and the picturesque ivy-covered tower of the **Parish
Church of Widcombe**, dedicated to St. Thomas á
Becket (see frontispiece). It was built between the
years 1499 and 1525, by a rate of 6d. in the pound,
ordered by the "chapel wardens" in 1502. This church
has been lately restored, and the chancel entirely rebuilt; the windows are filled with painted glass, the
gifts of many donors. As figures were not permitted,
the subjects are selections from the various shrubs
and flowers mentioned in the Bible. An elaborate
stone screen divides the chancel from the vestry, and
a beautiful window, which may be called a "Jesse
window," lights the chancel eastward. A new stone
pulpit utilises the staircase turret, that once led to the
rood loft. A singularly beautiful view is afforded

from the churchyard on the south. It was a favourite resort of Savage Landor, who purchased there a plot of earth for his last resting-place. His body, however, lies in another land.[*]

To the south is Prior Park; on the east are the grounds and mansion of "Crowe Hall," the residence of H. W. Tugwell, Esq., while Lyncombe Hill, with its diversified scenery, completes the picture.

The **Catholic Burying Ground**, separated from the so-called Abbey Cemetery by a wall only, is in excellent taste. A conspicuous object in this cemetery is the Mortuary Chapel of Count Eyre, with its elaborate altar, designed by Mr. Charles Hansom, and executed in alabaster by Bolton, of Cheltenham.

PRIOR PARK

CAN be approached either by the Carriage Road, or by Pope's Walk, through the archway. The associations connected with this celebrated spot, and its many distinguished occupants, will afford pleasure to the intelligent mind, and fancy, in her sportive moments, will repeople it with the spirits of the illustrious dead.

"A mile a this syde Bathe," says old Leland, "by south est, I saw 2 parks enclosyd with a ruinus stone wall now withe out dere. One longyd to the byshoppe, and other to the prior of Bathe." This park, from the circumstance of its belonging to the priory, received the name by which it is still known,

* Mr. Landor died and is buried at Florence.

and at the dissolution was included in the lands
bought of the king by Humphrey Colles.

The mansion, with which the park is crowned,
was designed and erected as a standing protest
against the reflections cast by London architects
upon the Bath oolite or freestone. With this view
a commission was given by Ralph Allen in 1738, to
Wood, the architect, to erect an edifice sufficiently
important in itself to command attention, and in its
construction to spare no expense, as a means of
showing to the world what could be done with such
valuable building material as that at his command.

For such a purpose it would have been difficult to
choose a better spot. The house, looking down a
vista of shady woods and undulating lawns through
the pretty glen of Widcombe, with its sheet of
water crossed by a Palladian bridge, is said to
comprise a more beautiful and varied view than any
other private residence in the kingdom, embracing
as it does an extensive prospect of the city and its
environs, with Lansdown, Beckford's Tower, and
Beacon Hill. Its lofty situation, its fine portico, and
the grandeur of its elevation, render it a conspicuous
and interesting object from almost every part of
the city.

The mansion, which occupies a natural terrace one
hundred feet below the summit level of Combe Down,
lies in front of the Wansdyke, here obliterated by
fir plantations and gardens. The house stands four
hundred feet above the level of the Avon. It con-

sists of a centre and two wings, united by arcades, and forms a beautiful line of building thirteen hundred feet long, describing the segment of a circle. The house, which is one hundred and fifty feet in breadth, is of the Corinthian order, elevated on a rustic basement, surmounted by a portico, and reached by a noble flight of steps. This portico was considered, at the time of its erection, to be the most beautiful and correct example of a six columned portico, in the kingdom.

Prior Park, after many vicissitudes, is for a second time occupied as a Catholic collegiate establishment. The College consists of three branches :—St. Peter's for younger boys, up to fourteen; St. Paul's for elder students, up to about eighteen; and the Seminary for those who, intending to embrace the ecclesiastical state, go through a complete course of philosophy and moral and dogmatic theology. The institution is primarily designed for lay education, but as many of the students intend to take orders, facilities are afforded for the ecclesiastical course.

The Church, which is being erected in the Corinthian style—the arrangement of which is similar to the old Basilica Churches—consists of nave, apse, aisles and six side chapels, the proportions of the columns being regulated accordingly. The structure is built with the lodge stile stone found on the estate.

The semi-dome of the apse and the panels surrounding the high altar are intended to be filled with

Venetian mosaics. A fine specimen of this work by
Salviati—the figure of St. John the Evangelist—may
be seen over the altar of one of the side chapels,
which has been finished as a memorial to the late
Dr. Bonomi.

The dimensions of the Church are 120 feet long
by 47 feet wide and 55 feet high. Two towers over
the west entrance rising to a height of 115 feet, and
overlooking the surrounding woods, will form, with
the body of the Church, an ornament to the College,
and a pleasing break to the sky line as seen from
Bath.

It was commenced by the late J. J. Scoles, Esq.,
of London, under whom the walls were partially
carried up, and after an interval of some years, is
being completed by his son, A. J. C. Scoles, Esq.

It is thought that it will be one of the finest, if not
the finest, specimens of pure classic style in the west
of England; it will be sufficiently advanced for
opening in 1876.

Prior Park is, however, especially deserving of
notice from having been the residence of a man
who did more for the permanent prosperity of Bath
than any of the worthies of the last century. It is
difficult to delineate the character of Ralph Allen,
without being unconsciously led away by the pane-
gyrics of contemporary writers. He was a good,
rather than a great man. Possessed of the most benevolent disposition, his celebrity, in a great measure,
rests upon the fact of his intimacy with, and un-

ostentatious acts of kindness towards men, who, at the outset of their career, needed a friend, and who, by their talents and exertions, subsequently became both good and great. The friend of Pope, Fielding, Smollett, Warburton, and Graves, is entitled to the admiration and respect of their admirers ; and when it is remembered that ample riches in his hands were not allowed to lie idle, but were constantly fructifying in deeds of undemonstrative benevolence, it is not surprising that Pope, in his Epilogue to the Satires, should thus speak of him (Dialogue i. v. 135–6) :—

> " Let humble Allen, with an awkward shame,
>   Do good by stealth, and blush to find it fame."

Ralph Allen* was born at St. Blazey, in Cornwall, in the year 1693. His father, who was a small innkeeper, had little to give him beyond a fair education. The son, after acting as clerk in the Exeter Post-office, was preferred to a similar appointment at Bath. Here, by vigilant observation, and by opening suspicious letters,† he obtained information

* There has been no trustworthy biography of Mr. Allen written. Many of the sketches given of him have been, for the most part, mere inventions. The best notice of his life we believe to be that written by the late Rev. Francis Kilvert, entitled "Ralph Allen and Prior Park," and published in his Posthumous Works.

† Some writers have attributed to Allen in this act an unwarrantable officiousness, but Mr. Kilvert says, and we think he is right, " it is probable that, at that critical juncture, the letters were suspected, and that Mr. Allen was authorised to open them." Whatever might have been the fact it is quite clear he acted with discretion.

of arms sent to Bath for the use of those who
favoured the Pretender. "When," says Dr. Harington, "the rebellion burst out, a numerous junto
in Bath took most active measures to aid the in-
surrection in the west of England; and Mr. Carte,
the minister of the Abbey parish when Allen detected
the plot, was glad to escape from the constables by
leaping in full canonicals from a window."

The intelligence thus acquired by Allen was
at once communicated by him to the celebrated
Marshal Wade, who at that time commanded the
Western district; and the Marshal was so pleased
with the act, that he procured for him the appointment of postmaster of Bath, and married him to his
natural daughter, Miss Earl.

In 1742, Allen filled the office of Mayor of
Bath, and, retiring from the Corporation in 1763,
presented the city with £500 towards the expense
of rebuilding the Guildhall. So unshaken was his
loyalty that, on the breaking out of the rebellion
in 1745, he clothed and equipped 100 Volunteers
at his own expense. Seven years later, in 1752, he
received the Princess Amelia as his guest at Prior
Park.

During Allen's connexion with the Post-office, he
applied himself to the establishment of cross-posts,
which he perfected, and having obtained a lease
from Government for twenty-one years, at £6,000
per annum, he found the speculation so profitable
that he was glad to obtain a renewal of the grant at an

increased annual rental of £20,000. The influence which, during this time, he acquired in the city was so great, that he was enabled to secure the election of men of his own choice as representatives in Parliament. As his wealth increased,[*] his house was opened to all the wits and literary characters of his age. Among others, he sought out Pope, and loaded him with kindness, but he was requited by him with ingratiude and contumely. Not content with Allen's great attention to himself, Pope wished him to give up the Manor House of Bathampton to Martha Blount, his *reputed* mistress.[†]

[*] Much of his wealth was no doubt acquired from the manner in which he developed the stone quarries upon his estate, and the business - like sagacity he displayed in this as in all other matters. He had his detractors, amongst whom was Thicknesse, one of the most ill-natured of mankind. He says : "While he was supposed to be gaining a princely fortune by digging stone from the *bowels* of the earth, he actually picked it off the *surface*, by traversing the whole kingdom with post horses." On this Mr. Kilvert says, that having regard to the magnitude of the contracts and their profitable nature, the insinuation that the business done was only a feint to cover his large, and by implication, illegitimate gains in connection with the government contract, is wholly groundless.

[†] The scandal here referred to was very generally believed during Pope's lifetime, and long afterwards ; but the reputation of Pope and Miss Blount have been amply vindicated, and their relations placed on a clear and just footing by the late Mr. Chas. Wentworth Dilke in a series of articles published in the *Athenæum* a quarter of a century ago, and re-published in his "Papers of a Critic" just issued (1875) by Mr. Murray. It by no means follows that Mr. Allen believed the stories then current with regard to Pope and Martha Blount, but supposing the refusal to allow Miss Blount to occupy his house to have been the true cause of the

Allen was, it is said, annoyed at the proposal, and positively refused to do so; upon which the poet quitted the house, spoke contemptuously of his best friend, and in his will ordered his executors to pay Allen the sum of £150, as the amount due for his entertainment at Prior Park. Allen paid this sum into the funds of the Bath General Hospital, quietly observing that, at the best of times, Mr. Pope was not a good accountant, and when he mentioned £150 as measuring the amount of his obligation, he had omitted a cipher in the amount. Allen also befriended Fielding, not with hospitality only, but with money; it is well known that whilst the *Squire Allworthy* of "Tom Jones" is intended for Allen, some of the finest descriptions of scenery in the novel are applicable to Prior Park.

Allen ably seconded Wood in the improvement of the city; and was one of the earliest supporters of the Bath Hospital, to which he not only contributed sums of money, but delivered, ready worked, at the building, all the stone required for its erection. One of the wards of that noble institution is appropriately named after him, and in the corridor of the principal floor a beautiful bust of white marble, from the chisel of William Hoare, was placed by Bishop

---

rupture, we can conceive many reasons to justify the refusal besides that assigned and generally accepted. Mr. Elwin, in his elaborate edition of Pope's Works now publishing, mercilessly exposes the vanity, trickery, and literary impostures of which he was guilty, but fully recognises the completeness of Mr. Dilke's exculpation of the Poet from the charge of immorality.

Warburton as a public record of the benevolence of
one who appears constantly to have kept in mind
Archbishop Whitgift's motto, on his noble foundation
at Croydon, in Surrey—

"He that giveth to the poor will never want."

In conclusion, it may be observed that riches in the
hands of such a man appear to have exerted their
legitimate influence, by dispensing happiness to all
around. His virtues deck his tomb with undying
honour. From the contemplation of such deeds
we arise to the consciousness that the philan-
thropist may be more worthy of respect than the
warrior, however glorious his victories.

Allen married as his second wife Elizabeth Holder,
and dying in 1764, at the age of 71, was buried
under a handsome mausoleum in Claverton churchyard.

Closely connected with the history of Prior Park
is the name of the celebrated Bishop Warburton.

William Warburton, descended from a knightly
family of the county palatine of Chester, was born
on Christmas eve, 1698, at Newark-upon-Trent,
where his father practised as a solicitor. In the year
1714, he was articled to Mr. Kirke, an attorney at
Great Markham. After devoting four years to the
study of the law, he applied himself to theology, was
ordained deacon in 1723, and priest in 1726. Presented in 1728, to the rectory of Brand Broughton,
in Lincolnshire, he resided there until 1746; and
during that period wrote his "Alliance between

Church and State," which was followed by the first and second volumes of his celebrated work, "The Divine Legation of Moses Demonstrated." With regard to the merits of the production, the judgment of contemporary critics was much divided. While some considered it a work of such profound learning, that, in the whole range of theological literature, it would be difficult to find its equal, others condemned it as deficient in proof; whilst a few maintained that the huge mass of learning brought to bear on the demonstration of that divine mission, tended to raise a doubt of its credibility from the apparent difficulty of the proof, and the immense labour taken to elucidate it.

Warburton, while at Broughton, defended Pope's fine poem, "The Essay on Man," from the attacks of a French critic, Monsieur de Crousaz. This led to his acquaintance with the poet, who procured for him the patronage of Mr. Murray, afterwards the great Lord Mansfield, and introduced him to the hospitable board of his friend, Ralph Allen.

It is strange upon what trivial circumstances the destinies of men appear to depend. Warburton's introduction to Allen was, of itself, perhaps, apparently unimportant, but it exercised a great influence on his future fortunes. First we see the man of letters employing his leisure hours in combating the attack of an unknown critic on a poem written by a stranger; then an invitation given by the author is accepted by his defender, Warburton,

who proposed at once to visit Pope at his Twick-
enham residence. It happened, however, that the
poet was absent and at Prior Park, and Warburton's
letter was handed to him whilst at dinner, whereupon he, agitated and perplexed, laid it on the table.
"What is the matter?" said Allen. "Oh, replied
he, "a Lincolnshire parson, to whom I am much
obliged, promises me a visit." "If that be all, let
him come here;" and this was Warburton's introduction to his future home!

In 1746, Warburton married Allen's favourite
niece, Gertrude Tucker, and resided at Prior Park.
He was not, however, long allowed to remain in
retirement, for, in the following year, he was elected
preacher at Lincoln's Inn. In 1747, he published
an edition of Shakspeare's Plays; in 1749, he vindicated Pope in the affair of Bolingbroke's Patriot
King; and, in 1750, published "Julian." In the
year 1751, he gave to the world an edition of
Pope's Works; and this was followed, in 1754, by
his "Principles of Natural and Revealed Religion."

Warburton's rise in the church had not hitherto
been rapid; but, in 1753, he was appointed to a stall
in Gloucester Cathedral, which, by Murray's interest,
he exchanged for one in Durham in 1755. Shortly
afterwards, Archbishop Herring gave him the degree
of D.D. It is not a little remarkable in the history
of an Anglican Prelate of modern times, that
throughout life he had no connexion with either
University.

In 1757, Warburton was made Dean of Bristol ; and in 1760, was raised to the see of Gloucester.* His subsequent labours consisted in preparing new editions of his works, with some lesser controversial writings directed against Bishop Lowth, John Wesley, and the Socinians. In right of his wife, he took possession of Prior Park at Allen's death ; and devoted himself so closely to literary pursuits, that the king, not having seen him at court for some time, asked him if he had just left his diocese ? Warburton was a shrewd man ; and, knowing wherein his power lay, replied, "No ; but I have, at Prior Park, been combating the enemies of that faith of which your Majesty is the zealous defender." He died on the 7th June, 1779, and was buried in Gloucester Cathedral.

"He was," says Dr. Johnson, "a man of vigorous faculties ; a mind fervent and vehement, supplied by incessant and unlimited enquiry, with wonderful extent and a variety of knowledge. To every work he brought a memory full fraught, together with a fancy fertile in original combinations, exerting the powers of the scholar, the reasoner, and the wit. But his knowledge was too multifarious to be always exact ; his pursuits too eager to be always cautious. His abilities gave him a haughty confidence, which he disdained to conceal or mollify. His impatience

* The works of Warburton, with a life by Bishop Hurd, were published in 7 vols., 4to., in 1788-94, and a selection from his unpublished papers was edited by the late Rev. F. Kilvert, and published 1841.

of opposition disposed him to treat his adversaries with such contemptuous superiority as made his readers his enemies, and excited against the advocate the wishes of some who favoured the cause. He used no allurements of gentle language, but wished to compel rather than persuade. His style is copious without selection, and forcible without neatness. He took his words as they presented themselves, and his sentences are unmeasured."

Dr. Hurd,* Bishop of Worcester, thus delineates his character:—" He possessed those virtues which are so important in society, truth, probity and honour, in the highest degree, with a frankness of temper very uncommon, and a friendship to those he loved which knew no bounds. Not suspicious or captious in the least; quick, indeed, in his resentment of real injuries, but then again (as is natural to such tempers) of the utmost placability. He had an ardent love of virtue, and the most sincere love of religion; was free from bigotry, intolerance and fanaticism. He venerated the civil constitution of the country, and was warmly attached to the Church of England. He was no party man, but the sincere advocate of toleration. As a writer and divine, it is not easy to find terms that will do justice to his merits: his reading was various and extensive, and his discernment exquisite; he saw and seized on what was just and useful in every science he culti-

* The late Rev. Francis Kilvert, it may here be mentioned, wrote the life of this able Prelate, published by Bentley in 1860.

vated, and in every book he read. His style was his own; its characters are freedom and force. He was the terror of the infidel and Socinian.*

"In mixed society he was extremely entertaining, but less guarded than men of the world usually are, disposed to take to himself a larger share of the conversation than good breeding would allow; yet few wished him to be more reserved, or less communicative, so abundant was the entertainment which his ready wit and extensive knowledge afforded. In private he was natural, easy and unpretending, at once the most agreeable and most useful companion. You saw to the bottom of his heart on any subject of discourse; his various literature, penetrating judgment, and quick recollection made him say the liveliest and justest things upon it."

It is, indeed, difficult to decide which of these sketches conveys to posterity the more accurate picture. While Dr. Hurd writes with too partial a pen, Dr. Johnson is, perhaps, too acrimonious; and yet we see throughout Dr. Hurd's remarks that truth compels him to admit many failings. The fact is, Bishop Warburton's works display an unnecessary and ostentatious parade of learning, where truth needs only close and convincing argument for its elucidation. His attacks on the Socinians are not the gentle corrections of a friend seeking to convince, but rather the castigations of an enemy

---

* In spite of Bishop Hurd, we may doubt whether he at all disturbed Gibbon in his complacent scepticism.

anxious to triumph. His works, erudite as they are, please no longer; and the negative merit must be accorded to him of having been a man who steadily maintained the doctrines of his church, without doing much for the advancement of vital and essential religion. His intentions were good, but his manner rendered them inoperative, so that his works are now perused rather for their learning than for edification or religious study. In his own day he enjoyed immense popularity. He sought in polemics for mere temporary honours, which his natural vanity taught him to consider eternal; so that his works, which were greatly praised during his life - time, are now consigned to comparative oblivion.

COMBE DOWN.

LEAVING Prior Park, we soon reach the gates of the Carriage Road, and, turning to the left, follow the highway for a short distance till we come to a gate, which conducts us to the Monument Field, so named from a triangular building, with a round tower, erected by Bishop Warburton, whereon was formerly a tablet, with a Latin inscription, in honour of Ralph Allen. It contains the remains of a circular staircase, now crumbling through neglect. The structure promises, at no distant date, to become a ruin. A portion of the Wansdyke may be seen, near the wall. From the brow of the hill, one of the most picturesque and perfect views of the city is obtained.

Immense blocks of stone are taken out of the freestone quarries on Combe Down, without the aid of blasting, and are at once worked into convenient forms for the builder.   The stone is at first soft and friable, but possesses the valuable property of hardening by exposure to the air.   It contains but few of what are popularly called fossils.   The nautilus, pinna marina, oyster, and pecten, are the principal.

This stone—called by geologists the great oolite— is found near the surface of the earth, in beds of about one hundred and thirty feet in thickness.   It is composed of marine shells aggregated together. These, from their globular shape, give the stone its generic name, which is derived from the Greek word ωον—an egg.   The effect of hydro-chloric acid on the oolite is effervescence.   There is but little residuum, and a slight animal odour is said to be exhaled.   The old quarries, which run under a considerable portion of the down, will well repay a visit ; light is admitted by circular shafts.

Combe Down, forming part of the parish of Monckton Combe, has long been celebrated for the purity and salubrity of the air.   The situation, on the brow of a hill, sloping to the south, together with its proximity to the city, renders it a delightful and convenient residence for invalids.   During the last few years many elegant villa residences have been built on the brow of the hill, commanding most beautiful prospects.   Its patrons affirm that it enjoys a protection from the cold north winds, which, in their passage over the warm vale of Bath, are assumed to be deprived of their severity. The Village lies open to the full sweep of the southerly and westerly winds, and a splendid and diversified view over a beautiful, undulating country, embracing Longleat, Clay Hill, the White Horse, Stourton Tower, Midford Castle, and the Wiltshire Downs, renders it desirable as a summer residence. Operations, we believe, have been begun, the object of which is to effect a better system of drainage, and obtain a better supply of pure water.

Very different is its aspect from what it was when Mr. Rack* wrote his description, in 1780. " The village of Combe Down," he says, " consists of eleven houses, built of the stone raised on the spot, each of which has a small garden in front, originally built for the workmen employed in the quarries. They are now let to invalids from Bath, who retire hither for the sake of a very fine air, from which many have derived essential benefit. The beautiful and extensive prospect, the wild but pleasing irregularities of the scenery, the extensive plantations of fir, which throw a solemn gloominess of shade, impervious to the sun and winds, over a fine soft turf free from underwood—all serve to render it a delightful summer retreat."

* The founder of the Bath and West of England Society; author of a volume of Essays and Poems; and an able collaborator of Collinson, in his compilation of the History of the County of Somerset.

The firs are nearly all gone, except within the walls of Prior Park. The **Church**, in the Perpendicular Gothic style, with a chaste and elegant spire, was consecrated in 1835. Near it stands a neat parsonage house. Formerly this district, as well as Monckton Combe, was part of the ecclesiastical parish of Southstoke, but the two districts were subdivided into Perpetual Curacies by the late rector, the Rev. H. Calverley. The Rev. G. Newnham has held the Perpetual Curacy of this district since 1842. A little below the Church, the road winds towards Monckton Combe. Few persons will probably pass the first curve, without pausing to admire a view, that to our thinking is of exceeding loveliness.

MONCKTON COMBE.

THIS Village lies in the valley below Combe Down, and consists of a single irregular street. The church, of which the Rev. Francis Pocock is the incumbent, has recently been re-built, the former edifice, erected in 1814, being found totally inadequate to the wants of the parish. The present structure consists of a west tower, nave, and south aisle. The style is that of the 13th century. The parsonage stands on a beautiful site at the west end of the village. A neat and commodious schoolroom has been built by the present incumbent for the use of his people.

The following lines, from the pen of Thomas

Campbell, are engraven on the monument of Mrs.
Shute and her daughters, who were accidentally
drowned at Chepstow, on Sunday, Sept. 20, 1812 :—
We quote only the first and last stanzas.

" In deep submission to the will above,
    Yet with no common cause for human tears,
    This stone, for the lost partner of his love,
    And for his children lost, a mourner rears.

Oh ! may each passer-by the lesson learn,
    Which can alone the bleeding heart sustain,
    (When friendship weeps at virtue's funeral urn)
    That to the pure in heart—' to die is gain.' "

Against the north wall of the chancel is a tablet
tomb, with a pediment terminating in three altars,
having three Latin verses, alternately hexameters
and pentameters. The following lines may serve to
convey the meaning :—

Rice Mansell, knight ; his daughter, Katheryne,
From home thou art, the wife of Basset's squire.
Bewper thy home ; and where they did enshrine
Morgan, the Briton's king, thou didst a babe respire.

Thy term of years was eight times ten ; but Time
Thine age sustained, and his, who was thy care ;
A youthful pair Love joined, and here they join
In death, who had of days and years an equal share.

His junior seven years ; when they had wedded been
That term of life, she was a widow seven ;
So that each had of time an equal share,
And the same day unlocked to both the gate of heaven.

William Bassett,	Katheryne Bassett,
Died A.D. 1586,	Died A.D. 1593,
Aged 80, March 10.	Aged 80, March 10.

Thomas Leyson, posuit.

The last line of this epitaph we transcribe for its exquisite beauty. It evidently alludes to their dying on the same day of the month, and, as will be seen, at the same age :—

" Vitæ ambo et mortis par fuit ipsa dies."

This old tablet tomb has been carefully placed at the end of the west aisle of the new church.

Collinson calls this village Combe Monkton ; but says that its name is simply Combe, the affix being added to mark it as the property of the Abbey of Bath. The mansion of Combe Grove, the property and residence of Major Vaughan Jenkins, lies on the brow of the hill north of the village. From the terrace a fine view of the valley of Midford is obtained.

In Domesday Book, this manor is called *Cume*, a word signifying a valley ; from time immemorial it was possessed by the Abbey of Bath. Its value at the Conquest was £8; at the Reformation, £20. Its rateable value, for apportioning Union expenditure, is £5,172, on an area of 540 statute acres. In 1780, it paid £103 poor rates, the population being 280. According to the last census, it contains 1,388 souls. The poor rates now average £324 yearly.

Proceeding through the village to the Somerset coal canal, we catch a glimpse of the Viaduct, and from this point are able to estimate all the quiet loveliness of the vale. In character, it is thoroughly English. Wooded uplands; a babbling brook, well

Railway Viaduct, near Midford.

stocked with coarse fish, and containing, especially in its higher part, a fair stock of trout; rich meadows, and glimpses of distant hills, constitute its claim to our notice. Nor is this all, for on the right is a chain of ponds,* half hid in a beautiful dell, spanned by a viaduct (see illustration), which forms part of the Somerset and Dorset line.

MIDFORD.

OF Midford, in 1588, Leland thus speaks :—" I cam to a village, and passid over a stone bridge they caullid *Milford* water. This broke risith yn the roots of *Mendip* hilles, about a 7 miles or more by west south-west from this bridge, and goith a mile lower into Avon."

The hamlet is remarkable for its modern castle, which occupies a commanding situation. It is of singular construction, being triangular, and having the angles rounded off, and embattled. Erected on a beautiful slope, the lower terrace is raised to a considerable height, and is surrounded by a balustrade. On the north and east there is a deep glen, the sides of which are clothed with fine coppice woods, intersected with walks, and ornamented with flowering shrubs.

When the house was erected, the owner built a Gothic priory on the brow of the hill, overlooking Horsecombe brook. At a little distance from it, in a thick mass of shade, stands a so-called hermitage,

* We have seen the lower one as clear and blue as a mountain tarn.

the effect of which is good and the scene below charming.

At Midford, prior to the opening of the railway, the produce of the coal-pits at Radstock was brought by tramway to the canal. Close to the village an ingenious contrivance for weighing a barge and its cargo may be seen.

The length of this ramble, if the tourist has not strayed far from the line of march indicated, may be between five and six miles, and as he is now within sight of the Midford Railway Station, we will, for the sake of convenience, assume that he there takes his ticket, and wends his way back to the city.

IN AND OUT OF BATH.

***

WALK THE FOURTH.

How we find our way out of the Town to
Southstoke; the Church; the Manor in
the Olden Time; on to Combe Hay; the
Mansion, Park, Church, and Graveyard;
the Poet Carrington: Biographical Sketch;
Home by Fortnight Hill and the Radstock
Road.

***

STARTING from the city, we pass down Southgate Street; cross the Old Bridge; mount the
steep ascent of Holloway; and following a road,
which runs nearly due south, reach the Cross Keys,
once a wayside hostelry of more note than at present.
A few yards beyond the inn is the parish lane
leading to

SOUTHSTOKE.

Passing by an ancient grange in the homestead of
a farm-house, we reach the church, repaired and

enlarged in 1845, under the direction of Mr.
Manners.   At the west end, the quadrangular embattled tower, having a turret and pinnacles, rises to
the height of fifty feet.   It is of the fifteenth
century, and was, in all probability, erected in the
reign of Henry VII., for Wharton relates that during
the wars of the roses, Somersetshire was decidedly
Lancasterian.   In return for the aid afforded by the
county, Henry rebuilt many of the churches.   The
northern doorway is a beautiful specimen of Norman
work.   There is also a Norman font.   The pulpit is
of stone, in the style of the church.   The alterations
reflect great credit on the then vicar, the late Rev.
H. Calverley, at whose expense, aided by a grant
from the Diocesan Society, they were brought to a
conclusion.   Mr. Calverley, at his own cost, also
erected, in 1840, a neat village school.   This gentleman died in 1874, and was succeeded by the Rev.
W. Acworth.

At the Conquest, this manor existed in two
separate lordships, as it had done in the reign of
Edward the Confessor.   William gave one to the
Bishop of Coutance, the other to Earl Morton ; the
former was taxed for seven hides, the latter for five
and a half, while a small portion was not taxed.

In an old lease, preserved in the Harleian MSS.,
the following memorandum occurs :—

"*That the vicar, for the time being, should have
going and pasturing freely with the farmer's beasts
there, for three beasts; whereof one shall be a horse,*

mare, or gelding, the second a kowe, and the third a
bullock; the first with the farmer's mares, his kowe
with the farmer's kine, and his bullock with the
farmer's bullocks, in certain leases and pastures, that
is to say, in Brode close, Grove close, and Shephouse
close, from time to time, as it has been used and
accustomed time owte of mind."

Descending by Hod's Hill, we reach the canal,
where, at the beginning of Combehay, the celebrated Weldon erected a caisson lock, in 1798, for
the ascent and descent of barges, the situation of
which is close to the residence of Mr. Hill, the
Engineer to the Somerset Coal Canal Company,
and the lower end of the chamber is marked by a
chestnut tree, planted by Mr. Hill's father.

The drop was sixty feet, and the walls are believed
to be still perfect, as when filled up. It consisted
of a wooden chamber, capable of containing a
barge, with a gate at each end. The vessel having
entered it, the gates were shut, a sufficient quantity
of water to float it being first admitted; it was then
either raised or lowered by appropriate machinery,
the perpendicular height from the surface of the
lower canal to that of the upper being 132 feet.
The caisson having proved a failure, the transit is
now effected by twenty-two ordinary locks, in the
space of rather more than a mile.

In 1871, the population was 355, and the poor
rates amount, on an average, to £150.

COMBEHAY, or HAWEY.

A lovely spot thou art Combehay ! Thy trees
With golden fruit, around each humble cot,
Are deeply laden, when Autumnal winds
Sweep o'er the well-reap'd fields, where corn has been,
Thy Winter is enlivened by the yew,
From which, in days gone by, strong bows were made ;
And sav'ry herbs, in sickness much extolled,
Grow 'midst the fragrant flowers of thy vale.

THIS was the only manor in Somerset given by
William to his half-brother, Odo, Bishop of Bayeux,
and Earl of Kent, reputed to be the wisest among
the Conqueror's generals, but who, in this and the
succeeding reign, was constantly involved in plots
and conspiracies. The manor, on the deprivation
of Odo, was given to the family of Hawey, from
whom it received its second appellation. It remained
in their possession until the reign of King Edward I.,
when an heiress brought it to the Stradlings, who held
it until 1684. It has since had a variety of owners,
and is now the property of Samuel Butler, Esq.

The mansion house is one of the most convenient
in the vicinity of Bath, and when in the possession of
the late Colonel Leigh, was honoured by the presence
of the Prince of Wales, afterwards George IV., and
other members of the Royal Family. It contains
some valuable pictures, and is situated on a lawn
sloping down to an ornamental piece of water. The
park contains a happy mixture of hill, dale, and wood.

The village church, which nestles close to the
house, is hid almost from view by evergreens, its

ivy-covered tower surmounting a modern nave and chancel. The whole body of the church has been restored; a new high-pitch open roof the whole length of the church from the tower, three arches, a new south aisle, and vestry, have been erected during the past year, at the sole expense of Mr. Butler; while stained glass windows have been added respectively by Mr. Hill, Mr. Webb, the Rector, Mr. Butler, and Mrs. Barnard, late of the parish, has also placed a very handsome one at the west end, *In Memoriam*, of her late husband, all of which are by Messrs. Bell and Son, Bristol; some handsomely carved stalls have been placed in the chancel at the cost of the Rector. The tower was built in the fifteenth, while the remainder of the building itself is of the eighteenth century. The Rev. C. C. Layard is the rector.

"Forty-one years ago the remains of N. T. Carrington, the gifted author of 'Dartmoor' and other descriptive poems, were interred at Combehay. Yet a stranger, visiting the spot and looking for his grave, would have sought it in vain, except by a reference to the old parish register, which faithfully records his burial and other less interesting facts for a period of more than 300 years. No slab, not even a headstone and scarcely a mound, marked the spot, where all that was mortal of the amiable poet lies commingled with its kindred dust among the rude forefathers of this picturesque hamlet. At a meeting held on the 22nd June, 1871, the members of the Bath Literary Club, anxious to do honour to his memory, and supported by the liberality of the Rev. John Buttanshaw, then rector of the parish, erected within the church, a handsome brass mural tablet, beautifully engraved and illuminated, bearing the following inscription :—

M. S.
N. T. CARRINGTON,
Poetæ,
Cui dulces in carmine musæ nomen insigne dederunt,
Vixit annos liii.,
Obiit die 2 Septembris, MDCCCXXX.
Amici quidam votem amabilem honorandi gratia,
hoc monumentum posuerunt."

Since the accomplishment of this generous act of the Literary Club, a beautiful Gothic tomb of Cheesering granite has been placed over the Poet's grave, bearing the following inscription :—

"Sacred to the Memory of the Poet,
N. T. CARRINGTON,
Who Died the 2nd September, 1830,
Aged 53 years."

This has been done by a younger son of the Poet, Mr. W. M. Carrington, of H.M.'s Dockyard, Devonport, and is alike creditable to his taste, and the filial respect and love to his father's memory, by which it was prompted.

The following brief biography is abstracted from the edition of his poems, published, in 1834, by the poet's eldest son, Mr. Henry Edmund Carrington.*

* The late Henry Edmund Carrington was for 28 years proprietor and editor of the *Bath Chronicle*. In describing the character of his father, he in many respects unconsciously pourtrayed his

"Carrington was born at Plymouth, in 1777, and at fifteen was apprenticed to Mr. Fox, a measurer in Plymouth dockyard. He was (as he himself said) totally unfit for the business. Mild by nature, fond of literary pursuits, and attached to reading, it was strange that a mechanical profession should have been chosen for him. Popular prejudice among the Plymouth lads in favour of the yard, and his father's being attached to it, were the cause of his taking a step, of which he soon repented. At the expiration of three years, he ran away; and, in a moment of desperation, entered on board a man-of-war, and was present at the battle off Cape St. Vincent in 1797, in commemoration of which he wrote some verses, which attracted the notice of his captain, who kindly sent him home. He then became a schoolmaster; and, in 1804, removed to Maidstone, where he married. At the pressing

---

own. The father lacked many qualities which the son possessed in an eminent degree, and which fitted him for the post he so ably filled. Great knowledge of human nature; an intuitive perception of the right thing to be said, and the best way of saying it; a vigorous understanding, combined with great culture and ability, and when occasion required, a determined spirit, which nothing could daunt—in him were happily united. He cared nothing for popularity, and never sought it, seldom or never taking part in the conflicts of party or of public life. But he none the less promoted the principles which he believed to be right in reference to both. Mr. Carrington died suddenly in 1859, and was followed to his last resting place at Swanswick by a large concourse of citizens of all ranks, parties, and religious persuasions, anxious to show their respect for so worthy a citizen.

solicitations of his friends, he returned to his native place in 1809, and there kept a school until within six months of his death, which occurred in 1830.

"Amidst the unceasing toil of a thirty-three years' scholastic experience, working early and late, he yet found time for literary composition. His boast was, that his business was never neglected. He possessed a winning manner and a kind heart; he was the child of nature, virtuous and independent, whose christianity was a holy influence, shedding a blessing on all around. Varied knowledge, great affability, and a modest demeanour, caused him, in society, to be listened to with pleasure and satisfaction. His 'Dartmoor' abounds with felicitous imagery, and great fidelity of description.

"He died in Bath, September 2, 1830, of pulmonary consumption. We may not inappropriately close this brief sketch in his own words.

'——— let ME rest
Like a tired bird in its own quiet nest ;
And find (how exquisite to find it !) there
Life's stormy noon crown'd with a sunset fair !' "

In Domesday Book the manor is called *Cume*, or *Cŵm*. It was then, with Twinney,* worth £10 13*s.* Its rateable value for Union expenditure is £1,959, on an area of 1,011 statute acres. The population, in 1871, was 172; and the poor rates average £120 per annum.

* The word Twinney is Celtic, and is identical in pronunciation with the word *Twynu*, still used in Wales, and meaning "the land of little hills."

IN AND OUT OF BATH.

WALK THE FIFTH.

BY RAIL TO MIDFORD; PLEASANT LOITERING TO
HINTON BY ROAD AND WOODLAND—THE ABBEY;
ON TO NORTON ST. PHILIP—THE PLACE IN
THE OLDEN TIME—THE GEORGE—THE FLEUR
DE LYS—JEFFERY FLOWER, GENTLEMAN—WE
WALK THE GROUND ON WHICH THE BATTLE
BETWEEN THE TROOPS OF THE DUKE OF MON-
MOUTH AND THOSE OF JAMES II. WAS FOUGHT.

CHARTERHOUSE HINTON.

THE liberty of Norton and Hinton—exempted
in the reign of Henry III. from the jurisdiction
of the hundred of Wellow, in consequence of its
having been bestowed by Ela, Countess of Salisbury,
on the Carthusian monastery, which she then founded
—contains many objects of interest.

As the places mentioned in this walk lie at a considerable distance from Bath, it would be advisable,

perhaps, to take the train to Midford, and commence the present ramble from that point.

Crossing the bridge, our way lies up a long hill, from which we obtain extensive views, embracing the hamlet and castle of Midford, with its Belgic-British stronghold, Combe Down and Southstoke, many a wood and neat farm-house embosomed in foliage, and the distant firs of Duncairn Hill, while winding southward through the valley, the newly constructed line of the Somerset and Dorset Railway, can be traced for many miles. If the air be still, the hooter of the Radstock Coal Works (distant some eight miles, in a south westerly direction) can be distinctly heard, and, in clear weather, the smoke of the engine fires may be seen.

At the Conquest, King William gave the liberty to Edward, Earl of Salisbury, from whom it obtained the prefix of " *Comitis*." Hinton was afterwards called Charterhouse-Hinton, from its Carthusian Priory. The Carthusian order having first settled in the desert of Chartreuse, near Grenoble, the general name of Charterhouse—a corruption of Chartreuse—was frequently applied to their convents, of which, at one time, the order possessed upwards of two hundred, the Charterhouse in London being one of them.

The Geologist, in ascending the hill, will have a good opportunity of observing the effects of denudation in the excavation of the valley.

The brook, in the bottom, has, in places, cut a channel into the harder beds of the lias, while the corresponding strata of the inferior oolite—fullers' earth, and the upper oolite, can be discovered on either side of the valley, giving us some idea of the giant scale on which Nature performs the excavator's work :

> " The hills are shadows, and they flow
> From form to form, and nothing stands ;
> They melt like mist, the solid lands,
> Like clouds they shape themselves and go."
>
> TENNYSON.

Archæologists, who are interested in the times, which geologists deem modern, will find many objects of interest in this ramble.

Half-way up, on the eastern side of the hill, is a Belgic-British fort; a second, stands near the lodge of Hinton Abbey. Above this is a beacon barrow, while the abbey is said to occupy the site of another sepulchral mound. There was a British settlement at Hinton, and the remains of a Roman entrenchment are still visible. In one portion, called the *Bulwarks*, coins and pottery have been found; and among the ruins of the abbey, Roman bricks and other relics are discovered. The village, which occupies a commanding position on the top of a hill, five miles from Bath, is about 400 feet above the level of the sea.

The church is chiefly in the early English style, presenting nothing worthy of notice, except its square tower, which differs from those of the neighbouring churches. This tower, though peculiar, is not as regards its upper story much more than a hundred years old. The church has been repaired under the superintendence of the late Mr. Elkington Gill. At the chancel end is the neat freestone sarcophagus of Mr. Symonds, of Hinton Abbey, who died in 1830. Within, are some memorials of the Hungerford family.

Near the church is the seat of the Hon. Mrs. Jones, from whose grounds to the east, we obtain extensive views of the Wiltshire hills—the White Horse, near Westbury, being distinctly seen in fine weather.

From this spot the landscape looks like a continuous plain to Winsley, and no trace of the river, or the valley which intervenes, can be discerned. Passing by railway through the valley of the Avon, it is difficult to realise that this immense excavation has been effected by denudation, but seen from this position, we learn how the once level surface has been cut through by the stream which we pass at Limpley Stoke and Freshford.

Following the church path, we proceed to the ruins of the old Carthusian Priory, now known as Hinton Abbey. This priory was founded in 1227 by Ela, Countess of Salisbury, in obedience to the will of her husband, William Longespée, son of King Henry II. and Fair Rosamond.

Ela was the only daughter of William de Eureux, Sheriff of Wilts and Earl of Salisbury, and on her marriage with Longespée, Richard Cœur de Lion created her husband Earl of Salisbury. King John made Longespée warden of the Marches of Wales, and one of the chief commanders of the fleet. Henry III. made him Sheriff of Hampshire, and Governor of the castles of Winchester and Dorchester. Rich and full of honours, Longespée seems to have been desirous of making the best of both worlds, and in his will not only enjoined on his widow the building of the priory in question, but left several valuable gifts for its endowment.

The Carthusians, brought hither by Ela, were first introduced into England by Henry II., and settled at Witham Friary, near Frome. They were an order in great esteem for the austerity of their rules, and held themselves as equals to kings and princes.

In the life of Hugo, Bishop of Lincoln, we find both Hugo and Einard, two poor brethren who came from Chartreuse, near Grenoble, to Witham Friary, addressing Henry as equals, and the latter giving the King a downright rating in good set terms.

The order of Carthusians was originally founded by St. Bruno, "a native of Cologne. He was des- "cended from noble and religious parents, and "completed his academical course with brilliant suc- "cess. After having held the highest offices in the "Church, both at Cologne and Rheims, he suddenly "resolved to quit the world, and to spend the re- "mainder of his days in monastic seclusion, and in "the year 1084, at the age of 23, retired with six

"companions to the desert of the Chartreuse, near
"Grenoble."—(*Lancelot's Tour.*)

He died in Calabria, Oct. 6th, 1101.   There is a
grand statue of St. Bruno, by Hondon, in the great
church of Sta Maria Degli Angeli at Rome, of which
Clement XIV. used to say, "He would speak if the
rules of his order did not forbid it."

" The cause to which tradition ascribes St. Bruno's
"converson is singular.   Whilst a canon at Paris,
"Bruno formed a peculiar intimacy with another
"canon of the name of Raymond Diocres. The latter
"is said to have been exceedingly social and agree-
"able, but not a decidedly religious character. One
"day they both dined together at a large party;
"after a very convivial meeting, Raymond was
"suddenly seized with an apoplectic fit, and fell
"on the floor without any signs of life. Bruno
"was deeply distressed. Preparations were made
"for the funeral; and as a particular friend of the
"deceased he was, of course, invited. The body
"was brought on a bier, in an open coffin, covered
"with a pall, by torch light. It was placed in
"the chapel, which was hung with black, and
"illuminated with a profusion of tapers. A solemn
"anthem was sung, and the priest began the
"service. After a little while, the pall, which
"covered the body, appeared to heave, and the sup-
"posed corpse slowly raised itself out of the coffin.
"Its eyes were glazed and fixed, and the paleness
"of death overspread its stiff and sharpened features,

"whilst with a look of deep anguish and horror, it
"uttered, in a slow and hollow voice, the following
"words—' By the just judgment of God I am cited,
"judged, and condemned.' He then sent forth a
"groan of unutterable anguish and despair, and fell
"down dead.

"The assembly were petrified with horror: the
"book fell from the priest's hands: each one stood
"motionless. In the midst of this awful silence,
"Bruno stepped forward, and prostrating himself on
"the ground, prayed aloud for mercy, and pro-
"nounced a solemn vow, dedicating himself hence-
"forth entirely to the service of God, who had
"given him to witness so unspeakably awful a
"judgment."—(*Lancelot's Tour.*)

St. Bruno did not institute any new rule; but
only revived the disused rule of St. Bennet in all its
primitive austerity.

Peter the Venerable was Abbot of Clugny, at
the period in which St. Bruno established his
order. Both he and Guignes, the first Prior, have
left an ample account of the early discipline observed
at Chartreuse. Every member of the community
had a separate cell with a little garden adjoining. In this cell he ate, slept, and worked;
except during the hours of out-door exercise,
which each monk passed in cultivating his little
garden. By this means the recluses, however
numerous, had no communication with each other.
They never met but at the hours of public service,

save on Sunday, when they received their portions of food for the week. Every one cooked his provisions in his own cell.

The rules of the order enjoined silence, solitude, and prayer. The use of linen was forbidden, and the monks, to judge from Hugo's Life, wore sheepskins in this country. Hugo's Biographer describes the pleasure with which the good Bishop of Lincoln used to quit his palace and robes of state, and, retiring to Witham Friary Convent, leap into his old sheepskin dress. At La Grande Chartreuse the monks, (pères) at the present time, wear a white cloth dress, whilst the servitors (frères) are dressed in brown.

The diet of the monks was very meagre, consisting, principally, of coarse brown bread and vegetables.

In case of illness they were allowed two spoonfuls of wine to a pint of water.

On high festivals a little cheese was allowed. In many instances they wore hair cloth next the skin, and whenever it was necessary to make a communication to their brethren, they did it, if possible, by signs.

Our fair friends will pardon our giving one of the rules of the order in the exact words of Prior Guignes. " Nons ne permettons jamais aux femmes " d' entrer dans notre enceinte ; car nons savons que " ni le sage, ni le prophète, ni le juge, ni l' hote de " Dieu, ni ses enfans, ni même le premier modèle " sert des ses mains, n' ont pu échapper aux câresses " on aux tromperies des femmes.

"Qu 'on se rappelle Salomon, David, Samson,
"Loth, et ceux qui ont pris les femmes qu 'ils avoient
"choisies, et Adam lui même; et qu'on sache bien
"que l' homme ne peut cacher du feu dans son sein
"sans que ses vêtemens soient embrasés, ni marcher
"sur des charbons ardents sans se brûler la plante
"des pieds."

The original building, erected by Ela, at Hinton,
consisted of a small chapel about twenty-four feet
long by sixteen feet wide, and was dedicated to the
Blessed Virgin Mary, St. John the Baptist, and All
Saints. It was subsequently enlarged, by the
addition of a chancel, the original window being
moved further back.

Afterwards a large chapel was erected, to the north,
the only remains of which are the Sedilia and the
spring of the chancel arch; the latter shows, however, that the building must have been of considerable size.

Ela's foundation was ratified by King Henry III.,
who ordained that the monks should be for ever
free from taxation, suit, service, and forest laws.
Their lands were increased by various benefactors,
and King Richard II. gave them annually an hogshead of wine from the port of Bristol.

Pope Innocent, by a deed, dated Lyons, 1245,
granted to the priory, rights of sanctuary as well as
other privileges.

In 1293, their estates were valued at £24 15s.; in
1444, at 76½ marks, or about £50 14s. 10d. In the
next century the value had increased to £248 19s. 2d.

The spot selected by St. Bruno for his own cell was among the eternal snows of the Alps—amid the wild and picturesque scenery of Dauphiné. Yet *here* the order chose a sunny spot, where nature smiles throughout the year, and seemed to court them to a life of ease and enjoyment. Did the bees whose busy hum proclaimed their right to enjoy life and gladness never taunt them with the dull inaction of monastic life?

But justice compels us to admit that these establishments were, at the time, the centres of hospitality, inns being almost unknown. Nor was this all, for during the earlier ages, religious houses were the nurseries of learning. Monkish industry belonged rather to the closet than to the busy world; but without it, our literature would not be so copious as it is. The good fathers preserved the literary treasures bequeathed to posterity by the poets, and orators of antiquity. The convents too were often the depositories of the archives of the kingdom.

At Hinton, a learned monk, Thomas Spencer, devoted many years to the composition of books, tending to promote Christianity. One of these, a Latin Commentary on St. Paul's Epistle to the Galatians, is favourably mentioned in Wood's Athenæ Oxoniensis.

Prior Hord surrendered the monastery to King Henry VIII. on the 31st March, 1540. At that time it contained nineteen monks, whose revenue was £250.

The present ivy-covered manor house was erected by the Hungerfords from the ruins of the abbey. It is a fair specimen of an Elizabethan mansion.

Of the Abbey* but a small portion remains. The chapel is well-proportioned, and, although overrun with ivy, its fine lancet-shaped windows can easily be traced. One of the detached portions, probably the refectory, exhibits a beautifully groined freestone roof, springing from central pillars. The lawn is surrounded by the original ditch and low stone wall.

At a short distance to the west is a large pond, which is supposed to have belonged to the Priory.

The site, on the suppression of the priory, was granted to John Bartlett, who sold it to Matthew Colthurst. Matthew Colthurst's son, in the 21st year of Queen Elizabeth, sold it to Walter Hungerford, who resided at Farleigh Castle, distant two miles, and owned a large part of the lands in the neighbourhood. Sir Edward Hungerford sold the property to the Robinsons, whose descendants, we believe, still possess the manor.

The rateable value of the parish of Hinton is now £4,046, on an area of 3,000 statute acres. The population is 566; the poor rates average about £257.

---

* The Abbey and grounds are private property, but permission to view them may be obtained on application at the residence.

NORTON ST. PHILIP.

THREE miles from the railway station at Freshford,
and about the same distance from Midford, upon
elevated ground, midway between Bath and Frome,
at the point where the road is crossed by another,
which connects Radstock and Trowbridge, equi-
distant, also, from both these places, stands this
interesting village.

It appears in the Domesday Book (1084) as
"Nortuna." At that time the manor, together with
that of Hinton, was held under the Crown by Edward
de Sarisberi (Salisbury), Sheriff of the county of
Wilts, in which that nobleman had very large estates.
He was standard bearer to Henry I., and was, in
that office, present at the battle of Brenneville, in
Normandy. In the Norman survey the place is
thus described :—

Edward himself holds Nortune. Iving held it in the time of
King Edward, and gelded for ten hides. The arable is ten carucates. In demesne are three carucates, and three servants, and
three villanes, and thirteen cottagers with three ploughs. There
is a mill of five shillings rent, and twenty acres of meadow, and
as many of pasture. Wood one mile long and as much broad.
It was formerly (worth) six pounds, and now seven pounds. Of
these ten hides King Edward (the Confessor) gave to the aforesaid
Iving two carucates of land.

It has been supposed that Ela, Countess of
Salisbury, was the foundress of Norton Church, but as
there are no signs of any architectural work of her
times to be traced in the building, such as are to be
found in the early English work of Hinton Church and

Abbey, the opinion is probably erroneous.   In 1284, according to a charter empowering the holding of weekly markets, the place was called *Norton Comitis*, with reference to the Comites, or Earls of Salisbury.

In the reign of Henry III. we find, that a license was issued to hold a fair "on ye Vigil, Feast, and Morrow of St. Philip and St. James," and, as the place probably, grew in importance, in the year 1284 (13th Edward), a charter was given to the monks of Hinton to hold a market every Friday in their manor of "Norton Charterhouse."   The fair used to be held at Hinton, but the monks complained, that their devotional services were interrupted by the "noise, disturbance, and insolence" of the fair, it being then held near their church of Hinton. In the 19th year of Edward III. (1345) another fair was granted to be ·held on "the Vigil and Feast of ye Decollation of John Baptist," *i.e.*, 28th and 29th Aug. ; afterwards called, in consequence of its nearness to the Dog Days, "Norton Dog Fair," a gathering recently given up.   In the 25th of Edward III. license was given to "change ye day of the May Fair from ye Vigil and Morrow to ye Feast and 2 preceding days :" this was what was afterwards called the "Wholesale Fair," and was held on the 27th April, as "May Fair" on the 1st May.

Collinson, in his history of Somerset, speaks only of "two fairs"—those of 1st May and 29th August.

In 1540, *Leland's Itinerary* speaks of "Phillipps Northtown, a pratie market towne," as "about a

mile from Farley Castle, and standeth in Somersetshire. This towne taketh the name of the dedication
of the church therein, that is, to Philip and Jacob.
There is a faire at this town on the feast of Philip
and Jacob."

A hundred years ago, a market cross stood at the
junction of the four roads, between the two principal
inns in the place, but in the last century, before the
days of "restorations," the stones were sold for
fifteen guineas, and the remains were ruthlessly
removed. About the same time the turnpike road
was altered in order to obviate an awkward bend
for the coaches, which passed daily through the
village : portions of the cross were, according to
the parish book, transferred to the churchyard,
in 1774.

Both these inns held their present names more
than two centuries ago. "The George" is a common sign in the neighbourhood, but the sign of the
"Fleur de Lys" was, perhaps, adapted by some one
when setting up an opposition to the older house,
named after the Patron Saint of England. As a
flower de luce was the crest of Jeffery Flower, it may
have had some connection with him in the reign of
James I. "*The Flower de Luce*" is thus mentioned
in an old MS. survey of Norton, dated 1644.—

" Richard Parsons, in right of Alice Parsons his mother, for
life of Jeffery Flower, and for 50 years after, by virtue of certain
letters patent under ye great seal of England, dat. at Westminster,
20 March, xxvi. Eliz."

Its more striking, and interesting rival, is thus referred to in the same survey, under date 1638,— a survey taken for "William Lord Craven, chief lorde of the same : "—

"Henry Tovie, Copyholder, claimeth to hold for term of his life, one tenement in Norton, being an ancient and common inn called by the name of the George, at 53s. 4d. The house, with the stables, out-houses, and a faire loft where the Lynnen cloth is sould at the Fair tymes : with the yarde, garden, and orchard, containeth 2 roods, 27 perches, and is worth by ye year £5."

The George Inn became the scene of some historical events not long after this survey was made, and has an interest attached to it, independent of the fact, that certain "Cloth and Lynnen faires" were held therein. It is a remarkable structure of the 15th century, which rarely escapes the notice of the traveller, as it did not escape that of the surveyor, when he called it, even in his times, "ancient." There is no appearance of its having been designed as a religious house; nor are there any armorial bearings sculptured on its walls to indicate that it belonged to some great county family. From the ecclesiastical character, however, of the lower windows, it must have been built under church influence; and as it was occupied by Henry Tovie, from Lord Craven, who received the Hinton Abbey Lands from the Crown, it was most likely built by the Monks, when they obtained their charter to hold a market and fair, as a hostel, in order to accommodate cloth sellers and frequenters of their market and fair. The building has just been repaired, and it is to be regretted that advantage of the opportunity was not taken to "restore" it more according to its original design, and to remove some of the too conspicuous additions. The steps outside are a modern excrescence, and, moreover, hide a handsome doorway.

A writer in the *Illustrated London News* of Jan. 27th, 1849, under the heading of "Nooks and Corners of Old England," calls it erroneously, "the Grange." He thus writes, "it has been greatly disfigured by modern hands, but that there is much left of its middle-age art. Its capacious porch, the designs of some of its windows, and its over-hanging upper stories (upon rude corbels), and its inner gallery leading to what once were bed chambers, all denote the pile to have been erected in the early portion of the 15th century. We miss 'the wind pipes of hospitality,' as chimneys have been happily styled; but we must recollect, that they were not requisite in the original appropriation of the structure, and, therefore, did not form a feature of the original design. At the point of each gable is a small campanile, or bell tower, of some architectural beauty, which makes us regret, that the building has not been preserved more intact, or has not attracted the attention of restorers."

It is clear, that in the village of Norton, the monks of Hinton had great interest. They had a charter of free warren in it, and a variety of other privileges. Originally, the living of Hinton was in the gift of

the Precentor of Wells, and Norton was entirely
independent of it; but in 1527 the monks threw
the responsibility of the cure of Hinton Church
on the Vicar of Norton, while they retained
their extensive property in Hinton, and arranged
that it should be tithe free. There is a document in the Registry of the Cathedral at Wells
concerning the "Union, appropriation, consolida-
tion, and incorporation of the parish churches of
Monks' Hinton and Norton St. Philip," in which
it appears, that the Prior and Convent formally
complained to the Bishop of the poverty of their
estate, in consequence of the expenses they had
incurred for repairs of the monastery, and of the
scandal caused by the "continual quarrels and disputes about various rights and particulars regarding
the tythes of a certain Grange, situate in the parish of
Norton St. Philip, to the said Priory belonging and
appertaining," and they, consequently, requested the
union of the two parishes. They represented, that
the perpetual vicarage of the parish church "is
notoriously bereaved of its fruits and profits, and is
insufficient to the support of the said Vicar," and
they request, that the "contiguous" parishes should
be incorporated. They succeeded in persuading the
Bishop's commissary, one John Pennande, to arrange
the difficulty; and, under conditions of certain
punctual payments of fees at Wells on the part of
the monastery, the Vicar of Norton was directed to
cease being troublesome about the tythes at the

N

Grange and at the mill, and to take charge of Hinton parish, and to rest content with certain gifts specifically set forth. The two parishes formed one cure until 1826, when they were divided by the Ecclesiastical Commissioners, and the patronage of the living of Hinton passed into the hands of the Vicar of Norton.

The M.S. book of the survey of the manors of Norton and Hinton, before referred to, under the date 1638, has references to both these "Granges," together with the mill at Norton, which, standing near the Norton Grange, would naturally be let with it. On the destruction of the monasteries, the site of the one at Hinton was granted to John Bartlett and Robert his son, on the 28th July, 37th Henry VIII., 1546; and, in 1577, it passed, first to Edmund Coulthurst, and then to Sir Walter Hungerford, of Farleigh Castle. His brother, Sir Edward Hungerford, dying 1607, left it (with other property) to his widow, who married the Earl of Rutland. It reverted to the Hungerford family, and was sold, at the breaking up of their estates, about 1684, to the Bayntuns, and was again disposed of to various persons about the year 1700. It consisted of 1,331 acres, together with the Farm, or Grange, "described as a large, ancient, well-built house, with barn, etc."

Norton Grange was Crown property in 1617, at which time it formed part of the maintenance of Prince Charles, son of James I. In 1638, it had been given to William, Lord Craven. Under him it was held, in

1638, by Jeffery Flower; the following description of it will clearly exclude the George Inn from the title of Grange :—

"Jeffery Flower, gent., claymeth to hould from the xxix. of March last past for term of xxviii. years the cappitall messuage mansion or manor house called or knowne by the name of the ffarme or graunge of Norton, with all the earrable lande pastures, meadows, close feedings and coppices there unto belonging, and payeth rent for the same p. annum £20 2s. od. A well-built house with the site thereof, with gardens, orchards, court-yards, vevy faire barnes, stables, graunaries, malt houses, and divers other convenient buildings, and whereof is converted into Tenements with a very profitable pigeon house."

In 1652, on account of having befriended Prince Charlie, afterwards Charles II., Lord Craven forfeited Norton Grange, and the property was sold to Mr. Water, of Westminster.

This farm of 800 acres was then estimated at a yearly value of £347, with a "present rent" of £20 2s. At the beginning of this century the farmstead was approached by a passage under the gate-house. The room was removed in order, probably, to admit the freer entry of laden wagons; but traces of the pillars, which supported the room, may still be seen on the two flanking cottages. Within the memory of men now living, also, gables, which must have made it a more picturesque looking building than it is, were removed from the roof of the Grange. The oak panels in one of the rooms, the substantial staircase and wide passages, together with the remarkable pigeon-house, speak to its having once been a residence of some importance. The "profitable pigeon-house," reminding us of the Roman Columbaria, is an Elizabethan building nearly 20 feet square, and contains holes for at least 600 nests, with only one outlet for the birds, besides the door.*

The Parish Register records that "Mr. Jeffery Flower was buried June 1st, 1644." Evidently, to some member of this family, if not to this identical Jeffery Flower, must be referred the following inscription, which was painted on the wall over the priest's door leading into the place now used as a vestry. It was necessarily removed at the recent restoration of the church,—

TE—FLOS—IAM—IUSTI
RAPUERUNT—STAMINA—FUSI
VIRTUTIS—REMANET
NOBILIS—VMBRA—TUÆ.

NOW—FLOWER—THE—FATES
HAVE—THEE—OF—LIFE—BEREFT
LARGE—SHADOW—OF—THY—VIR
TUES—THOU—HAST—LEFT.

This Jeffery Flower was, we may believe, a man of piety and substance, since he is noticed in a History of Bath as the donor of one of the windows in the Abbey :—

"Benefactors to the Repairinge of the Ruines of Bath-Abbey." *Warner's History of Bath.*

"Jefferay Flower of Philips Norton, in this countie of Somersett, gentleman, at whose only charge was built up the nave wall, with

* The Lord of the Manor, as such, formerly possessed certain rights in the dovecote, which have now lapsed.

doore therein at the east ende of the north allie of the quire."—
The door, in the Bath Abbey Church, has been lately restored
(1874.) In the spandrils of the doorway are the letters ɪ. F., and
a *flower de luce.**

Not far from this homestead, which has of late
years been again called "Manor Farm," stands the
𝕮𝖍𝖚𝖗𝖈𝖍. It is dedicated to St. Philip and St. James,
and shows signs of having belonged to the "late
decorated" order of architecture, and of having been
subsequently reconstructed and enlarged in the perpendicular style of the Tudors. These alterations
would account for the remarkable irregularity of
several of the arches on either side the nave, some
being flat, and others pointed. The difference in the
forms of some of the pillars would, also, indicate
that the aisles were added to the nave at different
times. Looking at the east windows of the aisles
we may observe that they are of two distinct
dates. The difference of the masonry outside
suggests that the tower and the south aisle were
built at different times; the workmanship of the
former being much superior to that of the latter.
The old pulpit of painted oak bore the date of 1607.

In 1847, the church being in a dilapidated and
unsatisfactory condition, the parishioners accepted

---

* The Abbey Church of Bath, for a long time after the dissolution of monasteries remained roofless and ruined. It had been the
Church of the Monks of Bath, and not a *Parish* Church. One
Colthurst, a great jobber in church property, gave it to the city
as a Parish Church. It was then repaired by degrees; but
chiefly in the time of King James I.

the proposal of their then vicar, the Rev. R. Palairet, to rebuild certain portions, to restore the roof, to reconstruct the sittings, and to make other alterations and improvements, he generously offering to secure the parish against all cost and responsibility. Under Sir Gilbert Scott's direction, and at an outlay of £4,218, which, saving eight subscriptions amounting to £122, was entirely provided by the vicar and some members of his family, the church has become one of the handsomest and most complete in the neighbourhood.

Besides the irregular arches and pillars, attention may be directed to the "squint,"* and to the stairs leading to the rood loft; also, to the position of the east window in the south aisle, which shews, by its height, by the two niches one on either side of it, and by the Piscina, that a chapel originally stood there. The old roof of the south porch is worth notice; as are also the narrow stairs within the wall, which must have led to a gallery over the door. The effigy in the south aisle which bears no name, is not intended, as Collinson states, to represent any woman, still less any woman of a "religious order;" but it must rather, from the dress, be considered the figure of some wealthy merchant, formerly, perhaps, a benefactor to the church. There are no other monuments of note. All the mural tablets were removed

---

* An opening through the wall in an oblique direction for the purpose of enabling persons in the transept or aisle to see the elevation of the Host.

from the body of the building and placed in the
tower, the oldest bears date 1641. But few of the
names on the tablets are borne by the present
inhabitants of Norton. The appearance of seven
or eight sculptured tombs in the churchyard,
some now defaced, and all unclaimed, would seem
to suggest that Norton had residents of more
substance two or three centuries ago than at
present—an idea strengthened by large handsome
mantelpieces being still seen in several of the old
houses in the village.

When standing within the church, it is impossible
not to feel that a most reverent care has watched
over the restoration, and has striven to secure
due honour for the House of God. The east
chancel window (by Wailes, costing £150,) represents our Lord, with St. Peter, St. Philip, St. James,
and St. Andrew: while the small subjects below,
give the incidents in the gospel narrative regarding
St. Philip. The north and south windows in the
chancel, and the west window of the tower, are
also by Wailes, and were put up at the same time,
namely in 1850. The east window in the north aisle
(by Horwood Brothers) is intended to illustrate *Praise;*
and the corresponding window in the opposite aisle
(by the same makers), presented by the parishioners
in 1858 as a thank-offering, is intended to suggest the
idea of *Sacrifice.* The first window in the south
aisle (by O'Connor), representing "St. Thomas
convinced," was an anonymous thank-offering in

1864.   The one next to it represents " The charge to St. Peter," (by Bell, of Bristol,) and was placed there by the parishioners "as a token of love and esteem for their late vicar, the Rev. R. Palairet, on his resignation" of the living, "October, 1866, after having officiated for twenty-nine years."   The west window in the same aisle (by Clayton and Bell, 1862), representing the " Baptism of Christ," and the " Blessing little children," throws the light of the setting sun upon the massive old font, which bears on one of its panels the device of a small, but very rudely cut, crucifix.

The tower, rising sixty-six feet to the leads, is in fine preservation: it contains a peal of six bells,* and a clock, which cost £250 (by Frodsham).   From its position in a hollow, the tower commands no view of the country around.   In the belfry are some curious

* Mr. Freeman, speaking of the tower, says "it is one of the most irregular he had ever seen—one that some man had designed out of his own head without reference to any other tower—quite unlike anything else, and incapable of being classed with any towers in the county.   It was not at all of the Somersetshire type, or any other type, that he was used to in different parts of England." This, Mr. Irvine says, is the result of the church having been " built mostly out of re-used older materials ; and accounts for the strange look and design so unlike ordinary Somerset towers. These old materials were probably obtained by pulling down the Priory Church of Hinton Charterhouse, near at hand.   A close inspection shows that the flat panelled work in the west front has no proper weather-plinth, and indeed that the whole is a tolerable working up of old wrought materials, somewhat as at the Bath Abbey the late organ gallery screen now forms the west lobby."

arrangements, which have been thought to indicate that there was at an earlier time a chapel
at or near the spot, when bell-ringing, perhaps, was
considered a more religious act than it is deemed
to be now. It may be as well to mention, that the
two stone heads placed in the tower below, and which
were removed from the chancel floor at the recent
restoration, came from the tomb of the two "Fair
maidens of Foscote," a neighbouring parish. A story
has been preserved by Collinson that these maids
were twins, born united to each other,—a fact for
which there is no other foundation than village
tradition.*

The School-house faces the western porch, and is
substantial and commodious, though not architec-
turally worthy of its close proximity to the beautiful

* Pepys, in his Diary, says :—" 1668, Salisbury, Friday 12th."—
"Up, finding our beds good, we set out, the reckoning and
servants coming to 9s. 6d., my guide thither 2s., coachman advanced 10s. So we rode a good way, lead to my great content
by our landlord to Philip's Norton, with great pleasure being now
come into Somersetshire, where my wife and Deb mightily joyed
there at ; I commending the county as indeed it deserves, and the
first town we came to was Beckington, where we stopping for
something for the horses, we called two or three little boys to us,
and pleased ourselves with their manner of speech. At Philip's
Norton I walked to the church, and there saw a very ancient
tomb of some Knight-Templar I think, and here saw the tombstone whereon there were only two heads cut, which the story
goes, and creditably, were two sisters, called the Fair Maids of
Foscott, that had two bodies upward and one stomach, and there
lie buried. Here is also a very fine ring of bells, and they mighty
tuneable. Having dined very well, 10s., we came before night
to Bath."

church.   In its origin it is interesting as being connected with the history of the senior partner in the well-known firm of silversmiths, "Rundell and Bridge." The father of the former lies buried in the churchyard near the south-east corner of the chancel, and to the memory of some members of his family there stands a tablet in the tower.

The name of Rundell often appears in the Register Book of a hundred years ago. There is, however, no one now of this name in the parish; but, it is believed, that the Rundell referred to was born Jan. 22, 1747, in the house south of the George Inn, and that he was brought up as a silversmith in Bath, in which city his elder brother was a member of the Corporation. Before that time it was the custom to send valuable diamonds over to Holland to be properly cut, the art not being well understood in England. Mr. Philip Rundell, having studied the subject and made himself master of it, removed to London; soon found himself in full employment, and in course of time became the principal jeweller in the city. He died in 1827, leaving what was then considered an immense fortune. When the news of his death reached Norton, those who considered themselves connected with him requested the Rev. H. Calverley, then vicar, to communicate with Joseph Neeld, Esq., Rundell's great nephew and residuary legatee, in the hope, that they might be remembered in the disposition of the property. The wants of the applicants promised to be so unlimited, that

Mr. Neeld, after visiting Norton, and consulting with the clergyman, decided that a school was the great want of the parish, and the most suitable gift considering the number of persons who believed themselves to be interested in the Rundell estate. He gave the exorbitant sum of £500 for the site, on which an old bakehouse stood, and erected the present building at a cost of £1,500, and endowed it with £50 a year, on condition that it should be called the "Neeld School."*

The parish owes the Infant School, which stands on the south side of the church, chiefly to the liberality of the late Vicar and his friends.

An account of Norton St. Philip would be in-complete without especial notice of the event which introduces its name into English history.

In an "Impartial History of the Life and Death of George, Lord Jeffreys," the fourth edition of which was published in 1693, only eight years after the battle of Sedgemoor, the writer, James Bent, gives the fol-lowing description of what took place there, as if he

---

* Greville, in his Journal, vol. 1, p. 90, Feb. 21st, 1827, says :— " Old Rundell (of the house of Rundell and Bridge, the great silver-smiths and jewellers), died last week, and appointed Robarts one of the executors. . . . . R. was 80 years old, and died worth between £1,400,000 and £1,500,000, the greater part of which is invested in the funds. He has left the bulk of his property to his great nephew. During the panic, he came to Robarts, who was his banker, and offered to place at his disposal any sum he might require. When his executors went to prove the will, they were told at Doctors' Commons that it was the largest sum that had been registered there."

were an eye-witness of it all.   After stating that the
Duke of Monmouth and his party left Amsterdam on
the 24th May, 1685; landed at Lyme on the 11th
June; marched, with a body of some 4,000 men,
through Taunton, Bridgwater, and Glastonbury, and
passed Bristol, he writes :—

"So we marched on to Bath, we lay before it in the afternoon,
and sent our trumpeter to demand the town, and they refused to
give us entrance, having a strong garrison, it being a stout people
and a strong place.   Having no mind to spare time in laying
seige, we marched on that day to a little town called *Philip's-
Norton*, and there lay that night, being now *Sunday* (this is a
mistake for Friday) the 26th of *June*, old style.   Saturday morning
preparing for *Frome*, we were drawing out our baggage for our
march, and on a sudden were alarmed with the appearance of the
army who had entered the town, and had lined all the hedges,
and begun to fire at us.   Here began the bitterest encounter we
yet had, and for an hour or more we had a brisk skirmish, but at
last we beat them back, killing about thirty which lay in the place,
and we lost about ten in all and a few wounded.   They, retreating
with their whole army, pitched within a mile of the town, and we
out also, and pitched near them, but out of musket shot, playing
canon on one another for some hours ; they killed us but one man
all the while, and with ours we did great execution, having the
advantage of the ground ; so at last they retreated, and I have
been told lost some hundreds of men in the battel, both killed and
wounded, so we marched on to *Frome*, a town where we were as
beloved as at Taunton, where we wanted for nothing but arms,
which were by a strategem taken from them a few days before our
entrance."

Monmouth was surprised at Norton by the Royal
Army, under Feversham.   It was his advanced guard,
consisting of about 500 men, under the young Duke
of Grafton, second son of Charles and the Duchess
of Cleveland, which made the attack of the 26th

of June, 1685. The charge is thus described by Lord Macaulay ;—

"Grafton* soon found himself in a deep lane, with fences on both sides of him, from which a galling fire of musketry was kept up. Still he pushed boldly on, till he came to the entrance of Philip's Norton. There his way was crossed by a barricade, from which a third fire met him, full in front. His men now lost heart, and made the best of their way back. Before they got out of the lane, more than a hundred of them had been killed, or wounded. Grafton's retreat was intercepted by some of the rebel cavalry ; but he cut his way gallantly through them, and came off safe. The advanced guard thus repulsed, fell back on the main body of the Royal forces. The two armies were now face to face, and a few shots were exchanged, which did little or no execution. Neither side was impatient to come to action. Feversham did not wish to fight till his artillery came up, and fell back to Bradford. Monmouth, as soon as the night closed in, quitted his position, marched southward, and by daybreak arrived at Frome, where he hoped to find reinforcements."

There is reason to believe, that Monmouth's head-quarters were at the George Inn. In the words of the Chronicler of " Nooks and Corners," before referred to, " the large projecting window " in the George " lights the apartment wherein Monmouth slept on the night of the battle," and the room is to this day known as the " King's Chamber."

* Monmouth was the illegitimate son of Charles 11, by Lucy Walters ; Grafton was the second son of Charles, by Barbara Villiers, Duchess of Cleveland. Her eldest son was created Duke of Cleveland, and her third and youngest Duke of Northumberland, but both these sons dying and leaving no male issue, their titles became extinct. The former married a daughter of Sir William Pulteney, of Misterton, co. Leicester, and had two daughters, one of whom, Lady Grace Fitzroy, married Harry, Lord Barnard, afterwards Earl of Darlington, who was an ancestor of the present ducal family of Cleveland.

There is an absurd tale told of a certain lane called Chevers Lane, having run with blood on that day.

The battle appears to have left a deep impression on the minds of the inhabitants. Not only have cannon balls of six and seven pounds weight been picked up, to keep alive the memory of the day,* but there are several fields called the "King's Field," "Spy Close," the "Monmouths," and "The Camp." The two former are on the high road from Bath, not far from the sixth milestone, and half-a-mile due west are the two latter fields, immediately under Baggeridge Farm; the one evidently the position of the rebels, and the other that of the King's forces, both within sight of each other, but out of musket shot,—the muskets of those days. The "King's Field" can be reached by a bridle road from Midford to Baggeridge. Of the 239 persons executed in the west of England for participation in this rebellion, six suffered at Bath, twelve at Frome, and twelve at Norton.

On a house behind the *Flower de Luce* Inn, is a stone shield with the arms of *Fortescue—a bend engrailed.* This connects Norton St. Philip with a very distinguished man, Sir John Fortescue, Chief Justice of the King's Bench, and Chancellor temp.

* The armour dug up in the parish must have belonged to some who took part in the "hard fighting" described by Clarendon in the Great Rebellion, when the troops, under Waller, were for some days marching out of, or falling back upon Bath, Bradford, Frome, and Wells, when Norton must have been the centre of operation.

Henry IV. He married Isabella, daughter and heiress of John James, of Philip's Norton, Esq. He was an eminent lawyer.* A field near Farleigh Lodge, on the Warminster Road (within the gates), but in Norton parish, is still called " James's Field."

The population, in 1871, amounted to 575, with about 180 houses. The survey of 1838 gives 914 acres of pasture, 504 acres of arable land, 59 acres of woods, 21 orchards, 27 roads,—in all 1,527 acres. The parish is now rated at £3,200. In 1638, there were 82 houses, 76 of which were valued at £103 10s. The rental, in 1856, was £1,148 10s. The living is in the gift of the Bishop of the Diocese. The Rev. H. B. Burney is the Vicar.

* The life of this eminent jurist was written, and printed for private circulation, in the year 1869.

IN AND OUT OF BATH.

WALK THE SIXTH.

WELLOW.

WE take our way from Bath by the Somerset and Dorset Railway to Wellow. The station is close to the Rose Gardens.

At Stoney Littleton, in this parish, in a sloping field, called *Round Hill Tining*, about three-quarters of a mile south-west from Wellow Church, Sir Richard Colt Hoare opened a tumulus, or sepulchre in 1816, and in the 19th vol. of the Archæologia gave the following description of it :—

"This singular burying-place is oblong, measuring 107 feet in length, 54 in breadth, and 13 in height. The entrance faces the south-west. A large stone, supported by two others, forms the lintel, having an aperture four feet high, which leads to a chamber six feet long, five feet high, and five wide. From thence a straight passage conducts to another cist, of equal size. This passage is forty-seven feet in length. There are, also, eight other small chambers, or recesses, facing each other, so as to form three transepts across the passage, and another at the extremity. The whole are composed of large stones, which show no mark of tools, or any appearance of cement. Each chamber might have contained three or four bodies."* Phelps, in his "History of Somerset," gives us an illustration of its entrance.

To reach this mound, we take the village road, which passes beneath what was once the tramway, and cross an ancient bridge of two arches; next we pass a Roman earthwork, which, it seems, has escaped antiquarian notice, and follow the road until we come to a gate, through which we pass in order to reach a clump of trees and some underwood in a field on the right. Near this point is the cemetery of Stoney Littleton.

In a field, called Wellow Hayes, and about half-a-mile from the village, several Roman tessellated

* In the Somersetshire Archæological Proceedings, vol. viii., p.p. 35 to 62, there is a very interesting paper, with illustrations, on this subject, by the Rev. Prebendary Scarth.

O

pavements have been discovered. They were first brought to light in 1685, and Gale has left us an account of them in his edition of the "Itinerary of Antoninus." In 1737, they were again laid open, when Virtue published three beautiful plates of them, at the expense of the Society of Antiquaries. They were exposed at this time to mischief, being apparently uncared for. In 1807 they were once more uncovered, when they attracted the notice of the Rev. Richard Warner, who published an elaborate description of them in his History of Bath.

Warner describes the villa to have been 100 feet long, by 50 in breadth. The patterns of the tessellæ are tasteful, diversified, and rich, having a border somewhat resembling a modern floor-cloth, while the centre contains allegorical figures and other ornaments, formed of square pieces, varying in size, from half an inch to nearly two inches. Five colours are seen; blue, formed of the Weston lias; white, from Newton; red, formed of Roman brick; purple, from St. Vincent's rocks; and grey, from the pennant, or silicious sandstone, overlaying the coal.

These tessellæ were laid together, so as to form the pattern intended, and then each separate portion was carefully removed and embedded in cement on a foundation or substratum of stone. The work, when closely examined, appears coarse to modern eyes; but, seen at a distance, presents a pleasing effect. "The general execution," says Warner, "its richness, and spirit, forbid us to assign to it a later date than the second century of the Christian era."*

In 1822, that laborious antiquary, the Rev. John Skinner, of Camerton, as the result of a careful examination, traced the foundations of a spacious villa, of a quadrangular form, with hypocausts, baths, and pavements.

The Romans, like the moderns, were fond of country residences. The family occupied the rooms facing south and west, while the domestics lived in those on the other sides, the whole opening upon a central quadrangle, protected from the weather by a covering resting on pillars, and removable at pleasure. The houses were warmed by flues made of pottery, built in the walls and under the floors. A passage ran round the interior of the quadrangle, and formed a promenade in unfavourable weather.

This pavement was, for the fifth time, laid open in 1843. It has suffered more from mischief than from time. A few coins, principally of the lower empire, have been found in the immediate neighbourhood.

---

* A coin of Augustus Cæsar, somewhat rare in Britain, was found in Wellow; and shows that Mr. Warner's opinion is, probably, correct. At the period of its discovery, three small and much-mutilated figures, sculptured on a slab of freestone, were also dug from the foundations of a wall.

Tradition relates that Wellow was a place of importance in the Saxon and Danish periods of our history, and that it possessed many churches. At Woodborough, during the last century, several stone coffins were found, such as we identify as belonging to those nations. There is also a large barrow, or tumulus, at the extremity of the parish. The tradition referred to, appears to be supported by the fact that, in the reign of Edward the Confessor, the parish contained no less than seven manors, the average annual value of each being about £13.

𝕿𝖍𝖊 𝕮𝖍𝖚𝖗𝖈𝖍 is a fine specimen of the work of the middle ages, and contains many beautiful examples of early ecclesiastical architecture. The interior shows the state of English churches prior to the Reformation. In the year 1845, during the incumbency of the late Rev. Charles Paul, it underwent considerable restoration and improvement.

The west window, formerly obscured by an unsightly screen which obstructed the light and injured the effect intended to be produced, was restored at the sole expense of the late Rev. Charles Paul. It is of the perpendicular style, with three lights, glazed with Powell's glass, in quarries of a greenish hue, with antique patterns in their centres. It contains the arms of England, emblazoned in the ancient manner, with those of the see, the then vicar, and the patron, together with the armorial bearings of the late Colonels Gore-Langton and Jolliffe, the late Walter Long, M.P., and the late

Mr. Wait. The roof is beautifully groined. The unique open seats are elaborately carved, and terminated by poppy-head finials. The ancient black oak roof is profuse in ornament of chaste and good character. The carved chancel screen is restored in accordance with the original design, and the carved reading desk, is panelled with crimson cloth. The chancel, slightly inclined to the northeast, is typical of the position of our Saviour's head on the cross—a symbolism common in our early churches. The octagonal early English font, with its decorated cover, is worthy of notice. It has a round shaft, divided into columns. The patronage of the living was vested in the Abbot and Convent of Cirencester, by King Henry I., in 1133.

The church was almost rebuilt in 1372, by Sir Walter Hungerford. Collinson, however, says that he was the original founder. His tomb is shown in the chapel, now called the Hungerford, or Lady Chapel, from a beautiful Gothic canopy which formerly surmounted a statue of the Virgin placed in its north-eastern corner. The wall is frescoed with a representation of Christ and his Apostles, with their appropriate emblems. The chapel contains various memorials of the Hungerford family, as well as a recessed monument of freestone, supporting a recumbent full-dressed effigy of Mrs. Popham, who died in 1614. Several children are represented below. The epitaph sets forth her many virtues. The monument was originally painted in accordance with the custom of the period. It has since been cleaned, and, although utterly out of character with the rest of the building, produces a pleasing effect.

There is a remarkably fine piscina, of a similar form to the font, at the angle in the eastern wall of the chancel, having a circular trefoiled fenestrella. Near its base, coins of Edward II. were discovered during the restoration of the church. The lay improprietors rebuilt the chancel. On the north side, the late vicar caused a recess, strictly in accordance with early models, to be formed for the reception of the fine unmutilated effigy of an ecclesiastic, discovered during the repairs. It is the only figure known which bears the incised Maltese cross on the forehead. The robes are gracefully disposed, and elaborated with great skill. The attitude is devotional and the countenance placid and resigned. On the breast is a chalice, and the feet are supported by the figure of a dog. The east window consists of a circular head, with three trefoils and three lights, and is glazed with cathedral glass. The north and south windows have been repaired. The chancel is the only portion of the church in which the pews have been retained. They are incongruous and misplaced, and interefere with the beauty of the *coup d'œil.*

From the chancel, the west window, and the pointed arch between the tower and nave may be seen to advantage.

There are other piscinæ in the church, remarkable

for containing the small shelf, or credence table, within the fenestrella. The organ is placed in the Hungerford chapel, which also serves as a vestry-room.

Externally, the church has a pleasing aspect. The height of the tower is about a hundred feet, and one of the turrets contains a staircase. The building is of the Perpendicular style, and was completed in the reign of Henry VII. The southern porch is surmounted by an elaborate canopy, once, in all probability, containing a figure of the Virgin. Near this point is the stair turret of the ancient rood loft.

The expenses of the restoration were about £800, of which £500 was raised by private subscription. Besides this sum, £100 was granted by the parish for essential repairs. The present vicar is the Rev. C. W. Horton.

Near the church stands the old manor house of the Hungerfords, now a farmstead. By the kindness of the tenant, we were shown a beautifully-carved mantel-piece, which has escaped disfigurement both from paint and mischief. The armorial bearings and grotesque figures are as sharp as when they left the carver's hands. The back-gate bears the date 1634, but from the general appearance of the mansion, we are inclined to believe this refers only to repairs.

In a cottage garden is the Holy Well of St. Julian, from which was wont to be taken the water for baptism. A legend tells us that when evil threatened the house of Hungerford, a white figure used to appear, mourning by the crystal stream. Since the extinction of the family, the ghostly visitant has disappeared, and now the "white ladye" and the legend are alike well-nigh forgotten.

Wellow, the largest parish in the Bath Union, contains 5,292 statute acres. The net rental is £9,201. The population, according to the census of 1871, amounts to 1,117.

DUNKERTON,

LYING two miles westward of Wellow, and four from Bath, is situated on the old Roman fosse-way, and derives its name from the British *Dun Cairn*— monument-hill.   It is interesting as having been one of the twenty manors in Somerset bestowed on a gallant follower by the Conqueror, in requital of services at the battle of Hastings.   He, when two Norman barons had declined to bear the standard, boldly accepted the honourable office ; in remembrance of which service, the "Tunstall" family still bear the Gallic cock, crowing "*Droit*" —*forwards*, as their crest, and their arms are en-circled by the Conqueror's own watchword, "*God is my Help.*"   A portrait of this stout soldier, copied from the Bayeux tapestry, is given in Knight's "Pictorial History of England."   His brother (after-wards the celebrated Archbishop Thurstan) was the first Norman abbot of Glastonbury; and his signature occurs as a witness to the sale of the bishopric of Bath to John of Tours.   William of Malmesbury, tells us that, wishing to introduce a favourite liturgy into his abbey—no uniformity having been previously observed in public worship —the Archbishop entered the church with an armed band, and a desperate conflict ensued, the result being that Oswald, Bishop of Salisbury agreed to compose a church service which subsequently became universal throughout the kingdom. It is not a little singular that in the reign of Henry VIII., Cuthbert Tunstall, bishop of London, friend of Erasmus, and one of the most learned men of his day, should have seen this liturgy superseded by the reformed ritual, for declining the use of which he was twice deprived of his bishopric.

In the reign of Edward III., the manor of Dunkerton passed by marriage into the possession of the Bampfylde family, and was sold by the late Lord Poltimore, in 1845.

𝕿𝖍𝖊 𝕮𝖍𝖚𝖗𝖈𝖍, with the exception of the tower, and east wall, was rebuilt, in 1859-60, by the late Patron and Rector, the Rev. F. Grosvenor, from the design of Mr. C. E. Davis, F.S.A., Bath. The church is dedicated to All Saints, and the present Patron and Rector is the Rev. Gerard Ludlow Hallett, B.C.L.

Internally there is nothing remarkable, except the following epitaph, recording the death, in 1634, of the Rev. John Dickes, rector of the parish :—

" Hic, hæc, hoc, hujus, huic, hunc, bonus, optima, clarum,
    Fulgor, Fama, Decus, vestit, adhœret, erit,
    Mente, animâ, oh ! requiem vivens ΑΙΟΕΚΛΕΤΟΣ ille
    Carpsit honore sacro'; jam super astra manet."

Dunkerton is in the Bath Union, and in the hundred of Wellow. According to the last census, the population amounted to 1,048, while the rateable value is £3,001 on an area of 1,233 acres.

CAMERTON.

SEVERAL learned Antiquaries, rejecting the claims of Colchester, in Essex, have sought to identify Camerton as the Camalodunum of antiquity. Be this as it may, we find that the Romans, when engaged in the conquest of Britain, soon occupied this county and entrenched themselves at Camerton, A.D. 43.

The camp at Camerton was traversed by the Fosse-road, and was so situated as to form an excellent centre for the defence of the district against the Cangi occupying the Quantock hills to the south, and the Brigantes and Silures to the north. The Romans were commanded by an able general, Aulus Plautius, who having defeated the Silures, commanded by Caractacus, drove them back into the mountains of Wales, and having received the submission of the Brigantes who inhabited the Severn valley, sent to request the Roman emperor, Claudius, to complete in person the conquest of Britain. This he is said to have accomplished in the short space of sixteen days, without a battle. The statement, however, is hardly probable, unless it be taken as referring to the south of England, including Somerset. In honour of his victory, however, it is certain that a temple called *Templum Claudii*, the Temple of Claudius, was

erected near Clutton, and hence the present desig-
nation, Temple Cloud. Soon afterwards, in A.D. 51,
Ostorius Scapula, another Roman general, made
further conquests and settled a colony of veteran
soldiers at Camerton, which the Rev. John Skinner
in an able essay, seeks to identify with Camalodunum, a theory which has many advocates, and is
rendered the more plausible by the ancient name
Camerlatone, not less than by the situation and
many confirmatory circumstances. Mr. Skinner, indeed, maintains, "That this district was actually
attached to the royal residence of Cynobelin, king
of the Belgæ, and father of Caractacus, spoken
of by Dion; and Camerton the identical spot occupied by the Roman colonists established by Ostorius
at Camalodunum."* Be this as it may, the whole
of the hill above Camerton is covered with Roman
remains. The several hills which formed the old
line of the Wansdyke were occupied by Roman
forts, and it is said that every ford on the Avon
was also a station of defence against the incursion
of the Silures from South Wales, who advanced up
the river in their coracles for the purpose of ravaging
the country.†

* Phelps' History of Somerset, vol. I., cap. iii.

† Tacitus says of the Roman general, Ostorius, "Cinctosque
Castris Avonam et Sabrinam fluvios cohibere parat,"—*i.e.*, having
guarded the rivers Avon and Severn with fortified camps, he
prepares to restrain the incursions of the enemy. These fortified
camps on the Avon were Portishead, Portbury, Clifton-down and
Leigh-down, Maesknoll, Englishcombe, Beacon hill, Hampton-
down, and Solsbury. Tac. Ann. lib. XIV.

Some years later the British tribe of the Iceni who lived in Norfolk and Suffolk, under their Queen Boadicea, rose in revolt while the Roman governor, Suetonius, was absent in the Island of Anglesea with his army, and so general was the rising among the Britons that they appear to have advanced to the West and sacked and burnt Camerton; that is supposing it to be the place meant by Camalodunum.*
When this revolt was suppressed, another spot seems to have been chosen for the site of a permanent settlement in this part of Britain, and the presence of health-giving springs, and probably also strategic reasons, connected with the great trunk roads, led to the building and fortification of Bath, then, as now—the Queen of the West.

𝕿𝖍𝖊 𝕮𝖍𝖚𝖗𝖈𝖍, of which the Rev. Edward Holland is the rector, is a handsome Gothic edifice, dedicated to St. Peter: it consists of a beautiful tower, nave, and chancel, with a side chapel remarkable for the elaborate tombs of the Carews, ranging from 1640 to 1750. Little has been done since 1848 to the parish church of Camerton. The situation, in close proximity to the picturesque domain of the Jarrett family, is one of singular beauty and interest.

The district of S. John Baptist, Peasedown, was formed in August, 1874, by the Ecclesiastical Commissioners, from adjacent portions of the three parishes of Camerton, Dunkerton, and Wellow.

* Phelps' History of Somerset, vol. I., p. 151.

When the proposed stone church is built and consecrated, these portions will form a separate ecclesiastical parish. The temporary 𝕴𝖗𝖔𝖓 𝕮𝖍𝖚𝖗𝖈𝖍, at
present used, has been tastefully fitted up by Mr.
Butterfield, and the building has been licensed for
Divine Service, and for the celebration of marriages.
The church was built by the Misses Jarrett, and
the endowment was also provided by them, with the
assistance of the vicar of Wellow (the Rev. C. W.
Horton), together with an annual grant of £50 from
the Church Building Commissioners.

The living, value £150 per annum, is, like that of
Camerton, in Miss Jarrett's gift. The Incumbent is .
the Rev. Chas. Hardy Little, M.A.

. Miss Jarrett is now building schools not far
from the church, and has also provided a parsonage
house for the Incumbent.

The parish of Camerton contains 1,728 acres.
The rateable value is £5,498; and the population
in 1871 amounted to 1,268 souls.

𝕿𝖍𝖊 𝕽𝖔𝖒𝖆𝖓 𝕱𝖔𝖘𝖘𝖊-𝖂𝖆𝖞, of which there are
numerous vestiges in the neighbourhood, has been
traced at intervals from the Humber in Lincolnshire
to the Sea Coast, at Seaton in Devonshire. It passed
through the island, transversely from East to West,
and its course from Cirencester to Bath may be easily
followed, as it is supposed to coincide very nearly
with the modern turnpike road, which, according to
a survey made in 1840, is said to present the dis-
tinguishing features of a Roman road, being raised

above the level of the adjoining land and being generally protected by a ditch on each side. In approaching Bath it runs between Marshfield and Colerne, equi-distant from both, passes the artificial cromlech, known as Shire-stones on Banner Down, at the junction of Wilts, Somerset, and Gloucestershire,*and descending by the western brow of the hill, enters Batheaston to the south-west of Elmhurst, where it met the *Via Julia*, another Roman road leading from Silchester to Bath. From Batheaston the two roads, parellel to each other, if not united, ran together by way of the present turnpike road to Walcot,† where the Via Julia, branching off through Guinea Lane, led by way of Weston, to Usk, on the river of that name. The Fosse-Way entering Bath through the north gate, left it at the south gate, and crossing the river by a bridge, ran up Holloway, to the Burnt House Gate (now removed), where it crossed the Wansdyke, at a spot where, in 1823,

---

* The present "cromlech" was erected by the late Melmoth Walters and his nephew, so recently as the year 1858, and owes nothing to antiquity but its form or shape; the very stones being new to the site.

† True to their practice of extra-mural and way-side sepulture, the Romans have left many traces of the kind contiguous to the road which ran from Batheaston to Bath. A notable example of the kind was furnished a few years ago by the discovery, in Mr. Sweetland's ground, near Cleveland Bridge, of three cists and a number of Roman coins. One struck by the moneyer of Julius Cæsar, being the coin of earliest date yet discovered in the neighbourhood, is now in the possession of Mr. F. Shum, F.S.A.

three skeletons were discovered. All trace of it is then lost in the new road, for half a mile, along which a charming view is obtained. Leaving the high road, the Fosse-Way proceeds straight to Dunkerton Bridge, running along a high ridge of land between Wellow and Camerton to Radstock, and a mile from thence is lost in the high road.

At the Red Posts, about seven miles from Bath, the remains of Roman buildings were discovered, which were probably vestiges of the first Roman posting station out of Bath. These were opened, and the results recorded, by the Rev. J. Skinner.* The word "The Fosse" is preserved in the name of the village "Stratton-on-the-Fosse."

To those who wish a nearer route from Wellow, there is not a more delightful country walk than that through Combehay Park up Fortnight Hill, where three farms, named respectively, Week, Fortnight, and Three Days farm, are a puzzle to the lovers of local tradition. Passing the once celebrated Fortnight School, we arrive at the top of the hill, and resting beneath the trees, can scan the beautiful and varied view before us.

The Bath Union workhouse—a building erected with due regard to the comfort, cleanliness, and health of its inmates, is situated on Odd Down. The chapel is a special object of interest, having been built by the inmates alone.

* Proceedings of the Somersetshire Archæological and Natural History Society, vol. 11., p.p. 174-186.

A little above Cottage Crescent is a deserted quarry, from which, as tradition relates, the stone was dug for building Bath Abbey.

𝕭𝖊𝖗𝖊𝖜𝖞𝖐𝖊 𝕮𝖆𝖒𝖕 occupies a projecting point of land opposite Cottage Crescent, between the old and new roads to Wells. Its remains are very imperfect; but its outer agger, with the ditch, may here and there be traced. The position commands both vales, and affords an uninterrupted view of Solsbury, Hampton, Lansdown, Englishcombe Barrow, Kelston, and the beacon on Mendip. It may have been originally a Belgic-British settlement, afterwards converted into a Roman outpost.

"Near the Wansdyke," says Collinson, "on the western part of Lyncombe, is a lofty eminence, called the *Barracks*, on which are several tumuli.* Beneath, stood the ancient village of Berewyke,† where, according to tradition, there was formerly a church, the tithes of which belonged to the vicar of St. Mary de Stall, in Bath." Finding no record of this village as a separate manor, we are of opinion that the church here spoken of, was one of the road-side chantrey chapels, erected for the convenience of pilgrims, journeying to or from the shrine of St. Joseph of Arimathea, at Glastonbury, which, in Romish

* The so-called tumuli are, there is reason to believe, old quarryings.

† In Domesday Book the Berewyks were members of some central manor. In many instances detached farms. Beria in Mediæval Latin means a wide open plain, and *Vicus* is the other component of the word. · See Duncange, "Voce, Beria."

times, drew a great concourse of people, for whom the church provided "hostels," or hospitals, where they were kindly entertained. To each of these a chapel was attached. On their departure, the rich gave a sum of money, then called a "dole;" while the poor proceeded without anything being demanded for their entertainment.

IN AND OUT OF BATH.

WALK THE SEVENTH.

Over the Old Bridge to Lyncombe and Widcombe; Beechen Cliff; Holloway; Magdalen Chapel and Hospital; St. Luke's
Church; the Quay; Avon Street; Kingsmead Square; Wesleyan Chapel; Trinity
Church; Hetling House.

LYNCOMBE.

" Oh, the charming parties made
   Some to walk the North Parade ;
   Some to Lyncombe's shady groves,
   Or to Simpson's proud alcoves."

ANSTEY.

HAVING passed the last few days in the
country we now propose to spend a short time
in the town and its immediate neighbourhood.

At the Conquest, Widcombe belonged to the king,
while Lyncombe was the property of the Bath Abbey.
In 1292, its revenues were rated at £8 17s. 6d. In
1236, it was given, with Widcombe and Berewyke, to

the vicarage of St. Mary de Stall, Bath. At the Reformation, the manors of Lyncombe and Widcombe were bestowed on Lord Russell, the ancestor of the present duke of Bedford, who disposed of them to the family of Biss. In 1638, Hugh Saxey, the founder of the hospital and school at Bruton, conveyed these manors to that establishment, and ordained that the parish should have the right to send two free scholars to be educated there. Hugh Saxey is said, by steady perseverance and meritorious conduct, to have raised himself from the condition of a stable boy, to the high and honourable post of auditor to Queen Elizabeth. The wealth that he gained he bestowed on the poor of his native town. The hospital receives ten women, eight men, and twelve boys ; the latter are kept until fourteen years old, and are then apprenticed.

"Lyncombe," says Britton, in his notes to Anstey's "New Bath Guide," "is a romantic narrow valley, which, in Anstey's time was a rural shady walk. Now," says he "it has changed its features ; and if not villified, is villa-fied, by a profusion of cottage ornées, mansions, gardens, etc. : and, although many of the valleys in the vicinity of the city abound with secluded and romantic beauties, that of Lyncombe is pre-eminent."

In Anstey's time, the vale boasted two places of public resort—the Bagatelle Gardens, and King James's Palace, so called from a tradition that the fugitive monarch concealed himself there, after his flight.

Wood gives an amusing account of the discovery of a mineral spring in Lyncombe, in the year 1737, as well as the causes of its failure. "The discovery of the Lyncombe spa," says he, "was owing to the following accident :—Mr. Charles Milsom, a cooper, in Bath, having, with four others, rented an old fishpond for twenty shillings a year, and there being leaks in the pond, he, in June, 1737, searched the ground at the head of it, in order to stop the chinks, at which time he perceived a void piece of ground, which as he approached, shook, and looked much like the spawn of toads. This, upon examination, he found to be glutinous, of a strong sulphurous smell, and the colour of ochre. On removing this with a shovel, he perceived several little springs boil up, emitting a black sand, which dried and turned grey. The other part of the soil was white. These things, together with the taste of the water, convinced him that he had made a discovery, and the next thing was to make it known. He forthwith adopts the title of "Doctor," and invites several of his neighbours, with their wives, to a party at the fishpond, and, making a bowl of punch from the water, he frightened his guests by turning the brandy a purple colour, which, they refusing to drink, he explained the circumstance to their satisfaction, when the punch was drank," as Wood says, "with no little mirth and jollity." The next year, one Dr. Hillary made a more particular inquiry, and induced the proprietor of the land to join him in the erection of a lofty edifice over the fountain, at an expense of £1,500; "but, alas!" says Wood, "the ground was weakened, so that the building destroyed the spring. And if Dr. Hillary had not taken on himself more of the architect than the physician in this work, Lyncombe spa had undoubtedly remained a fructile spring to the proprietors, to the great advantage of mankind in general."

𝔅𝔢𝔢𝔠𝔥𝔢𝔫 ℭ𝔩𝔦𝔣𝔣, or Bleak Leigh, rises to a considerable elevation above the "meander Avon," as Henry Chapman calls it. The best way of reaching it is by the lane behind Pope's villa, at the bottom of Lyncombe Hill. From the summit the view is very striking.

No word painting can adequately describe its beauties. Syer's Views, however, of the town and surrounding country are effective. At our feet lies the city, with its crescents, churches, and streets rising from the river well nigh to the summit of Lansdown. To the east are Grosvenor Place, and the hills of Solsbury and Hampton. Sham Castle, Claverton Road, Bathwick Hill, and the river creeping through the valley, diversify the prospect. A few steps onward, Widcombe Church, Crowe Hall, Combe Down, and Prior Park, the Cemetery, and Warner's pretty cottage, wherein he wrote his "History of Bath," come well in sight. Englishcombe Barrow rises towards the south, while Berewyke Camp, and Cottage Crescent, Twerton, the Weston Villas, and Kelston Roundhill, complete the picture.

A walk along the edge of Beechen Cliff leads us to Holloway, or, as it was formerly called, Haul Down, a portion of the Roman Fosse Way. On the north side of the road stands 𝔖𝔱. 𝔐𝔞𝔤𝔡𝔞𝔩𝔢𝔫'𝔰 𝔆𝔥𝔞𝔭𝔢𝔩 𝔞𝔫𝔡 𝔥𝔬𝔰𝔭𝔦𝔱𝔞𝔩.

MAGDALEN CHAPEL, HOLLOWAY.

It was by this route that Leland came to Bath. "I came down," says he, "a rocky hill, full of fair springs of water; and on this rocky hill is set a fair street, as a suburb to the city, and in this street is a chapel of St. Mary Magdalen." This house and chapel were given to the Abbey of Bath in the reign of Henry I., by Walter Hosate, on condition that the chapel should be thoroughly repaired; and Tanner, in his "*Notitia Monastica*," tells us that, in 1332, an indulgence of twenty days was granted to the benefactors of the hospital. Prior Cantlow rebuilt the chapel in 1495. On the east side of the porch is the following inscription :—

Thys.chapell.floryschyd.wt.formosyte.spectabyll.
In.the.honowre.of.M.Magdalen.prior.Cantlow.hath.edyfyde.
Desyring.yow.to.pray.for.him.wt.yowre.prygers.delectabyll.
That.sche.will.inhabit.him.in.hevyn.ther.evyr.to.abyde.

The meaning of the first line is, that it was ornamented with beautiful designs.

The chapel has little to recommend it to a stranger's notice except its antiquity. At the west end it has a small embattled tower, with one bell. There is every reason to believe that, prior to the Reformation, it was extra parochial, and that it was served by a monk, appointed for the purpose.

In the east window is some good stained glass, the subjects being the Virgin and Child, Prior Cantlow, St. Bartholomew, and Mary Magdalen. On either side of the nave is a perpendicular canopied niche, and another near the chancel. This building has been several times suffered to dilapidate. It was repaired in 1760, when it was fitted up for divine service. In 1823, after long neglect, it was again restored, but was closed again from 1833 until 1837, when the Rev. John Allen having been appointed master, service has since been regularly performed.

Of the hospital Wood speaks thus :—"It is a poor cottage for the reception of idiots; but there are few maintained therein, the nurse's stipend, for the support of herself and the objects of her care, being but £15 per annum.　Whoever" he continues, "enters it, will see enough to cure his pride, and excite his gratitude for the blessings he enjoys." It was rebuilt in 1761, and one idiot was, until recently, maintained in it.

At present there is no benevolent institution connected with the chapel.　The hospital (without inmates) is now governed by the Public Act 19th and 20th Victoria, chapter 45, and, under the directions of that Act, all surplus income is to be accumulated until the sum of £5,000 stock, at the least, has been raised, when a building is to be erected as near as may be to the chapel, and such hospital is to be established for the reception, maintenance, and improvement of poor idiots.　It does not follow that this will be carried into effect, because under the powers of the Endowed Schools' Act of 1869 the Trustees have made application for the conversion of the charity into an educational endowment, and if the application be granted, the funds will be applied, under the 74th section of the scheme regulating King Edward's School, Bath, to the education of girls.

S. Luke's Church.　This was built in 1867 as a district church for the accomodation of the inhabitants of South Lyncombe, a rapidly increasing suburb. It occupies a most convenient site between Hatfield

Place and Devonshire Buildings, and is designed in the early decorative style by Messrs. Hickes and Isaac, of Bath. There are 384 sittings, of which 128 are free. The Rev. Robert Tapson is the incumbent, and the patronage is vested in the Simeon Trustees.

The parish of Lyncombe and Widcombe has increased considerably in population during the present century. In 1801 it contained 2,790 souls. From the last census we find it contains 11,020 inhabitants. The area is 1,846 acres. The poor rates which before the Union were £2,018 are now increased to £2,248. The parish is included in the City and Borough of Bath by the Reform Act.

Let us return by the Quay. Avon street, with its once beautiful ceilings and noble staircases, is now the abode of the poor, where idlers congregate in squalid groups at doors, round which powdered footmen formerly waited. Close at hand is Kingsmead Square, at the western corner of which is the once elegant mansion of the Chapman family, now let in tenements. Herschel lived at 13, New King Street, where he first made those observations which subsequently led to the discovery of the Georgium Sidus. One evening, as he and Palmer, the architect, were conversing at the door, he pointed out that planet to the latter as a star not depicted on the charts.

The Wesleyan Chapel, in New King Street, of which John Wesley laid the first stone in 1780, was restored during the year 1847, in the decorated Gothic of the fourteenth century, after a design of

Mr. Wilson. The interior is fitted with open seats. Behind the stone pulpit is a recess forming an organ gallery, and on either side a stained glass window; light is admitted to the body of the building by an arrangement of quatrefoil windows in the clerestory.

In this street, Lord Nelson spent some of his boyish days. His father, the Rev. Horatio Nelson, kept a school at the corner house, No. 1.

𝔗𝔯𝔦𝔫𝔦𝔱𝔶 𝔠𝔥𝔲𝔯𝔠𝔥, erected in 1820, stands in James Street. The Rev. James Murray Dixon, is the Rector.* A portion of the parish has been annexed to the Ecclesiastical District of St. Paul, under the scheme sanctioned by the late Bishop, Lord Auckland.

Considerable improvements have recently been made in the street accommodation of this neighbourhood. The increasing traffic, arising from the branch line which connects the Midland Railway with the city, rendered improved means of traffic imperative. The terminus forms a handsome addition to Green Park Buildings. The former, as well as the latter, deserves a visit.

A handsome specimen of mediæval domestic architecture lies within a short distance of this locality, and is well worthy of a visit. It was erected in the reign of Queen Elizabeth, in whose time Sir Walter Hungerford, of Farleigh, is said to have "built himself a town house overlooking the

---

* The patron of the Living was formerly the late Rev. S. H. Widdrington, Rector of Walcot, who, in 1864, disposed of it to Trustees, in whom it is at present vested.

western borough walls." This mansion (since called Hetling House) was erected on a portion of land belonging to St. John's Hospital, near the Hot Bath. A drawing and description of its chimney-piece may be seen in the "Builder," No. 150.

To this mansion was attached a postern gate. A subterranean passage, now choked up, led to the gardens and pleasure grounds without the city walls. In 1643, Sir Edward Hungerford, the "spendthrift," garrisoned it with the retainers of the King's party, the large upper apartment forming a barrack room. Many tobacco pipes, with E. H. on the stems, have been dug up in the city ditch near the old postern.

In 1694 it was the property of Lord Lexington, who gave it to Mrs. Savil, in lieu of a legacy of £100. The lady married Mr. Skrine, an apothecary, when the house was called Skrine's lower house. In 1746, the Princess Caroline, with her sister the Princess of Hesse, occupied it.

A portion of the house is now used by the fraternity of Odd Fellows, and is called the Odd Fellows' Hall.

IN AND OUT OF BATH.

WALK THE EIGHTH.

BATH AS IT WAS; THE BEAR INN; IMPROVEMENTS; THE BRYMER CHAPEL; BLUE-COAT SCHOOL; BEAU NASH; UNITARIAN CHAPEL; THE THEATRE; QUEEN SQUARE; BATH AND COUNTY CLUB; PERCY CHAPEL; MORAVIAN CHAPEL; SAVINGS' BANK.

THE approach from the fashionable part of Bath to what may be called "the Old Town" was, until the commencement of the present century, very bad. Union Street was not then built. Within the last sixty years Quiet Street, which has recently been considerably improved, was almost overshadowed with trees, in which was a rookery. Old Bond Street was, to use a questionable phrase, a respectable thoroughfare; but Barton Street was narrow and unpaved.

At the time of which we write, 𝕿𝖍𝖊 𝕭𝖊𝖆𝖗 was the principal inn; so, of course, Anstey's hero, Simpkin Blunderhead, arrives there, and thus narrates his experiences.

> "And sure you'll rejoice, my dear mother, to hear,
> We are safely arrived at the sign of the Bear;
>
> .   .   .   .
>
> What though at Devizes I fed pretty hearty,
> And made a good meal, like the rest of the party,
> When I came here to Bath not a bit could I eat,
> Though the man at the Bear had provided a treat."

Matthew Bramble thus describes the inn :—" The communication to the baths is through the yard of an inn, where the poor trembling valetudinarian is carried in a chair betwixt the heels of double rows of horses, wincing under the curry-combs of grooms and postillions, over and above the hazard of being obstructed, or overturned, by the carriages, which are continually making their exits or entrances."

In the year 1800, the Corporation set themselves in earnest to the work of improvement. Union Street displaced the Bear Yard; Marchant's Court gave way to Northumberland Passage; Frog Lane to New Bond Street; Lock's Lane to Union Passage, while other alterations were the result of public and private enterprize; among others was the Corridor, leading from Union Street to the Guildhall. It was erected by the late Mr. H. E. Goodridge in 1825.

𝕮𝖍𝖆𝖕𝖊𝖑 𝖔𝖋 𝖙𝖍𝖊 𝕸𝖎𝖓𝖊𝖗𝖆𝖑 𝖂𝖆𝖙𝖊𝖗 𝕳𝖔𝖘𝖕𝖎𝖙𝖆𝖑.* We ought not to pass this institution a second time

* The Hospital is fully described on pages 70-73.

without paying a visit to the chapel. On the left-hand side of the entrance is a brass bearing the following inscription :—" The late James S. Brymer, Esq., presented £500 to be specially applied to the holy adornment of this chapel, and for the promotion of the more reverent worship of Almighty God, 1859." Opposite this brass is a memorial

THE BRYMER CHAPEL.

window to the donor, given by the Governors of the Hospital as a testimony to his worth and unostentatious generosity. It is divided into three compartments, the subject being the practical charity of the Good Samaritan; it is by Wailes, of Newcastle-on-Tyne, as are also the other windows of the building. Three arches divide the ante-chapel from the chapel. The caps of the pilasters are delicately carved. Without entering minutely into the decorations of the edifice, or the subjects of the other windows, it may be sufficient to say that the ornamentation is neither gaudy nor showy, but that all is graceful, in good taste, and in perfect keeping. The carving was executed by the late Mr. Ezard, under the direction of the late Mr. J. E. Gill. The chapel, which is 25 feet by 55 feet, accommodates 150 persons. The present chaplain is the Rev. T. Tyers.

Close to the Hospital is **The Blue Coat School**, founded in 1712, by Robert Nelson, the author of "Fasts and Festivals of the Church." The objects of the school are the education, clothing, and apprenticeship of the children of the poorer members of the Church of England. The old school-house was pulled down in 1859, and the present Elizabethan structure built in its place by Messrs. Manners and Gill, and opened in 1860. The tesselated pavement discovered when the foundation of the school was excavated, is re-laid in the lobby of the present building.

One hundred and twenty children (60 boys and 60 girls), of honest and industrious parents, who are resident householders of the several parishes of Bath,—St. Peter and St. Paul's, St. James's, St. Michael's, Walcot (St. Swithin's), St. Saviour's, Trinity, St. Paul's, Lyncombe, Widcombe, St. Luke's, and Bathwick. They are instructed in the principles of the Christian Religion, according to the doctrine and discipline of the Church of England, and in reading, writing, arithmetic, geography, history, and drawing. The girls are also taught sewing, knitting, household work, and the use of the sewing machine. The children are yearly provided with one suit of clothes, two pairs of shoes, and three pairs of stockings. They are admitted upon the recommendation of subscribers, when between eight and eleven years old, and at the age of fourteen are, by the Trustees, apprenticed to trades or placed in such services as appear most suitable to their several capacities ; a sum of £6 being paid with every boy, and £5 with every girl.

BEAU NASH.

AMONG the many persons of note who flourished during the eighteenth century, no one exercised so large an influence on the manners and customs of the higher classes in the city as Beau Nash, the titular king of Bath.

Nash was born at Swansea, on the 18th October, 1674, of respectable parentage. He was first sent to school at Carmarthen; subsequently matriculated at Jesus College, Oxford, and ultimately joined the army. But the restraints of a military life possessing no charms for one of his gay and volatile disposition, he resigned his commission, and entered the Temple, where his talents for conducting court revels induced King William to offer him knighthood, an honour which he had the good sense to decline.* At this period, the Inns of Court were a common resort for men of independence and fashion, and Nash became a gambler on a small scale and an idler of the first water. Pleasure was the business of his life; this pursuit he somewhat improved by his talents. Queen

* Queen Anne once asked him why he refused this honour, to which he replied, " Lest Sir W. Read, the mountebank, who has been knighted, should call me brother."

Anne's visit to Bath caused the city to become the focus of attraction for the gay, the wealthy, and the idle; and hither Nash repaired in 1704. Shortly after his arrival, he found that a leader in the path of pleasure was required. His ambition could now be gratified, and he entered' with spirit upon the performance of his self-imposed duties. Commencing as the servant of the great, he soon possessed absolute power. He caused gentlemen when in the ball room to abstain from oaths,* swords, and top-boots. The assemblies were attended by ladies in full court dress—precedence was never forgotten, so that in the arrangement of the dances all were gratified by the attentions which they received. His power was by these means firmly established. Unlike beaux in general, Nash was awkward in person, and naturally ungainly. To cover these defects, he affected stateliness of carriage, combined with extravagance in dress. Among other peculiarities, he constantly wore a white hat.

The Bath Mineral Water Hospital owes not a little to his efforts in obtaining funds for its erection. He was undoubtedly what, in modern phraseology, would be called a "good beggar," and when the hospital was completed, he stimulated the beneficence of the nobility and gentry, headed by King

---

* Nash did not always observe his own rule in this matter, for on various occasions he swore like a trooper in the presence of, and sometimes *at*, ladies when in the Ball Room. It must be allowed, too, that his veracity was little to be relied on.

Q

George II. and his Queen, in endowing and supporting it. His purse, it is said, was always open to
the claims of the sick poor, and many anecdotes are
related of his charitable disposition ;* at the same
time he outshone his contemporaries in dress,† establishment, and equipage, 'and defrayed all his ex-

* This disposition he often gratified by the liberal use of other
people's purses, a vicarious system of benevolence which has not
been unfashionable at other times.

† There is a doubt as to the authorship of a part of the following well-known epigram, although little as to the truth it expressed :

> "Immortal *Newton* never spoke
>   More truth than here you'll find ;
> Nor *Pope* himself e'er pen'd a joke
>   Severer on mankind.
>
> This picture placed these busts between,
>   Gives satire its full strength ;
> *Wisdom* and *Wit* are little seen,
>   But *Folly* at full length."

It is certain the lines were suggested by the position occupied by
the portrait of Nash between the busts of Newton and Pope in
Wiltshire's Ball-room. The two verses have been generally
attributed to Lord Chesterfield, but there is no evidence whatever
to show that he wrote them, beyond the unsupported statement
of Goldsmith. In a correspondence which appeared in the
Bath Chronicle in September, 1856, the authorship is claimed for
Mrs. Brereton. Southey, in his Specimens of the Later English
poets, 8vo. edition, page 392, quotes a satirical poem, consisting
of six verses, on Nash, by that lady, the last of which, with slight
alteration, is the second verse above given, but the first verse is
not included. If, therefore, Mrs. Brereton wrote the verse, which
contains the wit and force of the epigram, who wrote the former ?
It is almost certain that the verse was written by Mrs. Brereton
herself for the sake of brevity, giving as it does unity and
completeness to the last verse, which no other verse in her poem

penses from the winnings of the gaming table. Such was Beau Nash, the man to whom Bath owed much of its celebrity. He procured for it an exemption from the quartering of soldiers. For fifty years he presided over its amusements, which, after a fashion, were well regulated. From eight until ten in the morning the company met in the Grand Pump Room to drink the waters, while a band of music* enlivened the promenade. At ten they

---

would do. It is clear that the two verses, as we have quoted them, obtained general currency long before Mrs. Brereton's death, which took place in 1740.

* Goldsmith, in his life of Nash, after speaking of the miserable state of Bath anterior to Nash's elevation to supreme authority, says :—"And to add to all this, one of the greatest physicians of his age conceived a design of ruining the city, by writing against the efficacy of the waters. It was from the resentment of some affronts he had received there that he took this resolution, and accordingly published a pamphlet, in which he said, *he would cast a toad in the spring*." He then adds that Nash, "hearing the threat, humourously assured the people, that if they would give him leave, he would charm away the poison of the doctor's toad, &c., &c., by music," and that this incident led to his being invested with his tinsel sovereignty. Mr. Earle copies this story, but does not give the name of the malignant physician. The story is very apocryphal. The physician referred to was Dr. Radcliffe, but the true story did not apply to Bath at all. In the Penny Cyclopædia, under an article on "Dr. Francis Willis," it is stated that physician "discovered the mineral spring at Astrop, Northamptonshire, and "made it very famous, till the people of the place offending the "well-known Dr. Radcliffe, made him declare that he would put "*a toad in their well*, which he did by decrying its virtues where- "ever he went." Dr. Radcliffe, it is probable, freely expressed his opinion, when Queen Anne and Prince George of Denmark

adjourned to the concert breakfast at the public rooms. The morning was employed in chit-chat, and in strolling about the Bowling Green and Parades.* Fashion dined at three, at the boarding tables, where sobriety and frugality were strictly enforced.† Private

---

came to Bath in 1702-3, that the waters were unsuitable to the Prince, but nothing more.

* In the *Quarterly Review*, No. 278, there is a charming article on the historian of Cornwall,—Borlase. He appears to have amassed a large number of MSS., now at Castle Horneck, from which some very interesting extracts, relating to Bath, are quoted. In these extracts we catch a few fresh glimpses of Bath society during the last century; those relating to Pope, Ralph Allen, and the celebrated physician, Dr. Oliver, being especially interesting. It has been generally stated that the obelisk placed in the Orange Grove was designed by Nash himself, but in the article referred to we are informed that the draft of the design was executed by Borlase. The article says " We must now return to the year 1730, and, leaving politics and local matters, must follow Borlase to Bath, whither he went to seek the benefit of the Bath waters, under the care of a friend and relation, William Oliver. Until the com-commencement of the eighteenth century, when the value of her mineral waters was recognised once more, the ancient city of Bath had scarcely overstepped the limits prescribed for her by the Roman furrow. But, once brought into notice, her fame quickly spread. She had become, writes Dr. Oliver, 'the universal hospital, not only of this but of other nations, and hither the physicians sent their patients when they knew no longer what to do with them. A club-house was founded ; street was added to street, and square to square. The Prince of Orange came, and departed with a new lease of life. Orange Grove, then the chief place of fashionable amusement, was called after his name, and a column erected in the midst, from a design furnished by the accomplished pencil of the Rector of Ludgvan' " (Borlase).

† This it is not difficult to believe, if it be true that twelve shillings weekly was the average charge.

parties were then unfashionable. At six, the rooms were opened for dancing and play. The M.C. led out the ladies in the order of precedence for the minuet. Tea was then served; country dances succeeded; and the company retired at eleven o'clock. This rule was invariably followed. Even the Princess Amelia was unable to obtain one more dance after that hour.

The foregoing account of Beau Nash, is (with some modification), Dr. Tunstall's abridgment of Goldsmith's Life of Nash,* and fairly represents popular information on the subject.

It may, however, be questioned whether Nash's influence for good upon Bath has not been greatly exaggerated. That he succeeded by adroitness and administrative skill in casting a decorous veil over the vices of the age, and rendering them less gross and repulsive than they otherwise would have been, is quite true; but it is equally true, that the very order and system to which he reduced them, gave sanction and vitality to a state of things against which public opinion, even in those days, revolted. Nash unquestionably made all his arrangements subservient to his own selfish ends.

* Goldsmith's Life of Nash is an amusing work, from which a tolerably accurate account of the Beau may be obtained. It was however, written not in the interest of literature, or because the subject was intrinsically worth writing about, but as a "bookseller's book"—to sell, though the Author has undoubtedly invested the work with some of the enchantments of his captivating style.

He did good service in repressing duelling, and displayed much discretion as an arbiter in cases of dispute and in questions of honour.

He did something also to curb the haughty spirit of the hectoring aristocrats of the day, and to reduce the habits and manners of the "fashionable world" from chaos into order, if not refinement. But he always knew how to profit by the result.

His most ardent admirers are bound to admit that he had no resources except the gaming table; that he remained a gambler so long as his wits were spared him, and when age and decrepitude overtook him he suffered from privation and neglect. Nash complained one day to Lord Chesterfield that he had lost £500, upon which the latter replied, "I do not wonder at your losing money, Nash, but all the world wonders where you get it to lose."

It would not, we think, be difficult to show that the growth and prosperity of Bath, during the last century, were due in a great degree to its unexampled natural advantages; to the manner in which Ralph Allen encouraged the public spirit and enterprise of the citizens; and to the genius of the two Woods, who covered Bath with palatial houses, imposing crescents, and exquisite squares—deemed even by Lord Macaulay to be deserving of his eloquent praise. In these, and in other ways, during Nash's reign, the city was made an attractive place of abode for distinguished persons who had no part or lot necessarily either with the "little king" or his "little people."

"The Bath of the middle of the last century is familiar to all readers of the light literature of that period. The city, early in the reign of Queen Anne, began to be frequented by people of fashion; but the nobility refused to associate with the gentry at any public entertainments. Gentlemen came to the balls in boots, and ladies in aprons. A dictator arose in the person of Mr. Richard Nash, who was elected Master of the Ceremonies, and presided over the company, who assembled in a booth to dance and game. During a reign of many years, this king of Bath had got his unruly subjects into tolerable order. He had compelled the squires to put off their boots when they came to the balls, and the ladies to forego their aprons. His dominions were the resort of *all the sharpers and dupes in the land*, when the London season was over. *Every game of chance was here played without restraint, and Nash had his full share of the spoil of the unwary.* At Tunbridge he established a colony; and, like a great monarch, he often travelled there in state to receive the homage of his subjects, drawn in a post chariot by six greys, with outriders, footmen, and French horns. All went merrily till a cruel legislature passed an Act to declare Basset and Hazard, and all other games of chance, illegal. The statute was evaded; and an amended law was next year passed to declare all games with one dice or more, or with any instrument with numbers thereon, to be illicit. The law-makers did not foresee that an instrument with letters thereon might be as effectual; and the well-known game of E. O. was invented, and first set up at Tunbridge. Nash brought the game to Bath, not to offend the decorum of the Assembly Rooms, but to be carried on snugly in *private houses, to which Nash introduced those who had money to lose, con-federating with the E. O. table-keepers for a share of their profits.* This answered for some time, until another statute effectually put down all gaming houses and gaming tables, as far as law could ac-complish their suppression. There was no resource for the persecuted people of quality, but to establish private clubs."†

There is little doubt that the system which Nash developed left its mark for many years on the cus-toms and habits of the people of Bath. The traditions of his reign, with their false halo of prosperity—although in the present day estimated at their real worth—exercised for generations a baneful influence on the city.

We do not believe that the reign of Nash left behind it a single germ of real permanent good, or any healthy social element, and the proof, if such were wanting, is to be found in the fact that the system, fortunately, collapsed with the sovereignty of the monarch who called it into existence.

* Goldsmith relates this more in detail.

† Knight's History of England, vol. 7, pages 100–1.

Beau Nash died at the age of 88, on the 12th of February, 1761, and was honoured with a. public •funeral at the expense of the city.

𝕿𝖍𝖊 𝖀𝖓𝖎𝖙𝖆𝖗𝖎𝖆𝖓 𝕮𝖍𝖆𝖕𝖊𝖑 is the oldest Nonconformist place of worship in Bath. The first regular congregation was established in 1688,* and in 1692 a chapel was built in Frog Lane, now New Bond Street. The Communion plate, still in use, is dated 1744. Dr. Bennett Stevenson, who officiated for thirty-seven years, took an active part in founding the Mineral Water Hospital, and was one of the first governors. In 1795, the present building in Trim Street was erected, at a cost of £2,500. The first minister of the present chapel was the Rev. David Jardine, father of the late David Jardine, Esq., first Recorder of Bath under the Municipal Corporations Act. During his ministry, one of the occasional preachers (1796) was the celebrated Samuel Taylor Coleridge, who for a short time officiated as Unitarian Minister at Shrewsbury.† To the Rev. David Jardine succeeded the Rev. Thomas Broadhurst, author of a translation of "Greek Funeral Orations," and other works. He was followed, for nearly twenty-five years, by the Rev. Joseph Hunter, who was highly distinguished as an historian and antiquary. As shewing the extent and character of his contributions to literature, especial mention may be made of "Hallamshire," "The Deanery of Doncaster," "English Monastic

* See Murch's History of Presbyterian Churches.

† Cottle's Early Recollections of Coleridge. Vol. i., p. 179.

Libraries," "The Life of Oliver Heywood," and "The Connection of Bath with the Literature and Science of England." Mr. Hunter was one of the most prominent founders of the Bath Royal Literary and Scientific Institution. Since the close of Mr. Hunter's ministry, several gentlemen have officiated in the chapel, eminent for their learning and services to the city.

Congregational registers of baptisms and deaths were kept from a very early period, and were deposited, on the passing of the Registration Act, at the Government office in London.

In 1860, the chapel was considerably altered, enlarged, and improved under the supervision of Mr. Green, of London.

The Cemetery connected with the Chapel, is in the vale of Lyncombe, and was the gift of the late Mr. H. E. Howse in 1819.

Trim Street is remarkable for some military trophies carved over the door of the house, No. 5, formerly occupied by the family of the celebrated General Wolfe.

THE BATH STAGE.*

WHEN Bath was rising in reputation as a place of fashionable resort, the Theatre, almost of necessity,

* Richard Brinsley Sheridan came to Bath in the days of its dramatic pre-eminence, and here he met the beautiful Cecilia Linley, a singer, celebrated as the "maid of Bath." In 1772, he eloped with this lady, whom he married in France. It was during his residence in Bath that Sheridan conceived his most celebrated drama, "*The School for Scandal.*" Society in Bath

held a prominent position among the amusements of the city.

The exact date at which theatrical representations were first given appears uncertain, as we are told, in an accurate and laborious work, entitled " Some Account of the English Stage from the Restoration in 1660 to 1830," " a gentleman, who had occasion to search the records of the General Hospital, found that it was built on the site of an old theatre." Hornby appears to have been the manager, and to have acted unsuccessfully in that arduous capacity.

at that time naturally suggested the characters of which the Play is chiefly composed. Mr. Earle says " the first rough notes for the dialogue were found under this heading, ' The Slanderers —a Pump Room Scene.' " Sheridan lived on the whole happily with his wife, of whom all her contemporaries spoke in rapturous terms. She died in 1792, at the age of 38, to the sincere grief of her husband. Prophetically, Mrs. Sheridan may be said to have been " the beautiful mother of a beautiful race," Besides her only son she had only one daughter, who died young, but the next generation justified the remark, for this son, he who in his day was commonly called " Tom Sheridan "—witty, clever, and eccentric,—was the father of one son, Richard Brinsley Sheridan, Esq. (of Frampton Court, Dorset, formerly M.P. for Shaftesbury, and High Sheriff of the county of Dorset), and three daughters, who inherit the beauty of their famous grandmother, and much of the genius of their still more famous grandfather. One married the late Lord Dufferin and Clanboye, whose eldest son is the present Earl Dufferin, Governor-General of the dominion of Canada, dis- tinguished as an author, orator, and statesman. She married, secondly, the Earl of Gilford, heir to the Marquisate of Tweed- dale. Another daughter is the Hon. Caroline Norton, poet and novelist, and the youngest, is the Duchess of Somerset, who, as Lady Seymour, presided as the " Queen of Beauty " at the Eglintoun Tournament in 1839. Sheridan married, secondly, Miss Ogle, daughter of the Dean of Winchester.

Passing over the question of the earliest local embodiment of the legitimate drama in Bath, it may not be out of place to notice that nearly every writer on Old Bath informs us that "mysteries were performed in the Church of St. Michael in the reign of Edward III."

The first regular Theatre in the city, however, of which there is a clear and circumstantial account, was built in Orchard Street, by subscription, in or about the year 1747, Mr. Palmer being the principal shareholder, and ultimately the sole proprietor. Previous to its erection, a company performed on the ground floor of the Rooms, at which Beau Nash presided, and here Mrs. Charke, as we gather from her biography, acted during some weeks as prompter.

These establishments were rivals for the favour of the public, till Mr. Palmer prudently compromised with the proprietor of the Rooms in question, from which time the Orchard Street Theatre reigned supreme.

In 1768, the prudent and energetic lessee obtained the first Act of Parliament passed in this country for the protection of theatrical property. From these letters patent are derived the prefix, "Royal."

Between 1747 and 1805, Bath had rapidly increased in population, wealth, and luxury, and the Theatre in Orchard Street was no longer adequate to the wants of the public. It was, moreover, situated in a narrow street, and at a considerable distance from the upper part of the town. The access for carriages was inconvenient, and when the play bills announced any representation of unusual attraction, the boxes were found. insufficient to accommodate those who wished to attend. On account of these reasons, a new Theatre was built in Beauford Square, from a design of Mr. George Dawe, architect. It was opened Oct. 26th, 1805, with " *The Castle Spectre.*" The house held between £250 and £300, but £200 was considered, even in the palmy days of Bath, "a good take."

No similar building in the kingdom, perhaps, ever attracted a larger measure of undivided praise. The stage was equal in size to that of Old Covent Garden ; the decorations were rich and tasteful; for acoustic properties it was well nigh perfect, and every part of the ,house afforded an uninterrupted view of the stage. The ceiling was ornamented with some fine paintings by Andrew Cassali, purchased at the sale of Fonthill Abbey, by Paul Methuen, Esq., who generously presented them to the Theatre.

In the spring of 1862, this favourite place of amusement was burnt down. But Bath could not do without its stage ; £12,000 were soon raised by subscription, and a new Theatre, from the design of Mr. C. J. Phipps, F.S.A., was commenced on the 1st of October of the same year, and was opened on the 4th of March, 1863, with " *Much Ado about Nothing,*" Mr. and Mrs. Charles Kean sustaining the principal parts.

The cost of erection was about £12,000. The house is elegant and commodious; the situation is central, and the carriage approaches are convenient. The dress circle contains 221 seats; the pit is spacious; and the upper boxes leave little to be desired. At the ordinary prices of admission, the present building is capable of holding about £124.

But this matter of fact history of the Bath Theatres conveys an inadequate idea of the interest the stage excited and maintained for the greater part of a century. That this was due to a variety of causes, which no longer operate, may be admitted, but it is certain that the ability and reputation of the performers contributed in a great degree to the passion which prevailed for dramatic representations.

To say that the Bath Theatre was, during the greater part of the period referred to, the nursery for the London boards, would be to repeat what has been repeated, *Usque ad nauseam*. It may suffice to say that Edwin, Henderson, King, Blisset, Dimond, Abingdon, Crawford, Braham, Siddons, Murray, and Ellison, were more or less *fils et filles du Theatre*. All actors and actresses of Metropolitan reputation were pleased to appear on the boards. Here, the elder Kean took the house by storm; here Macready, with more studied grace, charmed the boxes, and evoked a storm of applause from the pit. At an earlier date, John Kemble and Mrs. Siddons were constantly before the Bath public. But these days have passed away, and it is probable that the

Theatre will never again permanently rank in public estimation as it has done.

It would be foreign to our subject to discuss why this is so, further than to say that the superfine morality of the present age—though advanced as the reason for non-attendance—has but little to do with it. Private parties, conversaziones, carpet dances, and the like, if they furnish less intellectual and perhaps more questionable amusement, have at least the merit of being cheaper.

It is difficult to trace the decline of the drama to any definite cause. Public taste changes, we cannot tell how or why; but it seems to us, paradoxical though it be, that the drama in its representative aspect has declined in proportion as its literary interest has increased. It is more than a supposition when we say, for instance, that twenty people read Shakespeare now for one who *read* him in the palmy days of the drama.

Harington Place was the town residence of Dr. Harington and his predecessors.*

* Henry Harington, M.D., like his more famous ancestor, Sir John Harington, of Kelston, was endowed with versatile gifts of mind and great intellectual powers. He was physician to the Bath Hospital, for the benefit of which he not only exerted his professional skill, but made his literary powers and labours subservient to its pecuniary interests. Eminent as he was in his profession, Dr. Harington especially excelled in the walks of literature and music. He was a man of gracious, winning manners, easy in carriage and address, and free from the smallest vanity. His analogical treatise on the "Doctrine of the Trinity" is ingenious rather than profound, but, nevertheless, it is a literary

At the north end of John Street, we see the last relic of antiquity in the neighbourhood. Barton Farm-house, said by tradition to have been the spot where Sherston, Mayor of Bath, entertained Queen Elizabeth, stood in its own farm-yard so late as 1752.

𝕼𝖚𝖊𝖊𝖓 𝕾𝖖𝖚𝖆𝖗𝖊 exhibits Wood's genius to the greatest advantage.

> " But then that *square*—within whose center rail'd
> Lies Taste upon an obelisk impal'd ;
> Mark, how from servile squeamish order free,
> The different buildings sweetly disagree ;
> This boasts a richer, that an humbler grace,
> Like courtiers in, and courtiers out of place."

We say no more. It would mar this felicitous description.

𝕿𝖍𝖊 𝕮𝖍𝖚𝖗𝖈𝖍 𝖔𝖋 𝕾𝖙. 𝕻𝖆𝖚𝖑, at the south-west corner of the Square, was consecrated by the Bishop of Bath and Wells in 1874. It occupies part of the site of a well-known inn, the Elephant and Castle, as well as part of the site of the Proprietary Chapel of St. Mary, which was built by Wood, the architect, in 1732, and was pulled down in order to increase the width of the approach to the Midland Station. The new church was erected to meet the wants of the parish of St. Paul, which has

---

curiosity. He wrote with ease and accuracy, and his poetry is not without merit. Perhaps, however, it was in music and musical composition that he displayed his highest power. In this he was *facile princeps*. To the end of his long life he devoted his many talents to the public good, sparing neither himself nor his purse in the furtherance of every object tending to elevate the public taste. Dr. Harington died at the age of 89, Jan. 15, 1826.

been carved out of the parishes of Trinity and St. James.* It is a Gothic structure, built in a style which prevailed in England during the latter part of the 12th century, and was designed by Messrs. Wilson, Wilcox and Wilson, of Bath. The internal dimensions are thirty-one feet wide by ninety-six feet long, and fifty feet high to the apex of the roof. The axis of the church does not stand east and west. The west aisle is only temporary. The cost has hitherto been about £4,000.

The Bath and County Club, situated at the north-west corner of the Square,† was established in 1858. At this time, there were two Clubs in Bath. " The York Club," founded in 1790, and " The New Club." The members of the former amalgamated with the Bath and County Club, and most of the members of the New Club were, in 1861, admitted without ballot into the younger Club. The number of members of the Bath and County Club is limited to 350. Visitors are admitted for four days by

* The scheme stipulates for the erection of a church in Avon Street.

† The obelisk in the enclosure was raised in honour of Frederick, Prince of Wales, and the Princess of Wales, and bears the following inscription, from the pen of Pope—a fact difficult to believe from its common-place character :—

" In memory of honours conferred, and in gratitude for benefits bestowed, on our City, by H.R.H., Frederick, Prince of Wales, and his Royal Consort, in the year 1737, this obelisk is erected by Richard Nash."

" Poor Fred who was alive, and is dead," was not a theme to evoke a spark from the genius of Pope.

R

permanent members. Temporary members are admitted for the season, or shorter periods, on the recommendation of permanent members. The entrance fee for permanent members is £10 10s. The annual subscription is £4 4s. It has all the conveniences of a Metropolitan club, and is one of the best provincial clubs in the United Kingdom. Lieut.-Colonel England is the present Honorary Secretary.

Percy Chapel. (Independent.) This chapel, situated in Charlotte Street, was built in 1854, and received its name from Percy Place, as a compliment to the late Rev. W. Jay, who resided there for many years. On the retirement of Mr. Jay from Argyle Chapel, after a ministry extending over fifty years, a large and influential body of his hearers seceded from the chapel, and combined to establish a separate congregation.

The Byzantine design of the building is of an elaborate character, and although its details and general appearance may be open to some objections, we believe that in acoustic properties and internal arrangements it is well adapted for public worship. It contains 1,000 sittings, of which 200 are free. The cost of the building was £5,000.

In 1868 some alterations and improvements being deemed desirable, they were carried out at an outlay of £700.

In Charlotte Street there are also other public buildings,—the **Savings Bank**, and the **Moravian Chapel**.

Victoria Park (Bath

IN AND OUT OF BATH.

WALK THE NINTH.

VICTORIA PARK; WESTON; NORTHSTOKE; BITTON;
HOME BY THE MIDLAND RAILWAY.

VICTORIA PARK.

AT the end of Queen's Parade is Rivers' gate, which forms the south-east entrance to the Victoria Park.

The idea of providing ornamental plantations, walks, and drives, in the immediate neighbourhood of the city was first entertained by a few public-spirited citizens in 1829, and so well was the scheme received, that nearly £5,000 was subscribed during the first year. The Park was formally opened by her present Majesty, then the Princess Victoria, in October, 1830. The site could hardly have been better chosen, commanding as it does varied and extensive views of the surrounding country. The ground was laid out under the direction of Mr. Edward Davis, and affords a favourable example of what may be effected in the way of landscape gardening. An old quarry was formed into a pretty dell : the surface springs of the field were collected into an ornamental pond, and a tasteful Gothic building was erected by the Corporation as a farm-house for that part of the Park belonging to the Freemen.

Besides its natural beauties, the Park is interesting as containing one of the best public arboreta in the United Kingdom. Owing to a favourable climate, and to the care of the Managing Committee, the city possesses a collection of acclimatised trees and shrubs almost unique in its completeness. Nearly every country is represented from Siberia to Cape Horn. It is unnecessary to enumerate the more interesting specimens, as the trees are conspicuously and correctly labelled. The collection of evergreens is especially good.

Through the Park is a footpath leading to the Weston Road.

WESTON.

THE village of Weston furnishes a fair excuse for an agreeable walk. The man for whom the present offers more attractions than the past, would probably take his way through the Park, while the scholar or the antiquary, might prefer to follow the carriage road, formed on the line of what was once a portion of the Via Julia. This military road ran through Walcot to the Severn. Roman Remains have from time to time been discovered along its course, and notably two Lares, now in the Royal Literary and Scientific Institution.

It is necessary to follow "Weston Lane" and its

branches, in order to notice the lines of handsome villas which have been erected in this parish during the last quarter of a century. About a hundred yards beyond the small gate at the north-west corner of the Park, a branch of the road, Park Lane, turns sharp off to the south, and a little below is crossed by another road which passes through the Park, to Park Gardens. This road sweeps to the west, and leads to Weston Park and to the village of Weston. Nearly along the entire line described are distributed, with more or less regularity, a large number of elegant and commodious villas, which form what may not inappropriately be called "New Weston." Among so many handsome residences it would be invidious to point out any as specially deserving of notice. Cranwells, however, the property and residence of Jerom Murch, Esq., can scarcely fail to attract attention.

In this suburb lived for many years Mr. Philip Duncan, for many years connected with the Oxford University, and Curator of the Ashmolean Museum. He was a ripe scholar and an accomplished gentleman. During his long residence here he identified himself with every useful and good work, and was an active promoter of every well considered scheme of philanthrophy and benevolence.

Weston proper is backed by an amphitheatre of gentle eminences, and is happier in its surroundings than in itself. To our thinking it is by no means charming, and looks rather like a small decayed country town than a modern model village.

At the Conquest it was divided into two manors, valued at £18, and contained a mile and a half of wood, two mills, and 120 acres of pasture lands. Of these manors, one belonged to the Abbey of Bath from time immemorial. The owner of the other was dispossessed by Norman William, who gave it to one of his followers. The manor, however, was purchased in 1106, by John of Tours, who gave it to the monastery, to which it remained attached until the dissolution.

Elphage, the first abbot appointed by King Edgar, was a native of this place, and holds a conspicuous position in the Saxon calendar for his piety and learning. Subsequently he became Bishop of Winchester, and afterwards Archbishop of Canterbury. He was stoned to death by the Danes at Greenwich, and his body, after being buried in London, was, by order of King Canute, removed to Canterbury Cathedral.

The Church, of which the Rev. Prebendary Bond is the vicar, stands on a rising ground in the centre of the village. It is of the Perpendicular order, having an embattled tower containing six bells; the nave and chancel were rebuilt in 1833, and various improvements and changes have, since that time, been made to adapt it to the present requirements of the parish. The living is a vicarage, in the patronage of the crown. In 1699, John Harington, of Kelston, endowed it with the rectorial tithes, on condition that the rector should be resident. Near it are the schools, substantial buildings, and well adapted for the purpose; in them 230 children receive instruction daily.

There is a public footpath through the churchyard, which in the mildest language, may be designated a public nuisance. The difficulties of diverting this right of way are, we assume, insuperable, or they would long ago have been grappled with. The arrangement is most irreverent.

According to the census of 1871, Weston contained a population of 3,570. The area of the parish is estimated at 2,600 statute acres, the rateable value being £20,570. The poor rates are at present a little over £1,260 per annum.

Following the course of Locksbrook, which, rising on the slopes of Lansdown, falls into the Avon, we reach the extremity of the village, where a road leads to Prospect Stile, and the race-course. A quarter of a mile beyond is North Stoke Lane, a continuation of the Via Julia.

From this point there is a glorious walk to Kelston Round Hill, or as it is sometimes called, Henstridge Hill. The view is superb. On either side lie the cities of Bath and Bristol; to the eastward, the eye wanders over the downs to Marlborough Forest; southward, over Salisbury Plain, into Dorset; westward, to the Mendip Hills, the Bristol Channel, and the Welsh coast; while to the north, the Forest of Dean darkens in the distance. Below are verdant hills and fertile valleys, with here and there a village.

NORTHSTOKE

Is a straggling village of antique farm-houses, pictu-resque in the highest degree. The 𝕮𝖍𝖚𝖗𝖈𝖍, of Norman foundation, is situated on a gentle eminence, and is remarkable for its utter want of beauty. A heavy square nondescript tower, having "William Britton, churchwarden, 1731," legibly engraven thereon, seems to have been built after his own design; it is thirty feet high. The font is Norman. The belfry contains a beautiful monument, representing a female figure sitting under a palm tree, and holding a palm-branch in her left hand. Above are the arms of Colonel Edward Brown, and below an in-scription to his memory. The chancel is divided from the nave by a wall, in which are two windows and a door. On either side of the porch is an ancient head. Rector, Rev. John Pedder.

The manor was given to the Abbey of Bath by Kenulf, King of Mercia, in 800. In 1120, Modbert de Stoke disputed the right; but, failing in proof, it was confirmed to the monks by Henry I. and Stephen. At the Reformation, it was given to Paulet Lord St. John; and, in Elizabeth's reign, to the manor of East Greenwich. The population is 150; the area, 660 acres. The poor rates average £80.

Returning through the village, we come to North-stoke Brow, from whence there is a charming view. Descending the field to the high road, we pass through the village of Swinford, where are some mills in full operation. A quarter of a mile further on is a lane which conducts us to

BITTON.

THIS parish is partly divided from Somerset by the River Avon. The vicarage was formerly annexed to the prebend of Bitton, in the Collegiate Church of Salisbury, from which it has been severed for many years, and is now in the gift of the Bishop of Gloucester and Bristol.

Bitton Church consists of a nave remarkable for its length, and a chancel separated from it by an elaborately beautiful Anglo-Norman arch, and terminated by a fine east window, containing stained glass. On either side is an emblematical carving, the one representing ears of corn, the other a vine branch. The church is very ancient, its foundation being Anglo-Norman, though the general character of the building is Perpendicular. The north chapel contains some elaborate sedilia of the Decorated style. In the north porch are preserved the effigies of Sir Walter de Bitton, and the Lady Emmote de Hastynges; they are good examples of the monuments of the thirteenth century. There are also some coffins, and other relics of antiquity. The tower consists of three stages, having diagonal buttresses, carrying crocketted pinnacles at each stage; it has an embattled parapet, with pinnacles. A very beautiful spire, restored by the Rev. H. T. Ellacombe, the former vicar, in 1842, surmounts the stair-turret. The drip corbels of the western doorway are supposed to represent Edward III., and his Queen.

During the last fifteen years the church has been improved by a handsome transverse beam roof of oak and cedar, resting on a series of stone corbels, beautifully carved with the plants mentioned in Scripture, and by the removal of the old high and narrow pews, and the substitution of new seats of solid oak, with richly carved ends. Several handsome memorial windows have been presented, the work of Hughes and Co., London.

The churchyard, which is a model of reverential care, contains some tombs after antique models.

Certain holders of land in this parish formerly possessed the right to pasture cattle in the meadows which skirt the Avon, from the Sunday after the 14th of August to the April following; the nominal owners having the right only to mow them. This day was one of high festivity. A white bull, decked with garlands, was led in with much ceremony. The custom has been long discontinued, but the practice of "shooting the meadows," as it is called, existed until 1864, when the ground was enclosed, and these ancient usages came to an end.

There are Roman Camps near the village, and several Roman remains have been found in different parts of the parish. A large ancient tumulus, of which the history is unknown, stands between the Church and the Railway.

There are two churches at Hanham, one at Kingswood, one at Oldland, and one at Warmley, each
with its separate parsonage house, school, and independent ecclesiastical and parochial organisation,
but all are Hamlets of Bitton.

˙ The admirable state of the church, and church
grounds is due to the late Vicar, the Rev. H. T.
Ellacombe, and his son, the present Vicar, the Rev.
N. A. Ellacombe, both of whom for many successive
years have bestowed upon them the most unremitting attention and care.

The Paper Mills, near Bitton, are worthy of notice
in themselves, and for the admirable management
of the proprietors.

The Bitton Station of the Midland Railway lies
about half-a-mile beyond the village.

The population, in 1871, was 2,577; the area is
3,355 acres; and the average poor rates are on a
rateable value of £11,444. The population of Oldland is 6,415; the area is 2,615 acres; and the average
poor rates are on a rateable value of £15,569.
The population of Hanham is 1,322; the area 1,195
acres; and the average poor rates are on a rateable
value of £5,186. The parish is rated in Keynsham
Union.

IN AND OUT OF BATH.

WALK THE TENTH.

The Upper Bristol Road; St. Michael's and Locksbrook Cemeteries; Partis College; The Church, Park, and Village of Kelston; Saltford; Corston; Newton St. Loe and Park; Home by the Lower Bristol Road through Twerton.

THE road at first is not very attractive, but we follow it for what it will give us an hour or two later, so we step rapidly on till abreast of the Gas Works, on the Upper Bristol Road, opposite which stands the **Church of S. John the Evangelist**, a chapel-of-ease to the parish church of Weston. Behind, lies **St. Michael's Cemetery**, a small burying-ground consisting of about two acres.

We pass the **County Sessions Court**, and a short distance beyond is **Locksbrook Cemetery**, belonging to the United Ecclesiastical Parishes of Walcot and St. Saviour.

From the front of the Mortuary Chapel a charming view is obtained. Everything that good taste can do to rob such a spot of its horrors, has been done. The extent of this great city of the dead is fifteen acres and a-half.

On the edge of Newbridge Hill, stands 𝕻𝖆𝖗𝖙𝖎𝖘 𝕮𝖔𝖑𝖑𝖊𝖌𝖊, erected by the widow of Fletcher Partis, Esq., in compliance with his will. This interesting building was completed in 1826, when it was opened for the reception of thirty decayed gentlewomen, each of whom receives an annuity of £30, and is provided with a separate residence. Ten of the number are required to be either daughters or widows of clergymen of the Established Church. Each of the annuitants must possess a secured income of a certain maximum amount. There is a resident chaplain; the Bishop of the Diocese is visitor, and the management is vested in thirteen Trustees.

KELSTON.

KELSTON, anciently called Kelweston, Kilweston, or Kelneston, names probably denoting its proximity to Weston, is the first village on our road. The views are rich in pastoral loveliness. The winding river, fringed with flowers; the deep green meadows, and the flashing weir, might charm a painter's eye. Kelston Round Hill, the ancient Henstridge Hill, shows well in the picture. Here was lit the Beacon fire, answering to that on the heights of Dundry—a fiery message to be telegraphed to Mendip, or Brandon Hill, and so downward to the coast.

The village is not without interest to the painter, the botanist, and the palæontologist The landscape is varied, and the woods which line the slopes of Lansdown, as well as those which hang above

the river, are full of wild flowers, some of which are
rare. The strata are extremely varied for so small an
area, reaching from the rhœtic beds through the lias
and the transition sands to the superior oolite.

The model cottages, fronted with escutcheons,
armorial bearings, and the suggestive inscription,
"In Memoriam," deserve notice. They were built
by the Lord and Lady of the Manor, Lieutenant-
Colonel and Mrs. Inigo Jones, who now reside at
Kelston Park.

This manor, formerly attached to Shaftesbury
Abbey, was taken by Henry the VIII. from the
Abbess, and given to Ethelreda Malte, supposed to
be his illegitimate daughter. The King protected
her, and gave her in marriage to a faithful follower
of his Court, John Harington,* to whom he granted
the manors of Batheaston and St. Catherine's Court.
These manors descended to the elder son of John
Harington, by his second marriage with the daughter
of Sir John Markham—the chivalrous, witty, and
learned knight, Sir John Harington, translator
of *Orlando Furioso*,† and author of *The Ajax*, a most

* We are in possession of the Harington pedigree to the
present time, but it is too long for our limited space, Branches
of the family still flourish in Devonshire and other parts of
England, while a few cling to the city of Bath, so long
associated with the historic interest attached to the founder
of the race. They have been well tried in the public service. In
the Church, the Army, and the Navy, the name of Harington has
always preserved its ancient lustre.

† The late Rev. E. D. Rhodes, at the time of his death,
possessed an original copy of this book as well as the *Ajax*.

pungent satire upon the Court. Sir John was Queen Elizabeth's "witty godson," and he gave her a brilliant reception when she paid him a brief visit during a summer excursion in 1591. Either at this time or on a subsequent occasion Her Majesty was entertained by the knight at St. Catherine's Court, and the bed in which she slept, as well as the furniture of the room, were until lately preserved there. Subsequently the Queen displayed some resentment*

* Sir John Harington was a man who loved good for its own sake. He had very definite aims, which he seems always to have kept in view, but he appears to have preferred his own peculiar and quaint method of action. He possessed an irresistible love of wit, epigram, and parable, and these he called to his aid on all occasions. His leading the good Bishop Montague into the roofless nave of the Abbey, for shelter in a storm, is an instance of his ready wit. By this obvious ruse, he obtained a more hearty and ready response for the "rotten folde" and the "poore sheepe" from the Bishop than he would have procured by any other method. It is more than probable that his first enforced absence from court was on account of some unseasonable exercise of his wit—some shaft of satire shot at random which wounded the Queen herself.

Sir John was appointed to a command in the Army, by Essex, at the especial desire of the Queen, when she sent that ill-fated nobleman as Lord-Lieutenant to Ireland, in 1599, and Sir John made a Report to "Queen Elizabeth, concerning the Earle of Essex's Journeys in Ireland, 1599," in a very characteristic document (Nugæ Antiquæ. vol. ii., p. 31). Essex "Knyghted this gentleman in the feilde, with many others; which provoked not a little the Queen at his return home;" so says Camden, but it is obscurely expressed. It seems scarcely possible to conceive why the Queen should have been angry with Harington for returning home, in other words, for following his leader, when no other course was possible. Yet it was so. The Queen evinced her displeasure towards all concerned. She seems towards Sir John, and banished him from the Court. Those who know "*The Ajax*" (a rare literary gem), will remember the illustration representing the philosophical mood in which he bore his punishment.

During the Queen's visit, she planted several trees, if not an entire grove. Some have decayed,

---

also to have been personally angry with the worthy Knight for acepting the honour, which, as Lord-Lieutenant of Ireland, Essex had a perfect right to confer. Harington acted well, and feeling acutely the *reflected disgrace* which the reckless imprudence of his patron had cast upon all concerned, deemed it wise not to appear at court.

This view of the cause of his later, and as it virtually turned out, final estrangement from Elizabeth's court, is partly confirmed by the following passage from a letter written by Sir Robert Sydney in 1600, to Harington :—

" Worthy Knight,—Your presente to the Queen was well ac-
" cepted of ; she did much commend your verse, nor did she less
" praise your prose ! Your Irish business is less talked of at her
" Highness's palace, for all agree, that you did go and do as you
" were bidden ; and, if the great Commanders went not where they
" ought, how should the Captains do better withouten order?
" But, mum, worthie Knyght, I crave all pardon for touching
" your galled back. The Queen hath tasted yonr dainties, and
" saith you have marvellous skill in cooking of good fruits." The Queen, whom Sir John saw once again in 1602, died in 1603, and he was called to court again by James I.

The Kelston Knight must not be confounded with the accomplished John Harington, head of the elder or Haverington branch, created Baron Harington of Exton by James I., to whose daughter, the Princess Elizabeth, he was tutor ; nor with the next lord, who, also, was a wit, a sonneteer, a *litterateur*, a courtier, and a man of great public and private virtues. He wrote many epigrams, which have been wrongly attributed to his Kelston cousin, who gives us an interesting account of this noble kinsman in the *Nugæ Antiquæ*, vol. 3.

but an oak, two yew trees, and some elms, still remain. Another tradition says she presented to the village a golden font, which being removed to Bristol for security in 1643, was seized by the party of the Parliament and converted into money.

At that time, the Harington 𝔐an𝔰𝔦𝔬𝔫 stood near the church. It was built by Sir John in 1587, from the designs of the famous Italian architect, Barozzi. Ravaged by both parties during the Civil Wars, it was never restored to its former grandeur, and was ultimately pulled down. Sir John died and was buried at Kelston in 1612.

The present mansion, of which Wood was the architect, was erected in 1760, on the brow of a hill, overhanging the river, by Sir Cæsar Hawkins physician to the King, from whose son, Edward, descended the eminent surgeon of that name, Dr. Francis Hawkins, physician to the Queen's Household, Dr. Edward Hawkins, provost of Oriel College, the late Sir John Cæsar Hawkins, and the present Baronet, who was, until lately, Rector of St. Albans, Herts. The mansion, which occupies the site of the old summer house, has been further enlarged by Lieut.-Colonel Inigo Jones.

The church was rebuilt in 1860. No part of the former structure remains, except the tower, the north porch, the massive door of entrance, the stone-work of the Elizabethan font, and two piscinæ. Some smaller relics of a still more ancient date exist, ·reaching back to Anglo-Saxon times.

One of the piscinæ, already mentioned, is of special interest. The heavy arch-stone above this basin, displaced in 1860 when the old church was razed, shewed that it had once formed the slab or top-stone of an ancient tomb, carved in relief with an eastern cross, with peculiar serrated shaft and arms, rendering it probable that when the early English Church was built, the materials of a more ancient building were re-used. At a still more remote date, there stood a cross, which, if not runic, retains the runic coil as part of its sculpture, similar to those in Ireland, and resembling the one in Carew churchyard,* Pembrokeshire. A fragment of the shaft remains, and is placed by the Rector in the chancel wall. Three sides of it are totally defaced; the fourth presents in symbol the doctrine of eternal life. " The tree of life " sculptured on it has for its roots the endless runic coil. Another relic is, probably, an ancient morse, or fastening of the priest's cope; it may be of Saxon or even Danish origin, at all events it is of bronze. The symbols on the brooch are strange, and have not as yet been interpreted. The tower, low and heavy, is of fine old masonry, about the time of Henry II., and is covered with ivy. The bells are four in number, a light-toned but melodious peal,

---

* At Crowcombe, West Somerset, two similar crosses exist. One stands in the churchyard ; the other, about the centre of the village. In architectural grace, the latter cross is not surpassed by any one in Iona. Crowcombe Court belongs to an ancient branch of the Carew family. The example nearest to the Kelston fragment now extant, is, it is believed, that at West Camel, Somerset.·

cast by a local founder, of well-earned repute in Somerset a century ago,—Bilby of Chewstoke.

The 𝕸𝖔𝖉𝖊𝖗𝖓 𝕮𝖍𝖚𝖗𝖈𝖍, of 1860, was built much in the style of that which preceded it, but is not quite so early, for the cusp and quartrefoil enrich its window tracery. The chancel lights are filled with painted glass, chiefly by Wailes of Newcastle, the gift of the families of Harington and Hudleston, in memory of their ancestors who repose at Kelston. Two more are specimens of ancient foreign art, and are not without merit. The western, or tower window light, is also antique and of stained glass; the subject being the Baptism of Christ in the River Jordan. The church is larger than it was formerly by the addition of a southern aisle, supported by massive pillars of Bath stone, each having the Lily leaf conventionally represented on the capital. The noted dead who rest within or round its walls are—Sir John Harington; Dr. Henry Harington, of Bath, who lived to the age of ninety, and of whom mention has been made; John Hudleston, esteemed in India as the friend and patron of the Missionary Schwartz; a daughter of the ancient House of Lee, Earls of Marlborough; and the late Dean of York, Sir William Cockburn, Bart., also Rector of Kelston for many years.

The Rev. F. J. Poynton is the Rector of the parish.

Our notice of this charming village must not close without a recommendation to strangers to take a peep at the ancient manor barn, the dovecote, and pretty village school, entered by a stately ancient porch, retained from the mansion dated 1566, which stood there until 1856, when the school was built on its site.

The total area of the parish is 1,045 acres. The population, in 1871, was 224; and the poor rates are assessed on a rateable value of £2,653. It forms a part of the Union of Keynsham.

SALTFORD.

LEAVING Kelston churchyard, we cross the fields to Saltford Ferry, near which are the brass mills, and two Stations; one on the Great Western Railway, the other on the Midland. Saltford is a pretty village, formerly belonging to the honour of Gloucester. The living is in the gift of the family of the present Rector, the Rev. W. Clarke Welsford. Saltford is five miles distant from Bath.

The Church, dedicated to S. Mary, is remarkable for an ancient heptagonal font, on which are seven angelic heads. The church was partially restored in 1851, and at the same time the tower—which is an inelegant structure—was "mended." The interior of the church is mean.

Near it is an ancient mansion of the Rodney family. The walls are four feet thick; the flooring is of unplaned oak. The circular headed window was modernized in the sixteenth century; the old door still remains, with a gabled porch, surmounted by a cross and sculptured corbels. A chimney piece bears the date of 1645. The roof has on its eastern gable a lion *sejant*, carved in stone.

According to the census of 1871, the population was 375; the rateable value is £5,849; and the acreage 823.

A pleasant walk of about a mile along the high road, brings us to the sequestered and pretty village of

CORSTON.

At the Conquest, it belonged to the Abbey of Bath, and was worth £8. In the reign of Henry I. it was alienated from the monastery to the family of St. Loe, and afterwards to the family of Inge. Subsequently it formed a portion of the Harington estates until the eighteenth century, when it was purchased by Joseph Langton, Esq., and, through his daughter, came into the possession of Col. William Gore-Langton.

The Church, of which the Rev. W. B. Doveton is the Vicar, is dedicated to All Saints, and stands in a well-kept churchyard.

The chancel is Early English; the nave is of later date. The tower is a plain square structure, with a short conical spire, and appears to have been erected in the year 1622. In 1865, the church was re-opened after having been thoroughly restored and enlarged by the addition of a north aisle of Early English architecture. It has now 254 sittings; before the enlargement, it had only 116. During the alteration, a very perfect piscina, with the fenestrella and a sedilia, was discovered behind the plaster of the chancel.

The living was formerly held by the Rev. Arthur Hele, son of the pious author of *Hele's Devotions*, and himself the writer of a Harmony of the Gospels. It is a Vicarage, in the gift of the Bishop of Bath and Wells, who is also the owner of the great tithes. The vicarial tithe is commuted for £170 per annum; there are about twelve acres of glebe. The ancient manor house, once inhabited by the Haringtons, is now the residence of a farmer. It was formerly used as a school, and the poet Southey received his early education under its roof. In his "Retrospect," he makes several allusions to Corston, its church and scenery.

The northern side of the parish is intersected by the Great Western Railway. The climate is very healthy and the soil fertile. Ammonites of large size have been frequently found in the fields, which are remarkably full of loose stones; it is believed they are of great service in keeping the ground moist in hot weather, and sheltering the crop from the wintry blasts.

In the centre of the village is the national school, erected in 1844.

The parish is in the hundred of Wellow, and the Union of Keynsham. The population, in 1871, was 445; the area 1,145 acres; and the average poor rates £300, on a rateable value of £4,342.

NEWTON ST. LOE.

A SHORT distance on the high road we cross a stile, and, ascending the hill, reach the churchyard

on its summit. The manor of Newton was one of
the many bestowed by the Conqueror on the Bishop
of Coutance; it afterwards came into the possession
for the family of St. Loe, or de Sancto Laude. In the
reign of King John, the sheriff assessed its owner,
Roger St. Loe, in the sum of £100 towards a levy
of that monarch; and when the barons rebelled,
this powerful lord is said to have imprisoned the
king in his castle at Newton. It subsequently passed
to the families of Botreaux, Burghersh, Hungerford,
Hastings, Neville; and ultimately, by purchase, to
Joseph Langton, Esq., whose only child and sole
heiress married Colonel William Gore, who assumed
in addition to his patronymic the name of Langton.

The **Church** is a remarkably handsome structure,
having a fine tower of the pure perpendicular style,
embattled, covered with ivy, and containing a peal
of five bells. Previous to its restoration twenty years
ago, by Mr. C. E. Davis, architect, it consisted
only of a nave and south aisle—from which the
double roof had been removed. It was at this time
spanned by an almost flat roof, which cut through
the east window of the south aisle, destroying the
tracery. The chancel was of very small dimension,
and was lighted with sash windows. In the north wall
were two square-headed perpendicular windows,
one of which is retained in the present vestry.
The arches dividing the aisle from the nave are
remarkable. The archless spaces in the south aisle
were lighted by tracery widows. In addition to

this, there was a south porch.   In the churchyard is a considerable fragment of the churchyard
Cross.   In addition to the nave, the church at
present has two aisles, the northern being exclusively the property of the Lord of the Manor.
It contains a fine Georgian marble monument,

NEWTON CHURCH.

railed off at the west end, commemorative .of the
first Langton who resided at Newton, and the last
owner, who lived in the moated castle in the park
before it was dismantled.*   All the woodwork of
the church is of massive oak, worked in good

* Of this Castle the tower and the outer bailie, gateways, (one
of them being very fine) and stables, only now remain.

taste. The church was nearly re-built and re-stored, at the expense of the late W. H. P. Gore - Langton, Esq., M.P.; the chancel is the gift of the present Rector, the Rev. George Gore. The whole building now forms a good type of a Somersetshire parish church. The pulpit is hand-some, and the carved stone screen is worthy of examination. A remarkable hagioscope was found during the alterations, and restored. It served the secondary purpose of a passage for the priest to minister at the "Altar of our Ladye" without having to pass from the chancel into the body of the church.

Near the church is a free school, built and endowed by Richard Jones, of Stowey, in 1698, but now in part supported by voluntary contributions.

Close to the village is the fine 𝔓𝔞𝔯𝔨. No lover of the country could fail to be pleased with the place and its surroundings—the archæologist, the botanist, or the mere admirer of pastoral scenery, might each find sufficient to interest him for a long summer day. The mansion is described by Collinson in laudatory terms.

Colonel Gore–Langton, who represented the county of Somerset for more than fifty years, died in 1847. His eldest son, William, married Jacintha Frances Dorothea, the only daughter and sole heiress of Henry Powell Collins, Esq., of Hatch Beauchamp, near Taunton, and died in his father's lifetime. His only son and sole heir, W. H. P. Gore-Langton, Esq.,

succeeded to the estates of his paternal grandfather
in 1847, and subsequently to the inheritance
of his maternal grandfather.   Mr. Gore-Langton
married the Lady Anna Eliza Mary, only daughter
of the late Duke of Buckingham; and represented
successively the Eastern and Western Divisions of this
county in Parliament.   He died in 1873, after a short
illness, and was succeeded by his eldest son, W.
Stephen Gore-Langton, Esq., who married a daughter
of Sir Graham Montgomery, Bart., and has issue.

The total area of the parish is 1,504 acres; the
population, in 1871, was 417.   The poor rates
are assessed on a rateable value of £6,593.

TWERTON.

TWERTON, formerly called Twiverton, but in Domesday Book *Twertone*—at which time it was divided into
two manors—was given by William the Conqueror
to the Bishop of Coutance.   In the reign of Henry
III. it was the property of the Bayeaux family,
through whom it came to the Rodneys, who held it
until 1590, when it was divided into a number of
estates.   In 1318, the church, valued at six marks,
was given to the nuns of Kington St. Michael, the
vicar being bound to pay the prioress 100 shillings
yearly, and as often as he failed in his payment he
was fined a mark towards the building of the Abbey
of Bath.   This deed, dated Evercreech, 1st August,
1242, is preserved in the registry of Wells.   The
nuns of Barrow had also a pension of two marks

from the rectory. The Rev. George Buckle, Prebendary of Wells, and Rural Dean, was appointed to the vicarage in 1852, and resigned it in 1875, on his appointment to the important incumbency of Weston-super-Mare.

Of the earlier 𝕮𝖍𝖚𝖗𝖈𝖍, which is dedicated to St. Michael, the font and tower alone remain; the former is Norman and octagonal, the latter embattled, and of the later perpendicular period. It contains six bells. The body of the church was rebuilt in 1839, after a design by Mr. Manners. The inscription—

"THIS IS NONE OTHER BUT THE HOUSE OF GOD ;
AND THIS IS THE GATE OF HEAVEN."

is of modern date.

Near the church are the celebrated Woollen Factories of Messrs. Carr, representing nearly all that is left of the ancient cloth manufacture at Bath, once celebrated throughout the world. For sometime after the Reformation, the prosperity of the city mainly depended upon it ; and at the restoration of King Charles II. there were no less than thirty-six looms at work in St. Michael's alone.

The increase of this now populous village may be gathered from Collinson, whose work was published in 1790. He says, " The village consists of one street half-a-mile in length ; the first house on the right was the residence of Henry Fielding when he wrote 'Tom Jones.'"* It stands at the east end of

* In his dedication Fielding says he has " endeavoured to laugh mankind out of their favourite follies and vices."

the village, and is but a poor dwelling, amid squalid surroundings. A crest still rests on a slab of stone over the doorway, but it may fairly be questioned whether the next neighbour knows even the name of the man who was once the cynosure of fashionable eyes.

Here too, is the City Prison, an establishment where a most efficient system of discipline is enforced. The present governor, Major Preston, is an officer of much firmness and judgment, combined with a judicious and admirable temper.

Rows of new houses are continually rising at the east end of the village in such numbers as threaten, before long, to unite it to Bath. To meet the religious wants of the increasing population, a plain building has been erected under the superintendance of Mr. C. E. Davis, which is intended to answer the double purpose of a Church and School; and another church is likely to be erected to meet the growing wants of the parish.

The eastern portion of the parish now constitutes a part of the Parliamentary Borough of Bath, under the Act of 1867.

Twerton is in the hundred of Wellow and Union of Bath. The population is 3,012; the area 971 statute acres; the rateable value, as supplied by the Union Assessment Committee, is £11,731; the poor rates, which were £306 before the Union, are now £949.

𝕿𝖍𝖊 𝕸𝖎𝖑𝖎𝖙𝖎𝖆 𝕭𝖆𝖗𝖗𝖆𝖈𝖐𝖘, the depôt and staff quarters of the Second Somerset Militia, adjoin the Cemetery.

The 𝕷𝖞𝖓𝖈𝖔𝖒𝖇𝖊, 𝖂𝖎𝖉𝖈𝖔𝖒𝖇𝖊 𝖆𝖓𝖉 𝕾. 𝕵𝖆𝖒𝖊𝖘'𝖘 𝕮𝖊𝖒𝖊𝖙𝖊𝖗𝖞, for the accommodation of the above united parishes,* was built from the designs of Mr. C. E. Davis, architect, and consecrated in 1862. It was laid out by Mr. Butler, and occupies an area of eight acres, part of which is appropriated to the use of Non-conformists.

We may return to Bath over the Victoria Suspension Bridge—a novelty in its time, — the principle of which is now, however, generally followed in all similar structures; or, we may cross the bridge of the Midland Railway Company, near the Station.

* A curious result of this arrangement occurred some years ago : a funeral from two of these parishes took place, and one clergyman discharged the two-fold duty. To economise time, and, presumably, trouble, he stood midway between the graves, and turning to each, alternately, shouted a sentence first to one and then to the other, with an effect infinitely more ludicrous than edifying. We have heard of political economy ; household economy, and other economies ; we should not like to give a name to this kind of economy.

IN AND OUT OF BATH.

———o○⟩⟨○○———

ENGLISHCOMBE.

CROSSING the Old Bridge and following the
Wells Road for something less than half a mile,
we turn into a lane on the right, and passing down
a narrow foot-path, enter the fields which lead direct
to the village of Englishcombe.

This name has been an unnecessary puzzle
to the antiquary, for a more perfect English
valley, could scarcely be found. Will the reader
accept the solution?* The manor was given to
the Bishop of Coutance at the Conquest, the
Saxon thane in occupation receiving a peremptory
notice to quit. It was then worth £10, having six
ploughs, two mills, twelve acres of meadow, one

* More natural than true, perhaps.

hundred acres of coppice wood, ten carucates of arable land, and three carucates in demesne. In the reign of King John, it was in the possession of the powerful family of De Gournay, one of whom made his youngest son heir, on the singular tenure of twelve cross-bow shots annually. Here stood one of their baronial castles; but Sir Thomas de Gournay being attainted for the murder of King Edward II., Englishcombe, with his other estates, was confiscated and bestowed on the Duchy of Cornwall, the Prince of Wales, in right of the said Duchy, being lord of the manor.

The Church is pleasantly situated on the brow of a hill, and presents a contrast to those which we have lately described, in having a central embattled tower, with pinnacles. The font is Norman, and square. On the north side of the tower, which contains five bells, are two finely preserved zigzag arches. The west window is of the decorated period, and contains stained glass. There are four shields in the mouldings : one of the Abbey of Bath ; another depicting a bugle horn ; the third a bow ; and the fourth a quiver of arrows. In the porch is a small decorated canopy, and near the altar a piscina. The south chapel has a square-headed decorated window, and on the wall between it and the nave is the figure of an angel supporting a coat-of-arms. Above is a window divided into two compartments, which contains some ancient stained glass. The church was thoroughly repaired in 1840, when sixty additional sittings were obtained. In the

graveyard is a decaying recumbent effigy, which
probably once occupied an altar-tomb in the chapel.
The Rev. C. Lloyd is the vicar.

Of the 𝕮𝖆𝖘𝖙𝖑𝖊 nothing remains except some
grassy mounds and the fosse in a field called *Culver-
hays.* Some years since, a large maple tree, which
stood on the spot, was cut down, under the idea that
treasure was concealed beneath it. Nothing, however,
but an ancient wall rewarded the search. The view
from the mound is very picturesque.

The 𝕸𝖆𝖓𝖔𝖗 𝕳𝖔𝖚𝖘𝖊 exists much in the same state
as when the unfortunate duke of Monmouth passed
through the village to Philip's Norton, from his
bivouac on Barrow Hill. The doorway, anciently
fastened with a strong bar of wood, has a small
window on either side, intended, perhaps, to guard
against surprise.

The 𝕽𝖊𝖈𝖙𝖔𝖗𝖎𝖆𝖑 𝕭𝖆𝖗𝖓, built out of the ruins of the
castle, is a fine example of the Gothic granaries of
the later period. A venerable pear tree is trained
against its buttresses; and in a hedge behind the
barn is a natural curiosity—two ancient yew trees,
which have grown together in the form of a lancet
arch.

In the orchard, near the church, the 𝖂𝖆𝖓𝖘𝖉𝖞𝖐𝖊
may be seen, and in the pasture lands, westward, it
exists in its pristine condition, namely, a long mound,
with a ditch on either side, varying in height from
nine to twelve feet. Few objects of antiquarian
research have caused more surmises than the

Wansdyke. In turn attributed to the Britons, Romans, and Saxons, it was probably an old Celtic boundary anterior to the irruption of the Belgæ. Throughout its course, from the Thames to the Severn, vestiges of it remain. Too feeble for an intrenchment in a thinly inhabited country, it was sufficiently durable as a landmark. Here and there, as at Avebury, in Wiltshire, it assumes the appearance of a fortification, but in every other portion of its course it could have answered no such purpose. Extending nearly in a direct line from the Thames, it enters Wiltshire at Great Bedwin, passing through Savernake Forest, and over Marlborough Downs by Calstone, Heddington, and Spye Park. It reaches the Avon at Benacre, traverses the fields, meets the river again at Bathampton, crosses Claverton Down, Prior Park, and Englishcombe, and passing Stantonbury Camp, through Publow to Maes Knoll, runs over Highbridge Common to the ancient haven of Portishead on the Severn.

𝕰𝖓𝖌𝖑𝖎𝖘𝖍𝖈𝖔𝖒𝖇𝖊 𝕭𝖆𝖗𝖗𝖔𝖜, half a mile from the village, is a remarkable mound. At the base it is 800 yards in circumference; the summit is 36 yards in diameter; the eastward slope is 104 yards and the perpendicular height 100 feet. Conjecture has sought in vain for the origin of this immense artificial mound. That it is so, all antiquarians agree, for its form and aspect differ materially from those of the neighbouring hills. From the summit is obtained a magnificent panoramic view of the vale of the Avon, embracing Bath and its suburbs, the Wiltshire and Gloucestershire hills, the Severn and the Welsh mountains.

The parish is in the hundred of Wellow and Union of Bath. The population, in 1871, was 533; the area is 1,852 statute acres, and the rateable value for apportioning Union expenses is £3,432.

Returning, we may follow the lane to the Wells Road, or cross the fields to Twerton. In either case the walk is very agreeable.

IN AND OUT OF BATH.

WALK THE TWELFTH.

Sion Hill—The Parry Family—a Group of Artists; Lansdown Crescent—J. H. Markland; Charlcombe; Royal School; Wesleyan College.

THE higher part of the city may be reached by Cavendish Place and Cavendish Crescent, to the north of which is Somerset Place, and to the west

SION HILL.

Summerhill, the residence of Robert Stickney Blaine, Esq., J.P., and formerly Mayor of the city, is a handsome house, built early in the present century, by Caleb Hillier Parry,* M.D., author of "The Elements of Pathology and Therapeutics." He was descended from a Pembrokeshire family, and was born on the 21st of October, 1755. In 1773, he went to Edinburgh, where he studied his profession. In 1775, he became a pupil of Dr. Denman, father of the first Lord Denman. In 1777 he returned to Edinburgh, took his degree, and subse-

* His father, Joshua Parry, whose memoirs were edited by Sir J. Eardley Wilmot, Bart., and published in 1872, was for many years Unitarian minister at Cirencester.

quently became president of the Royal Medical Society, the charter for which he was chiefly instrumental in obtaining.

Dr. Parry settled in this city in 1779, and soon took the commanding position among his cotemporaries to which his talents and acquirements entitled him.   He was a musician, poet, and painter; a correspondent of Burke and Wyndham on political subjects, and in various publications distinguished himself by his practical knowledge of agriculture. Dr. Parry devoted much attention to his merino flock, and succeeded in improving the texture of wools.   He was the friend and correspondent of Herschel and Dr. Jenner.   He read much, was a good mathematician, and a ripe scholar, and so greatly was he respected, that, on his death, he was followed to the grave by his friends and fellow-practitioners, who erected a tablet to his memory, in the Bath Abbey.

Dr. Parry was the father of the distinguished arctic navigator, Sir Edward Parry,* and also of Dr. Charles Henry Parry, who lived and practised for many years in the Circus.   The latter compiled a work of much research on "The Parliaments and Councils of England."

Dr. C. H. Parry, sometime before his death, presented the library collected by his father, to the Royal United Hospital.

* Sir Edward had two sons, Capt. Parry, R.N., the biographer of his father; and the present Dr. Parry, Suffragan Bishop of Dover.

At the south-east corner of Sion Hill stands 𝔇𝔬𝔯𝔦𝔠 𝔥𝔬𝔲𝔰𝔢, once the residence of 𝔗𝔥𝔬𝔪𝔞𝔰 𝔅𝔞𝔯𝔨𝔢𝔯, the painter, a man of precocious genius and considerable originality. His earliest success, it may be said, was, to a great extent, the barrier to his subsequent progress. In early youth he produced "The Woodman,"* a picture which astonished the cognoscenti of the city. This early successful effort was the theme of exaggerated praise, which, it is said, was not without the usual effect. Sir E. Harington, son of Dr. Henry Harington, wrote a pamphlet in praise of this work, entitled " A Schizzo on the Genius of Man," 8vo., 1793. It was natural that Barker's subsequent efforts should be estimated by the standard of his early work, and the comparison was generally to his disadvantage. An artist who produces his *chef d'œuvre* in youth, commits, practically, professional suicide.

Mr. Spackman, a coach builder, of Bath, and a man of artistic taste, conceived a warm friendship for the clever young painter, improved his education, and instructed him in the elements of his art. Mr. Spackman then sent his *protégé* to Rome, where he applied himself diligently to the

* Macklin, the celebrated Art Publisher, first purchased this picture, which he engraved. Afterwards Boydell bought it for, it is said, £735. It is now, we believe, in the South Kensington Museum.

A very fine copy of the picture, on a smaller scale, by Mr. Barker, was purchased at the sale of the late Mr. Charles Empson's collection, by D. Michael, Esq., and is now in that gentleman's possession. There are other copies in existence.

study of his profession. On returning to England he took the house above mentioned, adding to it a Picture Gallery, the walls of which he adorned with a fresco—"The Massacre of the Sciotes," a work as remarkable for originality of conception and brilliancy of execution, as for apparent durability. Mr. Barker, in this respect, claimed to have re-discovered a partially lost art, and his work, despite the fact that it has been covered by a film of varnish, at present exhibits, so far as colouring is concerned, all its pristine freshness. It is a subject of some interest at the present time to know that the success of Barker in this peculiar style of art, led to his being consulted when it was proposed to adorn the Houses of Parliament with frescoes. It may be assumed that if Barker imparted a full knowledge of the process which he himself adopted, it was disregarded, when we bear in mind the condition of several of the frescoes now on the walls of the Westminster Palace.

Barker produced a large number of paintings, but none so popular as the "Woodman," and often displayed symptoms of disappointment and impatience at the neglect he experienced, and that want of appreciation of his works which he felt conscious they deserved. He was a man of quick intelligence, a brilliant talker, and an excellent scholar.

Since Mr. Barker's death in 1842, a more just estimate has been formed of his genius and paintings, and his best examples are being sought with avidity by collectors. The late Sir W. S. R. Cockburn, at the time of his death, possessed many of the artist's best works.* Barker's figures in etching are very interesting, though they bear no comparison with the etchings of the present day, more especially with those of the French School which, in this branch of art, has attained great perfection.

Benjamin Barker was the younger brother of Thos. Barker. He, too, was an artist, less ambitious and less distinguished than his brother, but a successful man. His subjects, chiefly landscapes, were much admired and sought after. Many of his sketches of Wick, and Hampton Down, &c., were reproduced in sepia and are indeed charming. Mr. B. Barker lived on Bathwick Hill, in a villa now called "Oakwood." Mr. Britton says, "At this delectable retreat I spent màny happy hours in company with some of the Bath 'Worthies', amongst whom was James Hewlett," a distinguished English flower painter, whose sister Barker married. Barker was born in 1776, and settled in Bath about 1807. His later days were clouded by pecuniary losses.

* The Life of Mr. Barker is still to be written. Materials for such a biography were collected by Mr. Barker's son, Mr. Thomas Jones Barker, and Mr. V. Irving, but the promise has never been fulfilled. The design has not been abandoned altogether, as we know that some of the materials are in the hands of Mr. Harrison Barker, a grandson, who proposes to write and publish such a book in quarto form, if adequately encouraged in the undertaking.

The productions of **Hewlett** were much and justly admired. In and before his day they had scarcely been surpassed. In this branch of art however, great advances have been made, and Bath can claim many eminent professors. Hewlett's works bear no comparison with those of the late Mr. G. Rosenberg or his sister, the late Mrs. J. D. Harris, whether in drawing, grouping, artistic grace, or colouring. Both these distinguished artists are no more, but their genius. lives in the bright creations of their pencils. During visits paid by Mr. Rosenberg to Norway, he made some drawings of the mountain scenery of that country, in which he displays the versatility of his artistic ability. The mountains of Norway, in summer, are described as unlike the mountains of any other country, in their glowing tints; and these he most successfully depicted, having invested the scenes with unusual interest and beauty. We have to regret the loss of two such artists, who possessed, what Carlyle calls genius, namely, an infinite capacity for taking pains. Mrs. Duffield—a Rosenberg by birth also—is a lady gifted with faculties of no ordinary character. She married the late Mr. Duffield, and, together with her husband, pursued her profession in Bath, and subsequently in London, with pre-eminent·success. At the time in which we write, this accomplished artist is unrivalled as a Flower Painter. Mr. Duffield was the pupil and friend of Lance, and it is no disparagement of the latter to say that in "still-life" Mr. Duffield scarcely suffers by comparison with his great master. Mr. Duffield's landscapes likewise are very fine. He died early—too early for art, but not before he had achieved enduring celebrity.

Lansdown Crescent, erected towards the close of the last century, was then called Spackman's Buildings, after the friend and patron of Thomas Barker. It boasts a suburban view rarely equalled, and still more rarely surpassed.

James Heywood Markland, F.S.A., F.R.S., D.C.L., and member of the Roxburgh Club, was a native of Ardwick Green, Manchester, was educated for the legal profession, and practised for some years as a solicitor in London. An ardent student of archæology, topography, and other kindred sciences, in early life he contributed several articles for Britton's work on the Beauties of England, as well as to the Architectural Antiquities. He also wrote various papers for the Society of Antiquaries. On his retirement from practice, he resided at No. 1, Lansdown Crescent, where he collected a very fine library of topographical, antiquarian, and theological works. Mr. Markland was generally regarded as an accurate and industrious compiler, but not a profound scholar. He wrote and published, during his residence in Bath, "Memorials of English Churches," a valuable contribution towards the revival of a more earnest interest in the monuments and antiquities of our churches. This was followed by another *brochure* on a kindred subject, entitled, "On the Reverence due to Holy Places;" he also edited an edition of Bishop Ken's admirable little book, "Prayers for the Use of the Sick." In addition to this, he was an occasional contributor to the *Oxford Archæological Journal.* Mr. Markland was an ardent High Churchman, and took a very keen interest in all the theological discussions and controversies of the day. He was an active member of many of the benevolent societies and institutions in the city, and was one of the founders of the Literary Club. Mr. Markland married a daughter of the late Sir F. Freeling, Bart., by whom he had one daughter. He died in 1865.

Immediately below Lansdown Crescent is 𝔄𝔩𝔩 𝔖𝔞𝔦𝔫𝔱𝔰' 𝔠𝔥𝔞𝔭𝔢𝔩, opened in 1794. It was erected from a plan by Mr. Palmer.

CHARLCOMBE,

WHICH lies in a valley east of Lansdown, belonged to the Abbey of Bath from immemorial time. In the Confessor's reign, the manor was worth fifty shillings. At the Conquest, William Hosate held it, when it was worth £6. There is an agreement extant between him and the convent, of which Collinson gives the following translation:—

"*In this writing is declared the agreement which William Hosate hath made with the abbot Ulfwold, the abbot Ælfrig, and the whole convent of Bath concerning the land of* CEORLCUMB; *that is to say,*

they have delivered into his hands the said land, with
ten oxen and sixty sheep, with an acre for sowing, on
condition that he pay the monastery every year £2
rent, and that he go to the king's bank, and pay tallage
to the king. This is done on condition that he be
faithful and obedient to each abbot, and all the brethren,
in all things; and if he shall violate the trust which
he hath pledged, he shall forfeit the land, and be cursed
by Christ, Saint Mary and Saint Peter, to whom this
monastery is dedicated."

The manor remained in the hands of the clergy
until the Reformation, and the church patronage
continued in the hands of the lord of the manor until
the Rev. Walter Robins annexed it to the Bath
Grammar School. The benefice is now in private
patronage, having been separated from the Grammar
School, by the Endowed School Commissioners.
Vide p. 65.

The 𝕮𝖍𝖚𝖗𝖈𝖍, which is dedicated to St. Mary, consists of nave, chancel, and south porch. It presents
marks of high antiquity, and was thoroughly repaired prior to the Reformation. The extreme
length is about 51 feet, and the width 21 feet. It
has 90 sittings, which are free. The present structure is mostly of the perpendicular work, with some
remains of earlier work in the tower-arch and chancel-
arch. There is a north doorway of Norman character,
which is now blocked up. The porch also, is of early
character, and the south door is supposed to be a
modern restoration of the old Norman door. The

font is of a cylindrical bowl-shaped form, and Norman in character, with a carved band of lilies round it.   Near the altar is a monument, by Ford, of Bath, to Lady Barbara Montague, who died in the year 1766.   There is a small bell tower at the west end, six feet square, corbelled out from the wall.

CHARLCOMBE CHURCH.

Originally it contained two bells, but only one now remains.   The church was restored a few years ago, when the chancel walls, and part of the south wall of the nave, were re-built, a new roof put on the nave, and the area re-seated.   The circular pulpit is of stone. The windows, with but one exception, are filled with stained glass, illustrating subjects from the life and miracles of our Lord. There is also a carved stone reredos, containing the symbols of the four Evangelists, Agnus Dei, &c. On the west side of the porch is a venerable yew tree. The churchyard is well kept. In it there are several monuments of good design, and many of the graves are planted with choice flowers. The Rev. E. T. Stubbs is the present Rector.

Though the road tempts us onward, it will be convenient to turn our steps once more towards the city; but before doing so, the stranger should pause a moment to gaze at one of the sweetest suburban views with which we are acquainted. On the right, is a green and quiet valley; on the left, a lofty and abrupt hill; before, a pleasant lane; beyond, the valley of the Avon, winding eastward; around, hills of many a shape and hue, while here and there a church tower tells of the neighbouring town, and serves to make nature all the sweeter from the contrast.

Retracing the Charlcombe Lane until it meets the Lansdown Road, we turn to the left, and find ourselves in front of The Royal School. The following is an abstract of the general rules. The daughters of all Officers in Her Majesty's Army, inclusive of Royal Marines, are eligible. Claims are founded on the services of the father and the pecuniary circumstances of the family. The ages of admission

are from ten to fifteen. No pupil can remain after
the age of eighteen, unless under special circumstances. Elections take place in June and December.
Pupils elected by the votes of Subscribers pay £12 per
annum. Those elected by the Committee pay £27
per annum and no extras. Patron, Her Majesty
the Queen. President, Field-Marshal H.R.H. the
Duke of Cambridge.

On the west side of the road are a large number
of villas, and as the south slopes of Lansdown offer
admirable sites for houses of this sort, it is probable
that at no distant date " Upper Lansdown" will become one of the most fashionable suburbs of the city.

Charlcombe is in the Bath Union, and contains
an area of 571 acres. The population, in 1791, was
50, and in 1871, was 577. In 1770 the poor rates
were £22, and now average £330 per annum.

The Wesleyan College, called New Kingswood
—in perpetuation of the name of the place where it
was originally founded by the late John Wesley, the
apostle of Methodism—stands on the brow of Lansdown, and is a handsome edifice, in the style peculiar
to the Tudor period. It was erected from the design
of Mr. James Wilson, and consists of a centre,
containing a dining hall; a west wing, school-
rooms, and other offices; the chapel, with the
governor's house, occupies the east wing.

IN AND OUT OF BATH.

WALK THE THIRTEENTH.

St. Stephen's Church; Christ Church; St. James's Square, Anstey; St. Andrew's Church; The Royal Crescent; Catherine Place— Haynes Bayly—W. S. Landor; Brock Street —Skating Rink; Assembly Rooms; Circus— Somersetshire College — The Falconer Family—Gainsborough; Gay Street—Mrs. Piozzi; Milsom Street—Octagon Chapel.

ON the east side of Lansdown Road stands 𝕾𝕥. 𝕾𝕥𝕖𝕡𝕙𝕖𝕟'𝕤 𝕮𝕙𝕦𝕣𝕔𝕙, at present a chapel-of-ease to Walcot. The style is Decorated, and the design cruciform. The tower is 120 feet high, and at its basement is a massive door-way which practically forms a porch. The east window is of stained glass, and in the western transept there is a font of florid Gothic, the gift of the Pindar family. The architect of the church is Mr. James Wilson, F.S.A. Situated on a lofty and commanding eminence St. Stephen's forms a striking object whether seen from the city or the adjacent hills.

𝕮𝖍𝖗𝖎𝖘𝖙 𝕮𝖍𝖚𝖗𝖈𝖍, which stands at the east end of Montpellier, was erected in 1798 through the exertions of the late Archdeacon Daubeny, and was chiefly designed for the accomodation of the poor. Within the last few years a chancel has been added to the building.   The joint incumbents are the Rev. James Wood, rural dean, and the Rev. J. H. Way.

𝕾𝖙. 𝕵𝖆𝖒𝖊𝖘'𝖘 𝕾𝖖𝖚𝖆𝖗𝖊 occupies what was once the poet Anstey's garden.*   He at one time resided in

* Christopher Anstey born in 1724, was educated at Eton and Cambridge.   He resided afterwards chiefly in this city.   About 1766 he published his famous satire "The New Bath Guide," which obtained immense popularity, and passed through many editions.   In 1830 the late Mr. Britton published an annotated edition, illustrated by Cruikshank and Williams.   The satire is directed against the peculiar phases of society which prevailed at the period, and in certain parts, especially those relating to the then new sect of methodists, is not only harsh and unjust, but coarse and indelicate.   Anstey was the writer of many other poems—the "Election Ball" &c. &c. which in 1808 were collected, and, with the "Guide," published, with a biographical essay by the Poet's son, in a bulky quarto volume.   "Doctor Bongout" and "The Priest Dissected" are not, for obvious reasons, included in the volume.   The former was never acknowledged by Mr. Anstey, but there is little or no doubt as to the authorship; while the latter appeared with Anstey's usual imprimatur. It virulently assails a clergyman for an alleged attack upon Anstey, who, after a few copies were issued, discovered that he had been misinformed, and suppressed the poem, which is, therefore, exceedingly scarce.

Some of Anstey's works, as already remarked, are disfigured by grossness and impurity, and these qualities excite the more surprise and regret, when we turn to his exquisite paraphrase of the 13th chapter of St. Paul's First Epistle to the Corinthians —on Charity, from which we quote the concluding verse.   The

the Royal Crescent. In 1790 he received notice to quit, in consequence of its being required for building ground, upon which occasion he wrote the following epigram :—

"Ye men of Bath, who stately mansions rear,
To wait for tenants from—the Lord knows where,
Would you pursue a plan that cannot fail,
Erect a madhouse and enlarge your gaol ?"

It happened that, at this period, the doors of the gaol were open, there being no prisoners, and he

poem in beauty of diction and felicitous versification is comparable with the best of Pope's compositions.

Whilst in these gloomy vales of life we stray,
Hope cheers our souls, and Faith directs our way ;
But when to yon bright realms of joy we soar,
Faith shall expire, and Hope be known no more :
Faith shall be lost in certainty's abyss,
And Hope absorbed in everlasting Bliss ;
But Thee, thou fairest Grace, nor death, nor doom,
Nor ever-rolling ages shall consume,
Thou with congenial spirits mix'd above
Shall fill all Heaven with Harmony and Love,
In splendor seen, and full perfection known
Thy station fix by God's eternal throne ;
There with compassion all our errors scan,
And plead the cause of frail and sinful man.

Anstey was not the only satirist who found scope for the play of his wit and trenchant humour. Fielding in "Tom Jones" and Smollett in "Humphrey Clinker" had ample materials on which to exercise the rich exuberance of their inimitable fancy and satire in the many salient points of intrigue, gambling, folly, and fashionable frivolity which characterized a large class of the community. Anstey died in 1805, and was buried in Walcot churchyard. A tablet is raised in the church to his memory. He is honoured also with a tablet in Westminster Abbey. Miss Austen, Miss Burney (Madame D'Arblay), and other writers represent another and a purer phase of society.

U

was thus answered :—

> "While crowds arrive, fast as our streets increase,
>   And the gaol only is an empty space ;
>   While health and ease here court the grave and gay,
>   Madmen and fools alone will keep away."

The beech trees, of which the poet was particularly fond, were transplanted to Mr. Wiltshire's grounds at Shockerwick.

St. Andrew's Church is situated at the west end of Rivers Street, upon a site long since destined for the purpose, as appears from an original map of the locality preserved among the papers of the Rivers' Estate. The design, however, was never carried out. The reserved piece of land was occupied by Harley House ; and the name of "Upper Church Street," remained as the only record of an abandoned intention. Private speculation supplied its place by a Proprietary Chapel, and about a hundred years passed by. This unseemly provision for public worship in the finest quarter of the city could then be no longer tolerated, and an appeal, made by the Rector of Walcot, the Rev. T. D. Bernard, received an immediate and encouraging response. The site was purchased for £2,670, and the first stone was laid by the Bishop of Bath and Wells (Lord Arthur Hervey) April 26, 1870. The building proceeded gradually as the funds were supplied, and was consecrated by the same Bishop, September 11, 1873.

The Church is built in the Early English Style, from the designs of Sir G. Gilbert Scott, and its details were carefully superintended by his son, Mr. John Scott; Mr. Bladwell was contractor for the work. The design includes a lofty spire, which, whenever it is erected, will be a great ornament to this quarter of the city. A separate fund has been commenced for completing the tower, which as yet, is only raised to the height of the nave roof.

The Church, consisting of a nave and two side aisles, a chancel and chancel aisle, organ chamber, and vestry, affords accommodation for above 1,000 worshippers. Its internal proportions are remarkably good, and give an impression of spaciousness and dignity. The reredos, the pulpit, and the font—all of alabaster and marble—are gifts from members of the congregation. The church contains no great amount of ornament, but what there is, is well executed. The internal carving is by Messrs. Brindley and Farmer, of London : the external carving is not yet completed. The organ is a fine-toned instrument, built by Messrs. Bryceson, of London, at an expense of about £600. The erection of the church, including the purchase of site, has, up to the present time, cost nearly £18,000, which (with the exception of £300 from the Diocesan Society) has been entirely supplied by voluntary contributions, chiefly from the members of the congregation themselves, none of the common contrivances for raising money having been resorted to.

The present legal status of the church is only that of a chapel-of-ease, but with all the privileges of a parish, in the administration of baptisms, the performance of marriages, &c.

The **Royal Crescent** is a splendid row of thirty houses, of the Ionic order, erected in 1769, by the younger Wood. The façades, which terminate it at either end, are very imposing. Madame D'Arblay spoke of it as adding " all the delights of nature which beautify the Parades to the excellences of architecture which adorn the Circus"—a high sounding panegyric with very little meaning.

The satirist praises it in verse with more point and humour, but praises it, as will presently be seen, at the expense of its neighbour, the Circus :—

> " Not thus the *Crescent* towers thro' the air,
>   The proud Ionic reigns unrivall'd there ;
>   Her pedestals are eas'd of half their trouble,
>   Like gen'rous steeds, unfit to carry double."

About a hundred yards to the north of Brock Street, lies Catherine Place. Here—something more than fifty years ago—resided Thomas Haynes Bayly, a man whose name was once a household word in half the upper and middle-class homes of England. As a writer of drawing-room songs, and as a literary pioneer in the then untrodden regions of *vers de société*, his popularity was considerable. These songs are of unequal merit, some being felicitous specimens of the modern ballad, while others are without literary merit.

No uncommon sight in the streets of Bath, a few years ago, was the figure of a man, whose name has been in many mouths, but more for blame than praise. A scholar, a poet, a gallant of many amours, a politician of the advanced type, a sympathiser with the French Revolution, and above all, a man of a violent temper—such were the characters under which 𝔚𝔞𝔩𝔱𝔢𝔯 𝔖𝔞𝔟𝔞𝔤𝔢 𝔏𝔞𝔫𝔡𝔬𝔯 figured in polite society. There are some curious stories told about his early years. Men rumoured that he had been expelled from school for thrashing the head-master, with whom he had quarrelled about a quantity in Latin verse, and that he had been ex-pelled from his University for shooting at a Fellow of a College. These stories found others to match them, when Landor passed from Bath to Wales, and from Wales to Florence. He had been out-lawed from England for knocking down a barrister, who had cross - examined him. He promised the authorities of Como a "bella bastonata:" and challenged the Secretary of the Legation at Florence for whistling in the streets when Mrs. Landor passed. Such were the stories told, some of them with a foundation of truth, others with none at all, but yet aptly representing the wild ex-travagance and impetuosity of Landor's career.

His character combined all the contradictions and inconsistencies which men of genius so often display, who dim their brilliant ability by deficient human sympathies, and mar the perfection of their literary gifts by the obvious imperfection of their lives. Those who met him in the streets, wondered at the

man, who could gambol down Catherine Place with
his dog, Pomero—the "mi Pomero," the "caro
figlio," to which he gave the warm-hearted tribute
on his tomb :—

> "Hoc intus est fidele ; nam cor est canis."

Those who met him in society, knew him as one
whose laugh was perfectly "leonine," a kind of
crescendo of roars, mixed with the barking of his dog:
as one, who though he used to frequent "balls, routs
and parties," was singularly annoyed at his inferiority
in dancing ; or, perhaps, as one who was no sooner
out of one "amour" than he tumbled into another ;
a man perpetually quarrelling with any person from
whom he had received some real or imaginary
affront.

So much the outside of the man revealed. It was
those alone who knew him better or saw deeper into
his character, who realised the tenderness with
which he could bend over his flowers :—

> "I never pluck the rose ; the violet's head
> Hath shaken with my breath upon its bank
> And not reproached me : the ever-sacred cup
> Of the pure lily hath between my hands
> Felt safe, unsoiled, nor lost one grain of gold."

Only those who study his character can connect
with it the acute sense of pain with which he
regarded the sufferings of an animal. "What
that bird must have suffered," he said, when
having shot a partridge one winter afternoon, he
found it alive the following morning, "I often

think of its look." Or his genuine affection to his
mother : "The misery of not being able to see you,
is by far the greatest I have ever suffered. Never
shall I forget the thousand acts of kindness and
affection I have received from you from my earliest
to my latest days." Or his intense love of his
children. "This is the first time I was ever a whole
day without seeing Arnold (his son). He is of all
living creatures the most engaging. What a pity it is
that such divine creatures should ever be men, and
subject to regrets and sorrows." It was no common
attachment to him which could make his scholar-
friend, Dr. Parr, leave his guests at a dinner table,
to ride over to Warwick to see him; or Southey,
when every other name was a blank in his memory,
repeat softly, over and over again, "Landor, my
Landor;" or Archdeacon Hare, two days before
his death, whisper "Dear Landor, I hope we shall
meet once more." It is necessary to bear these facts
in mind when passing judgment on this singular
man, in order to qualify the attributes of "unsocial,
quarrelsome, misanthropic," so generally applied to
him. There were many reasons why such epithets
were deserved. To the ordinary observer they gave
the whole truth about him. But, like all men
of strong unregulated feelings, and clear critical
minds, there was a double character within him.
Merciless criticism of himself was combined with
headlong indulgence, and at times, Landor could
see his own mistakes as clearly as the most severe

of his contemporary judges. "I do not say I shall never be happy;" he says, "I shall be often so if I live, but I shall never be at rest. My evil genius dogs me through existence, against the current of my best inclinations. I have practised self-denial, because it gives me a momentary and false idea that I am firm; and I have done other things not amiss in compliance with my heart; but my most virtuous hopes and sentiments have uniformly led to misery, and I have never been happy, but in consequence of some weakness or vice." No judgment could be harsher than this. A friendly critic says of him: "He worked hard, and with tools of his own invention and fashioning; he whistled off ten thousand strong and importunate temptations—he dashed the dice-box from the jewelled hand of Chance, the cup from Pleasure's, and trod under foot the sorceries of each: he ascended steadily the precipices of danger, and looked down with intrepidity from the summit; he overcame arrogance with sedateness; he seized by the horn and overleaped low violence, and he fairly swung fortune round. This is not the doctrine," he continues, "of the silkenly and lawnly religious; it wears the coarse texture of the fisherman, and walks uprightly and straightforwardly under it."

The facts of his life may be told in few words. He was born in 1775, of an old Staffordshire race, which became united, when his father married his mother, with the Savages of Warwickshire. Passing his school-boy life at Rugby, he entered Trinity College, Oxford, in 1793, which he left without taking his degree. Then, for some three years, he resided at Tenby and Swansea, where he published his first long poem, entitled "Gebir." In 1805, began his first residency in Bath, broken by his Spanish enthusiasm which led him to serve as a volunteer in the Peninsular rising in 1808. In 1811 he married a lady, named Thuillier, as he describes her, "without a sixpence, and with few accomplishments: but pretty, graceful and good tempered: one who has no pretensions of any kind, and whose want of fortune was the very thing which determined me to marry her." Not much happiness, however, resulted from this union, and it is hardly to be wondered that his character was almost incomprehensible to his wife.

After a brief experience of country life at Llanthony, in Monmouthshire, Landor resided at Como, at Pisa, and Florence. In 1832, we find him again in England, and from 1836 principally in Bath,* which he left in 1858 to spend the remainder of his life abroad. He died September 17, 1864, at Florence, an exile from his country.

His relations to contemporary politics are more noticeable for the asperity and bitterness which

* Landor loved Bath, praised Bath, with all the energy of his nature. There were but two places, he was accustomed to say, he could live in—Bath and Florence, and he loved Bath because it was so much like Florence, and Florence because it was so much like Bath.

he managed to throw into them, than for any real elements of his character thereby revealed, or any effect they had on the social state around him. His revolutionary sympathies of course incurred suspicion and hostility on all sides, which his own violence towards individual statesmen, greatly aggravated. His estimate of Mr. Fox was as follows :—"To the principles of a Frenchman, he added the habits of a Malay, in idleness, drunkenness and gaming; in middle life he was precisely the opposite of whoever was in power, until he could spring forward to the same station. Whenever Mr. Pitt was wrong, Mr. Fox was right, and then only." His bitter epitaph on Lord Eldon is as clever as it is scurrilous :—

OFFICIOSUS ERGA OMNES POTENTES PRÆTER DEUM
QUEM SATIS EI ERAT ADJURARE.

He went even so far as to defend tyrannicide, and offered a pension to the widow of any one who would murder a despot. Napoleon Bonaparte,* he first thought the incarnation of the republican spirit; then his opinion changed to one of intense personal animosity. "He has the fewest virtues," he said,

* During Louis Napoleon's nine months' residence in Bath he sedulously cultivated the old poet's friendship and intimacy, and partly succeeded in diminishing his antipathy to the Bonaparte dynasty; after the *coup d'etat* of December, Landor poured the full vials of his bitter indignation upon its author. Nothing could exceed the eloquent indignation with which he denounced his quondam friend. After 1852, Landor said, "Why did we not kill him when we had him here?"

"and the faintest semblances of them of any man that has risen by his own efforts to power."

It is not, however, as a political writer, but as a man who possessed literary abilities of the highest order, that the name of Walter Savage Landor is worthy of our reverence. His poetical writings, both in English and in Latin, reveal the delicacy and perfection of his work. He was a born scholar, one of those whose appreciation of form, apart from matter, and whose critical insight and intimate sympathy with the feelings and thoughts of a past stage of civilization, gave to all his work the finish, and subtilty, and grace, which we connect with a classical, rather than a scientific training. It was especially in Latin that he excelled, possessing a style peculiar to himself, unlike Catullus, Virgil, Ovid, or Horace, but one marked by his own idiosyncrasy, and his own talent. Greek he learnt later, but his rare powers of intellectual sympathy are never shewn to greater advantage than in his "Hellenica," and, above all, in his "Conversations between Pericles and Aspasia." His principal English works are the poem of "Gebir," produced in 1798; "The Tragedy of Count Julian," which was the outcome of his Spanish campaign; and "The Imaginary Conversations of Literary Men and Statesmen," on which he was engaged between 1820 and 1830. The judgment of Lord Houghton on his style is worth recording. "Abounding in strong, even passionate diction, it is never vague or convulsive; magnificent as declamation can demand, it is never pompous or turgid ; humourous throughout, it avoids contortion and abhors caricature. Its chief characteristic is self-command."

It would have been happier for Landor if this self-command had accompanied him into active life. But "antipathy was the presiding genius of his life," and the rough nobility of his mind brings this out into clearer relief. Such men, in the isolation of their self-sufficiency, must bear their burdens alone, untouched by the broader sympathies of humanity ; a high type of mankind they undoubtedly present, yet one which deserves our sincerest pity.

The character we have depicted is common. Given a strong and cultivated intellect and an eager but undisciplined nature, and the results may be foreseen. Possessed of such qualities their owner will almost inevitably make warm friends and bitter enemies. He plays however a losing game with time. As the noon of his life fades into evening, the night side of his nature deepens and darkens.   His power of attraction diminishes ; his force of repulsion increases ; friends of brighter days die off, or perhaps fall from him.   Foes accumulate.   Such a man realises the fable of "the scorpion girt by the fire," which, poetically at least, is said to turn its desperate sting into its own breast ; and so the end comes, in coldness and neglect; in bitterness and misanthropy. Such an end was that of Walter Savage Landor.

Landor, during his later residence in Bath, lived in Rivers Street.

Margaret's Chapel, in Brock Street, was opened by Dr. Dodd, of unhappy memory, in 1770. It has been recently converted into a Skating Rink, and is called 𝕸argaret's 𝕳all 𝕾kating 𝕽ink.

𝕿he 𝕬ssembly 𝕽ooms, situated between Alfred and Bennett Streets, are still among the finest suites of public rooms in the kingdom. They were erected in 1771, by the younger Wood, at an expense of £20,000, raised among seventy subscribers. The site, which is central and convenient, presented little temptation for external architectural display. Wood understood his business too well to make useless sacrifices, and bent his whole powers to render the interior arrangement what it has been pronounced to be, " simply perfect." After more than 100 years, these rooms maintain their supremacy in point of grace, design, and suitability to the purposes for which they were especially intended. In his " Historic Guide to Bath," Mr. Wright thus describes them :—

" These constitute the noblest suite of apartments of the class in England, whether we regard the simplicity and elegance of the design, the fullness of their convenience, or the taste employed in interior decorations. The ball room, 106 feet in length, is adorned with 40 columns and pilasters 12 feet high, with an entablature, curiously enriched, above which is a plinth, ornamented with a Vitruvian scroll, whence rises the cove 12 feet ; the soffit is divided into compartments, decorated with garlands, palm and laurel branches; the ceiling is also divided into a like number of panels, with embossed reeds, from which gaseliers are suspended. Thirteen windows admit sufficient light, opposite which are the orchestra and niches for figures.

"The octagon room has a diameter of 48 feet, and is finished in the manner of the ball room. In panels prepared for the purpose are the portraits of Captain Wade, by Gainsborough; of Nash and Heaviside, by Shaw; and of Tyson, by James. The concert or tea room is 60 feet long, 42 wide, and has a colonnade of the Ionic order, nearly 12 feet high, the entablature of which is continued round the room. These columns support a Corinthian colonnade, forming the orchestra, the same lighter order being carried all round, and consisting of thirty columns and pilasters, with festooned capitals; the entablature is in stucco; the line of the cove is received by a swelling soffit of laurel leaves and berries, continued from column to column, across and along the ceiling, forming a net work, embellished with garlands, vines, laurels, and wreaths of flowers. The whole of the apartments are of equal height, namely, 43 feet."*　　Mr. C. W. Oliver is the present lessee.†

* In 1708, Harrison built and conducted the Lower Assembly Rooms on the Walks; while Mrs. Linley, a celebrated singer, conducted a rival establishment in the immediate neighbourhood. Mrs. Hayes, who succeeded Harrison, made a large fortune, and married Lord Hawley. The Lower Rooms, with the exception of the portico, were destroyed by fire in 1820. The greater part of York Street is built on the site of Linley's Ball Rooms.

† A List of the M.C.'s is given in the Appendix.

In the year 1754, Wood laid out the ground for 𝕲𝖆𝖞 𝕾𝖙𝖗𝖊𝖊𝖙 and the 𝕮𝖎𝖗𝖈𝖚𝖘. The latter is a magnificent circle of houses, its stages being of the Doric, Ionic, and Corinthian orders, presenting, says Collinson, every ornament of each. The pillars of the principal story support a cornice decorated with a series of ornaments cut in stone. " It is worthy," says Smollett, " to be called the Cestus of Venus ;" and it has been compared to the Coliseum of Rome turned outside in. The late Sir John Soane, R.A., professor of architecture, in one of his lectures, in order to give an idea of the immense size of the Coliseum, had two models made, placing that of the Circus at Bath within the area of the latter. In its centre is a reservoir, which might with advantage be removed. At present the appearance of the enclosure is gloomy, and offers abundant room for improvement.

> " A *Circus* that three ranks of columns boasts,—
> Three ranks of columns, like three rows of posts ;
> Where none to dang'rous merit make pretence,
> Or seek a painful, sad pre-eminence.
> No kind pilaster at that giddy height
> Dispels our terror or relieves our sight,
> Because we're told ('tho different the name)
> That massive and majestic are the same."

The poet does not seem to have been impressed with the beauty of the building.

The 𝕾𝖔𝖒𝖊𝖗𝖘𝖊𝖙𝖘𝖍𝖎𝖗𝖊 𝕮𝖔𝖑𝖑𝖊𝖌𝖊 was instituted in the year 1858. Its objects, according to the terms of

its original prospectus, were to provide sons of
gentlemen with a liberal education in classics and
mathematics, as a preparation for the Universities,
and the Army—objects towards which it has directed
its attention up to the present time. With an average
of ninety boys, its successes since the year 1861
have been as follows :—

University Honours :—Three fellowships; nineteen open scholarships; twelve first classes; nineteen
second classes; three University prizes, together with
several College prizes and third classes.

Honours at Woolwich :—

Fourth, fifth, seventh, and thirty-third places
in Entrance Examination ; first commission Royal
Engineers; Pollock Medal and Regulation Sword;
seventh commission Royal Engineers; fifth commission Royal Artillery.

Also two admissions to the India Civil Service.

So large a percentage of success during so short
a period is due to many causes. The number of
masters in proportion to scholars is greater, probably,
than at any other school, there being at present no
less than twelve on the staff. This enables the
teacher to exercise a closer surveillance over each
individual pupil, and at the same time, enables him
to give greater attention to boys of promise. But
still more, perhaps, is due to the energy and con-
scientiousness of those to whom the college owes its
foundation, and especially to the Rev. Hay S. Escott,
the late head-master.

The present head-master is Mr. W. L. Courtney, M.A., late Fellow of Merton College, Oxford.

Among many distinguished men who have resided in the Circus may be mentioned William Falconer, M.D., F.R.S., and the Rev. Thomas Falconer, M.A. and M.D., both of whom lived and died at No. 29. William Falconer was the younger of the two surviving sons of William Falconer, Recorder of Chester, and nephew of Randle Wilbraham, Esq., an eminent counsel. He was born in that ancient city, February 13, 1744, and settled at Bath in January, 1770. He was elected Physician to the Bath General Hospital, May 12, 1784, and resigned February 10, 1819. He died August 31, 1824, and was buried at Weston. Dr. Wm. Falconer was a man of great erudition. His treatise on the "Use, Application, and Success of the Bath Waters in Rheumatic Cases," published in 1795, and which is difficult to procure, is one of his many works.

The Rev. Thomas Falconer, born December 24, 1771, in Duke Street, in the parish of St. James, in this city, was the only child of William Falconer. After a careful education, he was elected a scholar of Corpus Christi College, Oxford, in 1788, became a Fellow in 1794, and entered Holy Orders. He then visited Edinburgh, and for two Sessions, attended the Medical Classes. He was a man of great acquirements as a scholar, and the author of some learned works. He edited the Geography of Strabo, printed

by the University of Oxford in two vols. folio.*
In 1810, he was Bampton Lecturer, the subject
being the Evidences of Christianity.   In 1823,
he took the degree of M.D., at Oxford.   For a
short time he was Curate of St. James, Bath.   All
contemporary accounts describe him as a high-
minded gentleman, and a. finished scholar.   His
love of justice, truth, and honour, were universally
recognised, and he was distinguished for his
knowledge and judgment.   Dr. Falconer was unremitting in his medical assistance to the poor,
and his disposition was liberal without ostentation.
He died in 1839, and rests near his father, in
Weston churchyard, where also several of his family
are buried.   Dr. Falconer left five sons and two
daughters, namely, the Rev. W. Falconer, Fellow of
Exeter Coll., Oxon, and Rector of Bushy, Alexander
Falconer, Esq., Thomas Falconer, Esq., the learned .
County Court Judge, of Usk, Randle Wilbraham
Falconer, M.D., D.C.L., of this city, Henrietta,
the wife of John Arthur Roebuck, Esq., Q.C.,
M.P., and another daughter who died unmarried.

At No. 24, lived Gainsborough, the Painter.   Of
all the eminent artists—and there are many—whose
lives and works have reflected lustre on the annals
of Bath, Gainsborough occupies the first and foremost place.   Among the great men of his day—

---

* A translation of this work by his son, the Rev. W. Falconer, is
included in one of Bohn's Standard Libraries.

Reynolds, Lawrence,* Wilson, and others—he occupied a distinguished position. Gainsborough was a
native of Sudbury, and was born in 1727. He had the
gift of painting, and in early youth furtively pursued
his studies in nature's studios—the woods and fields.
Denied the advantage enjoyed by some of his contemporaries and rivals, namely, that of having studied
his profession in the great continental schools, he
naturally fell into some conventional errors in drawing, and upon these incidental and almost unavoidable
defects, certain critics have based an imputation of
general slovenliness. Thicknesse brought him to
Bath, and it at least speaks well for Gainsborough's
disposition that he could for the briefest period
have endured so ungenial a patron. The artist
soon displayed those rare powers of portraiture, and
treatment of rustic subjects and landscapes which
have made his name and works so famous. He
realised in his pictures the critic's simple formulary,
"the cream of life and bloom of nature."† The

* Sir T. Lawrence spent his youth in Bath. As a boy of
thirteen he lived at 2, Alfred Street, and at that time his portraits
in crayons were valued at from two to three guineas each. It appears that before he was eighteen he supported his parents and
family from his professional gains. In "Warner's Recollections"
are copies of four of Sir Thomas's letters, alluding to his connection with Bath, the price of his pictures, &c., and also an account
of Mr. Barker giving the future president of the Royal Academy
his first instructions for setting his palette.—*Britton*.

† In sweetness, grace, and spontaneity, Gainsborough has
never been excelled, and in these characteristics he reminds
us of a passage in Hazlitt's "Plain Speaker":—"There are
two persons who always appear to me to have worked under

peculiar characteristics of his portraits are life-like fidelity, sweetness, and grace—the idealism of the painter's genius. He who could make a pleasing subject of Queen Charlotte, without doing violence to . artistic or facial fidelity, must at least have been a clever artist. Gainsborough, perhaps, attained his highest powers in Bath. During his residence in this city from 1758 to 1774,* he produced

this involuntary, silent impulse more than any others; I mean Rembrandt and Correggio. It is not known that Correggio ever saw a picture of any great master. He lived and died obscurely in an obscure village. We have few of his works, but they are all perfect. What truth, what grace, what angelic sweetness are there ! Not one line or tone that is not divinely soft or exquisitely fair ; the painter's mind rejecting, by a natural process, all that is discordant, coarse, or unpleasing. The whole is an emanation of pure thought. The work grew under his hand as if of itself, and came out without a flaw, like the diamond from the rock. He knew not what he did ; and looked at each modest grace as it stole from the canvas with anxious delight and wonder."

* Mr. Wiltshire, his friend and contemporary, has been spoken of repeatedly as Gainsborough's patron. He was a kind, firm friend, but not in any sense a *patron*, and in return for his friendship and services, the painter presented him with the famous pictures, which were sold after the death of the late Mr. John Wiltshire in 1867. Gainsborough for some reason did not sell many of his landscapes, and they were not dispersed until after his death. It would be interesting to see a full and trustworthy list of Gainsborough's works, and the respective collections they adorn. Some of his pictures are now located as follows :— National Gallery—Mrs. Siddons ; The Parish Clerk ; Dr. Ralph Schomberg ; The Market Cart ; The Watering Place ; Musidora (S. K. M.) Hampton Court Palace—Fischer, the Musician ; Col. St. Leger ; Copy of Portrait by Rembrandt. Picture Gallery, Edinburgh — Mrs. Graham. Collection of Sir R. Wallace — Several Fine Portraits. These are typical of his style, and perhaps

many of the works which after his death became celebrated. In personal character he was amiable, genial, and friendly, although at times somewhat reserved. Few great men in art, literature, or arms, are free from small failings. Turner was a miser and a recluse; Goldsmith was so loquacious, that Garrick said of him " he wrote like an angel and talked like ' poor Poll '"; Wolfe and Nelson seemed like great children, except when under the inspiration of their respective professions. Gainsborough's foible was an inordinate love of music. He tried his skill with indifferent success on a variety of instruments, forgetting sometimes he was a great painter, while cherishing the strange delusion that he was a great musician.

In Gay Street is a house profusely ornamented with wreaths carved from the Bath stone, which was for many years occupied by Mrs. Piozzi,* the friend of Dr. Samuel Johnson.

---

the most highly esteemed of his works, but they bear a very small proportion to the number of fine works produced by this distinguished artist. Besides the pictures enumerated by Fulcher in his " Life of Gainsborough," and which are also referred to in Mr. F. Shum's interesting notice of the painter, there would seem to be several still in obscurity, if Mr. Britton's memory is to be trusted, for he says, in his autobiography, that he saw "at a house in the Circus more than fifty paintings and sketches there in 1801." The late Mr. Gardiner, of Bath, left at his death some choice pictures of Gainsborough, and these are now in possession of his widow, but have not seen the daylight for many years.

* Mrs. Piozzi came to Bath in 1780 with her former husband, Mr. Thrale, the wealthy Streatham brewer, of whom Dr. Johnson said, when the new brewery was being built and the old one

𝕰𝖉𝖌𝖆𝖗 𝕭𝖚𝖎𝖑𝖉𝖎𝖓𝖌𝖘 were built in 1761, on a plot of ground called Town Acre.

𝕸𝖎𝖑𝖘𝖔𝖒 𝕾𝖙𝖗𝖊𝖊𝖙, which was intended for private residences, was erected in 1764. It forms a fashionable promenade, and contains some of the finest shops in the city.

𝕿𝖍𝖊 𝕺𝖈𝖙𝖆𝖌𝖔𝖓 𝕻𝖗𝖔𝖕𝖗𝖎𝖊𝖙𝖆𝖗𝖞 𝕮𝖍𝖆𝖕𝖊𝖑, opened in 1767, stands on the east side of Milsom Street, and is approached by a long passage. It was built by the Rev. Dr. Dechier, the architect being Mr. Lightholder. It probably attained its greatest popularity during the long incumbency of the late Dr. Gardiner, who died in 1838. At that time, the opulent and noble, who visited Bath, attended this place of worship. Dr. Gardiner was a man of courtly and dignified manners, who, while observing all the amenities of society, never forgot the more important responsibilities of his sacred office. On his death he was succeeded by the Rev. George Gardiner, now of St. Leonards. During the greater part of his

---

enlarged, that they would be the source of "potential riches which would exceed the dreams of avarice." Mr. Thrale had great resources in dinner giving, and he gratified his friend the doctor in this respect without stint. "They were dinners to ask a man to, Sir." After Mr. Thrale's death, his widow married Mr. Piozzi, to the surprise of nobody, but to the disgust of all, and at his death in 1809, adopted Bath as her permanent abode. Here, says a writer in the "Cornhill," "she appears to have sojourned for some seven years in a state of rampant senility, retaining all her wit to the last, but none of her wisdom, if she ever had any." She, no doubt, was a vain, loquacious, but amiable woman. Miss Burney cut her, after her marriage with Piozzi.

incumbency, from 1838 to 1851, the late Rev. Fountain Elwin was his coadjutor. The late Rev. Edward Mangin said of him that he was the most accomplished pulpit orator he had ever heard. The natural grace and charm of his manner certainly lent power and effect to the persuasive earnestness and simplicity of his preaching. After Mr. Gardiner left the Octagon, in 1851, Mr. Elwin, for some time, continued his ministrations in conjunction with one who has since attained to a very distinguished position in the Church—

The Right Rev. 𝕎illiam Connor 𝕄agee, D.D., Bishop of Peterborough,* was born at Cork, in 1821, being son of the Rev. John Magee, curate of the Cathedral Parish, Cork. At the age of thirteen he entered Trinity College, Dublin, and subsequently obtained a scholarship, besides other academical honours. In due course he took holy orders, and after holding a curacy in a Dublin parish for some time, he was obliged to relinquish it, and to proceed to Malaga for the benefit of his health, where he remained two years. On his return, in 1848, he accepted the curacy of St. Saviour, Bath, which he held about two years. In 1850 he was appointed joint incumbent, and shortly after sole incumbent of the Octagon Chapel. When the Liberation Society was organised, a counter-society was formed, called

* Having written this sketch of the Bishop for " Men of the Time," we do not scruple to appropriate it to our present purpose.

the "Bath Church Defence Association," in connection with which Dr. Magee delivered an able
lecture on "The Voluntary System, can it Supply.
the place of the Established Church?"   Such was
the effect of this address, that similar societies sprang
up throughout the country. Subsequently Dr. Magee
published "Christ the Light of all Scripture," an
Act Sermon preached in the chapel of Trinity College,
Dublin, June, 1860; "The Gospel and the Age."
delivered at the Ordination in Whitehall Chapel,
1860; and "The Church's Fear and the Church's
Hope," preached in Wells Cathedral, 1864, and "Rebuilding the Walls in Troublous Times," preached
at St. Andrew's, Dublin, 1866.   At Oxford, Dr.
Magee on several occasions was one of the Lent
Lecturers, and in August, 1861, he delivered a
thoughtful address to the clergy at Radley, in the
diocese of Oxford, on "The Relation of the Atone-
ment to the Divine Justice."   At Cambridge and
also in London, he frequently took part in preaching and speaking on behalf of Church societies, and
published several lectures delivered at various meetings—"Scepticism," "Baxter and his Times," and
"The Uses of Prophecy." The Bishop of Bath and
Wells (Lord Auckland) conferred on Dr. Magee the
honorary rank of Prebendary of Wells some time
before he left Bath.   In 1860, he succeeded Dean
Goulburn as minister of Quebec Chapel, London,
and in the following February was removed to
the Rectory of Enniskillen by the University of

Dublin. In 1864, he was appointed Dean of Cork, and shortly afterwards Dean of the Chapel Royal, Dublin. He became Donellan Lecturer for 1865-66, a position in Dublin analogous to that of Bampton Lecturer at Oxford. Dr. Magee was frequently selected as one of the special preachers at St. Paul's, Westminster Abbey, the Chapel Royal, and Whitehall, as well as at Windsor, before her Majesty. In July, 1867, he delivered a closely-reasoned address to the clergy of Oxford on " The Rule of Faith." He was also selected in 1868, to preach before the British Association at Norwich and the Church Congress at Dublin. Both these sermons were published, under the respective titles of " The Christian Theory of the Origin of the Christian Life," and "The Breaking Net." On the death of Dr. Jeune, in 1868, Dr. Magee was nominated Bishop of Peterborough, being, it is said, the only Dublin University man ever appointed to an English See. Bishop Magee has from time to time taken part in the debates of the House of Lords on ecclesiastical subjects, and his speech against the Bill for the Disestablishment of the Irish Church was a masterpiece of impassioned eloquence. In 1871 he published four discourses preached at Norwich Cathedral on "Christianity and Free-thought," "Christianity and Scepticism," "Christianity and Faith," and "The Demonstration of the Spirit." In 1872, he delivered and published a "Charge at his Primary Visitation," in which he treats of the Athanasian

Creed with great force and ability. In 1875, he published his Charge at his Second Visitation in that year.

Dr. Magee was succeeded, in the Octagon Chapel, by the Rev. J. H. Crowder, an accomplished gentleman and an excellent preacher, who, during his incumbency, published a volume of Sermons, entitled ". Truth and Love." Between Mr. Crowder and the present minister, other able men have officiated, among whom especial mention may be made of the Rev. R. Hayes Robinson, who published " Thought and Deed," an able volume of discourses, now in its second edition. The present incumbent is the Rev. W. Anderson, M.A., First Scholar of his year at Trinity College, Dublin, First Senior Moderator and Gold Medallist in Classics, Third Senior Moderator and Gold Medallist in Logic and Ethics in the University of Dublin ; a Life-Member of the Senate of that University, and formerly Prebendary of Derry and Rector of Upper Cumber. Since his connection with the Octagon, he has published a small volume, entitled " Reasons for our Faith," being a reply to some of the theories propounded by Mr. Matthew Arnold in " Religion and Dogma." Mr. Anderson is an active member of various organizations connected with the Church, and sustains his part with becoming moderation and distinguished ability.

The altar piece was painted by William Hoare, his remuneration being a pew in the chapel for life and a sum of £100.

William Herschel was by profession a musician, and from 1767 until he left Bath, officiated as organist in this chapel. Some of the music and score supposed to have been used by him are still to be seen.

IN AND OUT OF BATH.

LANSDOWN.

A PLEASANT walk of a mile from St. Stephen's
Church leads to 𝔅𝔢𝔠𝔨𝔣𝔬𝔯𝔡'𝔰 𝔗𝔬𝔴𝔢𝔯. On the
right hand lies the village of Charlcombe, with the
hills to the eastward, while Bannerdown, Kingsdown, and Hampton Down, bound the view, which
is of rare loveliness.

𝔐𝔯. 𝔅𝔢𝔠𝔨𝔣𝔬𝔯𝔡,* the only son of the celebrated
Alderman Beckford, was born in the year 1760.

* A writer in the *Cornhill* refers to the " Memoirs of William
Beckford of Fonthill, published anonymously in 1859, by Mr.
Skeet." The author was Cyrus Redding, and it is difficult to
understand how a man, who had been sub-editor of the New
Monthly Magazine, during the editorship of Campbell the
Poet, could have written, even with the scant materials at his disposal, so wretched a book. It would be no easy task to pick out
the best biography ever written, but any one who has had the
misfortune to read this book, may safely pronounce it to be

While he was still a child his father died, bequeath-
ing to him a very large fortune, consisting of property
in the West Indies, besides the estate of Fonthill
in Wiltshire. He evinced unusual intellectual pre-
cocity, which developed itself especially in the
direction of the fine arts and the literature connected
with the subject. When he was twenty, he published
" Biographical Memoirs of Extraordinary Painters,"
a pungent satire upon some of the artists of the
day, and an unsparing exposure of the cant which
prevailed in the art criticisms of the period.
After visiting Paris, where he met Voltaire, he
spent a considerable time in Flanders, Germany, and
Italy, developing that knowledge of art, which
in him was almost an intuitive gift. Subsequently,
he travelled in Portugal and Spain. In 1783, he
married Lady Margaret Gordon,* daughter of the

---

the worst. We are told that he and his wife paid a visit to
Mr. Beckford, who thought the best thing he could do with his
visitors was to pack them up in his closed carriage and cause
them to be trotted about the streets of Bath for the day. Possibly
Mr. Beckford felt a pre-visionary dread that he might one day
be the subject of a biography at the hands of Mr. Redding, and
incarcerated him by way of revenge.

* Lady Margaret died at the Castle de-la-Tour, in the Pays de
Vaud, 23rd May, 1786, leaving issue two daughters, the elder of
whom married the Duke of Hamilton ; the younger, General Ord,
by which she incurred her father's life-long displeasure. On his
death-bed he sent for her—his brief ominous words, " Come, come
quickly," indicating that he had arrived at that period, when the
aspiration engraved on his tomb was about to be put to its one
and only practical test.

Earl of Aboyne, and in the year following entered
Parliament as one of the Members for Wells.   In the
same year, as he himself tells us, he wrote "Vathek"
in French, at one sitting, comprising three days and
two nights, during which time he never took off
his clothes.   The consequence was a very severe
illness.   The work was afterwards translated into
English, but by whom Mr. Beckford never knew,
though it was admirably done.   Byron said of this
work "that in beauty of diction and gorgeousness
of description, and the splendour of its imagery,
it surpassed Dr. Johnson's 'Rasselas.'"   Be this as it
may, it takes a permanent place amongst the finest
English classics.   In 1790, he again sat in Parliament for Hindon, but politics were little to his taste,
and his love of change took him to Portugal for the
second time, when he built the magnificent palace
referred to by Byron in "Childe Harold."   He soon
after left the country, and, in 1801, returned to his
estate at Fonthill and disposed of the furniture and
fine collection of pictures and curiosities, purchased
partly by himself and partly by his father.   Subsequently, he erected the Abbey, at Fonthill,
the tower of which was 260 feet high.   The
rooms and appointments were of the most gorgeous
description ; and he then began to make that rare
collection of books, curiosities, and articles of virtu,*
which surpassed almost every other private collection

---

* He had, at this time, a great fancy for collecting china, and
conceived a plan for building a place for its reception, similar to
the palace at Cintra.

in the kingdom, not excepting those at Stow and Strawberry Hill. Whether prompted by necessity, or by one of those irresistible vagaries which seemed to characterise his conduct through life, we cannot 'tell, but, in 1822, he sold these costly treasures by auction ;* the estate and mansion being purchased by Mr. Farquhar. Shortly after, the great central tower fell, owing to the rapidity with which it was built, and the insecurity of the foundation. The property now belongs to Mr. Morrison.

In the same year he took up his residence in Bath, connecting the last house in Lansdown Crescent by a spacious corridor with the next house in the West Wing, and immediately proceeded to indulge

---

* The diligent and amiable Mr. Britton published a most interesting account of this place in a handsome quarto volume. In his gossiping autobiography, a book comprising his varied experience, extending over a long life of literary activity, he tells us "the auctioneer (Christie) prepared a catalogue for the sale of the estate and the house, with its splendid, and ever-gorgeous, contents. The auctioneer first made an exhibition of the place in the summer of 1822, fixing the price of admission at one guinea for each person. Thousands flocked to see, admire, and wonder ; and Fonthill continued 'the rage' for some months. During this gala I was a resident in the Abbey, with an artist, for nearly a month, for the purpose of writing and publishing a volume illustrative and descriptive of the place." He adds that "'during these singular transactions Mr. Beckford was storing his twin-houses, at Bath, with some of the choicest articles from his old libraries and cabinets," and that "it was not long after the property was sold, and the old miser (Farquhar) had occupied it, that Mr. Beckford's telescope, on Lansdown tower, failed to present within its field of view the tower of Fonthill, for it had fallen upon, and crushed, other parts of the building during a stormy night."

his consummate taste in enriching his new abode
with the choicest works of art.   He employed
the late Mr. H. E. Goodridge, architect, to build

BECKFORD'S TOWER.

the Tower, now standing on Lansdown.   The plans
and specifications having been completed, the building, up to the cornice under the Belvedere, was

erected in the short space of twenty-eight days. It is a plain square Italian tower, up to the Belvedere, above which it is crowned with an octagon lantern of a Greek character enriched with a floreated finial after the Choragic Monument of Lysicrates at Athens. The building connected with the tower contained several rooms, known as the Scarlet Drawing Room, the Sanctuary—with the statue of St. Anthony—the Crimson Room, and the Etruscan Library. Here were collected the choicest pictures, furniture, cabinets, and articles of *vertu*. Above the terrace the tower rises to a height of 130 feet.

Mr. Beckford died in 1844, and his last collection was brought to the hammer, in Bath, in the early part of 1845.

In 1847—three years after Mr. Beckford's death— the place on which he had lavished so much taste and expense, was sold, and narrowly escaped the degradation of being converted into a beer-shop and tea-gardens. Mr. Beckford's daughter, the Duchess of Hamilton, however, prevented this consummation, by repurchasing the property, and vesting it in the Rector of Walcot (the late Rev. S. H. Widdrington) and his successors, for the purpose to which it is now appropriated,—a Cemetery, and as a writer in the *Cornhill* says, "a very beautiful cemetery it is," but it does not, as he implies, *belong to the City of Bath.*

The grounds are entered through an arched gateway, elaborately enriched, and surmounted

w

by a belfry, the effect being enhanced by the
introduction of the piers and railings along the
wing walls on either side, which had previously
surrounded Mr. Beckford's tomb in the Abbey
Cemetery. His remains are now removed from
thence, and deposited on the precise spot desired by
himself. The beautiful red granite sarcophagus, an
appropriate tomb, was made under his own directions.
It bears his arms and the following epitaph :—

> " WILLIAM BECKFORD, Esq.,
> Late of Fonthill, Wilts,
> Died 2nd May, 1844,
> Aged 84."

> " ————————Eternal Power,
> Grant me, through obvious clouds, one transient gleam
> Of thy bright essence in my dying hour ! "

The lines are from Vathek. The tomb and the
entrance were both designed by Mr. Goodridge.

Mr. Beckford's life and career are neither easy
nor pleasant to analyse. Of his abilities we have
ample evidence, but they were obscured by his
contempt for society, and by his misanthropy. His
taste in art was perfect, and his knowledge great ;
but they were made to minister solely to his
own gratification. His disposition was reserved,
and his temper imperious. Occasional glimpses
of graciousness illumined his conduct towards his
inferiors, but they seemed only to render his
general bearing and character more gloomy. When
age and physical incapacity diminished the energy
of his earlier manhood, he came to Bath, his ini-

crocosm then consisting of the house in which he lived, and the secluded ride he made to the tower on Lansdown. He was unquestionably a liberal patron to men of ability in the city he adopted as his final home; and, we are told, he was kind to his servants, his dogs and horses, all in much the same degree, and for the same reason—they were essential to his comfort.

There are some points of resemblance between Mr. Beckford and Mr. Landor. Both were men of genius; both were highly cultivated; both possessed literary habits and refined tastes; both were imperious and passionate. Here the comparison ends. While the former evinced narrow sympathies and cold indifference for all around him, the latter amidst all his eccentricities, waywardness, and occasional outbursts of violent invective, displayed the tenderest regard for suffering humanity, and was capable of deep attachments and lasting friendships. Landor enriched English literature with works of enduring value; while Beckford, with all his capacity, frittered away his intellectual powers and the best of his days in dilettanteism, in building fantastic mansions and towers, rightly designated "follies," and collecting treasures to be seen by no eye except his own, and which in the end were distributed amongst a thousand owners.

> " Those golden pallaces, those gorgeous halles,
>   With fourniture superfluouslie faire ;
> Those statelie courts, those sky-encountring walles,
>   Evanish all like vapours in the aire."

Between the age of 22 and 62, he published nothing, and mankind are neither wiser nor better for what he published in his old age.*   A writer in the *Cornhill* says : " Mr. Beckford was as little a benefactor to his fellows as any man who ever lived so many years and spent so much money " (July, 1873).   The mysterious stories told of him were absurd, and are scarcely worthy of contradiction ; but Mr. Beckford in this respect shared only the usual fate of men who like him, adopt habits of unusual and selfish seclusion.

" One touch of nature makes the whole world kin."

This " touch " he never knew, and as the old Somersetshire poet, Samuel Daniel, said—

" Unless above himself he can
Erect himself, how poor a thing is man."

The productions of his later years were unworthy the author of Vathek.   The exquisite sentiment from that work, engraven on his tombstone, was penned when he was twenty-two; it was, however, but a transient sentiment of the moment, an "intellectual" inspiration, and, so far as we can judge, expressed in no degree what may be called his belief.

Passing Beckford's Tower, the Down becomes more open, and a mile beyond, stands 𝕮𝖍𝖆𝖕𝖊𝖑 𝕱𝖆𝖗𝖒, so called

* " Visits to the Monasteries of Alcobaca and Botalha," 2 vols. 8vo., published when he was sixty-three. " Italy ; with Sketches of Spain and Portugal," 2 vols. 8vo., published when he was eighty. Of the Satire, " Extraordinary Painters," a good account is to be seen in the " Retrospective Review," vol. 10.

from its having been, in ancient times, a hospital for poor pilgrims journeying to and from Glastonbury. This chapel, prior to the Reformation, belonged to the monks of Bath, who were lords of the manor of Lansdown. All that remains is a decorated window; the farm house was erected in the reign of James I. Near it, on St. Lawrence's Day, August 10th, a large fair is annually held, principally for the sale of cattle and cheese.

In 1551, the manor together with that of Woolley, was granted to Fyennes, Lord Saye, Lord High Admiral, by letters patent from Edward VI.; he subsequently sold it, and after passing through various hands, it ultimately became the property of the Blathwayt family,* to whom it now belongs, and is held under the manor of East Greenwich, which possesses the royalties of this and several adjacent manors.

Leaving what was once the Cricket Ground, we pass through a gate on the opposite side of the road leading to Weston, in order to visit St. Elphage's Well, the water of which is of singular purity, and

---

* The Blathwayt family of Dyrham Park. The house at Dyrham is a fine old mansion, thoroughly restored by the late Colonel G. W. Blathwayt thirty-five years ago. It is in a direct line by the road from the spot now described, but lies beyond the limits of the distance comprehended in this volume. Beyond it again is the mansion and domain of Dodington, the residence of Lady Georgiana and Sir Gerald Codrington, Bart., and about three miles further is Badminton, the palatial residence of the Duke of Beaufort; and eastward of this is Lye Grove, the property and residence of H. Hartley Hartley, Esq.

flows into an ancient stone coffin. There are many of these holy springs in different parts of the county.

Near the fourth milestone is the 𝕸onument, "erected," says Wood, "by Lord Lansdown in 1720, to the memory of his grandfather, Sir Bevil Grenville, near the spot on which he fell. This trophy, he continues, consists of two quadrangular pedestals, set on each other, without any proportion or harmony betwixt them; and these being surmounted by an Attic base, a cap of dignity, bearing the figure of a griffon passant, whose breast is supported by a shield, finishes the top of the monument. The arms of England, resting on the joint arms of the Duke of Albemarle and the Earl of Bath, Sir Bevil's son, with military ornaments under them, adorn the right side of the body of the pedestal, and were intended to allude to the restoration of King Charles II. The left side has a *bas-relief*, referring to the actions of Lord Lansdown in Hungary, consisting of military trophies; the Grenville arms, borne on a Roman eagle, with inscriptions, and the date Sept. 12, 1683, occupy the centre. On the north side are some verses, to the memory of Sir Bevil, signed William Cartwright, 1643; while others, written by Martin Llewellen, refer to the deeds of Sir Richard Grenville, "who," says Wood, "in a single ship fought the whole Spanish armada, in 1591!"* A quota-

---

* We need scarcely observe that this does not refer to *the* armada, but to a subsequent affair, in which, though Grenville displayed the utmost gallantry and devotion, he lost his ship and

tion, from Lord Clarendon's History of the Rebellion, is cut on the front of the pedestal.

The **Battle of Lansdown**, fought July 5th, 1643, is thus described in Green's " History of the English People " :—

"While Essex lingered and manœuvered, Charles boldly detached a part of his small force at Oxford to strengthen a Royalist rising in the west. Nowhere was the royal cause to take so brave or noble a form as among the Cornishmen. Cornwall stood apart from the general life of England : cut off from it, not only by differences of blood and speech, but by the feudal tendencies of its people, who clung with a Celtic loyalty to their local chieftains, and suffered their fidelity to the crown to determine their own. They had as yet done little more than keep the war out of their own country ; but the march of a small parliamentary force under Lord Stamford upon Launceston, forced them into action. A little band of Cornishmen gathered round the chivalrous Sir Bevil Grenville, ' so destitute of provisions that the best officers had but a biscuit a day,' and with only a handful of powder for the whole force ; but starving and outnumbered as they were, they scaled the steep rise of Stratton Hill,

---

his life. See *Knight's History of England*, vol. iii., p. 261. This Sir Richard Grenville was the grandfather of Sir Bevil. In *Westward Ho !* Kingsley gives a vivid description of that chivalrous age, and the stirring events in which the deeds of Grenville, Drake, Lee, and Hawkins were conspicuous.

sword in hand, and drove Stamford back on Exeter, with a loss of two thousand men, his ordnance and baggage train. Sir Ralph Hopton, the best of the Royalist generals, took the command of their army as it advanced into Somerset, and drew the stress of the war into the west. Essex despatched a picked force under Sir William Waller to check their advance; but Somerset was already lost ere he reached Bath, and the Cornishmen stormed his strong position on Lansdown Hill in the teeth of his guns. But the stubborn fight robbed the victors of their leaders. Hopton was wounded, Grenville slain, and with them fell the two heroes of the little army, Sir Nicholas Slanning, and Sir John Trevanion, 'both young, neither of them above eight-and-twenty, of entire friendship to one another, and to Sir Bevil Grenville.' Waller, beaten as he was, hung on their weakened force as it moved for aid upon Oxford, and succeeded in cooping up the foot in Devizes. But, on the 13th of the same month, the horse broke through, and joined an army which had been sent to their relief under Wilmot, afterwards Lord Rochester, and dashed Waller's army to pieces in a fresh victory on Roundway Down."

Lansdown is covered with ancient earthworks of various dimensions, and the high road near the Monument passes through a Roman camp.

A little below the Monument to the right of the road, is the residence of A. W. Macdougall, Esq.— "Battlefield," so called from its occupying the site of the fortified post scaled by Grenville's troops just before the final charge. It is a lovely spot, and interesting in connection with the historical associations of the neighbourhood.

The neighbouring coverts form one of the favourite "Meets" of the Duke of Beaufort's hounds.

In the valley, about two miles beyond, lies 𝕿𝖗𝖆𝖈𝖊𝖞 𝕻𝖆𝖗𝖐, the property and residence of the Rev. C. R. Davey, who possesses a small but very choice collection of pictures, of which special mention may be made of the following :—

"View of Verona," Canaletti ; " Portraits of Henry Arthington and his Wife," Vandyck ; " Descent of the Great Dragon," Rubens ; " Interior of Cabaret," Van Harp ; and fine examples of De Vries, Storck, Wilson, Victors, Berghem, Cuyp, C. Jansens, Luini, Chambers, T. Barker, Palamedes, Van Goyen, Hobbema.

A pleasant walk of about a mile leads to the village of

WICK,

Remarkable for its romantic valley and rocks,* celebrated not only for their picturesque beauty, but also for their geological structure. A deep rugged glen, three quarters of a mile in length, opens suddenly on a low country, and presents a singular contrast to the adjacent fertility. Through the rift a little stream dashes over a stony bed ; and although the quiet is disturbed by noisy mills,

* The pencil of B. Barker was constantly employed in depicting the natural beauties of this place, which was his favourite resort.

enough remains to make it attractive to the painter, the antiquary, and the geologist.

The 𝔅𝔬𝔠𝔨𝔰 belong to the carboniferous series, and by their presence indicate the probable eastern boundary of the Gloucestershire and Somerset-

WICK BRIDGE.

shire coal basin—which is clearly defined by the limestone of the same age, which fringes the Mendip Hills and those of Clevedon and Leigh Down, having its northern exposure at Cromhall, from whence it returns on the eastern side by way of Wickwar and Chipping Sodbury. From the latter point, owing to the thick covering of more recent secondary beds which encroach upon the coal measures on the eastern side, its extension from Sodbury tò Frome would have been unknown but for the disturbance which has brought up the limestone at Wick, with other slight exposures of the same beds at Doynton, Codrington, and Grammar Rocks under Lansdown. The gorge at Wick passes through the centre of this limestone, which is exposed on either side some 200 feet in thickness, dipping at an angle of about 60 degrees. Both east and west of the limestone the millstone grit succeeds, and there is little doubt the coal measures follow not far below the superficial beds of new red sandstone between Wick and Warmley.

Among the organic remains in the limestone may be found Spirifera, Productus, and many corals, though rarely in good condition. When the surface of the layers of millstone grit are exposed, they are seen to retain the ripple marks of the ancient coasts on which they were deposited, with occasional traces of the vegetation of the period.

A square Roman camp, containing an area of twelve acres, defended by a broad ditch and double earthwork, crowns the northern cliff. Many Roman coins, and other antiquities, have been discovered. No visitor to Bath should omit an excursion to this interesting spot.

The Church is of modern date, in the Early English style, and is dedicated to St. Bartholomew. There is a Church also at Abson, dedicated to St.

James.   These two churches constitute a Chapelry,
annexed to Pucklechurch, of which the Rev. Canon
Coney is the incumbent.   The united parishes are
in the Union of Keynsham, and the population,
according to the census of 1871, is 833.

A walk of some three miles brings the tourist to the
Warmley Railway Station, and once in the train, a
quarter of an hour takes him to Bath.—The length
of this ramble is about ten miles.

IN AND OUT OF BATH.

WALK THE FIFTEENTH.

THE ROAD TO LANGRIDGE — THE CHURCH; WOOLLEY; SOLSBURY CAMP; SWAINSWICK — THE CHURCH—WILLIAM PRYNNE.

ONCE more on Lansdown. About a mile beyond Beckford's Tower a country lane opens into the right of the main road, and leads to the village of

LANGRIDGE,

Which, hanging on the brow of the hill, commands a wide and varied view. At the conquest it was given by Norman William to the Bishop of Coutance, and was valued at sixty shillings yearly. In the reign of Edward II., it came into the possession of the family of Walsh, who retained it for several centuries. Subsequently it passed to the Walronds, one of whom sold it, probably in the reign of Queen Anne, to William Blathwayt, of Dyrham, in whose family the manor and advowson still remain. The place probably derives its name from the long ridge which intersects the valley—hence *Langridge.* A similar natural ridge, or as it is sometimes called " Hog's-

back, extends from Hinton across the valley as far
as Wellow, as shown on the Map.

The old 𝕸anor 𝕳ouse is an almost unique example
in this part of the country of the fortified, or rather
"security" tower of the 13th century, but which is
frequently found in the north of England. The
dimensions of the building are small, and could
scarcely have admitted the residence of a family.
Probably it was connected with other offices of a
temporary character which have long since passed
away. It was enlarged in the 16th century and also
at a later period, and now forms a picturesque farm
house.

The 𝕮hurch, which is dedicated to St. Mary Mag-
dalene, is small, consisting of a western tower, with
a saddle roof. Norman in form, it has a nave, north
porch, and chancel, to which an apse has recently
been added to correspond in some measure with a
very fine Norman arch. This arch from the sub-
sidence of its piers became elliptical; and it was
long a matter of dispute whether it had ever been
semi-circular. A few years ago, showing symptoms
of decay, it was carefully taken down, under the
direction of Mr. C. E. Davis. Each stone was
measured, and nothing being found missing, the arch
was restored to its original form. Within the tower
was a mutilated group of figures of the 11th or 12th
century, representing either the first and second persons of the Trinity, or, as some suppose, the Virgin
and Saviour. The former conjecture is more likely

to be correct as the sitting or principal figure is represented in the act of benediction. This group is now placed, as it is believed, in its original position, within a recess immediately above the chancel arch. The church has been partly restored. A pulpit of the seventeenth century continues the architectural history of the church commenced in the 11th, down to the repairs in the past and present century. In the tower are three ancient bells, bearing inscriptions. Near the arch are two monumental brasses, or rather coppers, one to the memory of Robert Walsh, who died 1427, and the other to that of his widow, Elizabeth, who died 1441.* The Rev. C. B. Barrow is the Rector of the parish.

Langridge is a small parish of 656 statute acres, with a population of 85 souls; it is in the Bath Union; the poor rates at present average £70 per annum.

Reference to the Map will direct the way to the village of

WOOLLEY.

At the Conquest it was called *Wilege*, and belonged, together with Bathwick, to the abbey of Wherwell, in Hampshire. At the Reformation, although the livings remained (and still are) consolidated, the manor has passed into other hands.

The Church, dedicated to All Saints, was built at the expense of Mrs. Parkin, about 1761. Al-

* See Appendix : List of Monumental Brasses.

though the architect was the famous John Wood, junior, it is unworthy of the praise bestowed upon it by Collinson.

The following inscription on parchment was found within the casing of the pulpit, when some alterations were made, in the year 1873 :—" Delapsurâ antiquâ capellâ hanc splendidiorem, solâ impensâ, Elizabetha Parkin de Ravenfield agro Eboracensi et hujus manerii Woollei Domina œdificari jussit anno Christi 1761."

Woolley contains a population of 64 souls. Its area is 366 acres; the poor rates average £60.

SWAINSWICK

Is not mentioned in Domesday Book. It is probable that the noble eminence of $\mathfrak{Solsbury}$* was a

* In his "Guide to the Knowledge of Bath, Ancient and Modern" the Rev. Prebendary Earle, after a very learned elucidation of the Archæological features of this interesting locality, says, "In estimating the importance of an ancient site, the Archæologist will always glance at the adjacent roads. Not at the modern highways of communication and traffic, but at those sequestered by-ways, where, if anywhere, the fairies frolic still. These are mostly of high antiquity, and they often point silently to spots once frequented and celebrated, now deserted and silent. The old road at Bathford, the ferry at Bathampton and the roads leading to it, may possibly contain a tacit allusion to the ancient greatness of Solsbury. We venture a surmise that if the system of Pre-Roman Roads in this part could be recovered, it would be found that this hill was the centre towards which they converged. In short, we shrink not from the responsibility of opining that Solsbury was something more than a hill-fort occupied merely on an emergency ; that it is the venerable site of a well-inhabited and populous British city. But not to urge this opinion

Danish camp in the time of Sweyn, king of Denmark, and that he gave his name to the village. This idea receives some confirmation from a Runic inscription discovered in Denmark, relating to one of the sea kings who died at Bath.

𝔖𝔬𝔩𝔰𝔟𝔲𝔯𝔤 𝔠𝔞𝔪𝔭 occupies the summit of a hill above the village. A deep defile encompasses it on three sides; on the fourth, the Avon, flows nearly at its base. The summit is surrounded by a'vallum, cut out of the escarpment of the hill, and contains nearly thirty acres. The western entrance is protected by an earthwork, opposite to which are some long barrows. On the south-eastern side there is another entrance. A large portion of the stones, which formed its northern agger, have been removed to repair the roads. This was one of the most important of ancient British camps. The view from the summit comprised Berewyke and Hampton Camps on the south-west; Mendip, Downhead, Maesbury, Pen Hill and Black Down on the south; Long Knoll and Alfred's Tower on the east; together with the Wiltshire Downs, and Bratton Castle. On

---

on the reader, we would assert no more than this, that in Solsbury we seem to find the first favourable condition for the congregation of a population in this valley. That Solsbury was once a city and that Bath was colonised by a migration therefrom, is a supposition that may be accepted or rejected; but that it was the *Arx* or "burg" of the Avon valley and of the city of Sul, is hardly likely to be disputed. It matters little whether it actually gave a population to the city beneath it, or only fostered the growth of the city by its facilities for retreat: in either case Solsbury must occupy the first chapter in a History of Bath."

X

the north, the view, is bounded by the Cotswold
Hills.   A beacon on Mendip, or Bratton, in Wiltshire, would have apprised all the camps of any danger
from the south.   The plateau is now a cornfield.

Camden in his "Brittannia" tells us:—"The
Saxons indeed about the 44th year after their landing
in Britain, by a breach of Articles renewing the war,
laid siege to this city, but being surpriz'd by the
warlike Arthur, they betook themselves to *Badon-
hill*, where (tho' in a desperate condition,) they
fought it out to the last, and were slain in great
numbers.   This seems to be the same hill with that
we now call *Lannesdown*, hanging over a little village
near the city, nam'd *Bathstone*, and showing at this
day it's bulwarks, and a rampire.   I know there are
some who seek for it in Yorkshire; but let *Gildas*
himself restore it to this place.   For in an old
Manuscript-Copy of his History, in the Cambridge
Library, where he treats of the victory of Aurelius
Ambrosius, he says; *To the year of* Badon-hill *siege,
which is not far from the mouth of Severn.*   But if
this will not convince them, let them understand
farther, that the adjoyning vale lying along the river
Avon for a great way together, is call'd in British
Nant-Badon, i. e. the vale of Badon; and where to
seek *Badon-hill* but near *Badon-valley*, I cannot tell."
—Gibson's Translation, 1753, 2 vols. folio, vol.
I., p. 89,

Below the Camp is the pretty vale of Chilcombe,
in which are reservoirs for the supply of the city.

Here too, may be seen the remains of intrench-
ments, which once defended the northern approaches to the strong hold of Solsbury.

The high ground to the North called Charmy
Down—remarkable for the beauty of the prospect it
affords—is occupied by the farm of the president
and governors of the Bath General Hospital. There
are some remains of British earthworks on the down.
In a field immediately behind the Farm-house are
the remains of a cromlech. Though only a single
stone is now to be seen, it is probable that excavation might bring others to light. In "Tumpy
Field," the plough has passed through several long
ridges of ancient stone heaps, and in it are four
barrows, the largest of which was found to be 100
yards in circumference and 20 feet high; these
probably will soon be obliterated. Keeping the
new road from the farm to the Gloucester Road,
which it joins four miles from Bath, another barrow
of a horse-shoe form may be seen on Hartley Down.
It has been conjectured that this somewhat unusual
form may be due to its having been opened at an
earlier period.

It should be observed that various opinions are
entertained as to the genuineness of the mounds on
Charmy Down, and that while some authorities
endorse the view given above, others are unwilling
to allow the origin claimed for them. In this conflict of opinion we must leave the reader to decide
on the character to be assigned to them.

𝔖𝔴𝔞𝔦𝔫𝔰𝔴𝔦𝔠𝔨 ℭ𝔥𝔲𝔯𝔠𝔥 presents many styles. The south porch is decorated, the door being Norman, with chevron ornament. The font is Norman; the tower, containing six bells, is massive and peculiar, and has no external opening. It is supported by

SWAINSWICK CHURCH.

three columns, with Early English capitals, the heads ornamenting them, forming two arches; the windows are of various periods. Near the south door is a decorated water-stoup, boarded over, with the exception of its upper portion. The arch between the nave and chancel is Early English, and the north aisle is divided from the nave by Perpendicular arches.* In the north-east corner is a chapel, separated from the chancel by a decorated arch. On the outside of the north door stands a fractured water-stoup, which formerly served for the special use of the family residing at the Manor, who entered the church by that door.† The building is dedicated to St. Mary.

The celebrated 𝕎illiam 𝕡rynne was born at the Manor House, in this village, in 1600. Educated at the Bath Grammar School, he matriculated at Oriel College at the age of 16, took his degree of B.A. in 1620, and subsequently studied at Lincoln's Inn. His mother was a daughter of William Sherston, who, after the charter of Queen Elizabeth, was eight times Mayor, and five times Member for the city. Prynne became a zealous adherent of the Puritan party. In 1632, he published his "Histrio-mastix; or, a Scourge for Stage Players"—a book remarkable for a certain kind of learning and research, but coarse, virulent, and fanatical in its tone. He was prosecuted in the Star Chamber, and sentenced to a fine of

* An illustration of a fine monumental brass in the church to Edmund Fforde, 1439, is given in the Autotype, representing also two others in Bradford Church. It is enumerated in the List in the Appendix.

† The Rector of Swainswick is the Rev. J. Earle, M.A., Prebendary of Wells, formerly Fellow and Tutor of Oriel College, and Professor of Anglo-Saxon in the University of Oxford. Mr. Earle is the author of "The Philology of the English Tongue;" "Two Saxon Chronicles, Parallel;" an edition of "The Merchant of Venice for Social Reading;" and a "Guide to the Knowledge of Bath, Ancient and Modern."

£5,000, the loss of both his ears in the pillory, ex-
pulsion from the bar, Oxford, and Lincoln's Inn; besides
this he was condemned to imprisonment for life. It
is very doubtful whether any member of the Star
Chamber had read the book, but it is said that Laud
and others read the index, and finding therein a very
strong phrase against "women actors," so "impudent
as to act, to speak publicly on a stage (perchance
in man's apparel and cut hair, here proved
sinful and abominable) in the presence of sundry
men and women," they determined that this was a
libel upon the Queen. The book had been seven
years in preparation, but unfortunately for Prynne
Her Majesty acted a part in a pastoral at Somerset
House only a short time before it appeared. Laud
and others, according to Whitelock, "had been
angered by some of Prynne's books against Ar-
minianism," and the King allowed them to revenge
themselves upon what he was told was a libel upon
his lively consort.* It is clear that the affair had, in
a great degree, become a personal quarrel between

* When Prynne wrote this book, he could have had no
intention of referring personally to the Queen, but as regards the
offence involved in the publication of the book, it makes little
difference whether he had any such intention or not. Just before
the book was issued, the Queen had taken part in a theatrical
performance, and therefore of necessity was brought under the
writer's general condemnation.

" Prynne, a lawyer of uncommon erudition, and a zealous
puritan, had printed a bulky volume, called Histrio-mastix,
full of invectives against the theatre, which he sustained by a
profusion of learning. In the course of this he adverted to the
appearance of courtesans on the Roman stage, and by a satirical

the Archbishop and the learned barrister, for in Laud's Diary we have an. entry that Mr. Prynne sent him "a very libellous letter about his censure in the Star Chamber for his 'Histrio-mastix.'" This memorandum is dated June 11th, 1634. On the previous 7th of May, Prynne had lost one ear in Palace Yard, and on the 10th, another ear in Cheapside.

Three years after, the pertinacious offender found means to publish from his prison another pamphlet, in which he assailed Laud,* and certain other bishops. For this he was again prosecuted; fined £5,000; pilloried—losing the stumps of ears the executioner had formerly spared —and branded on both cheeks with the letters S. L. ("Seditious Libeller.") If he did not bear his sufferings with meekness, he displayed a heroic and unfaltering courage under injuries and degradations scarcely endured by any other victim

reference in his index seemed to range all female actors in the class. The Queen, unfortunately, six weeks *after* the publication of Prynne's book, had performed a part in a mask at Court. This passage was accordingly dragged to light by the malice of Peter Heylin, a Chaplain of Laud, on whom the Archbishop devolved the burthen of reading this heavy volume in order to detect its offences. Heylin, a bigoted enemy to everything puritanical, and not scrupulous as to veracity, may be suspected of having aggravated, if not misrepresented, the tendency of a book much more tiresome than seditious."—*Hallam*.

* In relation to Laud and his fate, most historians agree in opinion that Prynne, after his release by the Long Parliament, was one of the most bitter and relentless enemies of Laud, and that he used every available means to promote and carry on the proceedings against the hapless Prelate, and that in so doing

of this iniquitous Court of Injustice.   After in-
carceration in Carnarvon, Dunster, and Pendennis
Castles, and subsequently in that of Mont Orgueil in
Jersey, he was released in 1641, by a warrant
of the Long Parliament then sitting.   Shortly
afterwards, he was elected member for New-
port, in Cornwall, and took an active part on the
popular side in the House of Commons.   In the
measures that followed, when the Monarchy and
Constitution were imperilled, he displayed a rare
magnanimity, forgot his own bitter injuries, and
resisted the proceedings against the Throne and the
King with all the ability and resources he could
command.   When Cromwell assumed supreme
power, Prynne assailed him with a virulence sur-
passing that he had used against the former Government, the consequence of which was several years'
imprisonment.   On the death of the Protector, he
interested himself zealously in the cause of the
Restoration, and was returned in conjunction with
Mr. Popham, as member for the city of Bath,* of
which he was restored to the recordership the follow-

---

he was wanting in those qualities of magnanimity he subsequently
displayed. Without touching upon the political aspects of the
question, it must be remembered that Prynne believed that the
Archbishop was the chief author of the Star Chamber proceedings
against him ; and it must be conceded that historians do not
write under the stimulating bias of cropped ears, slit noses,
ruinous fines, and sentences of life-long imprisonment.

* From the 10th section of his *Brevia Parliamentaria Rediviva*,
the portion relating to Bath in the Chapman Collection, we obtain
all the indentures relating to the election of members for Bath,

ing year, having by one of the sentences passed upon him, been deprived of that office.

In summing up the career and character of Prynne, it must be confessed that they present some singular and inconsistent aspects. The times in which

---

which were then extant in the Tower Rolls and Petty Bag office, he having been appointed at the Restoration keeper of the Tower Records. One of these, issued in the first year of Queen Mary's reign, is curious, for she is therein styled "Supreme head on earth of the church of England and Ireland," a title which few are aware that she used. He also gives us some curious particulars of his own election, for Bath, in 1660. In this year, it appears that, without any solicitation, he and Alexander Popham were to be elected, upon which two other candidates sent letters to the corporation, offering their services. These being disregarded, a petition was sent to the king, who summoned the mayor before the privy council, to answer the allegations; the mayor, in his justification, pleaded that he was detained in London, and, therefore, not responsible for the proceedings. During the mayor's absence, a precept from the sheriff, for the election, was obtained by the malcontents, so that it might take place before his return. The mayor, being released, hurried down, and Popham and Prynne were returned by him and the assembled corporation. Henry Chapman, on behalf of the opposing party, then demanded that all the freemen's votes should be taken; and on the mayor's refusal, Chapman, being captain of the trained band, ordered his drummer to beat through the city, summoning the freemen to meet at the Guildhall, and proceed to an election. "At that time," says Prynne, "there were 200 householders in the city, of whom forty attended, and returned the other two candidates." This return the mayor refused to seal, so the captain sealed it with his own and companions' seals. The sheriff made a double return to the House of Commons, but Popham and Prynne were declared to be the sitting members The captain seems to have carried things with a high hand, for he seized the mayor and eleven citizens, members of the corporation, under the plea of their being disaffected, and committed them to prison.

he lived, and the stormy scenes in which he moved, developed the contradictory attributes of his nature, in which ultimately the reasonable and the good prevailed. Conscientiously devoted to the cause of liberty, he saw at the outset of his stormy public life, the dangers of the policy pursued by Charles I., and this policy he traced, or thought he traced, to the combined influence of Laud and Wentworth. Be this as it may, when these counsellors were removed, he protested that enough had been done, and he foresaw that the death of Charles, instead of securing the supremacy of law and constitutional liberty, must, at least for a time, result in an iron despotism under Cromwell.

The question of Charles's execution is obviously beyond our province, but most modern statesmen and historians who justify that event on the grounds of law and justice, condemn it as impolitic and as a stupendous blunder. Prynne thought that, after the decisive triumph of the Parliament, whether the professions made by Charles to abstain from fresh aggressions upon the laws and to rule within the limits of the Constitution, were to be trusted or not, such restrictions might be imposed upon him, and enforced by public law and parliamentary energy, as would effectually check any further attempt to govern by his own arbitrary will and kingly prerogative. There can be no doubt as to Prynne's sincerity and honest patriotism ; he buried his own personal wrongs—his unexampled sufferings and degradations—in oblivion, and sought by every possible means to restore peace, and turn once more the public policy of the nation into the Constitutional channels of law and order. He was not, however, equal to the task. If he had possessed the calm energy, the statesman-like intellect, the consummate ability, the loveable personal qualities, the unequalled power of persuasion of Hampden, he must at this juncture have failed. But Prynne was not a statesman, not even a recognised leader; he was a vehement politician with narrow views. He met aggression with violence, and had but one remedy for the alleged intolerance of Laud and the government, and that was a Draconic intolerance many degrees more intolerable than the evil he combated. He lacked the comprehensive grasp and serene patience of a statesman, and on the slightest provocation had recourse to his fatal expedient, violent political diatribe, which brought upon him the vengeance of his enemies. Prynne was like a brave but unskilful commander who rushes upon the enemy with the certainty of defeat. When time and bitter disappointment convinced him of the mistakes of the past, and when he would have saved the monarchy, the king and the constitution, he was powerless; he could only look with dismay upon the scene; his errors and violence rose up in judgment against him; the revolutionary spirit he had done so much to evoke, swept away in its fury the king, the church, and the constitution, and with them, the liberties for which he had struggled, fought, and suffered.

When Cromwell was made Protector, Prynne became a thorn in his side. It was soon felt by the nation that the "little finger of Cromwell was thicker than Charles' loins," and Prynne employed his trenchant pen against the usurper, and for this suffered his last and longest imprisonment.

There is no reason to doubt that he retained, to the very last, his religious convictions, which were of the narrowest type of Calvinistic Puritanism; and yet, surviving Cromwell, he took an active part in the restoration of Charles II., and under his goverment became a placeman.* No

* The office conferred upon him was that of Keeper of the Records in the Tower, in which capacity he compiled many valuable papers illustrative of Constitutional and Parliamentary History. A copy of "Prynne's Records," 3 vols. 4to., was sold Nov. 18th, 1875, by Messrs. Sotheby, Wilkinson, and Hodge, from the Library of John Dunn Gardner, Esq., for £164—the largest price the work has ever produced. A history of Prynne's Books would be more interesting than many of the books themselves.

Prynne died in 1669, and bequeathed his voluminous writings to the Library of Lincoln's Inn, in the Chapel of which he is buried. A list of the books by Prynne now in the Abbey Collection will be found in the Appendix.

In his Essay on the "Connection of Bath with the Science and Literature of England," the late accomplished writer, the Rev. Joseph Hunter says: "Nor let any one be startled if the first name that presents itself is that of William Prynne: for although

Rege sub Augusto fas sit laudare Catonem,

I am not about to speak of him as the enemy of royalty and prelacy, or even in his other character as the castigator of the stage. I look upon this as a very inferior part of a very extraordinary character, and as in some measure belonging to the age rather than to the man. I look upon him as the great historical lawyer of his ᵗime; as acquainted, perhaps, beyond all his contemporaries with serious reflection was ever made upon his conduct, nor were any unworthy motives imputed to him. In the office he held, he did good service to the nation and to posterity in the valuable state papers he compiled; but from the nature and principles of the man as revealed in his previous career, his spirit must have been sorely vexed at the unrestrained licentiousness of the Court, the alternate truculence, truckling, and subserviency, and the profligacy of the Government he had assisted in restoring. He possibly arrived at the conclusion that these evils were incidental—the inevitable reaction from the previous *regime*, which in time would cure themselves—that so long as the Constitution was to some extent respected, there remained hope and the germ of national regeneration and independence. He perhaps little thought that the days of the race he had done so much to ruin and so much to restore, were numbered, and that the inherent folly of the dynasty would occasion its ultimate downfall and extinction.

Swainswick is in the Bath Union. The population

the constitutional law of England; as a man of immense industry; as the devoted investigator of our diplomatic antiquities; and as one who preferred a dark chamber in the Tower before the most sumptuous and lightsome apartment. I look upon him with great respect as a man who has rendered accessible to the public much of the contents of that great national repository of records, and who has incidentally thrown light upon almost every subject of English historical inquiry."

* Once he was twitted in the House of Commons with tergiversation, but he significantly pointed to his mutilated person as a proof of what he had *suffered* for liberty.

which in 1841 was 572, on an area of 845 acres, is, according to the census of 1871, 599. Its poor rates in 1778 were £15; they now average £245 per annum. It contains the populous manor of Tatwick, existing in two portions in Edward the Confessor's time, when they were worth together twenty shillings, At the Conquest they were given to the Abbey of Bath, being then valued at forty-five shillings.

An hour's walk from the Camp brings us into the London Road, near the eastern end of Grosvenor Place. Here, a turning to the left, leads to the Suspension Bridge, a pleasant spot in sunshine and fair weather; gay with many a skiff and four-oar, and affording a pretty view of the river and the valley.

The length of this walk is probably little less than ten miles.

IN AND OUT OF BATH.

WALK THE SIXTEENTH.

St. Catherine; the Church; St. Catherine's Court; Batheaston Church; Home through Walcot.

ST. CATHERINE.

THE views as we ascend Holt Down are very pleasing. The hills which form a natural amphitheatre enclose the vale where the Priors of Bath had a grange; the manor has been in the possession of the Church from time immemorial. It is not mentioned in Domesday Book, but its 𝕮𝖍𝖚𝖗𝖈𝖍 dedicated to St. Catherine, the patron saint of the citizens of Bath, bears marks of remote antiquity, although nearly rebuilt by Prior John Cantlow in 1499.

Its square embattled tower, which contains four bells, is connected with the nave by an arch resting on Norman capitals of peculiar design, and has a small Norman window. The square font of Caen

stone is adorned with interlacing circular sculpture.
The nave is 27 feet long; in it is a beautiful
pulpit placed against the north wall, still retaining
a portion of its decorations, which appear to resemble in style and colouring the screen at Wellow.
Above the arch, between the nave and chancel, the
ten commandments are painted. The chancel,
which is eighteen feet long contains the tomb of
William Blanchard, who lived in the seventeenth
century. It consists of a pediment and cornice,
supported by two Corinthian columns, their capitals
being gilt. The male figure is clothed in the half-
armour of King Charles's time, the female being at-
tired in the dress of the period. Both kneel; on
the pediment are three daughters, with the son
kneeling at a reading desk. The epitaph on the
tablet bears the date of 1631. The chancel contains
memorials of the Blanchards and Parrys, lords of the
manor. The east window bears the name of the
builder (Prior Cantlow), and the date, with the arms
of the Abbey—St. Peter's key crossed by a sword,
and the prior's mitre : in the smaller compartments
are roses, with the midday sun frequently repeated.
The other windows are emblazoned with them, and
also with an eagle having a scroll from his beak
bearing the words Prior Cantlow. The exterior of
the church is very pleasing, from the regularity of
the architecture and the square perpendicular windows. The interior was repaired during the year
1847, when a new communion table, of polished

ST. CATHERINE'S CHURCH.

cedar, with velvet cover and monogram, and a service of communion plate, were presented by the Hon. Emily Anne Strutt, in accordance with the will of her father. Near it is the Prior's barn of a cruciform shape, looking from a distance like a chapel with transepts.

Of **St. Catherine's Court**, built also by Cantlow, we have the following curious account, from a lease granted by the Prior, in 1524, to Thomas Llewellyn:— "The capital messuage called Katherine's court, stands near the church; the court of the same between the church hey and the house, and coming in an entry. On the right hand a hall, and behind the hall a whitehouse (the dairy), and on the side a parlor and a buttery, with a chimney both in the hall and in the parlor. Between the whitehouse and parlor, stairs of stone going into a chamber ceiled over the parlor, with a chimney in it; over the hall a wool loft, over the entry a chamber, by the entry a vacant ground; and over and under chambers; and also another hall with a vault underneath, and over a malt loft adjoining the same, two chambers. At the end of the hall another malt loft, with a mill called a quyver, and a place underneath to winnow malt; all this under one roof." At the Reformation it formed a portion of King Henry's gift to his daughter, Ethelreda Malte, who brought it in marriage to John Harington, whose son, Sir John, in consequence of the great expense entailed upon him by the visit of Queen Elizabeth at Kelston, sold it to William Blanchard. From the Blanchards it came by marriage into the possession of James Walters, of Batheaston. His heiress brought it to the family of Parry, whose heiress marrying Hamilton Earl, it became his property, and was subsequently sold to the Hon. Colonel Strutt.

The house is now divided into two portions, the farm and the court-house; the latter has an old garden with terraces, and a beautiful porch of the period of Charles I., who is said by tradition to have once passed a night in the house. The hall contains a fountain supplied from St. Catherine's Well, and an elaborate screen, surmounted by the arms of King Henry VII.—the united roses, with the garter, supported by the lion and dragon—for England and Wales. On either side of it are the letters C. R., placed there, it is believed, by Capt. William Blanchard, who was a loyalist in the civil wars. The drawing-room has a pleasant bay window facing the south, and in it is a fine sideboard of black oak ornamented with ancient carving, representing the implements of Hebrew worship.

St. Catherine is a vicarage attached to Batheaston; prior to the Reformation it was a chapelry. The population in 1841 was 159; the area 1041 acres, paying a net rental of £1540; the poor rates in 1771 were £12; in 1780 they were £26; prior to the formation of the Bath Union they were £114, and are now on an average £230 yearly. The population, according to the census of 1871, is 160.

BATHEASTON

Is very beautiful, and the neighbourhood is rich in wild flowers. Among the grassy slopes ferns and mosses luxuriate, and a rivulet, once rich in trout, wends its way through the meadows. Here and there a cluster of neat cottages or a gable roofed farm-house is disclosed to view by a sudden turn in the road.

The parish of Batheaston, with Amorel, formed a liberty exempt from the county jurisdiction, and was divided into two manors before the Conquest; one belonged to the king, the other to the church of Bath. The royal portion formed part of the lands sold by William Rufus to John of Tours, who reserved to the bishop the superior royalties, although he gave the lands to the convent. The Husseys, Fitzurzes, the Devereux, Scroops, Botelers, and Blunts, held it in succession under the bishops. In Queen Mary's reign it was given to the Earl of Northumberland. In 1667 the manorial rights were sold for £600. No court has been held here for nearly a century, nor have any manorial rights been claimed.

By Pope Nicholas's survey, in 1292, the Church, belonging to the Abbey of Bath, was valued at twelve marks, thus settling the dispute between the monks and the vicar with reference to the tithes, which, by agreement in 1262, were given to the vicar, together with a house near the church, on condition that he should sustain all burdens, and maintain a chaplain for St. Catherine's, whilst the Prior and convent agreed to build a residence for him, and allow him seven bushels of wheat annually, in lieu of the rectorial tithes, which they reserved to themselves. The church, a fine building, dedicated to St. John the Baptist, retains traces of the original structure, *circa* 1260, and is in its main features referable to the perpendicular period, having a nave, chancel, north and south aisles; the north aisle was rebuilt in 1833, when the whole edifice underwent thorough repair. The south porch has a decorated arch, above which is a perpendicular canopied niche, and on either side of the door a lavatorium. The nave is perpendicular, divided from the chancel by an arch. Near the altar is a piscina, having a bracket supported by a corbel, with a quartrefoil; on the south side is a niche for a statue. On the roof, between the nave and chancel, is a plain campanile, formerly containing the sanctus bell. The tower is of the perpendicular period, quadrangular in four stages, and embattled, one of the buttresses containing a stair turret, surmounted by a beautiful pinnacle. The tower is 100 feet high, and contains a niche on the east side, in which is the statue of an ecclesiastic, erroneously supposed to be the patron saint. The living is a vicarage in the gift of Christ Church, Oxford. The Rev. T. P. Rogers, M.A., is the present incumbent.

A recent addition to the internal attractions of the church is the Robertson Memorial Chamber, erected by the filial piety of Capt. Struan Robertson, of The Grove, in this parish, to the memory of his father, Captain F. Robertson, R.A., who, after active service in field and fort was, under the *nom de plume* of "Ubique," the contributor of many pleasing sketches to the military periodicals of his day, but whose chief and pardonable pride was his paternal relationship to the Rev. F. W. Robertson of Brighton, who, dying all too soon for the church and the world, but not for fame, has left behind him a collection of published sermons and essays of remarkable power and eloquence, and of world-wide popularity and usefulness. Capt. Robertson, who passed the evening of his days in calm and cheerful retirement in the bosom of his son's family at The Grove, was greatly beloved for his genial affability; and at times when in the confidence of friendship he became "the old man eloquent," he poured forth the treasures of a well cultivated mind and richly stored memory, with singular vivacity and felicity of expression. The organ chamber erected to his memory is built in the style of the latter part of the thirteenth century, in order to harmonize with the chancel, which it adjoins. It is about 19 feet long, by 16 feet wide, and the space not occupied by the organ forms a vestry. One of the two-light windows formerly in the north wall of the chancel was removed to make way for this chamber, and is rebuilt in the north wall, the stained glass being again inserted. Between the organ chamber and chancel are two handsome arches, elaborately moulded, supported in the centre by a red Mansfield stone shaft, having a carved capital and moulded base. An archway of similar character divides the chamber from the north aisle. Underneath the vestry a new heating chamber has been constructed. The design of the work was furnished by Mr. Frederick Preedy, of London, under whose direction the chancel, nave, and north aisle were restored a few years ago. The work has been well carried out by Mr. W. H. Newman.

Among the memorial windows which at once decorate and solemnize the interior of the church, is one dedicated to his late wife by J. Miller, Esq., the present owner of Batheaston Villa, a gentleman of the same name, but not in any way connected with the family which a century ago held poetical revels there. Conspicuous among the mural tablets in the church is one to the memory of the Rev. J. J. Conybeare, professor of poetry and Anglo-Saxon in the University of Oxford, and for many years vicar of this parish.

· Near the church—known by an eagle in stone—is the country seat of John Wood, the architect,*whose memory the citizens of Bath must always revere. The parish schools, erected by the parishioners, with

---

* Those who want to know anything of this distinguished man, and what he did for the city of Bath, are referred to "An Essay towards a Description of the City of Bath," 8vo., 1742. Mr. Wood, the elder, was an accomplished architect, and if his designs could have been recorded by a Warner, or an Earle, their excellence would have been rendered all the more apparent. In a weak moment, however, he attempted to write the early

aid from government, in 1858, are conveniently situated at no great distance from the rectory.

From the church there is a delightful walk to Bath, across the fields below Cliffe, leading to Lower Swainswick and Grosvenor.

𝔅𝔞𝔱𝔥𝔢𝔞𝔰𝔱𝔬𝔫 𝔐𝔦𝔩𝔩, situated on the Avon, is of remote antiquity. The remains of a paved path leading from it to St. Catherine's and called locally the Drungway, may still be traced, except where it has been obliterated by the highway. Some forty years ago, several Norman remains were discovered in the walls of the old mill. In the southern wall of the new building, two portions of sculptured capitals have been preserved, one representing the good and bad spirit striving for a soul, the other the scourging of Our Lord. Several portions of Norman columns, similar to those found at the Abbey of Bath, were also built into the walls.

The old 𝔉𝔢𝔯𝔯𝔶 to Bathampton Mill has been superseded by a handsome stone 𝔅𝔯𝔦𝔡𝔤𝔢 of several arches, erected by Messrs. Hickes and Isaac in 1872.

Overlooking the road to the river, at a short distance from the high road, is 𝔅𝔞𝔱𝔥𝔢𝔞𝔰𝔱𝔬𝔫 𝔙𝔦𝔩𝔩𝔞, where Lady Miller once presided as the high priestess of poetry.

---

history of Bath, and to describe his own works. Wood did great things in architecture, but in literature he was as intelligible as "the palpable obscure."

Landor, in a note to his Imaginery Conversation between Pericles and Sophocles says, in speaking of Queen Square and the Circus, Wood's masterpieces, that there is nothing in Rome or the world equal to them. Landor admired the Crescent also, the work of the younger Wood.

Here, too, was to be seen the celebrated vase, found in 1769 near Cicero's villa, at Frascati. The custom was for the company to meet every fortnight, when their compositions, consisting of enigmas, sonnets, and a French species of composition called *bouts rimés*, wherein terminal rhymes were given for verses to be attached to them—were read aloud, and the authors of the most approved compositions were rewarded with a sprig or chaplet of myrtle.

The following, written by Garrick, are now published for the first time, through the kind permission of Mrs. H. Hensley, who possesses the original MSS. There is no date on either.

"UPON CHARITY—THE SUBJECT GIVEN AT BATH-EASTON FOR YE PASSION WEEK."

"The Vase speaking:—"

"For Heaven's sake bestow on me
A little wit—and that would be
Indeed an Act of Charity!"

"N.B.—It was slipt into ye vase but treated wh great contempt, while reverend Tawdry* was rewarded."

On receiving back his sarcastic lines, Garrick wrote on the back of the M.S. this metrical comment :—

"UPON BATHEASTON PRIZE."

"What the proverb has taught and wise men alledge,
Bath Easton has now great in force,
That *This* Man is hanged if he look o'er a hedge,
While safely *that* man steals a horse :
In ye face of ye day and before all our eyes,
(Such doings my satire provoke)
A Parson Sir Tawdry was crowned with a Prize,
While Sir Sedley was burnt for a joke. "

* Rev. Dr. Whalley.

"THE PLEASURES OF MAY AT BATHEASTON."

1.

"Oh! spread thy green mantle, sweet May o'er the ground,
  Drive the blasts of chill Winter away ;
Let the birds sweetly carrol, thy flow'rets smile round,
  And let *us* with all nature be gay.

2.

Let spleen, spite and envy, those clouds of the mind,
  Be dispersed by the sunshine of joy ;
The pleasures of Eden had blessed human mind
  Had no fiend enter'd thère to destroy.

3.

As May with her magick can warm the cold earth,
  Let each fair with the season improve ;
Be widows restored from their mourning to mirth,
  And hard-hearted maids yield to love.

4.

The Soldier turned Shepherd soft passion shall learn,
  And breathe out his vows in the shade ;
The Divine* become warlike, in frolick shall turn
  The stiff band to a sprightly cockade.

5.

Tho' the red coat and black coat this season transforms,
  And melts marble hearts into sighs ;
Sweet May can do more, for it wakens and warms,
  And gives spirit to Beaux and to flies.

6.

Bring roses and myrtles to crown the gay feast,
  It's joy let each bosom impart ;
When pleasure is given and felt by each guest,
  'Tis the May of the mind and the heart."

* "Mr. Hardcastle (a clergyman) was at ye Masquerade like a French officer."

The following quotation from Boswell's Life of Johnson, by Croker, vol. v., p. 277, will explain the solemnities:—"Lady Miller's collection of verses by fashionable people, which were put into her vase at Batheaston Villa,* near Bath, in competition for honorary prizes, being mentioned, he (Dr. Johnson) held them very cheap. '*Bouts Rimés,*' said he, 'is a mere conceit, and an *old* conceit *now*,—I wonder how people were persuaded to write in that manner for this lady.' I (Boswell) named a gentleman of his acquaintance who wrote for the vase.—Johnson : ' He was a blockhead for his pains.'—Boswell: 'The Duchess of Northumberland wrote.'—Johnson: 'Sir the Duchess of Northumberland may do what she pleases; nobody will say anything to a lady of her high rank. But I should be apt to throw ——'s verses in his face.'"

* "You must know," says Horace Walpole, in one of his letters, "that near Bath is erected a new Parnassus, composed of three laurels, a myrtle tree, a weeping willow, and a view of the Avon, which has been new christened *Helicon.* They hold a Parnassus fair every Thursday,† give out rhymes and themes, and all the flux of quality at Bath contend for the prizes. A Roman vase, dressed with pink ribbons and myrtles, receives the poetry, which is drawn out every festival; six judges of these Olympic games retire and select the brightest composition, which the respective successful acknowledge, kneel to Mrs. Calliope (Miller,) kiss her fair hand, and are crowned by it with myrtle, with—I don't know what. You may think this a fiction or exaggeration. Be dumb, unbeliever! The collection is printed, published, — yes, on my faith! There are *bouts rimés* on a buttered muffin, by her grace the Duchess of Northumberland."

The collection is published in 2 vols. 12mo.

† Other authorities, Anna Seward included, say "every fortnight."

The following lines from a contemporary Satire, entitled "Bath: its Beauties and Amusements," evince a somewhat disparaging estimate of the poetic effusions which issued from this famous vase :—*

" But soft—behold, new game appears in view—
Observe that busy, fluttering, noisy crew !
They're all *Apollo's* sons, from top to bottom—
Tho' poor *Apollo* wonders where he got 'em !
See how they hurry to that hallow'd shrine—
That sacred seat of *Sappho* and the nine ;
Where, plac'd on quarries of the purest stone,
The red brick shines unrivall'd and alone ;
Bless us !— what toil, what cost has been bestow'd,
To give that prospect—of the *London* road !
Our admiration knows not where to fix !
Here a Cascade, and there a coach and six !
Within, a mystic vase with laurel crown'd—
Hence, ye profane !—'tis consecrated ground !
Here *Sappho's* hands the last sad rites dispense
To mangled poetry, and murder'd sense ;
Here jests are heard, "at which e'en *Juno* smil'd
"When crack'd by *Jove* magnificently mild ;"
Jests, so sublimely void of sense and thought,
Poor simple mortals cannot find them out ;
Rhimes,—like Scotch cousins,—in such order plac'd,
The first scarce claims acquaintance with the last ! ".

Returning to the city by the London Road we pass many charming villas ; Bailbrook House is now a private asylum.

At the end of Grosvenor Place (built in 1790) is a footway leading to the Suspension Bridge, erected, in 1830, by the late Mr. Thomas Shew, in order to open a communication with the pathway leading to the city by the banks of the Canal.

* Among other contributors were Anstey, Mason, Graves, Pratt, Garrick, Meyler, Whalley, Miss Seward, and other minor celebrities.

This eastern suburb, though parochially in the parish of Walcot, constitutes the independent ecclesiastical parish of St. Saviour's.

The Church is behind Beaufort Buildings. It consists of a tower of three stages, embattled, with pinnacles, and contains a peal of eight bells, the gift of the late Mr. William Hooper. The nave is separated from the side aisles by ten pillars, supporting a canopied roof ornamented with bosses, and lighted by ten windows. The chancel has a stained glass window of five lights. The pulpit and reading desk are on opposite sides, and of equal height. The font, which is incongruous and out of character, formerly stood in the church of Walcot St. Swithin. This building was erected in 1832, after a design by Mr. Pinch, on a site given by Miss Tanner. It contains 1,100 sittings, of which 700 are free. The building was designed before the revival of Gothic taste. The windows have heads, forming corbels, but the canopy over the doorway might have been omitted. The Rev. W. J. Pollock is the Rector, the patronage being vested in the Church Patronage Society.

The School connected with the church is a neat Tudor building.

In Kensington Place there is an Episcopal Proprietary Chapel, opened in 1795, and near it is the Walcot old Poor-house, now known as the Sutcliffe Industrial School. At the bottom of Snow Hill stands Walcot House, whose pleasure grounds

are now a stone yard; yet it still retains a relic of its
better days in the graceful sphinxes which surmount
the columns at the entrance gate.

The Eastern Dispensary, in Cleveland Place,
established 1832, is a well-arranged building, erected
in 1845, from a design by the late Mr. Goodridge.
It is attended daily by a physician and surgeon, the
medical staff consisting of three physicians, three
surgeons, and a resident medical officer. The object of the institution is to aid with medical advice
the sick poor from any parish in or near Bath, who
bring a subscriber's recommendation, but it confines
its home attendance to those only who reside in the
parishes of Walcot St. Swithin's, St. Saviour's, and
Bathwick.

Opposite Walcot Parade, whereon was formerly a
grange belonging to the Bath Abbey, is a commodious
Wesleyan Chapel, erected in 1815.

The ancient Manor of Walcot is not mentioned
in Domesday Book. It derives its name from two
Saxon words, *wealde*, a wood, and *cote*, a dwelling;
or as some suppose from " *wall*," a word which frequently enters into the names of places adjacent to
ancient Roman roads. In Bishop Roberts' grant of
land to the priory in 1280, the name was spelt Worle-
quet. By this grant the monastery possessed much land
in the parish. Sherston, the first mayor under Queen
Elizabeth's charter, induced his royal guest to include
the greater portion of the manor within the liberties
of the city. From 1691 to 1698, as appears from

parish records, it was so thinly inhabited that only six baptisms took place, and there were neither funerals nor marriages during that period. In 1730, it was obliged to maintain a pauper of another parish, having none of its own; it was then a village, with two cloth mills, and but eighty houses.

The Church, dedicated to St. Swithin, Bishop of Winchester, and Confessor to King Ethelwolf, was built in 1780, at the junction of the Fosse-Way and Via Julia. Like many Bath churches it has been more than once rebuilt. Here is a tablet to the memory of James Hare, M.P., the inscription on which was written by Georgiana, Duchess of Devonshire, famous for her wit, her beauty, and the matchless graces of her character. In the church is buried Sir Edward Berry, Nelson's friend and companion in arms, who for many years, after the close of his active career, lived in Gay Street. Here, also, is a tablet to Christopher Anstey, and several members of his family. The poet will scarcely be suspected of having written his own epitaph. Besides these there are many other monuments of more or less merit, some of which must be allowed exclusively to speak for themselves. A tablet to the memory of General D'Arblay, bears an inscription written by his widow (neé Fanny Burney) in terms of pardonable exaggeration. Near it is one to herself and her son, the Rev. Alexandre Piochard D'Arblay. At the east end, is a tablet to Thomas Pownall, formerly governor of Carolina and other British dependencies, and an eminent antiquary. The services of another valuable public servant, Mr. Brooke, are also briefly recorded on a tablet in the north gallery. He was commonly called Governor Brooke, from his having been governor of St. Helena.

Wood, in speaking of the Church preceding the present, says :—It was "a structure, before it was rebuilt, which answered the exact size and form of *Moses' Tabernacle!* Which form had been still preserved, and the size of the church encreased to that of the tabernacle, so as to have made it a perfect sample of that glorious edifice, if the rebuilding the church had not been made a job of and the jobber supported in his schemes by the refuse of the inhabitants of the parish, in direct opposition to the inclination of the principal parishioners.—The body of this church, as it is now built, is 40 feet in length and 30 feet in breadth; under which there is a room to bury the dead in, separated from the church by a timber floor, instead of a stone arch!"*

Walcot Street stands on the line of the old Fosse-Way.† It is partly in the parish from which it takes its name, and partly in the parish of St. Michael.

The first object that strikes us is the Old Cemetery, which is situated to the south-east of the church, and is now closed. Standing by the side of the ancient Roman highway, it is not surprising

---

* The laws of health were little observed in those days. "Sanitas sanitatum omnia sanitas" did not involve a policy for Walcot, nor, as will be seen, for the good people of St. Michael's.

† See page 205 for a fuller account of this ancient road.

that the ground should contain remains of Roman sepulture. Several cinerary urns and other relics have been discovered at various times on the spot.

Cornwell Buildings derive their name from the old conduit, Carn Well.

In Ladymead is that excellent institution, the **Female Home and Penitentiary**, carried on under admirable rules and with most judicious zeal. It is deserving of sympathy and pecuniary aid.

On the opposite side is a very handsome **Drinking Fountain**, designed by Mr. C. E. Davis, and erected at the cost of Mrs. Landon, of the Royal Crescent.

THE FOUNTAIN IN LADYMEAD.

The **Corn Market** is contiguous.

The population of Walcot, in 1871, was 25,779; the area 1234 acres; the rateable value £124,744; and the average amount of the poor rates about

z

£7,396. These figures include the whole parish, which, for ecclesiastical purposes, has been divided into three—St. Swithin's, St. Saviour's, and Trinity.

The **St. Michael's Old Burying Ground**, situated at the bottom of Walcot Street, is now closed.

Dr. Johnson visited Bath in 1776, and resided at the Pelican Inn.* During his stay in Bath, he was visited by his friend Boswell, who thus records the fact in his "Life of Johnson":—"Soon after this day, he (Dr. Johnson) went to Bath with Mr. and Mrs. Thrale. I had never seen that beautiful city, and wished to take the opportunity of visiting it, while Johnson was there. On the 26th of April I went to Bath; and on my arrival at the Pelican Inn, found lying for me an obliging invitation from Mr. and Mrs. Thrale, by whom I was obligingly entertained almost constantly during my stay. They were gone to the Rooms; but there was a kind note from Dr. Johnson, that he should sit at home all the evening. I went to him directly, and before Mr. and Mrs. Thrale returned, we had by ourselves some hours of tea-drinking and talk."

The Vineyards, were during the early part of the last century, noted for the production of Black cluster and Muscadine grapes. Two vines, planted together, were trained on stakes, at right angles, six feet apart. The produce was considerable; in 1719, sixty-nine hogsheads of wine were shipped from Bristol, at a price of ten guineas a hogshead.

* Now called "The Three Cups."

About 1730 the crops began to fail, the reason assigned for it being that, as the spring seasons were more backward than they used to be, the grapes did not mature before the winter. The circumstance is singular, as shewing the change of climate that has taken place.

Lady Huntingdon's Chapel was erected in 1765, together with a house for the minister, on some land purchased by the Countess for the purpose. The chapel was opened on the 6th October, the celebrated Whitfield preaching in the morning, and the Rev. Joseph Townsend,* Rector of Pewsey, in the evening. Romaine and Fletcher also occasionally preached, and in the next year John Wesley frequently officiated. "At this period," says the author of the "Life and Times of Selina, Countess of Huntingdon," "Horace Walpole was in Bath, and thus described the chapel: 'They have boys and girls with charming voices, that sing hymns in parts. At the upper end is a broad *hautpas* of four steps advancing in the middle; at each end two eagles, with red cushions, for the parson and clerk; behind them three more steps, with an eagle for a pulpit; scarlet arm chairs to all three ;† on either hand a balcony for ladies; the rest of the congregation sit on forms. Wesley is an elderly man, fresh-colored, his hair smoothly combed,

* An eminent geologist.

† There is a little confusion of language here for which the editor is not responsible. Walpole has mixed up eagles, cushions, "parson and clerk," and arm chairs in such delightful confusion, that the sentence is left for the reader as a sort of grammatical puzzle to be unravelled.

with a little *soupçon* of curl at the ends. Wondrous
clever, he spoke his sermon so fast, and with so
little accent, that it was like a lesson; there were
parts and eloquence in it, but towards the end he
exalted his voice, and acted very vulgar enthusiasm."'
The amusing old cynic adds that, at this time in Bath,
there was quite a rage among persons in high life to
make parties to hear the different preachers who supplied the chapel; among others he enumerates Lord
Chancellor Camden. "There was one thing," says
the author, in a foot note, "which he did not know
of, a seat for bishops, a curtained pew inside the door,
where they could hear without being seen; which the
facetious Lady Betty Cobbe, the Countess's cousin,
used to call 'Nicodemus's corner.'" In November,
Whitfield administered the sacrament, using, he says,
no less than eight bottles of wine. "Such a numerous
assembly," says he, "of the mighty and noble* I
never saw attend before in Bath." He was shortly
after succeeded by the celebrated Henry Venn; afterwards the service was performed by her ladyship's
chaplains alternately.

Near it stands the 𝕮𝖆𝖙𝖍𝖔𝖑𝖎𝖈 𝕬𝖕𝖔𝖘𝖙𝖔𝖑𝖎𝖈 𝕮𝖍𝖚𝖗𝖈𝖍, built
by the late Mr. G. P. Manners in 1840.

In Guinea Lane, near this, are the 𝕻𝖆𝖗𝖔𝖈𝖍𝖎𝖆𝖑
𝕾𝖈𝖍𝖔𝖔𝖑𝖘 of Walcot St. Swithin's, erected after a
design by Mr. Wilson, in three stages, to suit the
inequality of the ground. It has a range of deep
recessed arches with two towers, and is capable

* Whitfield, it seems, had a weak place—"the mighty and
noble," evidently, impressed him with great awe.

of accommodating 1000 children; 400 infants occupy the lower school, 300 boys the centre, and 300 girls the upper, each class having a separate entrance. The houses in the Vineyards were formerly called Harlequin Row, in consequence of some of them being built in courses of brick and stone alternately; they are now uniform in appearance.

On the opposite side are respectively The Paragon and Bladud's Buildings. They were erected during the last century.

At No. 33, is the **School of Art.** It was established in May, 1854, in connection with the Government Department of Science and Art. The institution owes its existence to a few public-spirited persons, who (aided by a grant of £200 from Government) purchased the present premises. It is well conducted; is of great practical value, and facilitates the cultivation of drawing and artistic taste amongst all classes.

Hay Hill Chapel is erected close to, if not actually upon, the site of a mediæval ecclesiastical chapel.[*] The present structure was erected by the Baptist community in 1869, at a cost, approximately, of £2,300. The place is an irregular wedge shape, with galleries on three sides. It is built in early pointed Gothic, and was designed by Messrs. Wilson and Willcox. There is a small vestry in the rear, and a school-room underneath.

* The Sanctuary Chapel, vide pages 40 and 41.

At the termination of the angle formed by Fountain Buildings is a 𝔇𝔯𝔦𝔫𝔨𝔦𝔫𝔤 𝔉𝔬𝔲𝔫𝔱𝔞𝔦𝔫, erected in 1860 by the Licensed Victuallers' Association, and the Society for the Prevention of Cruelty to Animals. The architect is Mr. C. J. Phipps.

IN AND OUT OF BATH.

————•o:◦:o•————

WALK THE SEVENTEENTH.

ST. MICHAEL'S CHURCH; MARKET PLACE; PARLIAMENTARY AND MUNICIPAL AFFAIRS; THE OLD AND PRESENT GUILDHALL; THE MARKET.

THE first mention of St. Michael's Church is in the charter granted by King Edward in 1361, wherein the city was directed to devote a sum of money yearly to its repair. It is supposed that the present is the fourth church on the same site. In 1438, as appears from Bishop Stafford's register at Wells, Thomas Short resigned the living, and was succeeded by a Carthusian friar, John de Bethlem. The immediate predecessor of the present church was a Roman building, erected on a faulty plan by John Harvey in 1731.* Being found both inadequate and expensive, it was replaced by the present one in 1836, after a design by Mr. Manners. It has a light and elegant spire, which forms a notable feature in every

* The name of the architect is given to refute the story that the churchwardens employed the sexton !

view of the city. The Rev. J. C. Burnett is the rector.*

Wood, it is well known, built Queen Square, and when it was proposed to build the church in 1731, he thus quaintly states the circumstances, and manages at the same time to express his own grievance :—
" This church, in the year 1730, being in a ruinous condition, Dr. Hunt, the late Rector of Bath, had thoughts of getting a brief to rebuild it, and to make it so large as to serve the parishioners, and the inhabitants of *Queen Square.* With this view I formed a design for a new church ; adapted seats for every one that had seats in the old church; and prepared a proposal, that if the parish would give me the materials of the old building, and the money that should be collected by a brief, I would, at my own charge, erect the intended fabric; provided the surplus pews could be secured to me, for the use of my tenants in and about *Queen Square;* and upon the 14th day of January, 1730-1, a vestry was called to take these matters into consideration : But when the parishioners met, the majority of them wou'd not hear of a brief, imagining it would be a reflection upon them and the city, nor would they listen to any proposal which tended to rebuild the church, for the benefit of others as well as themselves : They were so charitable, however, as to recommend it to me to erect a *chapel* on my own ground, for the use of my own tenants ; and then declared, that when

* See page 127 for the description of the separation of St. Michael's from the Rectory of Bath.

there shou'd be occasion to rebuild their church, they were both *able* and *willing* to do it of themselves, without the assistance of any body."

He then describes the church which was built without his professional aid, with a "timber floor," as in Walcot Church, "to separate the living from the dead."* Being unable to secure specific accommodation for "my tenants," he built St. Mary's Chapel, in Queen Square, to which reference has already been made.

The muniments of the parish contain the churchwardens' accounts as far back as the reign of Edward III., which are therefore almost as old as any in the kingdom, and are curious. They are set out in detail in the Appendix to Warner's Bath.

Parliamentary and Municipal.

There have been many conflicting theories on the subject of early municipal government, and it would seem that, as regards the electoral franchise in boroughs and cities, it was exercised in early times by different classes of the community. In the election of parliamentary representatives, Sir J. Macintosh says :—" In some places the freemen, in others the officers of a Corporation; elsewhere freeholders, burgage tenants, inhabitants contributing to public expense ;—these, and combinations of various sorts of them, were the principal classes among whom the elective franchise was in the earliest times shared."

---

* His strictures were evidently deserved, for a more wretched church was never erected.

The charters, previous to the reign of Henry VI., were not charters of incorporation, and as a rule in boroughs every freeman, who became a resident householder capable of paying scot and bearing lot (*i.e.*, paying his share of local taxation and discharging in turn the local offices,) became a burgess. The first charter of incorporation was given by Henry VI. to Hull, and other instances followed. In course of time, the Mayor and leading men of the Corporate bodies, acting by the Corporate seal and for the whole body, soon began to monopolise authority, and to exercise the power of selecting the burgesses, frequently among non-residents. The Crown also began to grant charters of incorporation, with clauses which gave exclusive powers to certain officers of the Corporation, or to certain select bodies.* By these means, and by the capricious growth and establishment of an infinite variety of local usages, the electoral as well as the municipal system of our boroughs became widely changed from its primitive character; and hence a crop of abuses and anomalies grew up, which was only eradicated by the Parliamentary and Reform Act of 1832 and Municipal Corporations' Act of 1835.

The first charter given to this city was by Richard I., but this charter conferred privileges, rather relating to trade than to local government. Henry III., in consideration of certain money payments, granted

* Hallam. Creasy.
  Macintosh. Forsyth.

another charter, enlarging the liberties and privileges of the previous charter, and also granting certain immunities and exemptions. Edward III., also in return for grants of money, agreed to confirm previous charters, and to extend to the city a special exemption from the domiciliary visits of odious and rapacious tax-gatherers, and gave to the local authorities the privilege of collecting the king's taxes as well as the local dues. Another clause protects the citizens against the encroachments of the Bristolians, who had established a rival fair for the sale of goods similar to those manufactured in Bath.

Henry VI. granted a charter to enable the citizens to elect their own Mayor, hitherto nominated by the sovereign, and in a second charter he granted additional liberties—enlarging the jurisdiction of the Mayor, and sanctioning the organisation of civic companies, and trading guilds.* Under these several

* Under this charter the only "Company" formed in Bath was The Drapers, about a century and a quarter ago—ten or twenty years before limitations on apprenticeship were proved unlawful. It was on the model of the London Companies, and had a sort of charter or deed-poll executed by the Mayor, &c. The original deed of the company was exhibited by Dr. Hunter to the Field Club.—See Transactions, vol. 7, No. 4, page 474.

In the early part of the sixteenth century, Trading Companies were formed by almost every class of traders, but they possessed no warrant either of charter or parliamentary authority. Nevertheless they assumed privileges themselves, and the right to transmit them to others on conditions of their own making. It is singular that these usurped powers and privileges were submitted to until 1765, when a Bath taylor, named Glazeby, having opened shop within their pretended jurisdiction—the question was tried, and the companies and their "rights" extinguished.

charters the city was governed until the reign of Elizabeth, when, in 1590, she granted the charter of incorporation under which—occasionally modified and supplemented by certain local acts—the city was governed for upwards of 200 years, and some of the privileges of which it enjoys to this day.

The constitution conferred by this charter was, owing to the sagacity and public spirit of Sherston, one of unusual comprehensiveness. It gave great scope for development, and when the city expanded so largely and so suddenly in the last century, the Corporation was fully equal to the increased responsibility, and unchecked by the restrictions of modern legislation, was enabled to foster and encourage, by liberal expenditure, the institutions of the day. The Corporate body, like many others, was not always consistent—it sometimes arrayed itself on the popular side, and sometimes, during civil commotions, displayed a time-serving spirit. It is curious to note that Bath was one of the first cities of importance that espoused the cause of the Parliament, and one of the first to tender its loyalty and welcome to Charles II.

The electoral franchise from the earliest times, down to the Charter of Queen Elizabeth, was of the simplest "scot and lot" character. It was never conferred either by charter or enactment. The earliest Charters to which reference has been made, conferred various rights and privileges, out of which, by degrees, grew a rough

kind of franchise, which was based on property
and certain conditions of citizenship, but it was in
those days necessarily limited to a very small number
of persons. The charter of Elizabeth not only recognized all previous rights, but gave a more definite
and a far more valuable municipal constitution.
It is a fact, however, to be observed, that this
charter conferred no direct electoral privilege upon
the citizens, other than those it conferred upon
the mayor, aldermen, and the citizen-councillors,
composing the first Corporate body, who possessed the power of self-election. This charter
of incorporation, however, was of immense value,
It gave legal powers to the body corporate to acquire
and sell property; to frame its by-laws; to regulate
the internal affairs of the city in trade and in local
taxation, as well as to assume the trust of all public
charities and institutions, and to direct public works.
The charter, moreover, gave an importance and dignity
to the city in the estimation of other towns and cities.
It became, under the charter, a "free city," and this
freedom enabled the supreme body to extend conditions of freedom to the citizens. These conditions were the holding of property, the serving an
apprenticeship of seven years, the due payment of
local taxes, and the discharge of public duties within
its jurisdiction. The freemen, in time—though no
specific powers were vested in them by the charter—
exercised considerable influence on the policy and
fortunes of the city through the Corporate body,

notwithstanding its independence and inherent right of self-election. There is little to show to what extent the freemen were permitted to exercise the Parliamentary franchise, but it is obvious that they did so, and that they acquired something like a recognized status in the time of Charles I., or probably before. After the restoration, it is manifest from the record of Prynne,* that the 200 freemen referred to as claiming to vote for the candidates opposed to himself and Popham, did not claim any new privilege, but a right that had been in some way conceded to, or acquired by, them and exercised previously. From this time forward, however, down to the Reform Bill, the corporation in its corporate capacity, chose the parliamentary representatives of the city without reference to the freemen, whose privileges were limited to the emoluments arising from the small estates then and still belonging to them, together with certain other advantages of a minor character.†

---

* See page 345.

† At a General Election in September, 1812, "Lord John Thynne and Lieutenant-Colonel Palmer were re-elected." Mr. John Allen, a citizen, "demanded a poll for himself and William Colleton Graves, insisting on the right of the freemen of the city to give their suffrages." After some very undignified proceedings, a legal decision was obtained, confirming that obtained in 1706. It is curious also to observe that the body of the freemen and the committee representing their interests, repudiated the attempt of Mr. Allen. The judgment of 1706 in substance was as follows:—
"The right of election for the city, by the established laws then in existence, was clearly defined, and declared to be vested in the Mayor, Aldermen, and Common Council."--*Mainwaring's Annals.*

The close corporation appears to have done its work with due regard to the interests of the city. It maintained through all the vicissitudes of party struggles a high regard for its own constitution, and a corresponding desire to do honour to the city in the men it chose to represent it in Parliament. Statesmen such as the great Pitt, Lord Bayham,* afterwards Earl of Brecknock, then Marquis Camden, and many other lesser magnates, add a lustre to the annals of the city, of which it may well be proud; and it is no small distinction that Pitt was sustained in the brilliant career, in which he acquired the

* Son of Lord Chief Justice, afterwards Lord Chancellor Camden, who, in the year 1759, when he was appointed Attorney-General, was also chosen Recorder of Bath. In 1775, and again in 1784, Bath elected his only son, the Hon. John-Jefferys Pratt (conjointly with Abel Moysey) as one of its parliamentary representatives. After the advancement of Lord Camden to the Viscounty of Bayham and Earldom of Camden, his son assumed the former title, and was again elected M.P. for the city in 1790, Viscount Weymouth being his colleague. On the death of Earl Camden, Lord Bayham succeeded as second Earl Camden. In 1812 he was created Earl of Brecknock and Marquis Camden. He was a man of singular uprightness of character and distinguished . ability. In 1798 he was appointed Lord-Lieutenant of Ireland; subsequently was made a K.G.; Teller of the Exchequer; Chancellor of the University of Cambridge; and Recorder of Bath, an office he held until the passing of the Municipal Corporations Act in 1835, so that two Peers, father and son, successively held this office. He died in 1840.

Camden Crescent was first called "Camden Place," after Lord Camden's residence in Kent. Why its name was changed is not easy to tell. The subordinate buildings which have adopted similar names, with the respective prefix of "Upper" and "Lower," should, it may be thought, have adopted other titles.

appellation of the "great commoner," by the un-
grudging support of the body who chose him.

All this is now changed. The exigencies of the
State demanded a new order of things. The Reform Bill called into existence conditions of national
life and energies which rendered it impossible
that the old municipal institution could co-exist
side by side with the enlarged basis of Parliamentary representation. If the result of the present
state of things, as many consider, is not perfect,
it must at least be remembered it is on the
whole very much what the citizens and burgesses
choose to have it.

The old Town Hall, which stood in the centre of
the Market Place, was built by Inigo Jones in 1625,
and pulled down in 1766. The building was of the
Doric and Ionic orders, resting on arches and ornamented with the statues of Kings Offa and Edgar,
which may now be seen over the door of a building
near the Hot Bath. The present Guildhall was built
by Baldwin, and completed in 1775, having various
apartments suitable for the offices connected with
the Corporation. The great hall is a noble room,
80 feet in length by 40 in breadth, and 31 in height,
containing portraits of Frederick, Prince of Wales,
and his Consort, George III. and Queen Charlotte,
Pitt — Earl of Chatham, Earl Camden, Anstey,
Ralph Allen, and Alderman Hunt. In the Mayor's
room is Turnerelli's bust of George III.; and in the
Council chamber one of Ralph Allen, set up during

his mayoralty. In this room also are duplicate portraits of George III. and Queen Charlotte. On the landing of the grand staircase is a fine portrait of Marshal Wade. In the lobby are two busts, one of the late Sir W. Tite,* M.P., and the other of the late T. Phinn, Esq., Q.C., who represented Bath (his native city) in Parliament from 1852 to 1855.

The Market well deserves a visit. It is eminently clean, commodious, and well supplied. Every Saturday it is kept open to a late hour and presents a busy and interesting scene. It was built in 1863, by Messrs. Hicks and Isaac, at a cost of about £6,000.

* A successful London architect. He built the Royal Exchange, and many other large edifices in London and elsewhere. In 1855, he was elected one of the representatives of Bath, and continued in that position until his death in 1873. Sir William was a collector of fine and curious books. At the time of his death, it is not too much to say, he possessed one of the most valuable private libraries in the kingdom.

IN AND OUT OF BATH.

WALK THE EIGHTEENTH.

Over the Down to Brass Knocker Hill; Limpley Stoke; Freshford; and Farleigh Hungerford.

LIMPLEY STOKE.

THE first part of the journey may be made either viâ Widcombe Hill or Bathwick Hill. The roads unite at the western edge of the plateau. From this point, the pedestrian can reach the brow of Brass Knocker Hill by the highway, or by a footpath to the right over the turf. The views from each are very charming.

At the top of Bathwick Hill is Grove House, formerly the residence of the Rev. James Pycroft, the author of some successful works, among which writers of fiction, when re-producing phases of thought more or less exceptional in the middle of the nineteenth century.·

One sort of literary gossip is apt to suggest another. Those who have read the fictions of Miss Pickering may remember the fresh colours in which she paints the charms of breezy uplands, where the turf is short and elastic, where the thyme and the harebell reach the maximum of odour and delicacy, and where the air is full of life and sweetness. This gifted writer was a native of Bath, and wrote the greater part of her works at the house of her mother in Prior Park Buildings. It is at least probable that many of these upland pictures were painted from nature on Claverton Down.

A view of infinite loveliness breaks upon us from the hill immediately above the viaduct. On the right is the valley of Midford. Half way up the opposite hill lies Monckton Combe peeping above the coppice wood, with here and there a pretty cottage or clustering hamlet. On the left are the Avon and the Canal, the former being crossed by means of a handsome aqueduct, under which passes the Wilts, Somerset, and Dorset Railway.

At the bottom of the hill, we can take the lower road which runs parallel with the railway, or cross the viaduct and ascend to the upper part of the are several novels. It is probable that the latter may serve as text books for future historians, and may furnish, half a century hence perhaps, materials for

village, from which a road to the left leads to the church.

Limpley Stoke lies about four miles from Bath by

STOKE BRIDGE AS IT WAS.

the road we have followed, and six by rail or the Warminster Road. It is one of the most pictur-esque villages in the neighbourhood of the city.

The houses are, for the most part, built with charming irregularity on the side of the hill. From the upper part of the village may be seen the picturesque bridge, which crosses the river near the railway station.

Stoke is derived from the Saxon, *stem*—place; but the prefix Limpley is a matter of conjecture. Tradition speaks of a Lady Limpley, who resided in a mansion near the church. The field in which the house is said to have stood is called Limpley Ground in the parish books. It is not unlikely, therefore, that the name Limpley Stoke may be derived from the family of Limpley, as Rodney Stoke derives its appellation from the Rodneys. The nomenclature of villages being frequently determined by the physical character of their respective localities, as for example Combe, Ford, Stoke, &c., it became necessary to distinguish various places of the same name by the appellation of some ancient family, or by some other prefix. No ancient records exist, but it is well known that the church lands, before the Reformation, belonged to the Abbey of Shaftesbury, and subsequently to the Dean and Chapter of Bristol.

The present Church, dedicated to St. Mary the Virgin, is a small, well-proportioned structure, consisting of nave, chancel, and tower. It is evidently placed on the site of one of more ancient date, probably the 13th century. From a Norman doorway, built up in the south wall, some idea can be formed

of the earlier structure. This doorway may have
been closed up when there was no further use for it.
From its position, and the traditional site of the
mansion of the Limpleys, it is not improbable that
the church, like many in the country, stood near
the mansion, and that the door in question formed
a private entrance for the family.

The tower, at the west end, seems an adjunct to
the church, there being an ancient campanile over
the chancel arch, in which were two bells. These,
according to the churchwardens' books, were sold in
the year 1781, and the proceeds (amounting to
£24 15s. 6d.) appropriated to defray the cost of the
pulpit, reading desk, font, &c. The bell in the
tower, which is of moderate size, bears the date
of 1596, and the letters w.p.i.a.f. These may have
been placed there when the tower was added to the
church. As the consecration crosses are cut in the
quoins of the nave on the north and south sides of
the tower, it is evident that it was not consecrated
with the church. Within the church, near the doorway, is an ancient stone pulpit projecting from the
wall, which was probably used as late as the year 1787.

That the church was dedicated to the Virgin
may be gathered from the niche recently discovered
over the doorway of the porch. The sides of
this niche are not perpendicular, and it seems to
have been made to suit the figure of the Virgin, who
is generally represented leaning her head a little to
the right, with the child on her right arm.

In the churchyard are several tombstones, as old probably as the 13th century. On the north side of the burial ground, fragments of Roman urns have been found. There was a *castra æstiva* in the immediate neighbourhood.

The chalice and paten used at the Holy Communion are curious and almost unique. The paten forms a cover to the chalice, and its handle, in the shape of a knob, is flattened at the top, so as to form a support when placed on the table. It has the date of 1577 engraved on it. The present vicar is the Rev. F. S. Forss.

The village, though small, has other objects of archæological interest besides the church. In Stoke Wood, above Chatley House, is a celebrated spring, called "Shingle Bell Well." It is immediately below the east end of a ruined building, long used as a barn. The stones of the walls having recently been removed for building purposes, little more than the foundations remain. From its position, shape, size, and general character, however, it was probably a chapel belonging to a small castle, traditionally known as Spy Castle. Standing near a point which commands an extensive view of the valley and surrounding hills, it may, perhaps, be not unreasonably conjectured that the name was derived from the site.

The waters in Shingle Bell Well have been held in great repute as efficacious in diseases of the eyes; tradition adds that sufferers, who received benefit from them, used to hang strips of rag or cloth on the branches of the surrounding trees as votive offerings.

Among the *debris* of a neighbouring quarry an ancient silver signet ring was found, in the shield of which was inserted a silver relic. Near the opening of the quarry, also, a pocket ring dial was discovered, similar to that described by Shakespeare in " As You Like It." Act II., Scene 7 :—

> "And then he drew a dial from his poke ;
> And, looking on it with lack-lustre eye,
> Says very wisely, ' It is ten o'clock :
> Thus may we see, quoth he, ' how the world wags.' "

Romantic legends, Christmas "mummeries," local ditties with quaint music, folk-lore, singular nomenclature, and a dash of superstitious simplicity among the humbler classes, seem to have been from the earliest times characteristic of this somewhat isolated village.

The remains of a Roman camp are to be seen on the hill near the lane leading from Upper Stoke to Midford. Many coins have been found in the field adjacent to the camp. In 1867, in grubbing up a brake, a bronze eagle was found. It is now in the Bath Literary Institution.

The West of England Hydropathic Establishment, under the general management of J. Smith, Esq., and an efficient medical staff, lies at a short distance from the Railway Station. The fine climate, pure water, and cheerful aspects of the spot, conduce materially to its success. The grounds, eighteen acres in extent, are tastefully laid out. Beside the appliances common to such an institution, there are Turkish and Electro-Chemical Baths.

The old **Manor House** is now converted into a **Reformatory** for Girls. The success which has attended this institution is due in a great measure to the excellent management, unwearied interest, and exertions of P. C. Sheppard, Esq., and Mrs. Sheppard, of Waterhouse.

The institution was certified Jan. 9th, 1861. From that time to the present (1876) the following summary will show the general results :—

Total Number of Juvenile Offenders Admitted ...		276
Finally Discharged—		
To Service 126		
Returned to Friends 68		
Emigrated from School 5		
Transferred to other Schools 3		
Died in School 4		
Sent to Union Workhouses 3		
To Gaols 2		
	——	211
Remaining in School 57		
Absent on Licence 8		
	—	65

The building now used as a Brewery is supposed to have been a portion of an **Old Monastery**, from the circumstance that mouldings and other ornamentations of an ecclesiastic design have been found, some of which still remain.

On excavating the site for the railway station, several skeletons, together with military accoutrements, apparently belonging to the 17th century, were found. It is probable that a skirmish between the Royalists and Roundheads occurred near the spot.

The population, in 1871, including the inmates of the Reformatory, was 452. The parish is in the Union of Bradford.

FRESHFORD.

THIS village, pretty in itself, its site, and its surroundings, lies on the Wilts, Somerset, and Dorset Railway, and is distant about six miles from Bath.

Passing the iron gates of a fine old house, the road leads, viâ the Post Office, to the Tyning, which forms the village promenade. Some part of the village is built on a dip of the ridgeway or "hogsback," which extends from Freshford almost to Wellow.*

A short distance beyond this high ground is Sharpstone, a mere cluster of cottages, situated near the banks of the River Frome. Close to this hamlet is a narrow passage, called the "drungway,"† leading into a quiet coombe, through which runs a footpath to Hinton Abbey, and the ruin mentioned in " My Mother and I."‡

The Hermitage deserves a visit, if only on account of the view it affords. From it may be seen

---

* This peculiar formation is shewn on the map, to which the reader is referred.

† A Somersetshire word meaning a path between two walls, or two hedges, from which there is no escape—a sort of Balaam's passage.

‡ The scene of this charming story lies chiefly at Freshford and the neighbourhood. It is scarcely necessary to say the author is Mrs. Craik (née Miss Muloch).

the Frome, meandering in its deep channel under Friary Wood, and beyond, the long line of Salisbury Plain, on the slope of which stands the White Horse. Eastwards lie Bradford and Devizes. Beneath, are the river, the railway, and the canal, running in almost parallel lines under Avoncliff, below which is an aqueduct, scarcely inferior to the one at Dundas. Behind the Hermitage is Park Corner, so called from its vicinity to the park or grounds of the Monastery at Hinton Charterhouse, and nearly half-a-mile further on is the hamlet of Pipehouse or Pipards.

Like Norton, Hinton, Iford, and Limpley Stoke, Freshford enjoyed its palmy days in the times when broad cloth was made by hand, and when the process was carried on in the cottages of the various work-people. The old, but still handsome houses in the village, were once the residences of wealthy clothiers. As a rule, the trade is now confined to towns, in which alone the large manufacturers of the present day find all the appliances necessary for a successful trade.

Freshford is rich in country walks. A path across the fields leads to Iford and Farleigh Castle. Iford House was the residence of the late Doctor Gaisford, an accomplished Greek Scholar, and Dean of Christ Church, Oxford. This stroll is full of pastoral loveliness. There is also a tempting path across the meadows to Avoncliff, from whence Bradford may be reached either by way of the aqueduct and the road which runs parallel with the railway, or by the towing path of the canal.

At the Conquest, Freshford consisted of four manors, namely, Iford, Freshford, which was divided, and *Undewiche* or Woodwick. In the latter there was formerly a parish church, and tomb-stones have been occasionally found in a place called Church Field. In 1448, Thomas Halle, of Bradford, the patron of the two livings, conjoined them, and Woodwick Church was allowed to decay. The two manors of Freshford were given to Hinton Abbey, to which they remained attached until the dissolution. They then passed through the families of Stringer, Davison, Ford, Ash and Methuen, into the possession of the Joyces, to whom Freshford House* still belongs.

Mementos of the former presence and influence of the Monks at Hinton survive in the names of Abbotsleigh, the Hermitage, and Friary.

The Church, of which the Rev. Thomas White-house is the rector, and the Simeon Trustees the patrons, is dedicated to St. Peter. It has an embattled perpendicular tower, forty-four feet high, containing a clock and four bells. The body is of the 18th century. The chancel was rebuilt in 1859.†

---

* This house was occupied for some years by the late Lieut.-General Sir William Napier, K.C.B. Here it was that he wrote the latter portion of his famous work, "The History of the Peninsular War." Lady Napier acted as amanuensis to her distinguished husband.

† In connection with this parish the name of John Curl, of Turleigh, in the parish of Bradford, Wilts, should not be for-

Freshford is in the hundred of Bathforum, and Union of Bradford. The population, at the census of 1871, was 584.

FARLEIGH HUNGERFORD.

ON a hill south of the ruins of the Castle are some slight remains of earthworks, which have been attributed to the old British period. On the slope of the hill in the year 1683, a Roman pavement was discovered. It was, however, little regarded until the late Mr. Skinner, of Camerton, visited it in the year 1822, when he laid bare the remains of a villa. In the Temple field, ten feet below the surface, he found a bath, and other apartments, with an almost perfect pavement, the walls stuccoed and painted green, and the flooring smooth and hard as marble. The remains, having been much injured by petty pilfering, are now covered up.* Traces of another

---

gotten, nor his remedy for the ecclesiastical abuse of non-residence. He seems to have been a man of a benevolent and religious spirit, as may be seen from his will, made Dec., 1703. Besides other legacies to the rector and the poor, he left a field called Eatons, and £100, to the rector for the time being, on condition that he should reside in Freshford, and officiate in the church twice every Lord's Day ; and in case he should not do so for the space of one month (sickness excepted) he was to lose all interest therein so long as he should be rector, and the money was to be given to the poor. He appears to have been interred at Freshford, for, according to an old register, " Mr. John Curl, of Turline, in the parrish of Bradford, was bury'd January the 5th, 1707."

* Some coins of Magnentius, Constantius, and Constans, were also discovered. For Plan of Bath, &c,, found here, see "Gentleman's Magazine," 1823.

Roman villa have also been found at the end of the ridge overlooking Stowford.

In the reign of the Confessor, this manor, then called in Domesday Book *Ferlege* but in some Anglo-Saxon documents "Færnlea," was worth twenty shillings, and belonged to Smewin, a Saxon. At the Conquest, it was given to Roger de Curcelles, then being only half of that value. At his death, William Rufus bestowed it on Hugh de Montfort, by whose descendants it was sold in A.D. 1337, to Lord Burghersh; but it retained the name of Farleigh Montfort until its purchase from Burghersh by Sir Thomas Hungerford, in 1383, in whose family it remained three hundred years; when Sir Edward the spendthrift sold it to the Bayntons, from whom it came by purchase to the Houltons, its present owners, in 1730. It is situated on the River Frome, eight miles from Bath, partly in Somerset and partly in Wilts, in the Frome union.

The Church, dedicated to St. Leonard, like the castle chapel (of which it was the substitute), was built by Walter Lord Hungerford, K.G., High Treasurer of England, *temp.* Henry VI., and together with the churchyard, was consecrated on St. Leonard's day, Nov. 6th, 1443. It is a neat edifice, consisting of a tower, about fifty-four feet high to the parapet, with a short pyramidal steeple covered with stone tiles. There are four bells.—Nave, and chancel, about ninety-six feet long, by thirty feet wide, complete the building. Over the south porch is a semi-circular stone, having a roughly incised cross, and the following inscription, rudely cut in old letters :—

MUNIAT HOC TEMPLŪ CRUCE GLORIFICANS MICROCOSMŪ:
Q̄ GENUIT XPM MISERI^S PCE FIAT ASILUM.*

Canon Jackson translates it thus:

" May he who by the cross glorifies man protect this church : May the mother of Christ become an asylum to the wretched by *her* prayer *for them !*"*

In the interior of the building, in the chancel, are four freestone monuments of the Houlton family. On the panels of the altar-rails, which are of oak, are carvings, representing—(beginning at the left) —1. The Manna descending.   2. The Seven-branched Candlestick.   3. Head of Moses.   4. A Loaf of Shewbread.   5. Two Loaves of Shewbread. These were placed there in 1836 by the late Colonel Houlton.

* The first line alludes to the Saviour ; the second to the Virgin Mary. This inscription has long exercised the wits of visitors. The words are contracted.   Written in full it runs thus : " Muniat hoc templum cruce glorificans microcosmum : Que (for quæ) genuit Christum miseris prece fiat asilum." The word " Micro-cosmus " (i.e. *little world*) was a term in medieval philosophy for *Man*, as opposed to the *Great World*, the *Globe*, mega-cosmus. Some ingenious expositors, not content with explaining things as they find them, would persuade us that above the rudely sculptured cross there *may have* been the figure of a globe, and that " Microcosmum " in the inscription *may* have referred to the said globe.   To such criticism the short answer is, that there is no trace whatever of any circle above the cross ; and that even if there ever had been one, the old Latinist knew what he was about better than to apply to the great world a term that had been specially invented to signify the little world !

The east window is made up of fragments of old glass, collected from different parts of the church. In the centre is St. Leonard carrying a chain; in the other lights, but very indistinct, are St. Anne and St. Christopher.

In the side windows are modern coats-of-arms, relating to the Houlton family, namely, on the north, Torriano and Houlton; on the south, White and Ellis.

In one of the south windows is an older coat, bearing the arms of Heytesbury and Hungerford quarterly: impaling 1 and 4. Zouche: 2. St. Maur and Lovell quarterly. 3. Cantelupe. This is the shield of a Sir Edward Hungerford, who died A.D. 1521 and Jane Zouche his wife.

In the top of the chancel windows, some of the old glass may be seen, viz., a knot of three sickles interlaced, with the coat of Hungerford in the centre.

The subjects of the two pictures against the east wall are, on the left, The Supper at Emmaus; on the right, the garden of Gethsemane.

One window displays, in almost every pane, the early crest of the Hungerfords, the sickle, and a square containing two triangles with a man's face, an ancient symbol of the Trinity; in another, on the south side of the nave, is a Knight's head, helmeted. commonly called Sir Thomas Hungerford.

Farleigh Castle is seated on a rocky terrace. On the south, the hill rises higher than the castle and commands it; it was, therefore, never regarded as a stronghold. In its most perfect state it consisted

Farleigh Castle.

of two wards, surrounded by a moat; the entrances were due east and west. The former, bearing the arms and initials of Edward Hungerford, was defended by a drawbridge and an embattled gatehouse, of which a great portion still stands. This led to the outer ward, in which were the offices, stables,

SOUTH-EAST GATEWAY FROM THE INSIDE OF THE COURT.*

guard-house, &c. Another gateway, guarded by two towers, led into an inner court-yard, which was flanked by four larger round towers, sixty feet high. Leland says, there was a common saying that one of the family built this part of the castle with the "praye

* The Autotype represents the Western Tower.

B b

of the Duke of Orleaunce,"* whom he had taken
prisoner.   In the lower ward, the four large towers
were connected by various apartments, some of
which were fine rooms used for State purposes, fitted
with painted glass, &c.   All these are now in ruins,
the only portion left entire being the larger chapel of
St. Leonard, and St. Anne's Chantry attached to it on
the south side.   Over the door, leading from the castle
yard into the chapel yard, is the Hungerford crest
in stone—a wheat-sheaf between two sickles.   On
the floor, near the west door, is the sculptured grave-
stone of one of the first Chantry priests.   The altar is
of breccia, on which is displayed a black letter Bible,
and above is a fresco of St. George and the Dragon.
At the south-east angle is a large altar-tomb, with
the following inscription:—" Tyme tryeth truth,
quod Walter Hungerford, Knyght, who lyeth here,
and Edward, hys sone, to God's mercy, in whom he
strust (*i.e.* trusts) for ever.   A.D. 1585, the vi. of
Desbr."   The copy of an autograph letter, of Oliver
Cromwell, stolen from an old chest in the castle
many years ago, is also preserved here.   Beneath
the arch dividing the chapel from the chantry is the
tomb of Sir Thomas Hungerford, one of the first recorded speakers of the House of Commons, and of
Joan his wife. He died in 1398; she in 1412. In the
centre of the chantry is a magnificent white marble
tomb of Sir Edward Hungerford, of Corsham, who
died 1648, and Margaret (Halliday) his wife, who

* Charles de Bourbon, taken at Agincourt, 1415.

founded the almshouse at Corsham, and died 1672. It bears their effigies, beautifully carved; he in armour with a wheatsheaf at his feet; she in a loose robe, her feet supported by a demi-lion, bearing an anchor. At the west end is a shield emblazoning fifteen coats-of-arms. The tomb is supported by black marble steps, and the figures are placed on a slab of the same material, eight feet long. Attached to the north wall is an altar-tomb of freestone, to the memory of an earlier Sir Edward, who died in 1607. Against the north-west corner is another altar-tomb, having the figures of a lady and her family kneeling, over which is a mural brass to the memory of the "right noble and vertuous Mrs. Mary Shaa," the daughter of the Lord Hungerford of Heytesbury, who was beheaded by Henry VIII.* She

* This nobleman brought little credit upon the family ; he was something of a Bluebeard. Three wives in succession complained of his cruel treatment, the last petitioning the king in piteous terms to be released from the tower in which her "lord" had imprisoned her, and where, as she alleges, her lord's chaplain had attempted to "poyson" her. Though the petition reached the king, it did not lead to her release. Probably the king conceded to his noble subject the right he claimed for himself of doing as he pleased with his own wives, and declined to interfere. Henry was, it seems, tolerant on the matter of "poysoning" a wife or two ; but not so on matters affecting his dignity. Hungerford soon after this offended his gracious master, who at once tried him on a frivolous pretext of treason, and applied his royal remedy for such offences or alleged offences, and cut off his noble subject's head on Tower Hill, 1540. This slight incident had the effect of releasing the fair captive of the Tower, who consoled herself for the inconsiderate treatment of her "first lord" by marrying another, viz., Sir R. Thockmorton of Coughton, who, it may be hoped, lavished

. died in 1613.   The ceiling retains some vestiges of
an old painting of the Resurrection, with portraits of
the Apostles.   The coats-of-arms, on the walls being
very nearly obliterated, were restored some years
ago.

Passing out of the chapel, the visitor should inspect,
the old family vault of the Hungerfords, under the
Chantry of St. Anne, in which are eight leaden
coffins, having the features of the face in relief.

The house, erected for the chantry priests of St.
Leonard's, is now a dairy farm, on the east side of
the chapel.

During the ownership of the Hungerford family,*
the castle was occasionally forfeited to the Crown.
In one of these intervals, Margaret Plantagenet,
daughter of George, Duke of Clarence, brother
to King Edward IV., was born in the castle, and
created Countess of Salisbury by Henry VIII.   She
married Sir Richard Pole, and became the mother

---

upon her the full measure of his affection, and was not sparing in
the number of "groats" he allowed her for pocket-money, which
had been so cruelly denied her by her former "lord."   The lady
was the daughter of Lord Hussey, and by her second marriage with
Sir R. Throckmorton had six children, namely, two sons and four
daughters ; the former died unmarried, all the daughters married :
Murial, to Sir Thomas Tresham ; Anne, to Sir William Catesby ;
Elizabeth, to Sir Anthony Tyringham ; Temperance, to Sir Randall
Brereton.

* The Hungerfords were a brave but intriguing race.   In the
Wars of the Roses, they espoused the Lancastrian cause, and
suffered in consequence.

of the celebrated Cardinal of that name. Involved in
the politics of the day, she was beheaded in the Tower
of London, in 1541. Her eldest son, Lord Montague, suffered the same fate in 1538. The castle
was reduced to its present ruinous condition in the
troublous times of Charles I. During the Rebellion,
Sir Edward Hungerford commanded the forces of
the Parliament, though the castle was garrisoned for
the king—a singular coincidence—by Col. Hungerford, but whether a relation or not, does not appear.
Sir Edward died in 1648, and was succeeded by his
nephew, Sir Edward, the "spendthrift," notorious
even in a notorious age for his wasteful prodigality
at the court of Charles II. Much credit is due to
the present owners of the property, for the manner
in which they have preserved what is left of so interesting a building.

About half a mile from the church is situated the
family mansion of the Houltons.

The visit to Farleigh Hungerford is supposed to be
within the compass of a summer day's ramble from
Bath. The walk there and back by road, over Brass
Knocker Hill and through Freshford, would be
about sixteen miles. It could be reduced to half
the distance mentioned, if the visitor took the rail
to Freshford.

The population of Farleigh, in 1841, was 154; in
1871, it amounted to 146. Farleigh is in the Union
of Frome.

IN AND OUT OF BATH.

———◦◦¦◦¦◦◦———

WALK THE NINETEENTH.

THE KENNET AND AVON CANAL; WINSLEY AND
TURLEIGH; BRADFORD; WESTWOOD.

~~~~~~~~~~~~~~~~~~~~~~~~~~~~~~~~

THE KENNET AND AVON CANAL.

ONE of the most agreeable walks in the neighbourhood is along the banks of the canal to the ancient
manufacturing town of Bradford-on-Avon.

The Canal follows the line of the Great Western
Railway to Bathampton. On the south are the
Hampton rocks and the new Warminster road. On
the north are Batheaston and Banner-down. To
the east are Bathford and Farleigh down, on the side
of which the Bradford road descends to its junction
with the London road. A little further on is a stone
wharf, formerly connected with the Hampton quarries
by a tramway. It is now disused. Then comes a

long stretch of rich meadow scenery and wooded hills. Close to Claverton is a bridge, and near it is a pathway leading to Warleigh Ferry. Presently Conkwell peeps out among the trees; then the aqueduct, beautiful even in these days of railway

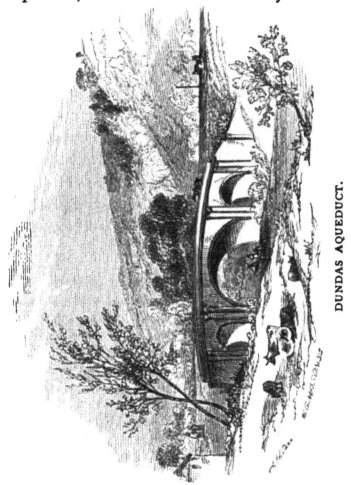

DUNDAS AQUEDUCT.

viaducts, claims something more than a passing notice; next, Stoke and Freshford are seen; and at length, Avonecliff, Turleigh, and Belcombe, help us on to Bradford.

WINSLEY AND TURLEIGH.

WINSLEY, or Wintersley, as it is called in Domesday
Book, deserves, if it does not derive, the name from
its high and exposed situation.   The parish contains
several hamlets, as Murhill, Conkwell, and Turleigh.
Turleigh House is a charming old residence.   Here,
Romaine wrote his " Walk and Triumph of Faith,"
nor is it improbable that the title was suggested by the
terrace on which he was wont to stroll and meditate.
The work was published 1771.   Here, too, Edmund
Burke,* was a frequent visitor to the same common
friend, Mr. Atwood.   In another house in the village
was born Sir Richard Atwood Glass, the constructor
of the Atlantic Telegraph Cable.

* In one of his visits to Bath, Burke was introduced to the family
of Dr. Christopher Nugent, a physician then residing in the Circus,
and married his daughter.   The union proved a happy one.   She
was a woman eminently calculated to confer happiness upon her
husband.   His portraiture of her is at once the most felicitous
and eloquent tribute ever paid by man to woman.   In the agita-
tion and anxiety of his busy and eventful life—anxiety intensified by
his sensitive nature—she was his comfort, his solace, and his joy.
As Mr. Smiles says in his work, entitled " Character "—" His domestic happiness more than compensated him for all the anxiety
consequent upon the strain and demands of his public life."   Burke
says of her—" She is handsome ; but it is a beauty not arising from
features, from complexion, or from shape.   She has all three in a
high degree, but it is not by these she touches the heart ; it is all
that sweetness of temper, benevolence, innocence, and sensibility,
which a face can express that forms her beauty,   She has a face
that just raises your attention at first sight ; it grows on you every

𝕸urħill, commands a noble view over hill and dale and swelling upland, and is a favourite spot for pic-nic parties.

---

moment, and you wonder it did no more than raise your attention at first. Her eyes have a mild light, but they awe when she pleases ; they command, like a good man out of office, not by authority but by virtue. Her stature is not tall ; she is not made to be the admiration of everybody, but the happiness of one. She has all the firmness that does not exclude delicacy ; she has all the softness that does not imply weakness. Her voice is a soft low music—not formed to rule in public assemblies, but to charm those who can distinguish a company from a crowd ; it has this advantage—*you must come close to her to hear it.* To describe her body describes her mind—one is the transcript of the other ; her understanding is not shown in the variety of matters it exerts itself on, but in the goodness of the choice she makes. She does not display it so much in saying or doing striking things, as in avoiding such as she ought not to say or do. No person of so few years can know the world better ; no person was ever less corrupted by the knowledge of it. Her politeness flows rather from a natural disposition to oblige, than from any rules on that subject, and therefore never fails to strike those who understand good breeding and those who do not. She has a steady and firm mind, which takes no more from the beauty of the female character than the solidity of marble does from its polish and lustre. She has such virtues as make us value the truly great of our own sex. She has all the winning graces that make us love even the faults we see in the weak and beautiful, in hers."—One son was the issue of the marriage. He lived to manhood, and his death forms one of the most touching episodes recorded in connection with Burke's domestic life. The effect, added to the mental strain upon his health, never robust, brought him to the verge of the grave, and it is not out of place to observe that as Bath was associated with his earlier career, so it was the last place in which he sought to recruit his shattered frame. He visited Bath in February, 1797, and placed himself under the care of Dr.

𝕮𝖔𝖓𝖐𝖜𝖊𝖑𝖑, which stands on the borders of Somerset and Wilts, is especially worthy of a visit. Placed, like Petra of old, in a cleft of the rocks, it exhibits, perhaps, greater marks of antiquity than almost any other cluster of houses in the kingdom. No admirer of sylvan scenery should visit Bath and leave this old world village unseen.

Near Winsley Church is a small gorge in the hill-side, called Danes-bottom, where, according to tradition, a battle was fought between these invaders and the troops of Alfred.

Parry. At the end of May, in that year, he returned home, and died at Gregories, near Beaconsfield, 9th July, 1797. His last letter from hence contains the following touching passage :—

" I have been to Bath these four months for no purpose, and am 'therefore to be removed to my own house at Beaconsfield to-'morrow, to be nearer a habitation more permanent ; humbly 'and fearfully hoping that my better part may find a better 'mansion." The church of Beaconsfield is the place of his burial. The grandeur of Burke's public character, his matchless abilities, and the moral beauty of his private life, were not appreciated by his own generation. His literary productions are only just beginning to be understood and estimated at their true value. Goldsmith, in his witty poem "Retaliation," little understood the character of the man of whom he wrote—half in irony, half in earnest :—

" Here lies our good Edmund, whose genius was such,
    We scarcely can praise it or blame it too much ;
    Who, born for the universe, narrow'd his mind,
    And to party gave up what was meant for mankind."

It is to be remarked that both political parties, since Burke wrote, when they wish to prove the truth of some great political principle, alike quote Burke. His apothegms and public sayings have become embodied in the literature and the wisdom of all nations.

𝔚𝔦𝔫𝔰𝔩𝔢𝔶 𝔠𝔥𝔲𝔯𝔠𝔥 is of recent date. The saddle-back tower which formerly stood at the west end of the old building, stands on the south side of the new structure. This tower is justly admired. One of the basement stones bears the date of 1161, referring, probably, to a still earlier tower. Winsley Church is among the few ecclesiastical edifices in the county dedicated to St. Nicholas. Tradition tells us that one of the three bells it boasts was brought from the Chapel of St. Catherine at Bradford.

In the Churchyard is a fine yew tree. Prior to the Reformation, Winsley and Limpley Stoke belonged to the Abbey of Shaftesbury. The neighbourhood is remarkable for its salubrity, the average mortality being only about one or one and a-quarter per cent. per annum.

Winsley and its three hamlets are in the Union of Bradford-on-Avon; in 1871, the united population lation was 1,074.

BRADFORD-ON-AVON,

A TOWN formerly celebrated as a manufactory of broad-cloth, but which latterly has become of less importance. It is situated almost at the foot of the Wiltshire Downs (whence it formerly derived its wool), between the old forests of Selwood and Braden. Of the former, some traces may still be observed at Longleat and Stourhead on the south; of the latter, vestiges may be seen in Spy Park and Bowood

on the north-east. St. Aldhelm, whilst Abbot
of Malmesbury, founded a monastery near the town
between 670 and 705, in which latter year he became
Bishop of Sherborne, "West of Selwood," his diocese being the five western counties. This monastery
was dedicated to St. Lawrence. In the tenth century,
Dunstan, Abbot of Glastonbury, at a "Wytan" held
at Bradford 957, was appointed Bishop of Worcester.
In 1001, Ethelred the King, gave Bradford and the
monastery to the Abbots of Shaftesbury; tradition
says "for a recompence of the murderinge of St.
Edward, his brother."

Bradford appears to have been a place of small importance until the fourteenth century, when it became
gradually more prosperous through the trade of the
"merchants of the staple." In the reign of Edward I.,
1295, it returned (by summons) two members to Parliament, namely, Thomas Dedans and William Wager.
After 1339, it ceased to be represented.

The monastery and town of Bradford were surrendered to Henry VIII., 1539, and in the thirty-
fourth year of his reign he granted the prebendal
manor and advowson to the Dean and Chapter of
Bristol, retaining the lay manor, which was leased by
Elizabeth to Henry, Earl of Pembroke, granting the
reversion to Sir Francis Walsingham. Possessed
alternately by the De Burghs, the Powletts, and the
Methuens, it was subsequently purchased by the
Cams, from whom it descended to the present possessor, Sir Charles Hobhouse, Bart.

Leland, in the reign of Henry VIII., mentions that Bradford "standith by cloth making," and it long continued this repute, which there is every reason to believe was much promoted by the family of the Halls, who lived at Bradford from the reign of Henry III. to the early part of the last century. The mansion* of this family is the most striking object in the town. It stands on a raised terrace, and is strikingly ornate in character, richer even than the building it so much resembles—Longleat, although very much smaller. The date of this building is the latter part of the sixteenth century.†

* Canon Jackson says Kingston House resembles Kirby Hall in Northamptonshire. Kirby Hall was a very interesting place. It was built by James I. in the heart of Rockingham Forest, and was used by him as an occasional hunting-box. James conferred it, together with a noble estate, upon the Finch family. The house was the occasional residence of the Earls of Winchilsea until the beginning of the present century. After years of neglect, it fell into decay, and the small portion of it now remaining is used as a shepherd's lodge.

† After the extinction of the Hall family, Kingston House became, through the last heiress, the property of the Dukes of Kingston, the last of whom married the notorious woman known as the Duchess of Kingston. After the Duke's death, a previous marriage with the Earl of Bristol was proved against her, but she succeeded in retaining the property the Duke had left her. She was a woman of audacity and craftiness. As Canon Jackson says in his paper in the *Wiltshire Magazine*, vol. I., p. 277 : "She resided occasionally at Kingston House, and no doubt by her fantastic performances infused a little vivacity into the orderly ideas of the townfolk of Bradford." The bulk of the landed estate belonging to the Duke at Bradford and elsewhere passed at the Duchess's death to the Duke's nephew, son of his sister—

Bradford is singularly rich in domestic architecture. The town is built in terraces, on the side of a hill, and presents a very picturesque appearance, three-fourths of the houses being gabled and mullioned. This style, generally abandoned in the eighteenth century, has here been continued almost down to the present time. There are two houses which still possess remains of the original plans—the central hall, porches, buttery, parlour, &c.—the best example being the one near the Town Hall, which a little care would suffice to re-establish in its former architectural beauty. At present the house is encumbered with work commonly called the Beatty Langley Gothic, which should be carefully removed. The barton farm, bridge, and barn, are worthy of study; the bridge is many arched, and without parapet. The group possesses a gateway, which scarcely retains a trace of its original form; the house, built within its former walls, is unfortunately still more transformed, but the barn at the back is nearly in the same state as the builders left it in the fourteenth century. It has double transepts, grand doorways, and wide buttressed walls, covered with stone tiles. There are few larger or handsomer barns in the kingdom.

Charles Meadows, who assumed the name and arms of Pierrepont, and was created Earl Manvers in 1806.

In 1848, Mr. Moulton purchased Kingston House, with about nine acres of land, and his first act—one for which he deserves the highest praise—was to put into complete repair all that remained of the North Wiltshire Hall of John Hall. Mr. Vivian's illustrations of the house are referred to at page 88.

The town bridge, near the railway station, is a very characteristic structure. Leland, in 1540, said it "had nine fair arches." Some of the arches are of ribbed construction, of the fourteenth or fifteenth century. The remainder have been reconstructed, probably at the same time the stone dome was built to cover the remnant of the old chapel which stood on a centre pier. "To what base uses we may return"—this chapel was turned into a blind-house or lock-up. The careful archæologist can trace the former building in general outline. Tradition assigns the dedication of this building to St. Catherine, and it is probably correct, as the chapel on the bridge at Bath was dedicated to the same patron saint.

The 𝔓arish 𝔠hurch and the 𝔙icarage, stand near the river, on the only level ground in Bradford. The former is a fine, although not an elegant building, of many periods and various styles. Ten years since it was carefully restored at an expense of nearly £6,000, under the superintendence of the late Mr. Gill of Bath. The tower is very plain, and the spire unusually blunt. The nave has a north aisle, which was added at different times in the fifteenth century, and is said to have contained two chantries, one to St. Nicholas, and one to St. Mary the Virgin. At the end of the nave, on the south side, is a small chantry chapel, built by a member of the Hall family. The chancel is of perpendicular character, with a good eastern window, filled with stained

glass, by O'Connor.   Remnants of every style are
to be found in this fine old church, of which a history
may be read in its progressive alterations.   There
are many good monuments, and a handsome brass
to the memory of Thomas Horton and Mary his
wife,* the diaper work on the figure of the latter is
good and characteristic.

Up to the year 1857 it was fully believed that the
𝕸onastery of 𝕾t. 𝕬ldhelm had totally perished.   In
that year the Wiltshire Archæological Society met at
Bradford, when the vicar, the Rev. Prebendary Jones,†
in pointing out the school adjoining the church, observed:—"That small arcade of semi-circular arches
which you may observe in the south wall—though it
may have been built in comparatively modern times
—does not look unlike a memorial of what the old
Saxon monastery may have been.   An examination
of the interior of the building, a short time ago, revealed a fragment of an arch, a large portion of which
had been cut away, which may have been the entrance to some large hall, or perhaps chapel."
These remarks led the way to future discovery.

* See List of Brasses in the Appendix, and Autotype Illustration.

† The Rev. W. H. Jones, M.A., Prebendary of Salisbury and
Vicar of Bradford-on-Avon, is a learned antiquary and archæologist. He has contributed a very interesting history of Bradford,
as well as an exhaustive account of the Saxon Church referred to
—besides other valuable papers—to the Wiltshire Magazine. He
is also the translator of the Domesday Book of Wiltshire, a work
of great research and information, published in 4to., by R. E.
Peach, Bath, in 1865.

Brass at Swainswick Church - near Bath.

Brass at Bradford-Church-Wilts.

At Bradford Church - Wilts.

AUTOTYPE, S.S & C°

After careful examination, Mr. C. E. Davis, of Bath, showed conclusively that the arcade was not modern as assumed by Mr. Jones, but that it was of great antiquity; that the arch was not the entrance to a hall or chapel, but the chancel arch of a church, and that the whole building was complete; a nave, chancel, and north porch being there, and an early round arch of a style antecedent to the Norman Conquest. Subsequent research established the belief that this was the church of the monastery of St. Aldhelm, the building mentioned by William of Malmesbury. It was dedicated to St. Lawrence, and existed in 1156. Considerable credit may be given to Mr. Davis for having first expressed his opinion so decidedly as to the antiquity of the church, an opinion borne out by the laborious researches of the Vicar, and confirmed by the judgment of eminent archæologists. The building is now under restoration, by public subscription. The figures of two angels, probably the earliest examples of *Christian* sculpture in England, have been carried to their original places over the chancel arch, but unfortunately the central figure, the Saviour, or the First Person of the Trinity, has been lost, so that the restoration will still be incomplete.

A careful restoration of this church carried out, so that the new work shall not be *confused* with the old, would form a shrine that many an architectural pilgrim might visit.

C C

WESTWOOD.

THIS ancient village stands on the top of a hill, two miles from Freshford. The Church has a perpendicular tower, with various fantastic monsters forming the drip corbels; the stair turret is surmounted by a beautiful pinnacle. The building consists of a nave, north aisle, and chancel, which contains a carved altar railing. The crucifixion, in ancient stained glass, ornaments the east window. The seats and roof in the north aisle have ornamental carved work. There is a piscina, of a rare kind, near the altar; the font is a plain Norman one, of an octagonal shape. The church is very interesting, and well worthy of a visit. Near it is an ancient Manor House, which bears marks of having been one of the ecclesiastical buildings attached to the abbey of Shaftesbury. It belongs, with much of the adjacent land, to H. W. Tugwell, Esq.

The living is a vicarage attached to that of Bradford.

The population, in 1871, was 543. The village is incorporated in the Bradford-on-Avon Union.

IN AND OUT OF BATH.

~~~~~~

WALK THE TWENTIETH.

THE VILLAGE OF BATHFORD; SHOCKERWICK;
WARLEIGH MANOR; BATHFORD VICARAGE AND
CHURCH.

BATHFORD, SHOCKERWICK, AND WARLEIGH.

** *The following, with the writer's kind permission,
has been abridged and adapted from Mr. Skrine's
paper, read before the Literary Club:—*

THE village of Bathford, about three miles
from Bath, lies on a steep declivity of Farleigh-
down, and overlooks the Avon and the Weaver, or
Box Brook.

The parish consists of three tithings or quasi
manors—Bathford in the centre, Shockerwick to the
north, Warleigh to the south.

The bounds of the manor given in an ancient
Charter A.D. 957, correspond very nearly with those
of the present time.* "First from the Avon along
the Strata or Fosse-way to the Onestone; thence to
Beonnan-lèhe (Banner-down; thence to the Weaver;
thence to Sibyrht-leáge ; thence to Hnæsleáge

* Codex Diplomaticus Ævi Saxonici, III. 451.

(Ashley); thence to Cunaca-leáge; (Conkwell; from Cunaca-leáge to the Avon."

The title of the manor was originally Forde, and it was thus designated down to the seventeenth century. The name was derived from a ford, which was, formerly, the usual means of communication between Bathford and Bathampton. It lay immediately below the church. On a rising ground, near this point is an old · pollard, which marks the site of a Roman villa,* the hypocaust of which was found about the middle of the seventeenth century.

The ford from which the village derived its name

* The following extract from "Aubrey's Monumenta Britanica" describes the Roman villa found in Forde in the seventeenth century :—"At Bathford (near the citie of Bathe) was found by digging of a drayning trench deeper than ordinarily in the grounds of one Mr. Skreene, in the year 1655, a roome underground, which was about 14 foot one way and 17 feet the other. The pavement of which was opus tesselatum (tesselated work) of small stones of several colours, viz., white (hard chalk), blue (liasse), and red (fine brick). In the middle of the floor was a blue bird, not well proportioned, and in each of the four angles a sort of knott. This ground and the whole manor did belong to the Abbey of Bath. Underneath this floor there is water. The floor is borne on pillars of stone about an ell distant the one from the other. On the pillars were laid plank stones on which the opus tesselatum was layd. The water issued out of the earth a little below, and many persuade themselves there is much water in it. This discovered place was so much frequented that it caused Mr. Skreene to cover it up again, because the great concourse of people, especially from Bathe, injured his grounds, but he would not cover it so soon but the people had torn up almost all the work before I came hither to see it, but his daughter-in-lawe hath described the whole floor with her needle in gobelin-stitch. Mr. Skreene told me there is such another floor adjoining yet untouched."

was connected with the Fosse-way, so often mentioned in these pages. Near Bathford, but on the
opposite side of the river, is a large meadow called
" Horselands," where, according to tradition, the
Roman cavalry were exercised. The road which
leads to Bannerdown is mentioned as "Strata" or
Fosse-way in a Saxon Charter of the tenth century,
relating to the manor, and still forms the boundary
of the parish. It may be taken for granted that
the village stood on this road, the importance
of which may be gathered from the following
facts. It ran from Cornwall to Lincoln, and from
thence to the North of England. It was therefore,
evidently, one of the greatest, perhaps the greatest
trunk line in England in Roman times. Much
of the commerce of the country in connection with
the tin and coal mines of Cornwall and Somerset
must have traversed it. There were but two or
three roads that could be depended on for crossing
the country and on these the Romans established
stations. It is only reasonable to conclude that
Forde was one of them.

But it was not merely on account of the roads
which passed through it, or of the fords over the
Avon and the Weaver, that Bathford derived its
importance. It was a Border Manor, bounded
by what the Saxons called the Mark or Border
Forest*—a waste of rough ground and brushwood,

* The Mark or Border Forest.—"Every community," says
Kemble, "not sheltered by walls, or the firmer defences of public

in which the tenants of the adjoining hamlets had
certain rights of pasture.

Shockerwick was that part of the district which
contained the Soke, or Court, held, probably, under
an oak, or near some ancient stone, to try offences
on the border or marches.   Such a stone is mentioned in the ancient Saxon Chartulary referred
to above.   The words are "Thone anne stein,"
to the one-stone, *i.e.* single stone.*   This stone, it
is said, not only marked the edge of the manor,
but also the boundaries of the Saxon kingdom of
Wessex, and the British kingdom of Damnonia,
and later still, the kingdoms of Wessex and Mercia.

This district was, in the times of the Belgæ and the
Romans, and during the Saxon invasion, doubly important as the strong border land of the south-
western British kingdom of Damnonia, and indeed
of all Britain, as against the Saxon invaders.   The
Avon—fringed by the long strip of forest territory
to the east, with Bath, as a great fortified city
and arsenal—formed, it may be assumed, the line of
defence.   In accordance with this view, and coup-
ling it with the fact that a distance of not more than
fourteen miles through the forest, either by the

"law, must have one to separate it from its neighbours and protect
"it from rivals. No matter how small or how large the community,
"it will still have a mark or space or boundary by which its right
"of jurisdiction is limited and the encroachments of others kept
"off, and therefore wherever we find an ancient Saxon settlement
"we find the Forest Mark, large or small, according to the size
"or nature of the district."

* See page 206 and also page 439.

Marlborough Road or the Fosse-way, would have brought the Saxons to Forde, there seems no inherent improbability in attributing to this site the account given by ancient writers of the Battle of Mons Badonicus, or Mount Badon, which is stated to have been fought at a place called " The Baths," near the mouth of the Severn.

King Edwy, A.D. 957, granted to the monastery of St. Peter, in Bath, on the petition of Wulfgar, abbot, " X mansas in loco ubi antiquorum relatû nominatūr Æt Forda," *i.e.*, " *Ten farms in the place which by the tradition of the elders is called the Ford.*" These farms occupied the whole of the central part of Bathford parish, but did not include either Warleigh or Shockerwick. The term, Bathford tithing, is still in use: ten farms making up the tithing both in name and fact.

It may be interesting to note that at the time of the dissolution of the monasteries, Cromwell, the minister of Henry VIII., under whose administration the Priory of Bath was surrendered, received the compliment of an annuity of £5 for his life, secured on the Manor of Forde.

The description of Bathford in Domesday Book is as follows: " The church itself holds Forde. In the time of King Edward (the Confessor) it paid Danegelt (or Dane-tax) for ten hides.* The arable

---

* If Kemble's theory be correct, thirty-three acres were equivalent to a hide, and therefore there must have been at least three hundred acres under cultivation, besides copse-wood and rough border pasture on the hill. The twelve acres of meadow were the

is nine carucates (or ploughlands) and six serfs, five villanes (bailiffs) and seven bordars (cottagers). There is a mill of ten shillings rent, and twelve acres of meadow, and of coppice-wood fenced one mile in length and breadth.

The number of houses at the date of the Domesday Book seems uncertain, but supposing the statement to mean only heads of families, there must have been eighteen houses or cottages in Bathford, seven or eight in Warleigh, and perhaps four or five in Shockerwick, and if so, we may reckon the inhabitants at a little over a hundred. In Collinson's time (1780) there were eighty-four houses and about four hundred inhabitants. At present there are two hundred and four houses and nine hundred inhabitants. The ratable value of the parish in 1771 was £818. In 1871, it amounted to £6,598 8s.

The Manor of Warleigh is thus described in Domesday, "Hugoline holds of the king *Herlei.*[*] Azor held it in the time of King Edward, and paid Danegelt for one hide. The arable is three carucates, with which are one villane and five bordars with two serfs. There is half an acre of meadow and three furlongs of coppice-wood in length and breadth.

---

paddocks near the homesteads of the farmers, about an acre and a quarter to each. The arable land and the pastures by the river were held in common, and cultivated by the tenants under mutually advantageous arrangements.

[*] The Saxon Charter calls it *Werlege.*

It was formerly and is now worth fifty shillings (that is to say) to let." The quantity of fenced woodland or coppice would seem identical with the extent of the wood now called Warleigh wood, but in the survey of 1605, South wood. The wood now above War-leigh Manor House probably formed part of the boundary waste in old times. Most of the ground between the wood and the meadows, about one hundred acres, must have been arable, the part near the river being used for feeding the cattle and sheep belonging to the tenants of Warleigh. Many of the meadows retain names shewing plough culture— Bean-leaze, What or Wheat-leaze, Wood-leaze, Sum-mer-leaze, and Hop-yard. Those fields which have been always meadow have the termination *mead*. The names were probably given by the Saxon cul-tivators before the Conquest.

Hugoline, who is here named as the lord of Warleigh was one of the three justiciaries of England who compiled or corrected the Domesday Book. Being noted for his clerkly skill and styled in-terpres or interpreter, he may have acted as secretary. As Treasurer of Edward the Confessor, he was in office at the Conquest, and was wisely made use of by William I. He had other manors in this neighbour-hood, as Claverton, Estone, and Hampton, which his son, Hugo Barbatus, or Hugh of the Beard (as Collinson says),* sold to John de Villula, Bishop of

* Mr. Hunter considers that Hugoline is the same person as Hugo Barbatus.

Bath and Wells,* by whom they were afterwards granted to the monastery of Bath, to assist in its maintenance, and to atone for his sins. Subsequently it seems to have been merged in the manor of Forde, and to have fallen into the hands of the Crown.

It is probable that in early times there was a chapel of some sort on the hill. It may have been only a cleft in the rocks. Be this as it may, down to the last eighty years revels, which imply the commemoration of a Christian dedication, were regularly held on Palm Sunday at a place above Warleigh House, not far from the Dry-arch, called *Cankery Hole*. This hole was supposed to lead through the hill to Farleigh. Could it have been a refuge from the storm of persecution in the time of Diocletian?

Near this spot human bones have been frequently found when stones were being quarried, and something very like a cromlech still exists.

These bones are popularly supposed to indicate the spot where the Battle of Warleigh was fought during the Civil Wars. This opinion may be due to the fact that the quarries in question are near the spot from which the Parliamentarians bombarded Claverton Manor House, a short time before the Battle of Lansdown.† It may be interesting to add that the ford, though now nameless, was originally called the Clot-ford, or the ford of the yellow water-lily, which is still found a little below. The opposite

---

* This fact is noticed in the early part of the present work.

† Vide page 91.

meadow on the Warleigh side of the river bears the name of Clot-mead. Mr. Barnes called the River Stour " Cloty Stour," because of its water-lilies.

> " Where wide and slow
> The stream did flow,
> And flags did grow and slightly flee,
> Below the grey-leaved withy tree ;
> Whilst clack clack clack from hour to hour
> Did go the mill by Cloty Stour."
>
> *Poems in the Dorset dialect.*

While on the subject of names it is not out of place to state that the term Warleigh (*Werlege* is the old Saxon name)seems to be derived from the "weir," which was at one time a valuable part of the property, when the lordly salmon lay at its foot. There are other Warleighs in England, all of which are situated near rivers abounding in fish, and one in particular, Warley in Devonshire, had a fishing weir from the earliest times.

Warleigh appears to have been held by the Prior of Bath, in demesne. A bridge, called the Prior's Bridge, existed there some three hundred years ago, as may be gathered from evidence given in a tithe suit, nearly two hundred and eighty years since. The fishery of Warleigh was a separate property from that of Forde, and was claimed as such by the ancestors of Mr. Skrine, the present lord of the manor.

In 1605, a survey of the manor was made by virtue of a commission from the Crown, of which the present owner possesses a copy. It is a document of much interest.

Twenty years after this survey was taken, the manor of Forde, including Warleigh, was purchased of William Rolfe, who claimed to hold it from Robert, Earl of Salisbury, "with the monies and in behalf of William Fisher of Batheaston, Thomas Skrine of Bathford, and Henry Skrine the elder, of Warleigh." The present proprietor of Warleigh inherits the whole of Warleigh Manor from the above-named Henry Skrine, and by purchase and exchange from time to time, his ancestors became possessed of the greater part of Thomas Skrine's share. In 1691, the surviving trustee and the representatives of the two co-purchasers, with Henry Skrine the elder, of the manor of Forde, conveyed to John Skrine, grandson of the said Henry Skrine, all the manorial rights of Forde. These rights were enjoyed down to the Inclosure Act of 1866. The remaining portions of the manor were sold to several persons, but Miss Briscoe, the descendant of William Fisher, one of the co-purchasers, still retains a portion of the estate allotted to her ancestors.

Bathford is a vicarage in the gift of the Dean and Chapter of Bristol, who also owned the rectorial tithes until the beginning of this century, when they were sold in order to redeem the land tax on the Chapter property elsewhere. The advowson was vested in the Chapter at the time of the dissolution of the monasteries under Henry VIII., at which time the then new See of Bristol was founded, and endowed with part of the spoils of the confiscated estates. The living was previously included in the manor of Forde, and formed part of the possessions of the Abbey of Bath from the earliest period of Church history. In the latter end of the last century the income of Forde was considered so insufficient that the vicarage of Hampton was united to it, which led to the ford over the Avon, being again much frequented. However advantageous in a pecuniary point of view this union may have been to the Vicar of Forde, it was far from being beneficial to the parishioners of either Forde or Hampton, who in respect of church privileges and pastoral care, had to be contented with only half of what they had previously enjoyed.*

The Church of Bathford, dedicated to St. Swithin, consists of a chancel, nave, north and south aisles, western tower, and south porch, and dates from a very early period. Collinson's description of the church in 1780, is that it was then "An old building, eighty feet in length and twenty in breadth, consisting of a nave, chancel, and porch *all tiled*. At the west end is a circular tower containing two bells. The nave is divided from the chancel by a clumsy Saxon arch." The "clumsy Saxon arch" has since that time been removed to make room for a lath and plaster construction. There is still a Norman font and doorway, and an early English arch to the porch. In 1856, some old steps belonging to a rood staircase were found in the north-west wall of the

* Vide Bathampton, page 96, for history of the re-separation.

nave, together with a mutilated statuette, supposed to be the effigy of a bishop. There is a handsomely carved oak pulpit, of the time of James I., which has the following text carved in gilt letters on the upper edge :—" Blessed are they which heare the worde of God and keepe it." The base is of stone, the four principal panels represent the four Evangelists in bas-relief; the designs are by Mr. Preedy. The Rev. E. J. Harford is the vicar.

Bathford is in the Union of Bath. The population, in 1871, was 964; the rateable value, on an area of 1,823 acres, is £6,626.

IN AND OUT OF BATH.

WALK THE TWENTY-FIRST.

To Box by Road or Rail—the Church; Hasel-
bury House; Chapel Plaster; Middle Hill;
Cheyney Court and Coles's Farm; Dit-
teridge; Colerne; Wormwood Farm; South
Wraxall Manor House and Church; Great
Chaldfield Manor House and Church; and
Monkton Farleigh.

BOX.

The village* is interesting; and its situation highly
picturesque. The valley is watered by a large brook,
and bounded by undulating hills, chequered with
hamlets, villas, and plantations. Here and there are
seen the farm-houses, peculiar to the seventeenth
century, which give to the valleys about Bath much

* This place forms the eastern limit of these Rambles, but
visitors to Bath should avail themselves of the facilities offered to
them on Tuesdays and Fridays to see Corsham Court (the seat of
Lord Methuen), and the fine Gallery of Pictures it contains.

of their interest. The freestone quarries, now extensively worked, are rich in cryptogamic plants.

The 𝕮𝖍𝖚𝖗𝖈𝖍, originally built in the early part of the 13th century, restored in 1713, and since enlarged, is an irregular structure, with embattled tower and late Perpendicular spire—the interior presenting in its general character many remains of the early English period. The font is octagonal, with centre ornaments in the panels. The arches dividing the nave from the north aisle have a peculiar running moulding, with only one quaint corbel remaining, but the roof is ornamented with bosses of a decorated character. At the end of the north aisle is a chapel with a groined arch, traditionally associated with the early lords of the manor. Between the nave and chancel are early English arches supporting the tower. The east window is filled with stained glass to the memory of the wife and children of the late Mr. G. Pinchin, of Hatt House; and in the chancel is an elegantly wrought mural tablet, in statuary marble, erected about 1739. Immediately above the chancel arch are emblazoned the arms of Queen Anne, during whose reign the church was much injured in its architectural features, in accordance with the debased notions then prevailing. Externally to the west end of the church are two stone coffins of the early Roman type. In an adjoining garden is a Roman pavement, now covered up; fragments of tessaræ were also discovered in a part of the churchyard, which was added about fifty years ago. A capacious Cemetery, with Mortuary Chapel, is among the recent additions to the village, and the incumbency of the present vicar has already been signalised by the erection of commodious School-rooms.

𝕳𝖆𝖘𝖊𝖑𝖇𝖚𝖗𝖞 𝕳𝖔𝖚𝖘𝖊, in the parish of Box, once a fine Elizabethan mansion, is much disfigured by alterations, supposed to be necessary for modern comfort. Early in the present century, several stone coffins were ploughed up on the site of the ancient church, long since destroyed. The great hall, which has been converted into rooms, has two fine arches. There are several good panelled wainscots, and one of the rooms has some painted canvas, in imitation of tapestry. This house, and the one formerly appropriated to the steward, are good specimens of the old English manorial residence.

Though no trace of the church remains, the Vicar of Box still receives £10 per annum from the lord of the manor. In the seventeenth century this manor belonged to a branch of the Speke family,* who also possessed a portion of the lordship of Box. The family became extinct 1682. The arms of Speke are still to be seen on the pillars at the entrance of the garden.

𝕮𝖍𝖆𝖕𝖊𝖑 𝕻𝖑𝖆𝖘𝖙𝖊𝖗, or *Plas-trew*—"the chapel in the woody place"—was one of the oratories erected

---

* The Spekes, of Jordans, near Ilminster, are another branch of the family above mentioned, and one of the most ancient in Somersetshire.

for the convenience of pilgrims journeying to and from the Abbey of Glastonbury.* It is situated in the deanery of Malmesbury. This interesting structure is in a ruinous condition. The remains consist of a porch, intended, probably, for the private devotion of those who passed during the period when no service was being celebrated, as there is an elegant and curious niche, in which formerly stood a statue of the Virgin. The nave and chancel together are twenty-nine feet long, by nine feet wide. At the western gable there is a bell turret. What would at first sight appear to be a north transept, is, more probably, the priest's room, or cell, as it was called before the Reformation. The records of these chapels are exceedingly scanty. This relic of our ancestors is, or was, an outhouse to a beer shop, and the grave-yard is a kitchen garden !†

* Similar to that referred to on Lansdown, page 325.

† Leland, in his journey through Wiltshire, says :—"I left on the left hand on the toppe of a litle hille, an hermitage withyn a litle as I turned down to Haselbyri." The name of Chapel Plaster and the place itself are wrapped in obscurity. Canon Jackson says :—"The building called 'Chapel Plaster': by tradition, a way-side chapel for pilgrims travelling from Malmsbury to Glastonbury. Aubrey calls it 'the Chapel of Playsters.' The meaning of the name is uncertain ; but it has nothing to do with the material of plaster ; being built of stone. It may either have been built by some one of the name of Plaster : or playster may be an old word for pilgrim : or it may mean the chapel built on the 'Plegstow,' play place or village green : as the 'Plestor Oak' in White's Selborne."

Ditteridge Church, near Box, Wilts.

From Box several interesting rambles may be taken. Across the brook is the pretty hamlet of 𝕸𝖎𝖉𝖉𝖑𝖊 𝕳𝖎𝖑𝖑, with its Spa. There are two mineral springs, one of which is an aperient chalybeate, the other sulphurous, containing a large proportion of carbonic acid.

At a short distance to the north, are two fine old mansions, namely, 𝕮𝖍𝖊𝖞𝖓𝖊𝖞 𝕮𝖔𝖚𝖗𝖙, near which the remains of a Roman villa were discovered in 1813; and 𝕮𝖔𝖑𝖊𝖘'𝖘 𝕱𝖆𝖗𝖒.—The former was erected towards the close of the reign of Elizabeth, and has some finely carved chimney-pieces. It belongs, together with the bulk of the Box Estate, to Col. Northey, and is used as a farm-house, though a portion of it is sometimes let as a gentleman's residence.—The latter, also containing some good chimney-pieces, is a gabled building, belonging to the family of Webb. It was built by an ancestor of the present owner in 1645.

The Rev. G. E. Gardiner is the Vicar of Box with Haselbury; which are in the Union of Chippenham. The population is 2,154. The church is dedicated to St. Thomas à Becket.

𝕯𝖎𝖙𝖙𝖊𝖗𝖎𝖉𝖌𝖊, or *Ditchbridge*,* is a small village near Box, containing a population of 95 persons. It is a Rectory in the gift of the Northey family; the Rev. W. N. Heathcote is the Incumbent. The 𝕮𝖍𝖚𝖗𝖈𝖍, which possesses many features of interest, consists of a Norman nave, chancel, and south porch, with a bell gable over the chancel arch. Various

* See Autotype Illustration.

additions and alterations have been made at
different periods. Some portions of the building
are the work of the thirteenth century, but the
windows are of later date. The chancel arch is
exceedingly narrow, and is doubly recessed and
chamfered. In the south wall of the chancel
there is a piscina, with a credence table; the font
has a circular basin, richly ornamented. The
stairs, formerly leading to the rood loft, are at the
north-east corner of the nave. Some parts of the
building are still covered with a thick daub of
whitewash. Mr. E. W. Godwin, the accomplished
archæologist and architect, thus describes a mural
painting discovered here :—

"The portion exposed is between seven and
eight feet high, and extends from the north window
about twelve feet westward. In the central compartment is a colossal figure of St. Christopher, a mer-
maid holding a mirror is introduced in front of the
saint's staff: the compartment to the right, representing a monk, or priest, holding a lantern, and
standing in the entrance of a church, apparently
forms a portion of the same subject. The figure in
the compartment to the left is intended to represent
St. Michael holding the scales of judgment, the image
of Sin is very expressive; the letters " ECCLE : A" in
this compartment have no connection with the subject, but probably refer to some text of Scripture
now destroyed, inasmuch as the ground work of the
letters is a fragment of the first coat which concealed

the mediæval pictures. The wavy pattern of the borders which separate the compartments is very bold and effective, but it is to be regretted that further means are not taken to remove more of the plaster and whitewash, which probably conceal other mural paintings of similar character." The church is dedicated to St. Christopher.

𝕮𝖔𝖑𝖊𝖗𝖓𝖊, or *Cold-horn*, stands on the summit of a hill. Among the high grounds which surround Bath, it would be difficult to find a more extensive, varied, and beautiful prospect that it commands. The church tower may be seen for many miles in various directions. The village, which is small and straggling, possesses scarcely any houses of importance, and few objects of interest.

The 𝕮𝖍𝖚𝖗𝖈𝖍 is dedicated to S. John the Baptist, and the parish is in the diocese of Gloucester and Bristol. The living is a small one, and the patronage is vested in the Warden of New College, Oxford.* The church consists of a nave of four bays,

* Historical Note.—It appears from the Colerne muniments, in the possession of New College, that the manor passed from Henry de Burghersh, Bishop of Lincoln, to Bartholomew de Burghersh, his nephew, who married for his second wife, Margaret, sister of Bartholomew, Lord Badlesmere, and that William of Wykeham purchased the reversion of the estate from Elizabeth, his daughter, wife of Edward le Despenser, for the sum of 700 marks, in the 11th year of Richard II., and conveyed it to the College in the following year.—Henry VI. granted to the warden and scholars of New College (A.D. 1447), a market at Colerne every Friday, and a fair for three days, on the vigil-day, and morrow of the decollation of St. John the Baptist (August 28, 29, 30).—*E. W. Godwin.*

north and south aisles, north chantry chapel, sanctuary, and south porch. The tower is placed at the west end of the nave, and is a very fine example of the indigenous Somersetshire perpendicular. The nave, and parts of the sanctuary, were built in the middle of the thirteenth century, and seem to show that this parish was once of importance. The capitals of the nave have been boldly and beautifully carved, and still retain the force and elegance of this early period of art. Some traces of French workmanship can be seen in the carving. It is singular that the north aisle is almost twice as wide as the south, though they are probably contemporary. When the site permitted, the reverse of this was usually the case, the old architects selecting the warmer aspect for the accommodation of the larger number. There are remains of beautiful piscinæ, both in the sanctuary and north chantry chapel, and also early arched tomb recesses in the south wall of the sanctuary and in the north wall of the chantry chapel. The nave roof was restored, and a new east window inserted, by a local architect a few years ago. This is little in comparison with what remains to be done. Fortunately the local gentry and the vicar have taken the matter in hand, and are fully alive to the necessity of the immediate and thorough restoration of this fine church. Under the careful direction of Messrs. Wilson and Willcox, it will be restored to its former beauty and dignity. The Rev. A. Turner is the Vicar.

Colerne is in the Chippenham Union. The population, in 1871, was 1096.

The high road passes Hunter's Hall, near which, at the end of the Rocks Estate,* stands the boundaries' pyramid.†‡ Bannerdown, with its ancient British earthworks, is traditionally said to have received its name of "holy hill" from having been the spot where St. Augustine met the British priests. The view is as bright and beautiful as any to be seen in merry England.

* It was formerly the property of the late Serjeant Wrangham. At his death, the estate was purchased by J. Taylor, Esq., to whom it at present belongs. The mansion is exceedingly interesting, and possesses a remarkably fine dining-room.

† See page 206.

‡ "Thone anne stein" or one stone, referred to on page 422, was near the site of this modern boundary mark.

IN AND OUT OF BATH.

WALK THE TWENTY-FIRST CONTINUED.

TO the south - east of Box lies 𝕿𝖔𝖗𝖒𝖜𝖔𝖔𝖉 𝕱𝖆𝖗𝖒, a gable-roofed building of the seventeenth century, a short distance from which is a veritable gem—𝖘𝖔𝖚𝖙𝖍 𝖂𝖗𝖆𝖝𝖆𝖑𝖑 𝕸𝖆𝖓𝖔𝖗 𝕳𝖔𝖚𝖘𝖊. This ancient manor house shows clearly the transition from the strength of the fifteenth to the comfort and elegance of the sixteenth century. The hall is fine even in its desolation. It was erected about the early period of the sixteenth century, by Robert Long, Squire to Lord Hungerford. The windows, according to Aubrey, were profusely decorated with stained glass, of which no vestige remains.* The springs of the arches terminate in coats-of-arms. The drawing-room is an Elizabethan addition. It

* In Aubrey's MS. Collections for North Wilts in the Ashmolean Museum, drawings are preserved of numerous armorial shields which once adorned the windows.

Fireplace at South Wraxall. Manor House.
Wilts.

is panelled, and has a beautiful ceiling. There is an elaborate chimney-piece,* enriched with caryatides and figures of Prudence and Justice, Arithmetic and Geometry, with various other carved work. It bears the date 1596, with an escutcheon and the marshal's fetterlock,†—the Long family holding the manor of Draycot Cerne in petty serjeanty by the right of officiating as marshal at coronations. Opposite to the chimney-piece is a projection, in which are seat recesses, with beautiful shell scrolls. In every chamber we see something to admire; old oak panelling, peculiar windows, or chimney-pieces; the porter's lodge with its oriel, the old bed-rooms, even the cellars, have each some object of interest. A few years ago it was occupied as a boys' school, with such results to the house as might be expected.

The mansion was formerly surrounded by a grove of oaks. These are now gone, and "it stands alone, like Adam's recollection of his fall." It was recently tenanted by a member of the Long family, but for a brief period only. The following anecdote

---

* See Autotype Illustration.

† Aubrey says this badge, which is a kind of padlock, was peculiar to the Longs as owners of Draycot. Mr. Jones, however, disproves this. He says:—"As the badge of the fetterlock was adopted by them, from the earliest period of their settlement at Wraxall—and certainly *before* they had anything to do with Draycot,—we venture, in opposition to the usually accepted tale, to submit that it was used as an emblem, appropriate enough, of the honourable office of bedel or bailiff, which they held there under the abbess of Shaftesbury, as Lady of the Hundred of Bradford."—See *Wiltshire Magazine*, vol. 13, page 280.

is related by Aubrey:—"Sir Walter Long's widow
made him a solemn promise that she would not marry
after his decease. Not long after, one Fox, a beautiful
young gentleman, did win her love, and she married
him at South Wraxhall, where the picture of Sir Walter
hung over the parlour door. As Fox led his bride
into the parlour, the picture fell on her shoulder,
and cracked in the fall."

The manor was granted by Agnes, abbess of
Shaftesbury, with the consent of her nuns, to the
monks of Farleigh, in 1252, having previously formed
a portion of the great manor of Bradford. It came
into the possession of the Longs, of Rood Ashton,
in the fifteenth century, in whose family it is still
vested. The population, according to the census of
1871, is 964.

South Wraxall Church, which has a saddle-backed
tower, was re-built a few years ago. Attached to it is
the Long chantry, containing an altar tomb, with a
mutilated recumbent effigy of a lady, without inscription, but with arms and the fetterlock badge. This
monument, probably, belongs to an early period of the
sixteenth century, as does the font, which is of an octangular form. The Rev. William Laxton is the Vicar.

About two miles from South Wraxall is Great
Chalfield, or *Chalfield*, Manor House,* and of this
interesting and extensive building the late Mr.
Hudson Turner says:—

"The very beautiful front of a Manor House, of

* See Autotype Illustration.

Great Chaldfield Church and Manor House.

(near Bradford-on-Avon.)

" the fifteenth century, has here been preserved; but
" unfortunately a part of the house was destroyed
" about twenty years ago. The porch has a good
" groined vault; the oriel window is particularly
" rich and elegant, and is well known by engravings.
" There is also a second oriel window, of a plainer
" character. The bay windows are particularly
" elegant, and the whole front is one of the most
" elaborate and finest that we have. The hall had
" a flat panelled ceiling of wood and plaster, with
" bosses at the intersections of the mouldings, and
" the wooden screen at the lower end also panelled,
" with two doors in it as usual. The shield of arms
" in the roof of the hall seems to shew that it was
" built by Thomas Tropenell, Esq., who married
" Agnes, fourth daughter of William Ludlow, lord of
" Hill Deverill, about 1450. The motto of the
" family—" *Le jong tira bellement*"—also occurred in
" several places on the roof of the hall. It is much
" richer, earlier in date, and far superior in every
" way to South Wraxall. The walls and roof of the
" hall, and back windows, remain perfect, though
" it is divided into small modern rooms; but the
" lord's chamber, or solar, at the upper end of the
" hall, with the cellars under it, have been pulled
" down, and the gable end, with the beautiful oriel
" window, alone preserved of this part. There are
" remains of a handsome groined passage at the end
" of the dais, leading to the staircase of the solar;
" and at the opposite end of the dais a projecting

"square bay, with a handsome groined vault, has
"been preserved : in the centre of the vault is a
"shield of arms. At the lower end of the hall is the
"usual passage behind the screens, leading from the
"porch to the servants' court; behind this is the
"kitchen, with its large chimney, though the fire-
"place is modernised. The offices are beyond, this
"is an unusual arrangement; we here pass through
"the kitchen to the offices, usually it is the reverse.
" The stables remain, but much altered, and the upper
"part of the gate-house has been turned into a
"pigeon-house. The barn also remains, but is much
"altered; its situation, however, shews that the prin-
"cipal entrance to this fine manor house was through
"the farm-yard, which was not an uncommon arrange-
"ment in the middle ages."

There are remains of flanking towers in the outer
walls next the moat, which show that the house was
slightly fortified. There are some curious *masks*, or
hollow figure heads in the solar, to enable the
inmates to survey strangers without themselves
being seen. These masks do not now occupy their
original positions.

The quaint little churchyard abuts on the farmyard,
and is only divided from it by a low wall. A small
but beautiful, perpendicular Church stands close by,
with its unique and ivy-clad bell cote. Just within
the doors, there is a fine perpendicular stone screen ;
also a good piscina and other interesting archæological remains. Incumbent, Rev. R. P. Little.

This quaint and remarkable manor house and church are well worth a visit. The parish is in the Union of Bradford-on-Avon. The population is 31; the ratable value is £999.

Returning to Wraxall, a pleasant walk, through an avenue of beech trees, leads to 𝔐onkton 𝔉ar-leigh, anciently called *Fern Leigh*.

The 𝔓riory of Monkton Farleigh was founded by Maud, Countess of Salisbury, about 1125, and was endowed by her with numerous estates. It is not certain that she commenced the building, but there can be little doubt that her son, Humphrey de Bohun, grandson of the first of that line, finished it and added to the endowment. It was dedicated to S. Mary Magdalen; belonged to the Cluniac monks of the order of S. Benedict, and was subordinate to to the Priory of Lewes, in Sussex. In this country the order of Cluni was founded by William de Warren and his wife, Lady Gundreda (daughter of the Conqueror), who introduced monks from the parent monastery at Cluni, in Burgundy, and erected the house at Lewes, about 1072. It was the most important establishment belonging to the order in this country, and was called one of the first "five daughters of Cluni." Though the Prior was appointed by the parent monastery in Burgundy, to which a small annual payment was made, the Lewes monastery enjoyed comparative independence, and controlled its own extensive revenues. There were twenty-seven houses of the order in England. The Priory at Monkton is intimately associated with the early history of this part of England. Bohun had declared for Matilda in opposition to Stephen. He built and garrisoned Trowbridge castle and made it sufficiently strong to resist the attacks of Stephen. This castle was, in fact, the stronghold of the Priory and its founders. Humphrey Bohun died in 1187, and was buried at Lanthony Priory,* founded about fifty years before by his wife's father on the banks of the Severn, close to the city of Gloucester. Besides the great wealth with which Monkton Priory was endowed, it possessed considerable Ecclesiastical patronage in various parts of Wiltshire and Gloucestershire.

The Bohuns were an ambitious race. The heads of the family were regarded as the patrons and pro- tectors of the Priory in secular matters, and they also assumed the right of nominating the Prior. This right was also claimed by the Prior of the superior house at Lewes. After some contention the dispute was settled by one of those fictions which determines that one party shall do a thing while another seems to do it. The fruits of victory practically remained with Bohun.

It has been already stated that the houses of Lewes and Farleigh were offsets of the monastery of Cluni. This foreign connection was, in cases of war, sometimes fatal to the alien Priories, whose

* A portion of the Priory still remains. A recumbent effigy of Bohun is to be seen in the south aisle of the nave of Gloucester Cathedral.

property was often confiscated. This insecurity rendered the connection between the Cluniac superior and Lewes and her dependents (including Farleigh), uncomfortable. After various narrow escapes, Lewes Priory was, in 1373, allowed to separate, and became enfranchised, *i.e.*, independent, by an act of naturalization. This emancipation from foreign jurisdiction encouraged Farleigh in the attempt to shake off allegiance to Lewes, but the impending change of the Reformation, as Canon Jackson says, put an end to both the establishments, and consigned mother and daughter to one common grave. Lodowick Millen was Prior at the dissolution. The Priory, with its estates, was conferred on Seymour, Earl of Hertford, subsequently Duke of Somerset and Protector.

Farleigh House is built on the site of the Priory, of which not a vestige is traceable. The estate, in 1550, was exchanged for other property by the Duke of Somerset, with the See of Salisbury. After many changes of ownership, the estate became the property of Mr. Daniel Webb, whose daughter and sole heiress married, in 1717, Sir Edward Seymour, who succeeded to the dukedom in 1749, and died in 1757. He was succeeded by his elder son, who died in 1792, when the title devolved upon his brother, Lord Webb Seymour, who had previously resided on the estate. He was grandfather of the present duke. It is remarkable that the property should thus have reverted again to the Seymours. At the end of the

last century, Mr. John Long, of Rood Ashton, purchased Farleigh, and in 1840 the late Mr. Wade
Brown bought it, and built the Tower of Observation for Government surveying purposes. After his
death, the estate was sold to various purchasers,
the house and largest part of the estate now being
the property of Sir Charles Hobhouse, Bart., who
resides at the mansion.

Of the former Church, little more than the tower
remains. During the incumbency of the late Rev.
E. Brown, in 1844, the body of the structure was
re-built, but the work has been recently advanced
by the present rector. The Norman doorway in
the north porch is preserved, and there is likewise
a Norman font. On the whole, the work has
been creditably executed. The windows are
small in proportion to the structure, and the effect
of the painted glass is to render the church gloomy—
a gloom exceeding the poet's fancy.

> . . . " storied windows richly dight,
> Casting a dim religious light."

The church is dedicated to S. Peter, and the
Rector is the Rev. T. H. Tooke. Patron, Bishop
of Salisbury.

The population, in 1871, was 326. The parish
lies in the Bradford-on-Avon Union. The ratable
value is £3,913 16s. 8d.

IN AND OUT OF BATH.

WALK THE TWENTY-SECOND.

KEYNSHAM — ROMAN REMAINS — THE CHURCH;
STANTON DREW—ANTIQUITIES—THE CHURCH.

KEYNSHAM.

THE distance by rail to the Keynsham Station is seven miles. The cuttings run through the lias. At Twerton, the tunnel traverses the new red sandstone, which overlays the pennant rock. The cutting at Saltford shows a section of lias which, at Keynsham, meets with a line of fault; on the western side carboniferous strata appear. The road passes through some delightful meadow scenery.

During the formation of the Great Western Railway in this parish, a 𝕽𝖔𝖒𝖆𝖓 𝖁𝖎𝖑𝖑𝖆, with a beautiful tesselated pavement, was discovered. The latter, having been carefully relaid, was for some years preserved at the Keynsham Station, but has since been transfered to the Literary Institution at Bristol.

The Rev. W. L. Nichols, in the introduction to his poem, called "*Horæ Romanæ*," gives the following description of these antiquities when first discovered :—" They are the remains of two buildings,

E e

the walls being constructed of the rough lias found in the neighbourhood. The lower and more important structure measured 102 feet by 55, but had been cut through by the high road which bounds it on the north. The entrance was on the eastern side, leading to a corridor communicating with the various apartments, beautifully paved, a large portion of the pattern remaining. Close to the road are the remains of a *hypocaust;* adjoining it a *sudatorium*, in the centre of which is a large pillar of stone. The *triclinium* measures 17 feet by 15, but seems to have been united to an adjoining room, of similar dimensions, by an *aulæum*, or curtain. The floor of the triclinium is ornamented with a tesselated pavement, in the centre of which is a circular compartment, bordered by a *guilloche* (an ornament like the curb-chain of a bridle); within this circle is a male figure, playing, with the hand, on a lyre-shaped instrument of music, with a dog fawning on him. In a concentric circle, of larger dimensions, are a stag, bull, leopard, panther, and lion, a tree being placed between each figure : architectural frets of various kinds complete· the plan, forming a very elegant and tasteful design.. The central figure has been supposed to be Orpheus, but with more probability Apollo, as the beasts are in a separate compartment, and form a very natural ornament of a sylvan villa ; and it is well known that the *triclinium* was sometimes named the Apollo. The pavements of the adjoining rooms are of a less elaborate character, and have been indented by the fall of the roof. The *tesseræ* are of five different colours, all from materials found in the immediate vicinity; red, of burnt tile, white and blue, from the neighbouring lias; the brown is the pennant grit, and the green a species of the lias marl, which occurs in abundance at Cully Hall, in Bitton parish. It is remarkable that the pavements were found carefully covered with the lias slabs. Numerous fragments of pottery, with relics of domestic life, pieces of the frescoes which adorned the walls, and glass, were dug from the ruins, with several coins; a denarius of Macrinus, an auræus of Honorius, and brass coins of Constans and Valentinian. The villa was probably occupied until the Romans finally withdrew from Britain." The following beautiful lines open Mr. Nichols' poem :—

> "Fragment of classic ground! that dost recal
> Visions of other days, and other men,
> Once rulers of the world! the past, stern teacher,
> Speaks from your relics: thrones have pass'd away,
> Nations have perish'd, languages have chang'd,
> And old Imperial Rome hath sunk to dust
> Since last the light of day shone on your walls.
> Memento of man's nothingness! ye bear
> Inscribed upon your ruins, *Vanity*—
> A nation's epitaph—yet leave half-told
> Your story, for in vain we ask—who was
> Your short-liv'd master? whose the taste that plann'd
> His Summer dwelling here on Avon side,
> Chamber, and corridor, and hypocaust, and whose
> The feet that fourteen hundred years ago
> Trod yonder pavements, mazes intricate
> Of dædal wreaths, and rich mosaic, match'd
> So curiously elaborate stone with stone?"

The portion of the remains preserved is the pavement of the *triclinium*, of which there is an accurate drawing in the Royal Literary Institution.

The town of Keynsham was once celebrated for its **Great Augustinian Abbey**, whose possessions extended over much of the neighbouring country. It was endowed with the whole Manor and Hundred of Keynsham ; some interesting remains have lately been discovered.

The **Abbey Church**, which was founded by William Earl of Gloucester, in 1170, for the Black Canons of St. Augustine, stood nearly due east of the present parish church, and not far from the Railway Station. When clearing a site for the erection of several small villas, some interesting remains of the monastic buildings were brought to light. The walls, and a pavement of encaustic tiles—parts of a chantry chapel of two-vaulted compartments—were laid open. The chapel seems to have been attached to the eastern end of the conventual church. Fragments of Early English mouldings, and several bold transitional capitals, together with some shrine or tabernacle work of rare beauty, were also discovered. Most of these remains may be referred to the reign of Edward I. A number of curiously incised monumental slabs were also found, some of which are inscribed with the names of brethren of the abbey. One or two of the most interesting of these relics have been presented to the Royal Literary Institution, and may be seen under the portico.

The 𝕮𝖍𝖚𝖗𝖈𝖍, dedicated to St. John, has recently been restored at a large expense. It is a spacious fabric. The stately tower, erected in 1635, from materials taken from the ruins of the adjoining abbey, replaced an older one which was destroyed by lightning, and forms a conspicuous object to persons travelling between Bath and Bristol. It is of mixed perpendicular and debased work, but very effective in its general character, and possesses a peal of eight musical bells. The chancel is of Early English architecture, and contains some fine monuments of the Brydges family (Dukes of Chandos). Within the communion rails, on a massive altar tomb, surmounted by a renaissance canopy, lies the armoured effigy of Henry Brydges, Esq., the first of that antient family buried here. He died in 1587.*

The site of the monastery was granted by the Crown, in 1552, to the above named Henry Brydges, by whom a spacious mansion was erected from its ruins. Of this the gateway-arch of the stables only now remains, the house having been pulled down in 1776.

Keynsham, according to a popular legend, derives its name from one of those saintly virgins, who, devoting their time to fasting and prayer, were assumed to possess miraculous gifts. St. Keyn, it is said,

* The property formerly held by this family ultimately passed, together with the title, through the last heiress to the ducal family of Buckingham. The present Duke of Buckingham and Chandos disposed of the estate a few years ago.

converted all the snakes in the neighbourhood into stones;—the whole parish being full of the ammonite, no doubt, gave rise to the tradition. In reality, the appellation, common to many other parishes, is derived from the local positions of its "hams" or meadows.

It has been recently determined to lay out a Cemetery for the use of the parish.

The Rev. J. H. Gray is the present Vicar.

Keynsham contains a population of 2,245, on an area of 4,171 acres; the poor rates average about £800 per annum.

STANTON DREW.

THE distance from Keynsham to Stanton Drew is about five or six miles, and the walk is delightful.

In the high road to Chew Magna is a large stone, called Hautville's Quoit, said by tradition to have been thrown from Maes Knoll by the redoubtable champion, Sir John Hautville, whose effigy, in Irish oak, is to be seen in Chew Magna Church. This stone was computed by Collinson to have originally weighed thirty tons. The largest circle lies 100 yards south of the Chew; scarcely two authors agree in its admeasurement. "Its greatest diameter," says Phelps, "is 126 yards from north to south; its lesser, 115 from east to west. Fourteen stones are visible, five stand, eight are recumbent, and eleven buried under the surface, whose situation may be seen in dry summers."

Authors have differed as to their number. Mus-grave, in the year 1718, makes them thirty-two; Wood, in 1740, thirty; Collinson fourteen; and, Seyer, twenty-seven. Phelps conceives Wood to be correct. Within the eastern circle, is the great altar-stone, as at Stonehenge. The second circle consists of eight stones, thirty-two yards in diameter. Four are still standing, the others lie on the ground. One of them is nine feet high, twenty-two feet in diameter, and is computed to weigh fifteen tons. The entrance was a semi-circular avenue, of which seven stones remain.

In the orchard, south of the church, is a circle consisting of twelve stones, called by Dr. Stukeley the Lunar Temple. They are rude and irregular. The diameter is 120 feet. This temple is situated about 150 yards from the largest circle; ten stones may still be seen. To the south-west of the church are three stones, of which one is recumbent, and two upright, one being very large. The fallen stone is fourteen feet long by ten wide. The tradition is that a bride on her way to the church, together with all her attendants, were converted into stones; in accordance with this fable the remains are called the Wedding. North-west from the cove,* in a field called Lower Tyning, are two flat stones.

This temple is supposed to have been erected by the Britons, under the superintendence of the Druids. Mr. Fergusson, F.S.A., attributes it to the Arthurian

* See Mr. Long's article in the Archæological Journal, vol. xv.

or post Roman period, as a memorial of King Arthur's 11th battle. Near it are Maes Knoll, Stantonbury Hill, Englishcombe, Camerton, and other British towns, with the important Wansdyke, and a village, called at the Norman Conquest Belgætown, now Belluton. Sir Richard Colt Hoare says the stones at Stanton Drew are more ancient than those at Stonehenge, and the Rev. J. B. Deane, F.S.A., in the 25th vol. of the Archæologia, says, "they are a *dracontium* or serpent temple," remarking "that wherever there was a serpent temple, there was a legend similar to that related of the holy virgin St. Keyn." Unfortunately for this hypothesis, there are "snake stones" at Keynsham, amply sufficient for the legend, had Stanton Drew never existed.

These circles in the south of England are classed with the remains at Avebury and Stonehenge, of which they are the smallest group. The Rev. W. L. Bowles has referred their origin to the worship of Teut, an astronomer, supposed to be a great grandson of Noah, who divided the year into 365 days; the first representation of Teut was a stone on a mound. Fourteen miles from these remains, on a vast natural mound, is situated a stone, called to this day Cleeve Teut, or Toot, and the various Chews are supposed to be corruptions of this name. There can be but little doubt that Stanton Drew was the centre of an important district, where the people assembled together, received their laws, their punishments, and their religious, moral, and

political instruction. It is not on the whole un-
reasonable to conclude that these British temples
were used both for secular and religious purposes.*

The **Church** stands between the Cove and the
Tyning. The square embattled tower, which is
placed on the north side, has a porch and a beautiful
decorated arch-way, above which is a canopied niche.
It contains, among others, the tomb of Sir Michael
Foster, one of the justices of the Court of King's
Bench, who died in 1763. The font is of a plain
bowl shape, hewn from a solid stone, without ornament, and is either Saxon or Norman. This church
was partially re-built, and badly restored, in 1847.
The old Rectory House is an interesting relic of
the middle ages. It contains a window, with curious
grotesque heads forming the corbels, and the arms
of Bishop Beckington, cut in stone. The church
is dedicated to S. Mary. The Incumbent of Stanton
Drew is the Rev. H. T. Perfect.

The Farm House, belonging to Mr. John Fowler,

---

* There are many theories on the subject of these megalithic
monuments. Among the most able of the older writers on
the subject may be mentioned Aubrey and Stukeley; of the
middle period, Keysler, Musgrave, Wood, Collinson, Hoare,
and Seyer; and of more recent date, Phelps, Rev. J. B. Deane,
Rev. Prebendary Scarth (see article in Somersetshire Archæological Journal, vol. xiv), and Mr. W. Long. The article from
the pen of the last mentioned gentleman, like that on Abury, is
an exhaustive treatise on the subject (see Archæological Journal,
vol. xv). He is at present engaged in preparing an article
on Stonehenge, which doubtless will be marked by his usual
care, knowledge, and research.

deserves notice; it contains an interesting Mediæval window.

During the last seven years a new Parsonage house has been built, under the superintendence of the present Vicar, and the benefice has been increased in value by the Ecclesiastical Commissioners.

The parish is in the Hundred of Keynsham, and the Union of Clutton. The population, in 1871, was 553; the poor rates, which were £225 in 1839, now average £400 yearly.

APPENDIX.

METEOROLOGY.

BATH, situated on the slopes of lofty hills, affords a considerable variety of climate, which resembles that of the West of England generally, but without sharing in its excessive rain-fall. An excellent paper on the Temperature and Rain-fall in this city was read by the Rev. Leonard Blomefield, at the Meeting of the British Association held in Bath in 1864. That gentleman has continued his observations up to the present time (1876), communicating his results to the Bath Natural History Club, and his experience leads him "to believe that though there is no great difference in temperature between this and other places in England, lying eastwards in about the same latitude in *moderate* seasons or during moderate weather, there is a marked difference when the weather becomes of an *extreme* character, the difference being greater in proportion to the excess of heat, if summer, or to the excess of cold, if winter, amounting on an average to five degrees in favour of Bath." Thus in June, 1858, when the thermometer at Oxford, Norwich and Gloucester rose to 90 degrees, at Nottingham to 92 degrees, and Greenwich to 94·5, at Bath it was never higher than 84 degrees. Again in the hot May of 1864, when the maximum temperature in other places ranged from 85 to 88 degrees, in Bath it was never higher than 79 degrees. So much then for this city being hotter than other places in summer, as is commonly supposed. In cases of severe cold there is as great a difference on the other side. Thus, on that notoriously cold day, Dec. 25th, 1860, when the thermometer at Nottingham and Cambridge fell to minus 8 degrees, at Bath it was not lower than plus eleven, showing a difference of 19 degrees. The weather registers, from which it is needless to quote further examples, invariably give the same indications.

The latest Blue Book, published by the Rivers' Pollution Commissioners, "on the Domestic Water Supply of Great Britain," contains a Map of the Country by which the rain-fall of any given district may be seen at a glance. It is shown that Bath enjoys, in common with the West and Midland Counties, a moderate and sufficient supply of from 25 to 30 inches yearly. This quantity increases rapidly as we go westward ; Bristol having a rain-fall of from 30 to 40 inches, which increases in Cornwall to from 40 to 50 inches, the higher parts of the county ranging from 50 to 75 inches.

During the past few years, the water supply of Bath has been supplemented at a large outlay, from springs in St. Catherine's valley, a distance of about five miles from the city. The quality of these springs, which are quoted in the Blue Book before referred to, as being amongst the purest in the Kingdom, is unexceptionable, and the quantity is sufficient to supply a population at least double that of Bath.

Subjoined is an analysis made by Charles Ekin, F.C.S., of water from the principal source, and which may be taken as a fair sample of the whole supply. It will be seen that though it is rather hard for washing purposes, it is only sufficiently so as to make it palatable and wholesome for drinking—a soft water, though of course better for washing, not being so wholesome as a harder water for drinking purposes, and *vice versa.*

The contents per gallon are as follows :—

	GRAINS.
Ammonia	0
Chlorine	1·03
Nitrogen as Nitrates	0·094
Nitrogen as Nitrites	0
Albuminoid Organic Matter	0·028
Total Solid Impurity	21·46
The Temporary Hardness is	15·2°
Permanent ditto	3·78°
Total ditto	18·98°

ON THE ANGLING ROUND BATH.

RAMBLES ABOUT BATH would, at least in our opinion, be imperfect without some account of the Angling to be found in the neighbourhood. All rambles are pleasant things, but to our thinking rambles, rod in hand, are delightful. Before describing the various waters which lie within the compass of an hour round the city, either by road or rail, it may be advisable to state that within the four seas of Britain there is no such thing, *de jure,* as "free fishing," unless it be on navigable rivers. Even this point is at the present moment *sub judice.*

Having thus placed ourselves on terms not adverse to the interests of riparian proprietors, we venture to hope that they will, as far as they can, exercise a merciful and liberal policy towards the lacklands of the rod who sue to them in *formâ pauperis.*

Between Bristol and Bath the Avon is navigable, and practically open to all comers. For a mile above, and for two miles below Keynsham, the river—sluggish and unpromising as it looks—affords fair angling, especially for carp and tench. This part of the Avon is rather heavily worked by fishermen from Bristol, who, nevertheless, often contrive to make good bags. From Bath to Bradford, leave is more or less required, especially near the different weirs. At these points some trout are always to be found, which for shape and size could not easily be matched on rivers of far greater sporting pretensions. The higher portion of the stream, say from Lacock upwards, offers first rate perch and jack fishing. The water is preserved, but leave may occasionally be obtained. The manufacturing refuse from the mills at Bradford and Trowbridge has done much to injure the river which, in our memory held trout, jack, carp; and tench, of exceptional weights. The gudgeon are probably the finest in the kingdom.

Next in importance—so far as the sporting public are concerned—is the Canal, the property of the Great Western Railway Company. The Chairman, we believe, is willing to grant permission for fair angling. The Company appear to exercise little prohibitory influence over this part of their property. At present it has no market value as a fishery. Passing through a charming pastoral country, the Kennet and Avon Canal boasts more agreeable scenery than the majority of such artificial water ways possess. It contains a fair stock of coarse fish, and rather more than the usual allowance of fine perch. With the minnow or spoon bait, excellent baskets may be made by skilful performers. We have seen many a take in which these fish averaged three quarters of a pound all round.

The principal trout streams round the city may be grouped as follows. To the north-east, Swainswick brook. To the north and east, Batheaston brook, and Box brook. To the south-west, Newton brook. To the south, Midford brook.

Swainswick brook crosses the London Road about fifty yards beyond Grosvenor Place. Above Woolley Church it holds rather a large stock of trout. The stream is so narrow and wooded that it is only suitable for some form of bait fishing. The water is jealously regarded by some of the farmers who, however, might —if taken in a pliant hour—give an occasional day's angling.

About two miles further on the London Road is the village of Batheaston, immediately beyond which the Batheaston Brook falls into the Avon. Some years ago this beau ideal of an English rivulet held an excellent stock of small trout. At present, poaching, and imperfect preservation, have reduced it to the level of a somewhat barren water farm.

The village of Box, about five miles from the city, gives its name to a stream which might, with little impropriety, be called a river. Its length is considerable, something probably like twelve or fourteen miles. Parts of this brook are carefully preserved. Few streams of its size offer more secure harbourage ; more abundant food ; or better spawning grounds. `If preserved, it would afford capital sport. Weaver-mead offers as pretty a stretch of fly fishing water as need be desired.

Newton brook crosses the Lower Bristol Road, about a quarter of a mile beyond the village of Twerton. It contains a few fair sized fish.

Three miles south of the city is Midford brook, which falls into the river near the Aqueduct. From this point to Midford it is full of coarse fish. Now and then it holds a few heavy river trout. Above the village it is a trout stream *pure et simple*. It is heavily wooded, and the banks are high. With these disadvantages, it requires a master of the art to make a good bag. Wellow—provided leave is obtained—would form the most suitable angling quarters. It is close to the water ; the valley is very lovely, and the Inn comfortable. Lodgings could be obtained in the village. It should be added that the brook receives a large tributary near Midford. This stream runs through, and far beyond Coombe Hay Park. In our salad days we have occasionally made five-and-twenty pound bags of roach, and perch, and chub, in this water. We have no knowledge of its present angling capabilities.

If the size of the city is taken into consideration, it may be pronounced fairly well supplied with fishing grounds. Almost every branch of the art may be employed. Were we compelled to offer an opinion as to the most killing baits on the smaller waters mentioned, we should name the minnow, wasp grub, ant eggs, and worm. These little brooks, hid away in quiet pastoral valleys, are wonderfully solitary. We have followed them, rod in hand, for days together without seeing man, woman, or child.

ROWING.

HAVING noticed very briefly the angling in the neighbourhood of Bath, it would be out of place to pass, *sub silentio*, a somewhat kindred pursuit.

The Avon though not a first rate river for Boating is by no means a bad one. It is sufficiently wide ; of a uniform depth ; without much weed, and carries the oarsman or canoeist through pleasant pastoral scenery.

The part of the water principally used for this purpose lies be-tween the Cleveland Bridge and the weir at Bathampton. Above this point the river really deserves the name of beautiful. The distance between the weir at Bathampton and the weir at Warleigh is, probably, something like four miles. Boats can easily be hauled over the former, and canoes could be carried across the meadows in order to pass the latter.

Below the city, the locks afford an easy passage to Bristol, giving a range of fifteen or sixteen miles.

There are several Boating Clubs. The principal places where skiffs, out-riggers, four oars, and canoes are kept, for hire, are the Villa Fields, Cleveland Bridge, and immediately above Pulteney Bridge. The entrance to the last named boat-house lies opposite St. Michael's Church. The river is dangerous to those who are unable to swim, from its depth, as well as from the formation of the banks.

LIST OF BOOKS, written by WILLIAM PRYNNE, now in the LIBRARY of the ABBEY CHURCH, BATH:—

The Perpetuitie of a Regenerate Man's Estate against the Saints' Total and Final Apostacy, 4to., London, 1627. God no Impostor nor Deluder, 4to., London, 1629. A Coppie of a Recantation of certain Errors raked out of the Dunghill of Poperie and Plagianisme, publiquely made by Maister Barret, of Kayes Colleged in Cambridge, the 10th day of May, 1595. The nine Assertions or Articles of Lambheth composed and agreed upon at Lambheth House, 20th Nov. 1595. Healthes, Sicknesse, or a compendious and brief Discourse, proving the Drinking and Pledging of Healthes to be sinfull and utterly unlawfull unto Christians. 4to., London, 1628.

An exact History of Pope's Intollerable Usurpations upon the Liberties of the Kings, and Subjects of England and Ireland. Books III. and IV. with an Appendix and three Indexes. Large folio. *(Commences page 227.) No title.*

An exact Chronological Vindication and Historical Demonstration of our British, Roman, Saxon, Danish, Norman, and English Kings' supream Ecclesiastical Jurisdiction over all Prelates, Persons, Causes within their Kingdomes, Dominions, &c. Large folio. *(To page 80), wants title. Bound with the foregoing.*

The First Part of a Brief Register, Kalendar and Survey of the several Kinds, Forms of all Parliamentary Writs. 4to., London, 1659.

A Breviate of the Life of William Laud; Archbishop of Canterbury. Extracted (for the most part) verbatim out of his owne Diary and other Writings under his owne hand. Imp. folio, London, 1644.

Canterburies Doome ; or, the First Part of a Compleat History of the Commitment Charges, Tryall, Condemnation—Execution of William Laud (late Archbishop of Canterbury). By William Prynne, of Lincolnes Inne, Esquire, specially deputed to this publike service by the House of Commons Order, dated 4th Martii, 1644. Imp. folio, London, 1646.

Brief Animadversions on, Amendments of, and Additional Explanatory Records to the Fourth Part of the Institutes. (Wants title.) Dedication dated May 29th, 1669. Imp. Folio.

The First, Second and Third Parts of a Seasonable, Legal and Historical Vindication of the good Old Fundamental Liberties, Franchises, Rights, Properties, Laws, and Government of all English Freemen. Small folio, 2 vols., London, 1654-57.

The following are bound in one volume, 4to. :—

The Popish Royall Favourite ; or, a Full Discovery of his Maj. Extraordinary Favour to, and Protection of, notorious Papists, Priests, Jesuits, &c., manifested by Sundry Letters of Grace, Warrants, &c. (Title wanting.)

Rome's Masterpiece ; or, the Grand Conspiracy of the Pope and his Jesuited Instruments to extirpate the Protestant Religion, re-establish Popery, subvert Lawes, Liberties, Peace, Parliaments, by kindling a Civill War in Scotland, &c. London, 1644.

A Moderate Apology against a Pretended Calumny. In answer to some Passages in the Preheminence of Parlement. London, 1644.

The Falsities and Forgeries of the Anonymous Author of a late
 Pamphlet (supposed to be printed at Oxford but in truth at London) 1644, intituled the Fallacies of Mr. William Prynne, discovered in a Short View of his Books—intituled The Soveraignty of Parliaments. The Opening of the Great Seal, &c. London, 1644.

A Gagge for Longe-Hair'd Rattle-Heads who Revile all Civill Round-Heads. 4 pages, 4to.

A Vindication of Psalme cv., 15, "Touch not mine Anointed, and doe my Prophets no Harme," from some *false glosses* obtruded on it by Royalists. 4to., London, 1644.

The Doome of Cowardisze and Treachery ; or, a Looking-Glasse for Cowardly or Corrupt Governours and Souldiers, who through Pusillanimity or Bribery betray their Trusts to the Publick Prejudice. 4to., London, 1643.

A True and Full Relation of the Prosecution, Arraignment, Tryall, and Condemnation of Nathaniell Fiennes, late Colonel and Governour of the City and Castle of Bristoll, &c. By William Prynne and Clement Walker. 4to., London, 1644.

Twelve Considerable Serious Questions touching Church Government (sadly propounded out of a Reall Desire of Unity and Tranquility in Church and State) to all sober-minded Christians, &c. 4to., London, 1644.

A Full Reply to certaine Briefe Observations and Antiqueries on Master Prynne's Twelve Questions about Church Government, &c. 4to., London, 1644.

Brief Animadversions on Mr. John Goodwin's Theomachia, &c. London, 1644.

Truth triumphing over Falshood, Antiquity over Novelty ; or, a Seasonable Vindication of the Undoubted Ecclesiastical Juris-diction, Right, Legislative, and Coercive Power of Christian Emperors, Kings, Magistrates, Parliaments, in matter of Religion, Church Government, &c.—in Refutation of John Goodwin's Innocencies, Triumph and his dear Brother Barton's Vindication of Churches commonly called Independent, &c. 4to., London, 1645.

A Fresh Discovery of some Prodigious New Wandring-Blasing Stars, and Firebrands Stiling themselves "New Lights Firing our Church and State into New Combustions," &c. 4to., London, 1645.

Transcript of a Letter lately written from the Sommer Islands, to William Prynne, of Lincolnes Inne, Esquire, relating the Schismaticall, Tyrannical, and Seditious Proceedings of the Independents there, &c.

A Soveraign Andtidote to Prevent, Appease, and determine our unnaturall and destructive Civill Warres and dissensions, &c. 4to., London, 1642.

A Vindication of four Serious Questions of Grand Importance Concerning Excommunication and Suspention from the Sacra-ment of the Lord's Supper. 4to., London, 1645.

The Lyar confounded, or a Briefe Refutation of John Lilburnes miserably-mistated Case, mistaken Law, Seditious Calumnies, and most malicious Lyes against the High Court of Parliament, &c. 4to., London, 1645. *(Three Leaves wanting at the end.)*

MONUMENTAL BRASSES.

A List of Monumental Brasses in the three Counties surrounding Bath, some of which are within easy distance from the city.

SOMERSETSHIRE.

PLACE.	DATE.	PLACE.	DATE.
Axbridge	1493	Langridge	c. 1427
Banwell	c. 1470	(Only inscription remaining,	
,,	1503	figure gone)	
,,	1554	,,	1441
Beckington	1475	Petherton (South)	c. 1420
Burnett	1575	,, ,,	1442
Cheddar (good)	c. 1440	S. Decumans	1572
Churchill	1572	Swainswick	1439
Crewkerne	1525	(See Autotype p. 416)	
Dunster	1497	Tintinhull	1464
Fivehead	c. 1550	Weare	c. 1490
Ilminster	1440	Wraxall	
,, (fine)	1618	Yeovil—on the Lectern	

WILTSHIRE.

PLACE.	DATE.	PLACE.	DATE.
Aldbourne	1508	Devizes	c. 1650
Alton Priors	1528	Fovant (curious)	1492
Beckington	c. 1470	Lavington (West)	c. 1559
Bedwyn (Great)	1510	Lacook	1501 ·
Bradford	15..	Mere	1398
(See Autotype p. 416.)		Monkton	1500
,,	1601	Preshute	1518
Broughton Gifford	1620	Salisbury—St. Thomas's	
Bromham	1516	Church	1570
,,	15..	Salisbury Cathedral	1375
,,	1574	,, ,,	1578
Charlton	1524	Seend	1498
Cliffe Pipard	1380	Tisbury	
Draycot Cerne	c. 1370	,,	1590
(Good—the Knight holds his		Wandborough	1402
wife's hand.)			

Monumental Brasses continued :—

GLOUCESTERSHIRE.

PLACE.	DATE.	PLACE.	DATE.
Alveston	15..	Deerhurst	1400
Bisley	1505	,,	1625
Bristol—S. John's	1478	Dowdeswell	c. 1500
,,　—S. Mary Redcliff	1439	Dyrham (good)	1401
,　　　　,,	1471	Eastington	1518
,,	148.	Fairford	1471
,,	1522	Gloucester—St. Michael	1519
..,,　—S. Peter's	1461	Leckhampton	1598
,,　—Temple	c. 1395	Lechlade	c. 144.
(Said to be palimpsest.)		,,	c. 150.
,,	c. 1460	Minchinhampton	1556
,,　—S. Werburgh's	1546		
Chipping Camden	1450	Newland	c, 1450
,,	1467	Northleach	c. 1400
,,	1484	,,	1447
,,　　(fine)	1401	,,	1458
Cheltenham—S. Mary	1513	,,	c. 1480
Cirencester	1360	,,	14..
,,	1427-34	,,	1493
,,	1438	,,	1501
,,	1442	,,	1525
,,　　(fine)	c. 1460	,,	c. 1530
,,	1462	Oldpien	
,,	1478	Rodmarton	·. 1471
..	14..	Thornbury	1571
,,	c. 1520	Tormarton	1493
,,	1529	Winterbourne	c. 1380
,,	1529	Wootten-under-Edge	1392
,,	1587	,,　　(fine)	1417
,,	1642	Yate	1590

MASTERS OF THE CEREMONIES OF BATH.

THE office, previous to the appointment of Nash, was not one of much importance, and the assemblies were of a far different character from what they afterwards became under his regime. The Balls, which seem more or less to have been previously a cloak for gaming, were held at the Town Hall. It is more than probable, in the absence of recorded facts, that Webster was the first who held the office permanently, and he was an adventurer—a coarse, unprincipled gambler, who reflected, the habits and manners of the society over which he presided.

As is shown in the notice of Nash, if these elements were not purified by him they were brought into order, and under his sway grew into that epoch of fashion which forms a notable chapter in the annals of Bath. Nash died in 1761. One trait of the Beau is not generally known. He was exceedingly fond of argument, especially on subjects of which he knew little, and cared less. Religious polemics he introduced in season and out of season, affecting a contemptuous unbelief in revealed religion. On one of these occasions when arguing with Bentley* the following epigram was written by a member of the party :—

> " On Reason, Faith, and mystery high,
>   Two wits harangue the table;
> Bentley believes he knows not why,
>   Nash swears 'tis all a fable.
>
> Peace Coxcombs, peace, and both agree!
>   Nash, kiss thy empty brother;
> Religion laughs at foes like thee,
>   And dreads a friend like t'other."

Mr. Collet was the immediate successor of Nash, in 1761. He retired in 1769, and was succeeded by Mr. Derrick. He was a very diminutive man, a fact which did not detract from his importance in his own estimation. Affecting a taste for literature, during occasional intervals he visited different parts of the country, and described his impressions in a series of letters addressed to various friends and correspondents. The style is affected and the matter commonplace; the tenuity of thought is in an inverse ratio to the pomposity of the language. Nevertheless Mr. Derrick was held in much esteem for his many good qualities.

At the death of Mr. Derrick in 1769, a schism occurred. Mr. Brereton was elected by a party, with, it was so alleged, undue if not indecent haste; and a rival, Mr. Plomer (Master of the Ceremonies at Bristol) was brought into the field, and a double election ensued. The dispute was arranged, by the

* Son of the famous Dr. Bentley.

retirement of both, in favour of Captain Wade, nephew of
Marshall Wade. Captain Wade, resigned in 1777 on accepting
a similar post at Brighton.

Mr. Brereton in the same year was re-installed in his old
position at the Lower Rooms, and Mr. Dawson was appointed to
the Upper Rooms. The former retired almost immediately, and
was succeeded by Mr. Tyson, from Tunbridge Wells. Mr. Dawson
abdicated in 1785, and Mr. Tyson transferred his sovereignty
from the Lower to the Upper Kingdom, where he reigned until
1805, and was followed by Mr. King, who had succeeded to
his throne at the Lower Rooms. Mr. King died, in 1816,
and Captain Wyke held the office until 1818; in 1819, Mr.
Heaveside was installed in the office, which he held until
1825. At the Lower Rooms Mr. Le Bas succeeded Mr. King,
in 1805, and presided there for some years, and was followed in
succession by Mr. Gwynette and Captain Marshall, the latter retaining the office until the destruction of the Lower Rooms, in 1820.

In 1825, Captain (afterwards Colonel, and then Major-General)
Jervois was installed in the office. He held the post until he
obtained the rank of a General Officer, in 1849, when he was
appointed Governor of Hong Kong. General Jervois was a
man of great tact and excellent judgment, and during his long
tenure of office as Master of the Ceremonies, discharged the
duties which devolved on him with singular prudence, and with
great advantage to the city. He gave dignity to the office by
his high-bred courtesy, and irreproachable character. Witty,
vivacious, well versed in books, and possessing a tenacious
memory, he was the "life and soul" of society. In conversation
he was apt in quotation, and always ready with a well-timed
illustration from his favourite authors, especially Shakspere.
He had a passion for books, and displayed no little skill in the
manner in which he illustrated such of them as afforded scope
for especial embellishment. At his death he left a collection of
books of much interest, and considerable value. He was followed
by Mr. Hodges Nugent, who resigned, in 1863, and was succeeded
by Mr. Emerson, who held the office for a very brief period.

The office remained in abeyance until 1875, when Lieutenant-
Colonel England was unanimously elected.

TERMINATIONS.

COMBE.

Charlcombe.
Combe (Down).
Combe (Hay).
Englishcombe.
Horsecombe.
Lyncombe.
Smallcombe.
Monckton Combe.
Widcombe.

DOWN.

Bannerdown.
Charmey Down.
Claverton Down.
Combe Down.
Farleigh Down.
Hampton Down.
Holt Down.
Kingsdown.
Lansdown.
Odd Down.

FORD.

Bathford.
Freshford.
Iford.
Hungerford.
Midford.
Bradford.
Saltford.
Shawford.
Slaughterford.
Swinford.

LEY.

Farley (leigh).
Tunley.
Turley (leigh).

LEY (Continued).

Warley (leigh).
Winsley.
Woolley.

RIDGE.

Langridge.
Ditteridge.

STOKE.

Limpley Stoke.
Northstoke.
Southstoke.

TON.

Bathampton.
Bitton.
Camerton.
Claverton.
Clutton.
Corston.
Dunkerton.
Hampton.
Hinton.
Kelston.
Newton.
Priston.
Stanton (Drew).
Stanton (Prior).
Twerton.
Upton.
Weston.
Wilmington.

WICK.

Bathwick.
Farley Wick.
Shockerwick.
Swainswick.
Tatwick.

We are indebted to Mr. T. W. Gibbs, for this list of terminations.

INDEX.

☞ In the note on the Sheridan Family, page 235, the name of
   the Earl of *Gifford* is, by a printer's error, spelt *Gilford*.

GOULD & SON, BATH.

ESTAB^D 1787   ESTAB^D 1787

23, Milson Street, & 2, George Street,

DEPARTMENTS.

TAILORING	Civil, Naval, and Military. Ladies' Riding Habits, Costumes, Jackets, &c. Clerical Robes, Liveries, &c., &c.
HATS	Velvet Nap—12s. to 23s. Felt—7s. 6d. to 12s. 6d. Ladies' Riding Hats; Boys' Hats, Caps, &c.
SHIRTS	Long Cloth—36s., 42s., 45s., and 48s. per Half-Dozen. Flannel, Oxford Gauze, Silk, &c. *Directions for Self-Measurement.*
GLOVES	Dent's Fownes', and Best French Makers Ladies' and Gentlemen's Kid, Cotton, and Tan. Gould and Son's Celebrated 2s. Gloves.
SCARVES	Long, Extra-Long, Silk, and Satin. Made-up Sailor's Knots, Danes, &c., &c. Mufflers and Ties of every description.
HOSIERY	Cotton, Merino, Silk, Lambswool, &c. Vests, Drawers, and Socks, in all Makes and Prices. Specialities made to order.
LEATHER	Portmanteaus, Hat Boxes, Ladies' and Gentlemen's Waterproof Coats and Leggings, Rugs, &c.
UMBRELLAS	Ladies' and Gentlemen's Silk and Alpaca. Natural and Carved Sticks, Ivory, &c. Carriage Umbrellas.

PRICE LISTS POST FREE.

1

DEPÔT FOR MINTON'S WARES.

ROBERT CAREY,

CRYSTAL TABLE GLASS,

AND

China, Earthenware, & Furnishing

SHOW ROOMS,

NORTHGATE STREET

And NORTHGATE LANE, BATH.

ESTABLISHED UPWARDS HALF-A-CENTURY.

THESE spacious Rooms contain a magnificent STOCK OF GOODS, comprising the choicest productions of the English, Dresden, Berlin, and the Oriental Markets, to the more simple and inexpensive Patterns, suitable alike to the Cottage or the Mansion.

Families about to Furnish, before deciding elsewhere, are invited to pay a visit and judge for themselves.

A FEW PRICES ARE SUBJOINED :—

	£	s.	d.		£	s.	d.
A good Stone China Dinner Set (for 12) ...	3	3	0	to	42	0	0
A China Breakfast Service (for 12)	1	10	0	,,	15	15	0
A China Tea and Coffee Service (for 12) ...	0	12	6	,,	15	15	0
A Ditto Dessert Set (for 12)	1	1	0	,,	25	15	0
A good Toilet Set (6 pieces)	0	6	6	,,	9	9	0
Cut Crystal Wine Glasses, per dozen ...	0	6	6	,,	3	3	0
,, Tumblers ,, ...	0	6	0	,,	3	3	0
,, Quart Decanters, per pair ...	0	8	6	,,	5	5	0
,, Claret Jugs, each	0	7	0	,,	3	10	0

The above Services, either in Glass or China, can have Crest or Monogram impressed at the Shortest Notice, Samples can be seen at the Show Rooms.

A large Stock of Goods, suitable for India and the Colonies, always kept in Stock ; and to show the manner in which these Orders are executed, numerous of the most flattering Testimonials from Officers of high rank can be seen on application.

Price List on Application ; and Estimates and List of Quantities for Military Messes, Clubs, Hotels, &c., SUPPLIED FREE OF CHARGE.

DISCOUNT FOR CASH PAYMENTS.

E. & H. VEZEY,

Coach  **Harness**

Builders **Makers**

(BY APPOINTMENT TO HER MAJESTY,)

LONG ACRE,

AND

19, MILSOM STREET,

BATH.

E. & H. VEZEY beg respectfully to call attention to their

NEWLY REGISTERED PATENT

FOR OPENING AND CLOSING THE HEADS OF LANDAUS.

Their arrangement to obtain the above great advantage is so simple and easy, that any person sitting inside can with the slightest effort, Open or Close either part of the Head, without the assistance of either Coachman or Footman, thus forming instantly an elegant and complete Summer or Winter Carriage.

E. & H. VEZEY having now sent out a great many of their PATENT LANDAUS, can guarantee every satisfaction being given.

SIDE LIGHT LANDAUS opened with the same arrangement.

VEZEYS'
NEWLY DESIGNED

ROUND FRONTED WAGONETTE
MELBOURNE PHAETON.
BEATRICE PHAETON.
STANHOPE PHAETON,
With moveable Hind Seat and Step.

AND SEVERAL OTHER IMPROVEMENTS.

McKenzie's Patent also fitted to Order, for Opening or Closing Landau Heads.

STILTON HOUSE,
8, PULTENEY BRIDGE, BATH.

S. J. STAFFORD,
PROVISION MERCHANT,
OIL AND ITALIAN WAREHOUSEMAN.

The finest quality Goods, rendered at the lowest remunerative Prices,

Viz. :—EVERY DESCRIPTION OF

ENGLISH AND FOREIGN CHEESE,
BACON, HAMS, TONGUES, CHAPS, CHINES, &C.

CHEESE.

STILTON	CREAM	GRUYERE
SOMERSET	BATH CREAM	GORGONZOLA
CHEDDAR	R. VICTORIA	PARMASAN
WILTSHIRE	YORK CHEESE	DUTCH
GLOUCESTER	NEUFCHATEL	AMERICAN
BERKELEY	CAMERNBERT	CANADIAN
DERBY	H. NORTHWICH	SCHABZWEIGAR
CHESHIRE	LIMBOURG	ROQUEFORT
	EDDISH.	

HAMS.

BATH	CUMBERLAND	WESTPHALIA
YORK	SUFFOLK	LIMERICK
WILTSHIRE	BRUNSWICK	MUTTON
	MONTACHES.	

BACON.

MILD CURED, SMOKED, OR PALE DRIED.

BATH	YORK
WILTSHIRE	STRASBOURG

TONGUES.

PICKLED	RUSSIAN OX
SMOKED	REINDEER

N.B.—Hams, Tongues, and Chaps prepared ready for Table Pic-nic, &c., in various ways, by Steam process.

FRESH BUTTER DAILY.

PRIMEST DORSET WEEKLY, in Casks or otherwise.

Every description of Pickles, Sauces, Sardines, & other specialities.

MELTON PIES, by the best makers, *Colin & Co.*

Cambridge Sausages daily during the season, from Sept. 1 to May 31.

Orders per Post, with Reference, punctually attended to, Carriage Paid, and Package Free on all Orders above £5 in value.

2

ESTABLISHED 1779.

STOKES, SONS & ROADHOUSE,

GENERAL DRAPERS,

LINEN MERCHANTS,

SILK MERCERS,

COSTUMIERS,

DRESSMEN,

HOSIERS,

HABERDASHERS,

GLOVERS,

FURRIERS,

CARPET WAREHOUSEMEN,

HOUSE · FURNISHERS,

AND

UNDERTAKERS.

FUNERALS conducted personally to any part of the United Kingdom.

ABBEY CHURCHYARD
AND
CHEAP STREET,
BATH.

MESSRS.

TYLEE & HILLIER,

Pharmaceutical Chemists,

7, BRIDGE STREET,

BATH.

ESTABLISHED 1805.

Somersetshire College, Bath.

Visitor:

The Very Rev. the DEAN OF NORWICH, D.D. (late Head Master
of Rugby), Chaplain in Ordinary to Her Majesty.

President:

The Right Hon. LORD PORTMAN, late Lord Lieutenant of the
County.

Vice-Presidents:

The Right Rev. the LORD BISHOP of BATH and WELLS.
Sir WALTER TREVELYAN, Bart., Nettlecombe Court, near
Taunton.
Sir ALEXANDER ACLAND HOOD, Bart., St. Audries, near
Bridgewater.
Rev. G. G. BRADLEY, M.A., Master of University College, Oxford
(late Head Master of Marlborough College).
F. H. DICKENSON, Esq., Kingsweston.
The Ven. the ARCHDEACON of BATH.
Colonel BURROWES, K.H., Bourton Court, near Bristol.
Rev. J. H. BLACKWOOD, D.D.
WILLIAM LONG, Esq., West Hay, Wrington, near Bristol.
H. D. SKRINE, Esq., Warleigh Manor, near Bath.
Rev. JAMES PYCROFT.
The Right Rev. the LORD BISHOP of PETERBOROUGH.
Sir JOHN KENNAWAY, Bart., M.P., Escot, near Ottery St. Mary.
Sir C. B. GRAVES SAWLE, Bart., Penrice, Cornwall.
The Ven. the ARCHDEACON of LLANDAFF.
AMBROSE G. LETHBRIDGE, Esq., Eastbrook House, Taunton.
Rev. CANON BERNARD, Bath.
R. WILBRAHAM FALCONER, Esq., M.D., Bath.
W. T. BLAIR, Esq., Bath.
Rev. E. P. VAUGHAN, Wraxall.
R. GUY EVERED, Esq., Hill House, near Bridgewater.
J. BLOMMART, Esq., Willett House, near Taunton.
Rev. Prebendary STEPHENSON, Lympsham Manor.
Major-General H. Y. D. SCOTT, C.B., R.E., Ealing, Middlesex.
Rev. HAY S. ESCOTT, South Luffenham Rectory, late Head Master.

Executive Committee:

Rev. CANON BERNARD.	H. D. SKRINE, Esq.
Rev. JAMES PYCROFT.	Rev. Prebendary STEPHENSON
R. WILBRAHAM FALCONER, Esq., M.D.	Rev. HAY S. ESCOTT.

Secretary:

P. C. SHEPPARD Esq., Waterhouse, Bath.

Head Master:

[7] L. COURTNEY, Esq., M.A., Fellow of Merton College, Oxford.

(SOMERSETSHIRE COLLEGE, continued.)

Bankers:
STUCKEY'S BANKING COMPANY.

Solicitors:
Messrs. INMAN and INMAN.

Staff of the College:

A. L. FRASER, M.A., 1st Mathematical Master.
T. M. BROMLEY, M.A., } Assistant Classical
J. B. BADDELEY, B.A., } Masters.
Rev. C. EVERITT, M.A., Lecturer in History.
Mons. S. PORCHAT, French Master.
Herr. O. SONDERMANN, German Master.
Mr. T. R. BENNETT, Geometrical Drawing Master.
Mr. E. GIFFORD, Free-hand Drawing Master.
Mr. GATEHOUSE, Chemistry Master.
Mr. MACINTOSH, } Masters of the Lower School.
Mr. C. YOUNG, }

THIS College was founded in 1858, with the view of providing a course of education similar to that of our best Public Schools, with more attention to individual Boys than the large forms of those Schools render possible. Whilst both Classics and Mathematics are thoroughly taught in preparation for the Universities, and the Woolwich and other Examinations, very considerable attention is paid to History and Geography, and to French; a class for Natural Science has been established and a laboratory provided; and every effort is made to instruct the Pupils in the Holy Scriptures, and to render that instruction practical. The effective character of the education is sufficiently attested both by the Reports of the Examiners, and also by the marked success of the Pupils who have proceeded directly from the College to the University, or to the Royal Academy, Woolwich.

Since October, 1861, the following honours have been attained :—

University Honours—

THREE FELLOWSHIPS,
NINETEEN OPEN SCHOLARSHIPS,
TWELVE FIRST CLASSES,

NINETEEN SECOND CLASSES,
THREE UNIVERSITY PRIZES,
AND SEVERAL COLLEGE PRIZES AND THIRD CLASSES.

Honours at Woolwich—

FOURTH, FIFTH, SIXTH, SEVENTH, AND THIRTY-THIRD PLACES IN ENTRANCE EXAMINATION;
FIRST COMMISSION ROYAL ENGINEERS;
POLLOCK MEDAL AND REGULATION SWORD;
FIFTH COMMISSION ROYAL ENGINEERS;
SEVENTH COMMISSION ROYAL ENGINEERS;
FIFTH COMMISSION ROYAL ARTILLERY.
ALSO, TWO ADMISSIONS TO THE INDIA CIVIL SERVICE.

The Pupils of the College have the use of a Gravelled Playing Ground, a covered Fives Court and Gymnasium, and a Cricket and Foot-ball Field of several acres.

Prospectuses, Examiners' Reports, and further Particulars may be obtained at the College, or upon application to W. L. COURTNEY, *Esq., Winifred House, Bath: or to the Secretary,* P. C. SHEPPARD, *Esq.. Waterhouse, near Bath; or to* Mr. R. E. PEACH, 8, *Bridge Street, Bath, Bookseller to the College.*

Bath Proprietary College,
SYDNEY PLACE.

Visitor:

The Right Hon. and Right Rev. the LORD BISHOP OF BATH
AND WELLS.

Trustees:

Rev. H. M. SCARTH, M.A. | W. THOMPSON, Esq.
H. ARGENT SIMMONS, Esq.

His Grace the DUKE OF CLEVELAND, *President of the Council.*
Rev. H. M. SCARTH, M.A., *Vice-President of the Council.*
Major-General KENNEDY, *Treasurer.*
JOHN THIRLWALL, Esq., *Honorary Secretary.*

Principal:

Rev. S. C. VOULES, M.A., *late Scholar of Lincoln College, Oxford,
late Assistant Master at Rossall, and Marlborough College.*

Vice-Principal:

W. H. SCOTT, Esq., M.A., *late Scholar of St. Peter's College, Cambridge,
with Six other Masters.*

---:o:---

THIS College is established with the design of providing for the
Sons of the Nobility, Clergy, and Gentry, a sound Classical, Mathematical, and General Education, in strict conformity with the
principles of the Church of England.

In the Classical Department the education is chiefly intended on
a preparation for the Universities, and is to a great extent classical.

In the Modern Department the teaching is based as far as possible on the requirements of the examinations for Woolwich, the
Line, Cooper's Hill, Civil Service, &c. This Department, too,
endeavours to meet the wants of a large class of Boys who are
destined for early Professional or Mercantile life.

This College also is recognised by the Secretary of State for India
in Council as possessing an efficient class for Civil Engineering.

A Public Examination is held before the Summer Vacation.

An Exhibition of £50 is awarded at this Examination to that
Pupil proceeding to the University of Oxford, Cambridge, or
Dublin, who shall be pronounced by the Public Examiners to have
shown sufficient proficiency in his studies.

One Scholarship of £20 a year, tenable for three years, and Two
of £15 a year, tenable for two years, if the Scholar remains a Pupil
of the College, with a free nomination, will be competed for in July.
These Scholarships are open to all, whether Pupils of the School,
or others eligible to become Pupils, whose age on the 1st July
shall not exceed 15 years.

TERMS :—For DAY BOYS, 10 to 18 Guineas; for BOARDERS
(inclusive of Tuition), 50 to 63 Guineas.

*All communications to be addressed to the Honorary Secretary, or the Principal,
Bath Proprietary College, from whom any information may be obtained.*

LADIES' COLLEGE,

27, CIRCUS, BATH,

Under a body of Patrons, Lady Referees, & an Executive Committee.

Lady Principal: Mdlle. HUBERT DE FONTENY.

————:o:————

THE Lady Principal of this College is a Member of the Church of England, and earnestly desires that the education given in it, should be based upon the only true foundation—the principles of the Gospel of Christ.

Believing the great aim of all education to be the training of the mind to habits of thoughtfulness and self-culture, she will do her utmost to promote this object, and for instruction in modern languages and general accomplishments, she has secured the assistance of the best Professors.

The College Classes for the Daughters of Gentlemen residing in Bath and the neighbourhood are conducted under the superintendence of the Lady Principal, and are held between the hours of Nine and Two.

BIBLE CLASS... ... ... REV. T. P. METHUEN, M.A.

ENGLISH LITERATURE, &c. ... MR. J. W. MORRIS.

Professor of the English and Latin Languages: MR. S. EDWARDS.

There is a Resident German Lady and a Resident English Governess.

Terms:

Under 14 Years of Age	15 Guineas per annum.
Above 14 Years of Age	20 ,, ,,

Optional Payments:

		Per Annum.
French, on M. Colart's and M. Roche's System	MDLLE. COUR ...	6 Guineas
German	FRAULEIN SCHULTZE ...	8 ,,
Italian	SIGNOR MOSCARDI ...	8 ,,
Pianoforte...	HERR ROECKEL ...	12 ,,
Ditto	FRAULEIN BOERNGEN ...	10 ,,
Ditto	MISS DONE ...	10 ,,
Singing	SIGNOR PIERACCINI ...	,,
Ditto	MISS BIANCHI TAYLOR ...	10 ,,
Singing Class	MISS BIANCHI TAYLOR ...	6 ,,
Drawing	MR. HOBSON	8 ,,
Lectures on Popular Subjects are given at stated periods		,,

The Vacations consist of Seven Weeks at Midsummer and Six Weeks at Christmas

Mdlle. HUBERT DE FONTENY receives a limited number of Boarders.

Terms, inclusive of College Fees ... ... 65 Guineas per annum.
Seat at Church ... 1 Guinea per annum | Laundress ... 6 Guineas per annum.

Capt. BRYAN HOLMF, St. George's Hill, Bathampton, } *Hon. Secs.*
G. J. ROBERTSON, Esq., 24, Grosvenor Place, Bath, }

Prospectuses may be obtained of Mr. PEACH, Bookseller to the College,
8, Bridge Street, Bath.

THE REV. W. G. LUCKMAN, M.A.,

(Queen's College, Cambridge,)

Seven Years Assistant and Boarding House Master of the Bath Proprietary College,

Receives Boys into his House, from the Age of Seven Years and upwards, to prepare for Public Schools, the Military, Naval, and Civil Service Examinations.

Terms :

For Boarders above 11 years of Age ...	80 Guineas per Annum.
,, ,, under 11 ,, ...	60 ,, ,,
Daily Boarders	30 ,, ,,
Daily Pupils...	16 ,, ,,

The Terms for Boarders include all Charges except Medical Attendance and Books.

Extras :

The following subjects are taught by experienced masters :—

French	4 Guineas per Annum.
German	6 ,, ,,
Drawing	6 ,,
Music	6 ,,

The School is divided into Three Terms. The Vacations are :—

Spring—Three Weeks, commencing the middle of April.

Summer—Seven Weeks, commencing last Week in July.

Christmas—Four Weeks.

A Term's Notice must be given of the intended removal of a Pupil, in default of which the full charge must be paid for the ensuing Term.

——:o:——

THE School Course consist of Religious Instruction, English History, Grammar, Reading and Spelling, Geography, Arithmetic, Latin, Greek, French, and Drawing ; the object being to give Boys, preparing for Public Schools, a good Elementary Education : as also a special preparation for Boys intended for the Military, Naval, and Civil Service Examinations.

There is a large Play-Ground and Cricket Field, consisting of Two Acres, attached to the House.

9, Johnstone Street, Bath.

Youth, Adult, and Private Tuition.

CITY ACADEMY,

34, MILSOM STREET, BATH,

SUPERINTENDED BY

LUTHER MUNDAY,

OF LONDON.

DAY SCHOLARS (exclusively) from Nine till Twelve,
and Two till Four.

Writing in Twelve Lessons.

FIRST CLASS TESTIMONIALS.

MISS AGNES MUNDAY'S
PREPARATORY SCHOOL.

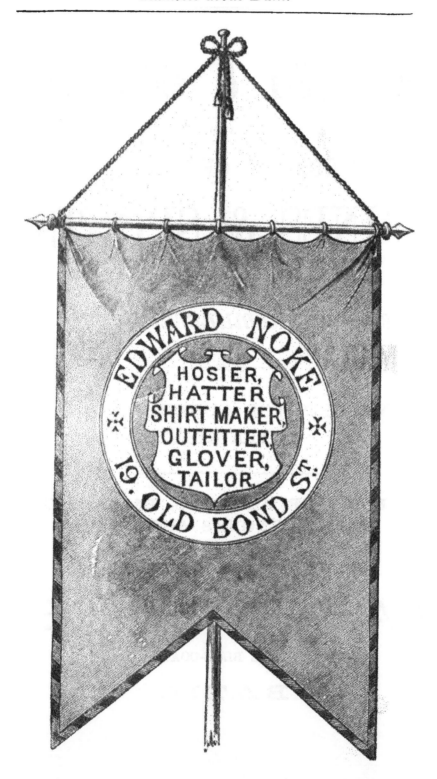

GEORGE BENJAMIN,
COAL MERCHANT.

OFFICE:
SAWCLOSE, Queen Square.

DEPOTS:
MIDLAND AND GREAT WESTERN
RAILWAYS,
BATH.

SOMERSETSHIRE, COALPIT HEATH,
LLANTWIT, DERBYSHIRE,
AND LEICESTERSHIRE COALS.

COKE AND FIREWOOD.

THE

𝔚ine, 𝔖pirit, and 𝔄le 𝔖tores.

———:o:———

W. & A. GILBEY,

WINE IMPORTERS

AND

DISTILLERS,

36, BROAD STREET, BATH.

———:o:———

THE undoubted good quality, and value of all Wines and Spirits, supplied by W. & A. GILBEY, is shown by the extent of their business, which is entirely without parallel, and amounts to an average sale throughout the entire year of

· 18,000 DOZENS WEEKLY.

Sole Agency for Truman, Hanbury, Buxton & Co.'s celebrated London Stout, and Burton-on-Trent Ales, all of which are supplied in 9-gallon casks, from 1s. per gallon.

BASS AND ALLSOPP'S INDIA PALE ALES.

FINEST CHAMPAGNE DEVONSHIRE CIDER.

DINNER SHERRY—A full flavoured good delicate SPANISH SHERRY, 22s. per dozen.

———:∞———

ADDRESS:

36, BROAD STREET, BATH.

ESTABLISHED 1850.

JOHN RUSSELL,

LADIES' AND GENTLEMEN'S

FASHIONABLE

BOOT & SHOE

MAKER,

7, ABBEY CHURCHYARD,

(OPPOSITE THE GRAND PUMP ROOM,)

BATH.

J. BATSTONE,

(Late TOULMIN,)

TAILOR, HATTER,

OUTFITTER,

AND

𝕻ractical 𝕾hirtmaker,

9 & 10, OLD BOND STREET,

BATH,

AND

12, PARK STREET, BRISTOL,

AGENT FOR CHRISTY'S SILK AND FELT HATS, and NICHOL'S OVERCOATS.

EDMUND WILLCOX,

Furnishing Ironmonger,

AND

MANUFACTURER,

34, MILSOM STREET, Bath.

LOCK, GAS, BELL, AND SMITHS' WORK BY EXPERIENCED WORKMEN.

TABLE LAMPS, GASELIERS, AND BATHS.

RANGES, REGISTER STOVES, BEDSTEADS.

Best Sheffield Cutlery and Electro-Plated Wares.

REPAIRS SPEEDILY EXECUTED.

————:o:————

AGENT FOR THE LUX SOLIS OIL.

6

RAND PUMP ROOM HOTEL,
BATH.

THIS Handsome Hotel is situated close to the Grand Pump Room, opposite the Abbey Church, and half-way between the two Railway Stations, the Great Western and Midland—five minutes' walk from either.

Attached to the Hotel is a magnificent suite of Baths supplied from the Mineral Springs.

High class accommodation.

For Tariff of Prices and other information apply to the
MANAGER.

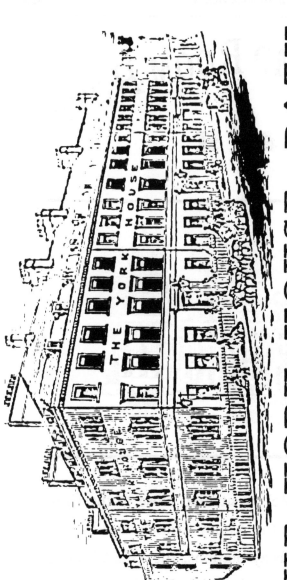

THE YORK HOUSE, BATH,
FOR GENTLEMEN AND FAMILIES,

Is situated in the best part of the City, and in the immediate neighbourhood of the Royal Victoria Park, Assembly R Theatre, Crescents, and principal streets, and about five minutes' drive from the Railway Stations.

Arrangements made at a fixed charge per week in Coffee Room and Private Apartments.

Wines and Spirits of the first quality.

The Proprietor, being the holder of a large stock of Wines and Spirits, is prepared to supply Private Families on the best t Terms and every information on application to J. ODLUM, Proprietor.

WHITE LION HOTEL,

BATH,

FOR FAMILIES AND GENTLEMEN,

F. P. FENNER,

Late of Cambridge, Proprietor.

THE "LION" is *not* a *Company* Hotel, but it is one of the oldest and best reputed of the many Hotels for which the West of England has been long distinguished.

It is spacious ; occupying an open and commanding position, and aims at being classed among the most comfortable resorts of this highly favoured and attractive locality. It is also in close proximity to the celebrated Baths, the Abbey, and all the approved centres of trade and fashion.

The comfort is guaranteed by the unvarying personal superintendence of the Proprietor and his family, with whom arrangements can be made at all seasons for the reception of families either by the week or month.

Cards, with Tariff, and View on application.

NIGHT PORTER.

47

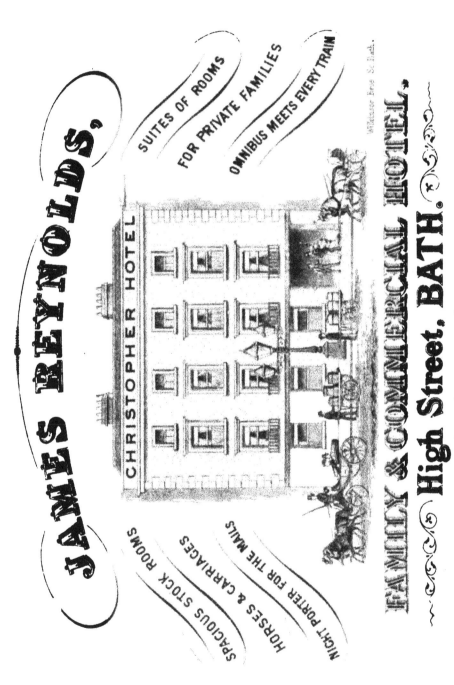

Private Lodging House,

3, MANVERS STREET,

Station Road, BATH.

STAFFORD'S

PRIVATE

BOARDING HOUSE,

ESTABLISHED 1827,

2, LAURA PLACE, BATH.

This Old Established Boarding House has been

NEWLY FURNISHED THROUGHOUT,

And is carried on by the

WIDOW OF THE LATE PROPRIETOR.

Visitors to Bath will find it replete with every comfort.

POWLETT HOUSE,

HENRIETTA STREET,

(NEAR GREAT PULTENEY STREET,)

BATH,

Private Select Boarding House

FOR

LADIES & GENTLEMEN.

This Establishment is acknowledged to be superior both as regards the Table and other appointments.

E. COOMBS,

PROPRIETRESS.

THE

SWAN HOTEL, WELLS,

SOMERSET.

(FACING THE CATHEDRAL.)

F. C. GEORGE,

PROPRIETOR.

Families and Tourists will find the Swan Hotel replete with every accommodation.

PRIVATE ENTRANCE TO THE CATHEDRAL.

POSTING IN ALL ITS BRANCHES.

7

JACOB SMITH, Jun.,
MEAT SALESMAN,
13, CHEAP STREET,
(OPPOSITE THE ABBEY CHURCH,)

BATH.

FAMILIES WAITED ON DAILY FOR ORDERS.
Meat Delivered to All Parts of Bath Daily.

Country Orders promptly attended to.

SPECIAL ARRANGEMENTS
MADE WITH SCHOOLS AND BUSINESS FIRMS.

CONTRACTS ENTERED INTO.

ALL ORDERS EXECUTED WITH DISPATCH.

WORKS PUBLISHED BY R. E. PEACH.

————:o:————

AQUÆ SOLIS, NOTICES OF ROMAN BATH. Being a Description of all the Roman Remains which have been found in and around the City, up to the present time, with Fifty-one Illustrations of the Vestiges of Temples and other Structures, also of Altars, Inscriptions, Tombs, Weapons, and Implements, Personal Ornaments, and other Remains, a Map of the City and Neighbourhood, beautifully coloured by hand, shewing the Roads, &c., of the Roman Period, and the Ground Plan of an Antient Roman Bath. By the Rev. H. M. SCARTH, M.A., Prebendary of Wells and Rector of Wrington.

DOMESDAY FOR WILTSHIRE: Translated and Edited, with Illustrative Notes, by the Rev. W. H. JONES, M.A., F.S.A., Vicar of Bradford-on-Avon. Handsomely printed in One Volume, Demy 4to., Cloth Boards. Price 31s. 6d.

SELECT READINGS (2 vols.) FROM THE POETS AND PROSE WRITERS OF EVERY COUNTRY, Edited by Rev. JAMES FLEMING, B.D., Incumbent of S. Michael's, Chester Square, London. First Series, 4s. 6d. Second Series, 3s. 6d. Sold separately.

OBJECTS OF INTEREST IN THE CITY OF BATH AND ITS NEIGHBOURHOOD. Fourth Edition—Revised and Enlarged. Price 6d., with Map, 9d. ; with Two Maps, 1s.

THE HISTORIC GUIDE TO BATH. With Map and Illustrations. By the Rev. G. N. Wright, M.A.

ON THE CONNECTION OF BATH WITH THE LITERATURE AND SCIENCE OF ENGLAND. By the Rev. Joseph Hunter, F.S.A. Price 3s.

THE LITERATURE AND LITERATI OF BATH. By George Monkland, Esq. 2 Vols. Price 6s.

THIRTY-EIGHT GRAPHIC VIEWS IN BATH AND ITS NEIGHBOURHOOD; with Introductory Notice. By James Tunstall, M.D., author of "Rambles about Bath and its Neighbourhood." Demy oblong, 8vo. Price, in Paper Covers, 5s. Cloth elegant, gilt edges, 7s. Cloth elegant, large paper demy, oblong 4to., 12s.

THE BATHS OF BATH. By Dr. Falconer. With Plans. Neat Cloth. New Edition in the Press.

MAP OF THE CITY AND BOROUGH OF BATH. Paper Covers 6d., Cloth 1s., Mounted on Canvas in Cloth 1s. 6d.

ARROWS.—A Series of Sermons. By the Rev. G. Tugwell, M.A., Rector of Bathwick. Price 4s.

8

Works Published by R. E. PEACH, *continued.*

———————:o:—————

By the Right Rev. W. C. MAGEE, D.D., Bishop of Peterborough.

THE VOLUNTARY SYSTEM: Can it supply the place of the Established Church? Fourth Edition. 2s.

CHRISTIAN SOCIALISM: A Charity Sermon, 8d.

THE BLESSING ON THE PURE IN HEART. A Sermon. 8d.

THE GOSPEL AND THE AGE: An Ordination Sermon, preached at Whitehall. 1s.

CHRIST THE LIGHT OF ALL SCRIPTURE: An Act Sermon, preached in the Chapel of Trinity College, Dublin. 1s.

SPEECH ON THE SABBATH QUESTION. In Reply to the advocates of the Sunday League. 3d.

REMAINS AND MEMOIR OF THE LATE REV. E. TOTTEN-HAM, B.D., Prebendary of Wells, and Minister of Laura Chapel, Bath. Crown 8vo., cloth, 7s. 6d.

AURICULAR CONFESSION: A Lecture. 1s.

TALKING TO TABLES: A Great Folly, or a Great Sin.- Third Edition. 6d.

LIGHTS OF THE MORNING; or Meditations for every Day in the Ecclesiastical Year. From the German of Frederick Arndt. With Preface, by the Right Rev. W. C. Magee, D.D., Bishop of Peterborough. 2 vols., 11s.

THE CHURCH'S FEAR AND THE CHURCH'S HOPE: A Sermon, preached in the Cathedral Church of Wells, at the Annual Meeting of the Bath and Wells Diocesan Societies, on Tuesday, October 4th, 1864. 1s.

———————

By the REV. R. HAYES ROBINSON.

Formerly Incumbent of the Octagon Chapel, Bath, and late Curate of Weston ; Secretary to the National Society.

THOUGHT AND DEED.—SERMONS ON FAITH AND DUTY, Second Edition, with Two Additional Chapters. Price 5s. Beautifully printed on Toned Paper, and strongly bound in Neat Cloth.

CONTENTS.—1. The Sacrifice of Christ. 2. The Wages and the Gift. 3. Ashamed of Christ. 4. Three Conditions of Christian Discipleship. 5. Sleeping for Sorrow. 6. Christ and History. 7. Wisdom in Simplicity. 8. The Blessedness of Giving. 9. Persecution and Martyrdom. 10. Thoughts on the Second Advent. 11. Christian Thanksgiving. 12. Many Crowns.

Works Published by R. E. PEACH, continued.

———:o:———

By the Rev. W. ANDERSON, M.A.,
Minister of the Octagon Chapel, Bath.

REASONS FOR OUR FAITH.—Six Lectures on Modern Misrepresentations of the Christian Religion and the Christian Evidences, with references and Notes. Price 3*s.*, cloth boards.

CONTENTS.—1. The Value of Dogmas and their place in the Christian System. 2. Christian Morality and its proposed Substitutes. 3. Christian Miracles, their Value as Evidence and their place in the Christian Religion. 4. The Meaning and the Power of Faith in Christ. 5. Mr. Arnold's Method of Interpreting the Bible. 6. Anti-Dogmatism Tested by the Writings of its Leading Advocates.

By the Rev. F. TILNEY BASSETT
Vicar of Dulverton.

CHRIST IN ETERNITY AND TIME.—Four Advent Sermons, preached in Old Widcombe Church, Bath, 1870. Price 2*s.* 6*d.*

"The Sermons are thoughtful and suggestive, rich in Divine truth, and written with much force and eloquence of language."—*Christian Advocate and Review.*

"The volume contains much valuable matter."—*Guardian.*

"Careful and scholarly Sermons." "True eloquence which springs out of a realization of the greatness of sacred truth."

"His remarks are such as might be expected from one who is so well versed in the original."—*Record.*

"Will be welcome to a wider circle of readers than that for whose behalf the volume was especially published."—*Bath Chronicle.*

"Much superior to the average." "Nor should we omit to notice the light the author, from his intimate acquaintance with the ancient text, has been enabled to shed incidentally upon various passages he has quoted."—*Bath Express.*

THE TEACHER'S TEXT BOOK : A Collection of some of the difficult passages in the Gospels, familiarly and easily explained. Price, in Paper Covers, 1*s.* 6*d.* Cloth, 2*s.*

SACRED ALLEGORIES AND THEIR LESSONS, IN VERSE. Price 2*s.* 6*d.*, Cloth elegant.

THINGS THAT MUST BE.—Four Advent Sermons, preached in Margaret's Chapel, Bath, 1872. I. The Beast. II. The Anti-Christ. III. The False Prophets. IV. The Second Advent. Cloth, 2*s.*

By the Rev. M. HOBART SEYMOUR.

REPLY TO THE STRICTURES OF THE REV. W. J. E. BENNET, ON THE CHARGE OF THE LORD BISHOP OF BATH AND· WELLS.

THE HOT

MINERAL SPRINGS OF BATH.

THE WATER used for BATHING is supplied directly from the MINERAL SPRINGS. The natural temperature of the Water, which is from 117° to 120°, being regulated by means of cooled Mineral Waters.

These Waters are peculiarly beneficial in cases of Rheumatism, Chronic Diseases of the Skin, and General Debility.

Payments for all the Baths must be made by Ticket only, which may be obtained at the Office adjoining the Grand Pump Room Hotel.

———:o:———

ARRANGEMENTS FOR DRINKING THE WATERS.

The Grand Pump Room is open each Week-day from 8.30 till 4.30, and on Sundays before and after Morning Service.

Charge—Single Glass, 2d.

R. B. CATER and CO.,
Sherry Wine Shippers.

R. B. CATER and CO.,
Port Wine Shippers.

R. B. CATER and CO.,
Claret Wine Shippers.

R. B. CATER and CO.,
Brandy Shippers.

R. B. CATER and CO.,
General Wine Merchants.

R. B. CATER and CO.,
Sole Agents for Brett's Eau de Vie.

R. B. CATER and CO.,
Agent for Bass's India and Burton Ales.

R. B. CATER and CO.,
Sole Agents for Rogers' A.K. Bitter Ales.

R. B. CATER and CO.,
Bottlers of Guinness's Extra Dublin Stout.

R. B. CATER and CO.,
Bottlers of Cater & Co.'s Sparkling Dinner Ales.

Five per Cent. allowed on Orders of £2 for Cash.

Postal Address—

R. B. CATER & COMPANY,
27, MARKET PLACE,
BATH.

JOLLY & SON,

Silk Mercers and Linen Merchants,

11 & 12, Milsom Street, Bath,

42 & 43, COLLEGE GREEN, BRISTOL.

LIST OF DEPARTMENTS:

BLACK AND COLOURED SILKS,
DRESS MATERIALS,
FURS,
SHAWLS,
MANTLES,
SILK AND MATERIAL COSTUMES,
MILLINERY,
CHILDREN'S DRESSES,
LADIES' LINGERIE,
LACE AND BALL DRESSES,
RIBBONS AND FANCY GOODS,
HOSIERY.

DAMASK,
IRISH LINENS,
TABLE LINEN,
HUCKABACKS & GLASS CLOTHS,
BLANKETS,
FLANNELS,
LONG CLOTHS,
CALICOES,
COTTON SHEETINGS,
MUSLIN CURTAINS.

IMPORTERS OF THE GUARANTEED BLACK SILKS.